Making Sight Words

Teaching Word Recognition from Phoneme Awareness to Fluency

How to help children read words effortlessly without memorization

Bruce Murray
Auburn University

Published by Linus Publications, Inc.
Ronkonkoma, NY 11779

Copyright © 2012 by Linus Publications

All Rights Reserved.

ISBN 10: 1-60797-284-0

ISBN 13: 978-1-60797-284-6

No part of this publication may be reproduced, stored in a retrieval system, or transmitted, in any form or by any means, electronic, mechanical, photocopying, recording, or otherwise, without the prior permission of the publisher.

Printed in the United States of America.

This book is printed on acid-free paper.

Print Numbers   5   4   3   2   1

TABLE OF CONTENTS

CHAPTER 1
A new view of sight words 1

CHAPTER 2
How alphabets work—a history 9

CHAPTER 3
How beginners develop the ability to read words 27

CHAPTER 4
The language processing system of skilled readers 51

CHAPTER 5
Preparing students to learn to read 69

CHAPTER 6
Learning to detect phonemes in spoken words 87

CHAPTER 7
How to teach phonics for sight word learning 113

CHAPTER 8
Choosing texts for reading instruction 137

CHAPTER 9
Moving from decoding to fluency 159

CHAPTER 10
Developing word recognition through spelling 179

CHAPTER 11
Looking ahead: Teaching vocabulary and comprehension strategies 193

CHAPTER 12
Epilogue: Landmarks and pitfalls in learning to read 213

PRACTICAL CHAPTER 1
How to introduce a new book 237

PRACTICAL CHAPTER 2
How to scaffold word learning during oral reading 245

PRACTICAL CHAPTER 3
How to teach a letterbox lesson 265

PRACTICAL CHAPTER 4
How to teach blending, concepts about print, and letter recognition 283

PRACTICAL CHAPTER 5
How to assess to find out where reading is breaking down 295

PRACTICAL CHAPTER 6
How to take a running record 319

PRACTICAL CHAPTER 7
How to develop fluency through repeated readings 327

PRACTICAL CHAPTER 8
How to teach spelling as wordmapping 339

PRACTICAL CHAPTER 9
How to write a literacy report 347

Glossary 357

References 367

Children's books cited 379

CHAPTER 1

A New View of Sight words

MAKING SIGHT WORDS

Does the title suggest a return to discredited whole word methods, the look-and-say approach, rote memorization of words by flashcard drill, and boring stories about Dick and Jane that repeat a few words dozens of times to pound them into children's memories?

Nothing could be further from the truth. This book tells the exciting story of how beginners can be taught to make sight words, words they can read effortlessly and automatically, not by memorization, but by understanding their alphabetic mappings. *Making sight words* is a journey from phoneme awareness to accurate, reliable decoding, and from there to the effortless word recognition of fluent reading so incredibly rapid that it surpasses the speed of speech. In short, making sight words means learning each new word so thoroughly and efficiently that after only a few learning trials, we can instantly and effortless read the word for the rest of our lives.

METHOD OR PROCESS?

The term *sight word* is typically used ambiguously as either a method or a process. A sight-word *method* means learning words by rote, i.e., by mechanical repetition without real understanding. With the exception of a few common, irregular words like *to* and *of* found in even the simplest text, beginners don't need drill and memorization methods to learn sight words because such methods are notoriously inefficient and unreliable. On the other hand, every reader needs a vast store of words that can be recognized instantly and effortlessly. Nearly all of our sight words are learned by a sight-word *process*. The process of making sight words by understanding alphabetic mappings is the topic of this book.

Why do we need sight words? To get the ideas in challenging texts, skilled readers—including you and me—need to marshal our mental resources for the task of comprehension. We must reduce a vast text to a compact gist, all the while relating new ideas in a text to our background knowledge, to reconstruct an internal model of the text. Building a text model requires us to recall previous information we've read, sometimes many chapters earlier, while drawing inferences about background knowledge and experiences typically signaled very briefly by authors. Skillful reading also involves a critical evaluation that continually weighs the qualifications and bias of writers, translates emotionally laden terms into neutral language, and considers the evidence for the claims made by the writer. All this concentrated mental labor must be liberated from any struggle with word identification. That means that for unencumbered reading comprehension, word recognition must be automatic, effortless, and instantaneous—nearly all the words in text must be sight words.

THE BLIND MEN AND THE ELEPHANT

Beginning reading has long been the most controversial area in all of education. Since the 1950s, educators and parents have fought pitched battles in a protracted reading war over how to teach beginners to read. One reason for the ferocity of the debate is that everyone agrees that reading is crucial. Failing to learn to read in first grade is far more serious than, say, failing to learn to sing on pitch or failing to draw a proportional figure in art class. Reading failure disposes a student to fail in every subject that depends on reading—science, history, even mathematics—with a potentially permanent debilitating influence on the whole of one's academic, social, and economic career.

Remember the folk tale of the blind men and the elephant? Six blind men in India had never seen an elephant. A kindly rajah, hearing of their plight, invited them to his palace to encounter a tame elephant first hand. One blind man felt the trunk and decided that the elephant is like a snake. This drew an immediate objection from the second blind man, who after running his hand along the elephant's tusk, pronounced the elephant to be something like a spear. The third blind man was feeling the elephant's ear; the elephant, he insisted, is nothing like a snake or a spear—it's like a fan. The fourth blind man, examining the elephant's leg, emphatically disagreed, likening the elephant to a tree. This made no sense to the fifth blind man, who after flattening his hands on the elephant's broad sides, declared that the elephant was like a wall. The sixth blind man, holding the elephant's tail, informed his colleagues that all of them were completely off base, and that the elephant in fact resembled a rope. Their debate grew in volume and intensity until the kindly rajah appeared and showed them that they were all partly right, but that they needed a more comprehensive view of the elephant—a whole-elephant view.

Similarly, in many long-standing and intractable controversies about reading, advocates focus on single aspects of reading and fail to appreciate the larger, developmental picture of how we learn to read. One side argues that children must learn to sound out words, only to encounter an equally determined opponent insisting that children must learn to recognize words by sight. One side will be adamant that children must read whole meaningful texts, but will run into stiff opposition from others emphasizing accurate reading of individual words. One side will demand explicit, systematic instruction for beginning readers, while opponents insist children learn to read by reading.

As with the blind men and the elephant, most of the conflicting views so vehemently advanced in our reading wars dissolve in the light of a larger, developmental view of reading. Each position carries an important element of truth, but each turns out to be a limited view, one aspect of a larger reading "elephant." Beginners do need to learn to sound out letters and blend phonemes to identify words, and they also need to develop a vast lexicon of words recognized instantly and effortlessly—an immense sight vocabulary. One of the key discoveries of recent reading research is that we make sight words most efficiently by decoding them. Reading whole texts is the best kind of reading practice because the student reads more words with much greater motivation under a natural time pressure to comprehend that helps us make sight words. However, there is no getting around the task of learning to identify individual words because texts are made of words. A long line of experimentation in reading demonstrates that beginners make optimal progress in learning to read under explicit, systematic instruction provided by skillful, responsive teachers. Yet every young reader reaches the point where the only way to acquire the independent reading vocabulary for reading the many unfamiliar words routinely encountered in meaningful texts is avid, independent, voluntary reading. Nearly everyone agrees about the goals of reading instruction. We all want children reading fluently, with enjoyment, and with keen, critical understanding. Where we disagree is in how to get children reading fluently, with enjoyment, and with keen, critical understanding. Fortunately, we have a way to resolve disagreements about effective practice: science.

RESOLVING QUESTIONS WITH SCIENCE

Teachers do well to align ourselves with psychologists, who use scientific methods to study how people learn. Imagine if the blind men had pursued their conjectures about the elephant by developing and testing predictions. If the elephant were like a rope, we should be able to tie the elephant in a knot. If the elephant were like a spear, we should be able to throw the elephant. If the elephant were like a tree, we should be able to climb the elephant and find leaves. The results of such experiments would have helped the blind men refine their understanding of elephants, in this case, by falsifying explanations inconsistent with other data on elephants.

How do we scientifically resolve questions of how to teach reading? Science is more than observation and measurement. Scientific inquiry begins with a proposed theory, usually a causal explanation of a phenomenon. Useful theories of reading propose connections between cause and effect, so that introducing the cause (e.g., teaching something in a certain way) brings about a desired effect (i.e., learning). For example, we might propose that learning to read requires the development of perceptual-motor coordination. Good theories generate specific, observable predictions about future events, allowing us to test a theory by devising experiments. For example, the theory that reading requires the development of perceptual-motor coordination suggests children who develop their perceptual-motor coordination by learning to walk a balance beam will improve their reading. To test this theory, we need to randomly select an experimental group of children for balance-beam training. If children learn to walk a balance beam and their reading doesn't improve, the theory is falsified—we can throw it out. Scientific progress is usually made by disproving the theories that don't work, thus advancing successful theories by clearing away the "dead wood."

Suppose children in our experimental group learn to walk a balance beam and their reading does improve: Has our theory been proven? No, because we haven't eliminated other explanations for their improvement. For instance, our participants may be getting good reading instruction in class that is spurring their learning, so that the balance beam work is incidental to their reading success. To rule out alternative explanations, we need a *control* group randomly selected from the same class who receive a comparable treatment not expected to improve reading (perhaps they can learn origami). If the balance beam group improves their reading ability more than the origami group (using statistical calculations to determine that the measured improvement exceeds what we could expect by chance alone), we have scientific evidence that our perceptual-motor treatment is causing gains in reading. Incidentally, developing perceptual motor skills has not been shown to improve reading (Saphier, 1973).

In general, we depend on scientific theories to guide our reading instruction. Theories are strengthened or weakened by experiments that test predictions based on those theories. As the science of reading education develops, we abandon theories that don't test out—that's progress. The result of this progress is that scientific understanding of reading becomes public knowledge, not private opinion. We accumulate knowledge of teaching procedures *shown* to bring about learning. This means that the best way for teachers to get students learning to read is to use methods shown to work in scientific studies of reading. Of course, theories can never precisely tell us what to do in the classroom. They simply provide general rules for effective teaching, and they steer us away from methods without demonstrable effectiveness. We have established clear landmarks—methods and activities of demonstrable effectiveness in carefully designed educational experiments—and pitfalls—methods and activities that don't work. Within the framework of tenable theory, guided by the landmarks and pitfalls identified by experimentation, teachers forge effective instruction, which always involves a measure of individual creativity.

Scientists in psychology, education, linguistics, anthropology, artificial intelligence, and many related fields have conducted scientific research on reading for over a century. Psychology is of particular interest to teachers because it includes the study of learning and memory, an inquiry closely related to teachers' efforts to help children learn and remember concepts and strategies. Reading is an important specialty area within the field of cognitive psychology, which has been the source of some of our best research on reading (Metsala & Ehri, 1998; Perfetti, 1985; Stanovich, 2000).

Today, we have a large body of public knowledge about learning to read, and about what sort of teaching is effective for causing children to learn. From time to time, influential syntheses have emerged to summarize our progress in understanding how children learn to read (Adams, 1990; Chall 1967; NRP, 2000; Snow, Griffith, & Burns, 1998). Of these syntheses, Marilyn Jager Adams's *Beginning to Read: Thinking and Learning About Print* (1990) has been particularly valuable not only for its scholarship and balance, but because an accompanying *Summary* (Stahl, Osborn, & Lehr, 1990) brought its practical conclusions to teaching professionals. I studied with the late Steve Stahl, who led the *Summary* team, at the University of Georgia soon after the book was published. However, *Beginning to Read* is now more than two decades old, and some of its conclusions are becoming dated.

Making Sight Words may be read as an update to Stahl et al.'s (1990) *Summary* of Adams's *Beginning to Read* (1990). Both books deal with broad questions about what to teach, why, and how. Understanding our public knowledge about how children learn to read and how they can be effectively taught will help preservice teachers evaluate teaching ideas from basals, magazines, internet sites, and classroom observations in the light of scientific research. *Making Sight Words* will update some of the ideas in light of more recent research, especially in the crucial area of phoneme awareness. In addition, I will intersperse practical techniques for teaching and assessing reading. These techniques will appear as practical chapters to prepare preservice teachers for teaching experiences as tutors with struggling readers in a lesson format adapted from Clay's Reading Recovery program (Clay, 1993; Pinnell, Fried, & Estice, 1990).

Teaching is both an art and a science. Teachers translate the findings of scientific research to the creative, practical task of teaching children, an art. Teaching can never be reduced to recipe knowledge, and *Making Sight Words* should not be viewed as a cookbook for teaching. Teaching is a complex profession, comparable to law or medicine. One can't learn to argue the law simply by observing courtroom examinations, or learn to practice medicine by observing doctors making their rounds. Learning any profession requires learning how the experts think, drawing on deep reserves of knowledge, and applying research-tested theory to solve practical problems. Teachers who read *Making Sight Words* will enhance their knowledge of how reading is taught and learned, and they will encounter many creative solutions translating research findings for the urgent task of teaching beginners how to read.

SOME BASIC TERMINOLOGY

The problem of learning to identify words is addressed in phonics, which can be simply defined as decoding instruction. Phonics is instruction in how to identify printed words from their spellings. The term phonics is used for instructional approaches and their content. Phonics is not the same as phonetics, which is a branch of linguistics that deals with characteristics of speech across languages and does not involve decoding written words at all. Identifying words means using conscious problem-solving to figure out a word unfamiliar in printed form. To identify a word by phonics means sounding out the phonemes (speech gestures) cued by elements of the spelling, and then blending the phonemes to approximate a recognizable pronunciation of a known word, close enough to access the word in context. In contrast, sight words are recognized, rather than identified. Once a word has entered our sight vocabulary, we know longer use problem-solving strategies to identify it; instead, we recognize it effortlessly and automatically. We also learn easier and less conscious routines for dealing with unfamiliar printed words efficiently. Encountering a pseudoword like *fratch* is no problem for skilled readers like us; we quickly generate a pronunciation without overt sounding out and blending. Thus, phonics strategies for identifying unfamiliar words develop into word recognition skills.

Though tensions have eased in the reading wars, phonics remains a controversial topic. One obvious reason, already noted, is that nearly everyone agrees on how crucial reading is to one's entire academic career. Disputes about phonics tend to suffer from the logic of the blind men and the elephant, failing to take a large-scale developmental view of reading. Our images of phonics may be wildly disparate, with some disputants thinking in terms of dreary seatwork in workbooks while others imagine an exciting and empowering unveiling of the mysteries of the alphabetic code. A basic problem is that educators often fail to use scientific methods to resolve their disputes. Disagreements are often taken to the political arena. Professional organizations may pass resolutions, legislatures may enact new laws, and university search committees may weed out candidates with opposing views, when what's really needed is a dispassionate examination of the empirical evidence allowing the development of a scientific consensus.

Often the question of whether to emphasize phonics is phrased too broadly. Phonics is decoding instruction, and there are as many varieties of instruction as there are teachers. The question for most teachers is not whether to have decoding instruction, but rather what kind of decoding instruction is effective. Just as there are better and worse methods of teaching arithmetic, some phonics programs and activities are effective and others decidedly less effective. Even strong advocates of phonics—and I am one—would recoil from packaged, teacherless programs of skill exercises like Hooked on Phonics. Effective phonics programs lead students earlier to the effortless word recognition of sight vocabulary, which improves comprehension and enjoyment of books. At its best, phonics initiates children into the secrets of the alphabetic code, showing them how spellings map out the pronunciations of words to make spellings easy to understand and remember.

Phonics aims at teaching students to identify words from spelling information alone. Does every reader need to learn to identify words from their spellings? The convergent conclusion of a vast scientific literature on reading development is that expert readers are expert at decoding (Ehri, 1998; Perfetti, 1985). To become an expert reader, every beginner needs to learn to identify words from their spellings. This is true regardless of instructional approach, whether children learn from a whole language approach, from a traditional basal reading series, or from an explicit phonics program (Griffith & Klesius, 1990). Thus, every would-be reader needs to learn what phonics tries to teach.

What about anecdotal reports of children who learn to read words without systematic, explicit phonics? It is undeniable that many children become avid, expert readers without much phonics teaching; it may well be that with high intelligence, well-developed phoneme awareness, and automatic letter recognition, some children can begin to decode with the most casual and incidental help of adults. Historically, however, the Phoenicians made the only discovery of the alphabet in history; where Phoenician traders exported the alphabet, as in Greece and Rome, alphabets took root; where they did not, as in East Asia and pre-Columbian America, alphabets never appeared.

The need for more explicit and systematic instruction depends on what children have already learned. Some children are like seeds already planted in rich soil, only waiting for sunshine to sprout and flower. But others are like seeds still in the package. They need to be planted in rich soil, watered, brought into sunlight, weeded, and sprayed with insecticide. These are the children who, without the expert help of a skilled and caring teacher, face the destiny of a lifetime of stunted reading.

SUMMARY

Although the term *sight word* is commonly used to refer to the method of memorizing word shapes or spellings, a sight word can mean any word recognized instantly and automatically—which for most of us includes every word in this chapter. The process of learning sight words involves learning to size up the alphabetic mapping recorded in the spelling and then storing the complete or near-complete spelling in memory as a sensible map of the pronunciation, easy to remember because it "looks" like the pronunciation of the word. The purpose of this book is to explain how we make sight words and to apply this understanding to make learning to read easier for young children challenged to make sight words.

Beginning reading has been the single most controversial area in education. An important reason for the protracted conflict over reading education has been a lack of developmental perspective on learning to read. Beginning reading, marked by a struggle to decode words, bears little resemblance to the effortless word reading of skilled readers engaged in a critical reading of the messages of texts. Though we all agree on the value of fluent reading focused on the ideas in texts, people often disagree about how to move from decoding to automatic word recognition. This book will show that decoding is a necessary step in the process of making sight words rather than a wrongheaded diversion from that goal.

Arguments over beginning reading instruction have been difficult to resolve because the issues have typically been addressed by political means, whether in newspaper debates, professional organizations, or legislatures, rather than by science. In the scientific method, we begin with a proposed theory that attempts to explain cause and effect. Scientists pit theory against theory by using each theory to generate hypotheses about what will happen in an experiment. In educational experiments, we randomly assign some students to the experimental condition we think will improve their reading, and others to a control condition that will help them in some other way. The theory that better predicts the experimental results is strengthened, while the unsuccessful theory is weakened. The theory of reading that survives in the arena of experimentation points to the causal factors teachers can influence to help children learn to read. While no theory can provide a roadmap to effective reading instruction, we have discovered instructional landmarks shown to be effective and pitfalls shown to have a negative effect on reading progress. Effective reading teachers chart a careful course though this educational terrain.

Since the 1960s, scientists in reading education have produced a succession of research syntheses that have guided teachers in planning research-based reading instruction. One of the most illuminating works was Adam's (1990) *Beginning to Read*, which was summarized for teachers by Stahl, Osborn, and Lehr (1990). *Making Sight Words* updates these older works, focuses them with the discoveries of Linnea Ehri (1998), supplements them with new information on phoneme awareness, and applies them with techniques like the letterbox lesson and wordmapping that offer practical guidance to teachers of beginning readers.

The term *phonics* continues to be tinged with notoriety. Phonics is simply decoding instruction, and since we learn words by decoding, children need effective phonics to learn to read words. This means that the key question is what sort of phonics is effective for teaching children to read words. Effective phonics shows how alphabetic writing maps out the pronunciations of words in spellings and makes spellings easy to remember for sight word reading. Every beginner needs what phonics tries to teach. While some children learn the alphabetic mapping system easily, the system is certainly not obvious. Historically, it was only discovered once; where Phoenician traders carried the idea of alphabets, alphabets thrived, and where they did not, alphabets never appeared. Most children need explicit instruction to make sense of the intricacies of the alphabetic code.

CHAPTER 2

How Alphabets Work—A History

WRITING AND CIVILIZATION

Writing and civilization began about the same time, roughly 3500 BC. This means we've only had any kind of writing for fewer than 6000 years. Given that people may have inhabited the planet for a million years, writing is quite a recent invention. The first writing appeared in the Sumerian civilization of ancient Mesopotamia, or what is now Iraq. It was made by pressing the wedge-shaped point of a stylus into a clay tablet, and it was called cuneiform.

The coincidence of writing and civilization was not accidental. A civilization is a culture capable of building cities, and cities require written laws and written contracts for stable trade. The first use of writing was probably to keep track of business contracts. Imagine a beer brewer who promised to produce 20 barrels of barley beer (invented about 10,000 BC) for a bronze sword. The brewer hadn't yet made the beer, and the swordsmith's bronze stores were still piles of tin and copper ore. So that neither would renege on the deal, the two craftsmen would press their agreement into clay, sign the tablet, and fire it in a kiln. If either came to regret his rash contract, the other could bring out the indelible agreement to hold him to his promise.

The unexpected result of the development of written language was how much writing improved our intelligence. Writing replaces the fleeting, ephemeral sound waves of the human voice with an artificial memory, freezing words into text for study and criticism. It brought about the first long distance communication, so that rather than travel in person, the brewer might send his barley order by sailboat up the Euphrates to a granary, and the swordsmith might similarly replenish his copper supplies. Not only could people send messages across great distances, they could be sent forward through time. Because of writing, we can receive messages from the dead and preserve our own ideas for our descendants. In this way, humanity could begin to accumulate an archive of knowledge, preserving what was painfully learned for the benefit of future generations. If Hittite raiders burned a village and destroyed its irrigation system, plans recorded on cuneiform tablets would allow its rebuilding, long after the inventor had passed away. The possession of a knowledge archive meant that humans could be taught by the world's finest teachers, even from the grave.

Logographies

Cuneiform, like its Egyptian cousin hieroglyphics, was a logography. A logography is a straightforward, intuitive system. If we needed a symbol for apple, a simple expedient is to develop a stylized apple with some resemblance to an actual apple, but easy enough for anyone to draw, e.g., Ó. A tree would be a standardized and stylized tree image, e.g., Ÿ. Beyond such concrete nouns, devising symbols gets a bit harder. To capture the verb take, we might improvise on the idea of a reaching hand, e.g., Ç. Combining these logographic symbols, we could create a message:

$$ÇÓŸ$$

Translation: Take an apple from the tree. Notice how a logography works: Each symbol stands for a whole word, but more precisely, a symbol represents the concept behind the word, irrespective of the particular spoken word. Thus my message could be read, "Prenez une pomme de l'arbre," or "Nehmen Sie einen Apfel vom Baum," or "Tome una manzana del árbol." In French, German, or Spanish, the idea is a constant. Modern Chinese has made good use of the idea of a logography. Though the northern dialect of Beijing is so different from the southern dialect of Canton as to be incomprehensible for spoken conversation, all literate Chinese can read the same writings, which don't depend on any particular way of pronouncing the words (see Figure 1).

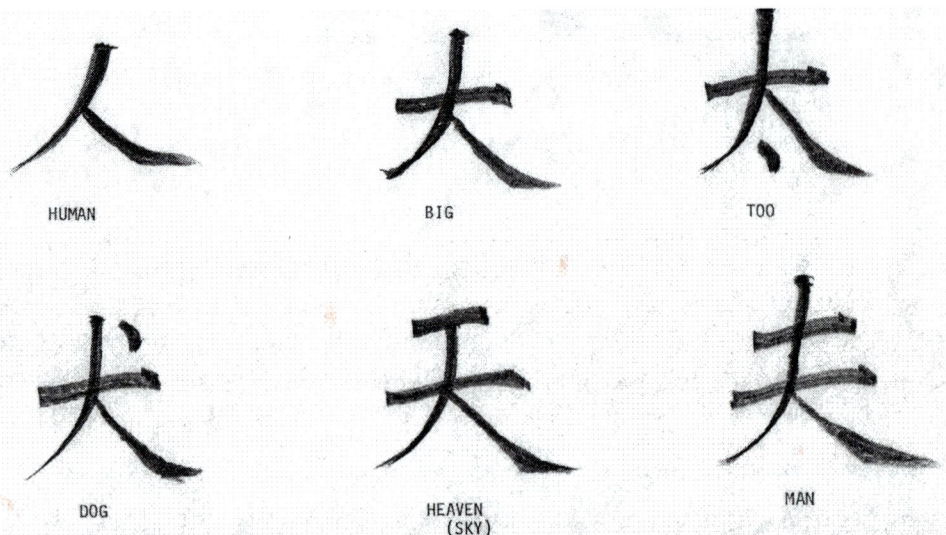

FIGURE 1: Chinese characters from the pen of Liqing Tao

We even make limited use of logographs in English. Our Arabic numerals are clearly logographic representations of concepts. The top row of the typing keyboard allows us to write such logographs as @, #, $, %, and &.

Logographic writing is so simple and straightforward that some have suggested that we teach English words as whole symbols. However, this presents several problems. Readers of Chinese require about 4000 symbols even to read the newspaper. Having to learn thousands of symbols greatly increases the time and effort for learning to read. Historically, it proved difficult for working-class Chinese to finance years of study to learn so many symbols, with the result that writing became a skill of the wealthy. English would be even worse: A conservative estimate counted 88,500 different words in printed school English (Nagy & Anderson, 1984). A further complication is that unlike Chinese logographs, English words are not unique symbols, but rather permutations of the same symbols. For example, *team, tame, meat*, and *mate* recycle the same four symbols in different orders, making them easily confusable as logographs.

Logographies also tend to be inflexible. Although "take an apple from the tree" was easy enough to represent, we run into real problems with "Jose took a good burrito from the cantina." Though concrete nouns are easy to represent, more abstract words (e.g., good) and other verb tenses are difficult to imagine, forcing us to memorize symbols with no natural relationship to their referents. Proper names like *Jose* and words of foreign origin (e.g., *burrito* and *cantina*) pose the problem of a virtually endless stream of new words entering the language, each of which needs to be learned by the literate. In short, logographies don't seem to be versatile enough to represent new words easily. In combination with the vast number of symbols for learning a logography, this most intuitive form of writing poses serious difficulties for universal literacy.

Syllabaries

Japanese scholars upgraded the Chinese logography by adding a *syllabary*. In a syllabary, a symbol stands for a syllable, the distinct chunk in a spoken word built around a vowel nucleus. A syllable is a speech sound with a distinct vowel nucleus. Adding a syllabary allowed the Japanese to write words that are hard to picture, such as names, by using sound-alikes. For example, we could write the names *Jose* as "hoe say" and *Barbara* as "bar bar rah," as illustrated in Figure 2:

FIGURE 2: Syllabary images for *Jose and Barbara*

Pretty silly, but you get the idea. We use a sequence of one-syllable *sound-alike* words to represent new words with more than one syllable.

Syllabaries work nicely for languages with a limited number of syllables. For example, spoken Japanese has only 70 syllables. Using 36 kana syllabary symbols, in combination with logographs borrowed from the Chinese, gives the Japanese great flexibility in adding new written words to the language. Notice that a syllabary changes the basic idea of a written language. With a syllabary we shift from representing universal *meaning* to representing *speech*. This makes writing much more versatile for representing new words, though it renders the symbols incomprehensible to those who don't understand the spoken language.

Could we teach syllables as symbols for spoken chunks of words in English to simplify learning to read, so that children would learn syllables like *syl*, *la*, and *bles*? Unfortunately, English has at least 5000 syllables, still too many to learn without years of diligent study. We would face the same problem we encountered in teaching English words as logographs—that the word chunks are not unique symbols, but rather reorderings of the same 26 symbols. But to make matters worse, symbol strings representing syllables have no meaning. Can we, in good conscience, ask children to learn 5000 meaningless sound symbols?

Alphabets

Some anonymous Phoenician genius solved the problem of a completely flexible and easy-to-learn writing system about 1500 BC. He developed the alphabet to encode speech while greatly reducing the number of symbols to learn by working at the level of phonemes. How do we know the alphabet came from a single brilliant mind? Historical records show that only regions visited by Phoenician traders (for example, Arabia, Greece, and Rome) developed alphabetic writing. Areas not visited by the Phoenicians (for example, east Asia or the Americas) did not develop alphabets. Cultures with alphabetic writing had a huge advantage in bringing literacy to the common people, thus enhancing the intelligence of the literate with artificial memory, long distance communication, verbal time travel, and the educational advantages of a knowledge archive. Widespread literacy encourages the development of wealth, scientific discovery, and the growth of democracy. It is not without justification that the alphabet has been called the greatest invention in the social history of the world.

The heart of this ingenious invention is the insight that spoken words are composed of a sequence of elemental vocal gestures, or *phonemes*. For example, to say *smooth*, we begin with a hissing of air across a flattened tongue, followed by pressing our lips together and humming, and then make a small opening between pursed lips while continuing to vocalize sound, and finally cutting off the flow of breath by placing the tongue between the teeth. These four gestures—/s/, /m/, /U/, and /th/—are executed to make one seamless sound, *smooth*. English speakers recycle about 40 such vocal gestures to make our 5 million English words, with a virtually limitless supply of pronounceable syllables and syllable combination available for future coinage.

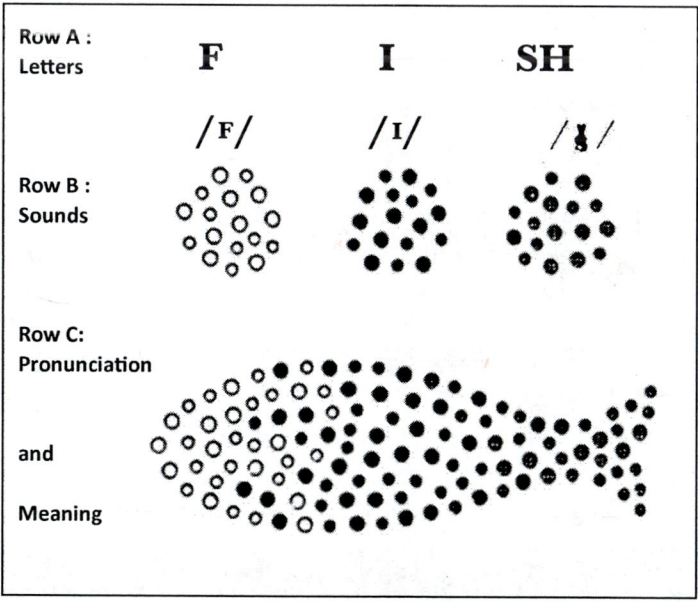

FIGURE 3: The spelling, phonemic structure, pronunciation, and meaning of the word *fish* (Lewkowicz, 1980)

The Alphabetic Principle

Figure 3 graphically illustrates how alphabets work. A logography would directly represent the meaning of fish with some sort of simple, stylized drawing, perhaps something like the outline of Row C. Our Phoenician genius realized that spoken words are composed of phonemes. In the example, the spoken word *fish* is created by blending the gestures /f/, /i/, and /sh/. In the image in Row C, notice that the white, black, and crosshatched dots are thoroughly blended, or coarticulated. There is no easy, mechanical way to separate the phonemes. To recognize the elemental gestures requires phoneme awareness, the ability to detect phonemes in spoken words. Realizing that spoken words were composed of phonemes, the Phoenician genius devised phoneme symbols—graphemes—to map out the sequence of phonemes in the spoken word. A *grapheme* is either a single letter or a digraph, a phoneme spelling with more than one letter. For example, in Figure 3, the letter *f* represents the gesture of touching the top teeth to the lower lip and blowing through the slight opening. The letter *i* represents the sound made by vocalizing while pushing the sides of the tongue through slightly open teeth. The digraph *sh* represents the phoneme made by pursing the lips, centering the tongue, and blowing air through the aperture. Placing these symbols in the order *f-i-sh* maps out the fluid movements we make in saying *fish*. In general, the alphabetic principle is the organizing idea of alphabetic writing: The sequence of letters in the written word maps out the sequence of phonemes in the spoken word.

Before leaving Figure 3, notice that moving from Row A to Row B to Row C represents a beginner's inexpert procedure for decoding. The beginner recognizes the graphemes (*f*, *i*, and *sh*) and sounds them out, i.e., generates phoneme approximations corresponding to the graphemes. Then he blends these phonemes together to generate a pronunciation close enough to *fish* to recognize the word. Moving in the reverse order from Row C to Row B to Row A represents early spelling. The beginner segments the spoken word into phonemes and then represents each phoneme with a letter. The relationship between Row A and Row B represents the traditional phonics curriculum: Sounding out the phonemes in words. However, children can't really understand phonics without the ability to move easily between Rows B and C, involving phoneme awareness. Going from Row B to C—blending—and going from Row C to B—segmentation—are critical components of decoding and spelling words. A recent breakthrough in understanding reading is that children can't make sense out of phonics lessons without phoneme awareness.

Types of Phonemes

All phonemes can be sorted into two basic types: vowels and consonants. These terms better describe phonemes than letters because many letters can represent either vowels or consonants. Vowels are phonemes made by vocalizing (making sounds with the vocal cords) with an open, shaped mouth. Just as the shape of a horn makes different sounds, so the shape of the mouth creates different vowels. Consonants are phonemes made by closing off part of the vocal channel to cause audible friction. Consonant graphemes provide powerful phonetic cues for recognizing words ("Cn y rd ths?"). However, we could not read as easily without vowels, because vowel graphemes complete alphabetic mappings. For example, the consonant graphemes in "Pt pt th pt n th pt" do not provide enough information for context-free word recognition, a hallmark of skilled reading (Perfetti, 1985).

Let's see how alphabetic writing matches up with other writing systems. Is the alphabet versatile enough to write any message? We'll let Lewis Carroll answer:

> Twas brillig, and the slithy toves/Did gyre and gimble in the wabe:
> All mimsy were the borogoves, /And the mome raths outgrabe.

Any message we can imagine, even nonsense words, can be written in an alphabetic system, and skilled readers can decode any message with amazing accuracy. As a skilled alphabetic reader, I'd wager anyone reading this book can read a word like *smedge*—which I made up—and come up with the same pronunciation I intended.

But is alphabetic writing easy to learn? In its favor, alphabets dramatically reduce the number of symbols to learn (there are only 26 letters in the Roman alphabet used to write English). When children catch on to alphabetic writing, they take off. Most children learn to read and write by age seven, and some children learn around age four (my daughter Ellen began to decode words shortly after her fourth birthday).

Difficulties with Alphabets

On the other hand, some very smart children don't catch on to alphabets. We call them dyslexics, reading disabled, or learning disabled: Children with normal intelligence who just can't seem to get the hang of alphabetic writing. They know about piñatas, marsupials, and feta cheese, but what does *g* mean? For such children, a letter seems to be strange, confusable symbol with a meaningless name (*gee*) for a weird mouth move (/g/). Try to show a child that *g* tells you to stop up your breath by pressing the middle of your tongue against the roof of your mouth, and then while vocalizing, releasing your tongue to let out your breath with a small explosion of sound, all as a fluid gesture during the production of a spoken word. Without an awareness of the phoneme /g/ in spoken word contexts, the symbol *g* remains essentially meaningless.

The trickiest part of using alphabetic writing is phoneme awareness; that is, recognition of the elemental vocal gestures of the language in spoken word contexts. For example, it requires phoneme awareness to recognize the phoneme /u/ hidden in the middle of *thumb*. One obvious reason phonemes are hard to recognize is that we make them incredibly fast, from 10 to 20 phonemes per second in normal speech (Liberman & Liberman, 1992). For instance, I can say, "He stuck in his thumb and pulled out a plum," with 28 phonemes, in about 2 seconds, without hurrying. The speech stream is ordinarily filled with such torrents. Another problem with phonemes is that they are coarticulated, or overlapping in spoken words. Try this experiment: Put your mouth in position to say the word *tip*. Now switch your mouth in position to say *trip*. Notice how your tongue pulled back and your lips pursed up? Both words begin with the phoneme /t/, but to say *trip*, you have to position your mouth to say /r/ even before you pronounce /t/. The vocal gestures are coarticulated.

The irregularity of English spelling is certainly a problem. Our 26 letters can't cover the more than 40 phonemes in English, so that some letters do double or triple duty, and many digraphs (2- and 3-letter graphemes) must be pressed into service. Letter position is a variable (compare the various phonemes for *y* in *you*, *gym*, *spy*, and *any*). Some letters serve a signaling function in spellings; for example, the silent *e* signals both the vowel and the final consonant in *rice* and *cage*. English spelling became complicated for several reasons. Through invasion and immigration, foreign words were added to the language, sometimes retaining their native spellings and pronunciations (e.g., *chauffeur*). Pronunciations changed over time, so that an initially regular pronunciation like the Anglo-Saxon word *of* mutated into a softer syllable, slightly easier to pronounce. But the irregularity problem is exaggerated. In highly regular orthographies like Finnish or Spanish, some children still struggle to learn to read. Skillful readers of English learn to mentally mark silent letters as they learn irregular words, realizing that all spellings map pronunciations with decent accuracy, even if a letter or two must be ignored or given an unusual pronunciation (e.g., in *listen* or *answer*). Skillful readers have no problem reading the following poem quoted in Adams (1990) from an anonymous letter published in the *London Sunday Times* (Jan. 3, 1965).

HINTS ON PRONUNCIATION FOR FOREIGNERS

I take it you already know
Of *tough* and *bough* and *cough* and *dough*?
Others may stumble but not you,
On *hiccough*, *thorough*, *laugh*, and *through*.
Well done! And now you wish, perhaps,
To learn of less familiar traps?
Beware of *heard*, a dreadful word
That looks like *beard* and sounds like *bird*,
And *dead*: It's said like *bed*, not *bead*—

For goodness' sake don't call it "deed"!
Watch out for *meat* and *great* and *threat*
(They rhyme with *suite* and *straight* and *debt*).
A moth is not a moth in *mother*
Nor *both* in *bother*, *broth* in *brother*,
And *here* is not a match for *there*
Nor *dear* and *fear* for *bear* and *pear*,
And then there's *dose* and *rose* and *lose*—
Just look them up—and *goose* and *choose*,
And *cork* and *work* and *card* and *ward*,
And *font* and *front* and *word* and *sword*,
And *do* and *go* and *thwart* and *cart*—
Come, come, I've hardly made a start!
A dreadful language? Man alive.
I'd mastered it when I was five.

My favorite part of the poem is its concluding couplet. With all its complications and irregularities, English can be mastered by young children, provided they can be helped to become aware of phonemes, receive some explicit help in learning to decode, and practice reading texts that encourage a decoding strategy.

READING INSTRUCTION IN AMERICAN HISTORY

Early American schools used no-frills reading instruction designed to rapidly introduce the alphabetic code. These schools worked under adverse educational conditions. Children of all ages were usually taught in a single classroom. They were equipped with chalk and slate, but few students had books. A typical student had access to a hornbook (a single sheet with the alphabet, decodable syllables, and prayers), a primer (an introductory reading book), Webster's Blue Back Speller, and the Bible.

Imagine what a lesson might have been like back then. A stern schoolmaster would have a class of beginners march forward to recite. The children would laboriously decode charming texts like *ba, be, bi, bo, bu* (be sure to use the short vowel pronunciations), *da, de, di, do, du*, and *ha, he, hi, ho, hu*. Then each child might return to work with an older tutor in spelling simple syllables. The teacher would likely motivate literacy study with corporal punishment for shirkers.

Horace Mann

Horace Mann took strong exception to this kind of schooling. Mann was the secretary to the Massachusetts Board of Education, or what we would now call the state superintendent of schools. After a six-month tour of European schools, Mann returned with the zeal of a reformer. He determined to replace one-room schools with larger elementary schools broken up by grade levels, with books appropriate to the instruction at each level. He helped establish normal schools, or what we would today call colleges of education. These were such important reforms that Mann is viewed today as the founder of America's public school system.

But Mann also called for a controversial reform. He wanted to replace the spelling and decoding of nonsense syllables with what he thought was a short cut: teaching children whole, meaningful words. Later, he reasoned, novice readers could analyze words learned as wholes and recognize their alphabetic mapping. Mann was a gifted writer who wrote persuasively and passionately about his reading shortcut. He argued that instruction in whole words "will be like an excursion to the fields of Elysium compared with the old method of plunging children, day by day, for months together, in the cold waters of oblivion, and compelling them to say falsely, that they love the chill and torpor of the immersion."

I doubt if the average reader knew exactly what Mann meant, but under the force of such rhetoric, it is easy to find yourself nodding in agreement. Here it is again, in plain language: Asking children to learn whole words will bring them to an educational paradise, whereas having them focus on the alphabetic code is like dunking them in cold water. But is that true? In Mann's method, children must be taught each new word by rote, which presents major problems. They must learn thousands of arbitrary matches between written and spoken words. The denizens of Mann's paradise lie immobilized, waiting for the teacher to help them take each painful step. In contrast, the children who emerge from the cold swim of phonics cavort and play happily in the freedom of literacy.

The phonics-whole word pendulum swung back and forth in American schools, sometimes advancing, sometimes retreating. However, by about 1930, when basal readers were introduced, the whole-word method became the dominant reading method in the public schools (see Balmuth, 1982). It's not that meaning-emphasis programs didn't teach phonics. Rather, the phonics they taught was analytic, incidental, and gradual.

In *analytic* phonics, children are asked first to memorize whole words and later to analyze them to understand how their spellings mapped out pronunciations. The rule in analytic phonics is never to pronounce phonemes in isolation. How would this work in practice? MacGinitie (1976) provides an example:

> The teacher is instructed to write the word *girls* on the board. The teacher then says, "You can find out what this word is. With what consonant does it begin? With what consonants does it end? You know the sounds that *g* and *r* and *l* and *s* stand for. I am going to say something and leave out this word at the

end. When I stop, think of a word that begins with a sound *g* stands for, ends with the sounds *r* and *l* and *s* stand for, and makes sense with what I said."

MacGinitie commented, "Obviously, that instruction is rather complex for most adults, let alone most six-year-olds." But of course, the lesson can *seem* a success by the simple expedient of providing a very heavy context: "In this class, there are many boys and . . . ?" But children's success in producing the word *girls* will have nothing to do with the impenetrably complex explanation mandated by analytic phonics, with its rule forbidding the teacher to pronounce phonemes to model how to sound out and blend.

Besides the method of analytic phonics, phonics was to be taught incidentally, without a planned order for introducing correspondences. There was to be no rigorous attempt to cover all correspondences in a planned sequence. Also, phonics was to be covered gradually, so that a new correspondence may be introduced every couple of weeks. This means that phonics instruction may well last into third or fourth grade. From our vantage point in the early 21st century, the meaning emphasis approach may seem dated, but features of this approach are not far from the mainstream. For instance, consider this poem, published in the leading practitioner journal in reading education (Warner, 1993):

INDEPENDENT STRATEGIES

When I get stuck on a word in a book,
There are lots of things to do.
I can do them all, please, by myself;
I don't need help from you.
I can look at the picture to get a hint,
Or think what the story's about.
I can "get my mouth ready" to say the first letter,
A kind of "sounding out."
I can chop the word into smaller parts,
Like *on* and *ing* and *ly*,
Or find smaller words in compound words
Like *raincoat* and *bumblebee*.
I can think of a word that makes sense in that place,
Guess or say "blank" and read on
Until the sentence has reached its end,
Then go back and try these on:
"Does it make sense?"

"Can we say it that way?"

"Does it look right to me?"

Chances are the right word will pop out like the sun

In my *own* mind, can't you see?

If I've thought of and tried out most of these things

And I *still* do not know what to do,

Then I may turn around and ask

For some help to get me through.

Do we really want children looking at the picture to guess a word? How will they remember the word without the picture? Is it enough to sound out the first letter? Plenty of words begin with the same letter. Does it really help to say "blank" and read on? Context is usually not powerful enough to elicit a word, unaided by decoding.

Rudolf Flesch

In 1955, Rudolf Flesch published a bestselling counterattack against whole word methods entitled *Why Johnny Can't Read* (Flesch, 1955, 1981). Flesch set forth his position with a strong appeal to common sense. Since English is an alphabetic language in which spellings map out the pronunciations of words, children must learn to decode and spell words from their spellings. He called for a return to explicit phonics and launched a no-holds-barred attack against the prevailing instructional consensus on the whole-word method. Like Mann, Flesch (1955) was a powerful and persuasive writer who communicated his passionate beliefs with great effect:

> It's a foolproof system all right. Every grade-school teacher in the country has to go to a teachers' college or school of education; every teachers' college gives at least one course on how to teach reading; every course on how to teach reading is based on a textbook; every one of those textbooks is written by one of the high priests of the word method. In the old days it was impossible to keep a good teacher from following her own common sense and practical knowledge; today the phonetic system of teaching reading is kept out of our schools as effectively as if we had a dictatorship with an all-powerful Ministry of Education.

Flesch's basic argument was well founded, but the arguments he used to make his case ignited an angry debate. He overstated the case, suggesting that explicit phonics will permanently cure all reading problems. He also minimized the difficulty of teaching phonics, suggesting that struggling readers can be set right with minimal instructional effort. In his zeal to reform reading, he attacked the motives of his opponents, arguing that there was a conspiracy to deny reading to children in order to employ remedial teachers and enrich publishers of plodding, repetitious texts.

Flesch's opponents fired back, accusing Flesch of wanting to destroy public education and reduce reading to meaningless drill. The battle lines were drawn for an escalating reading war that engulfed the latter half of the twentieth century. Like any war, the reading war has had its casualties—children kept from the most effective reading methods because of ideology. Passions run high because the stakes are so high. Success in learning to read is critical to a student's entire educational career.

Jeanne Chall

The beginning of détente came with the publication of *Learning to Read: The Great Debate*, by Jeanne Chall, a professor of education at Harvard and a leading scientist of reading education (Chall, 1967). By synthesizing the experimental evidence comparing phonics and whole-word methods, Chall demonstrated that explicit, systematic phonics was more effective than whole-word methods of teaching reading. Children taught explicit phonics in first grade were more successful in learning to read words. The experimental literature showed that explicit phonics in first grade builds an advantage in reading comprehension, at least through third grade. Chall coined the terms *code-emphasis* and *meaning-emphasis* to capture the contrasting instructional positions (See Figure 4).

Chall interpreted the experimental literature on reading instruction to support instruction featuring explicit, systematic, and intensive phonics. In explicit phonics, children are taught to sound out the phonemes signaled by graphemes and to blend the phonemes into recognizable words. This implies that phonemes must be pronounced in isolation (i.e., sounded out) in order for the teacher to model and for children to practice decoding. A systematic phonics program teaches the content of phonics—about 80 regular correspondences between graphemes and phonemes—in a planned order. Usually this means following up instruction in single consonants with the study of short vowels, consonant digraphs, long vowels signaled by silent *e*, long vowel digraphs, and other digraph vowel patterns. The program proceeds at an intensive instructional pace so that most students are well equipped with decoding tools by the middle of second grade.

Meaning emphasis	Code emphasis
Analytic or implicit phonics: First have children memorize a whole word and later analyze the spelling. Never pronounce phonemes in isolation.	*Explicit* or synthetic phonics: Model how to sound out and blend and then guide practice in decoding. Pronounce phonemes in isolation.
Incidental phonics: Take up phonics as children seem to need it.	*Systematic* phonics: Cover all major correspondences in a planned sequence.
Gradual phonics: Don't hurry children; develop phonics knowledge throughout elementary school.	*Intensive* phonics: Teach two correspondences per week and finish by second grade.

FIGURE 4: Meaning Versus Code Emphasis

It is instructive to note the tone with which Chall (1967, p. 309) conveyed her conclusions:

> My review of the research from the laboratory, the classroom, and the clinic points to the need for a correction in beginning reading instructional methods. Most schoolchildren in the United States are taught to read by what I have termed a meaning-emphasis method. Yet the research from 1912 to 1965 indicates that a code-emphasis method—i.e., one that views beginning reading as essentially different from mature reading and emphasizes learning of the printed code for the spoken language—produces better results, at least up to the point where sufficient evidence seems to be available, the end of the third grade.

Note the unmistakable tone of the scientist in Chall's writing. No effort is made to persuade the reader with powerful rhetoric. The scientist lets the data persuade.

LARGE-SCALE PROGRAM COMPARISONS

Chall's synthesis certainly did not settle the phonics debate, but it moved the debate into the court of scientific inquiry. Chall's synthesis of the experimental literature on the effectiveness of phonics had concluded that code-emphasis approaches lead to greater success in learning to read. Given the continuing disparity favoring meaning-emphasis programs (about 85% of all reading programs) over code-emphasis programs (about 15%), people asked Congress for answers, and Congress responded by sponsoring two large-scale experimental studies of beginning reading: the USOE First-Grade Studies (Bond & Dykstra, 1967) and Project Follow Through (Stebbins, St. Pierre, Proper, Anderson, & Cerva, 1977).

The First-Grade Studies (formally, the U. S. Office of Education Cooperative Research Program in First-Grade Reading Instruction) was in progress at the same time as Chall's review of the literature, 1964-1967. The goal was to compare the effectiveness of major competing approaches for teaching children how to read. These included meaning-emphasis basals, code-emphasis basals, linguistic programs, the language-experience approach (a forerunner of whole language), and the initial teaching alphabet (an attempt to regularize English spelling with a special alphabet). The researchers coordinated 27 separate projects, all of which used the same terminology, identifying information, program duration, data-collection schedule, experimental controls, pretests, and outcome measures.

Three factors characterized the most successful first grades (Bond & Dykstra, 1967). First, consistent with Chall's analysis, successful programs included explicit, systematic phonics instruction. Second, they emphasized reading stories and books, not workbook pages or flashcards. Third, they included writing as a partner with reading instruction. As later research demonstrated (Clarke, 1988), daily writing with invented spelling improves children's phoneme awareness, with positive effects on both reading and spelling ability.

Several other interesting conclusions emerged from the USOE First-Grade Studies. The effectiveness of systematic phonics programs did not depend on the readiness of children; slow children and bright children made similar gains. The best predictor of success in learning to read was not intelligence, but letter recognition. Children who could name upper and lowercase letters by the time they entered first grade tended to be the better readers by the end of the year. No single reading method worked for everyone. Every program had both its successes and its failures, which is understandable given that phonics is instruction, and some kinds of decoding instruction are better than others. Finally, teacher skill explained as much variability as instructional method and materials. Programs and materials don't teach themselves: A good reading program needs a good teacher. It should comes as no surprise that skillful teachers are vital agents in children's success in learning how to read. For example, the ability to manage children's behavior so that they remain on task and learning is itself a critical success factor in helping children learn.

The Follow Through studies (Stebbins et al., 1977) were commissioned by Congress to follow up graduates of Head Start, a preschool program to help poor children get off to a good start in school. The problem with Head Start is that preschool gains often disappear in first grade. Thus the question driving the Follow Through studies was: What sort of first-grade program can "follow through" on the achievements of Head Start to maintain the "head start" into later schooling?

The 22 programs compared in the Follow Through studies focused on either skills, intelligence, or motivation. Some programs tried to teach basic academic skills—the traditional "3 Rs" of reading, writing, and arithmetic. Some tried to stimulate children's intelligence with field trips, guest speakers, and science demonstrations in the classroom. Some programs tried to improve children's motivation using child-centered activities aimed at increasing children's self-esteem. The data from the Follow Through studies (Stebbins et al., 1977) showed that children at risk of reading failure get the greatest advantage from programs that teach basic academic skills. The most spectacular success came from a program called DISTAR, which featured explicit, systematic phonics with highly structured, scripted lessons and fast-paced interactions between teachers and students. Children who followed up Head Start with DISTAR made permanent gains in their reading achievement over the other programs. They were more likely to succeed in later content-area courses, complete high school, and pursue a postsecondary education.

The effectiveness of explicit, systematic instruction has been demonstrated in every major synthesis of the research on beginning reading since the large-scale research studies of the 1960s and 1970s: *Becoming a Nation of Readers* (Anderson, Hiebert, Scott, & Wilkinson, 1985), *Beginning to Read* (Adams, 1990), *Preventing Reading Difficulties in Young Children* (Snow, Burns, & Griffin, 1998), and the *Report of the National Reading Panel* (NRP, 2000). Explicit, systematic phonics instruction is one of the landmarks of effective instruction, an approach shown to work in over 60 years of educational research.

What does the research tell us about the kinds of beginning reading instruction that gets kids off to a fast start? To summarize, children make the greatest gains in code-emphasis programs featuring explicit, systematic, intensive phonics instruction, led by a skillful teacher, including lots of reading of books and daily writing. Under such instruction, children gain independence earlier, allowing them to learn new words by reading. By moving quickly to a decoding strategy, they learn sight words faster and more easily, so that after only a few encounters, they can recognize words instantly and automatically. A growing sight vocabulary frees up their minds to think about the meaning of the texts they read, thereby improving sight vocabulary.

Is the ultimate goal of phonics to learn to sound out and blend words? Laborious decoding is only an interim step. The real goal of phonics is effortless word recognition—sight vocabulary—that allows young readers to work full-time at the meaning of texts. In the next chapter, we look at the basic research that shows how beginning readers learn to make sight words.

SUMMARY

Writing and civilization coincide because developing writing is an essential step toward creating an economy capable of sustaining cities. The development of writing empowered humanity with artificial memory, long-distance communication, an archive of knowledge, and the essential tools for education.

The first writing was logographic, using symbols that directly represent the meanings of words. However, logographies require learners to memorize thousands of symbols, and they do not have the flexibility to readily incorporate foreign words and proper names. These problems are somewhat alleviated with a syllabary, i.e., a writing system that encodes the sounds of syllables rather than meanings, but most languages have too many syllables to make a syllabary practicable.

The most efficient system for representing language is an alphabet. The alphabetic principle is that the sequence of letters in a spelling maps out the sequence of phonemes in the spoken word. Because the number of phonemes is limited (there are only about 40 in English), the number of letters can be limited to a manageable number (26 in English). With alphabetic writing, we can read words we've never seen before and write any message of interest, including nonsense. However, learning to use alphabetic writing requires beginners to detect the phonemes in spoken language that are represented by letters. For some children, the challenge of phoneme awareness poses a major barrier in learning to read.

In the one-room schools of the nineteenth century, teachers taught the alphabetic code with drill methods that focused on spelling and reading basic syllables. Educational reformer Horace Mann ridiculed such methods and urged the teaching of whole, meaningful words. By the 1930s, most American schools taught reading with a meaning-emphasis method that featured analytic phonics. In analytic phonics, children memorize whole words and later analyze them to understand their alphabetic mapping, under the rule never to pronounce phonemes in isolation.

In the 1950s, the popular writer Rudolf Flesch galvanized public opinion against whole-word methods with the book *Why Johnny Can't Read*. Flesch correctly argued that alphabetic writing requires decoding instruction, but by minimizing the difficulties of phonics and vilifying opponents, he ignited a war over beginning reading methods. The debate over phonics took a more serious turn when Jeanne Chall synthesized the extant research literature to show that a code-emphasis method featuring explicit, systematic, intensive phonics is more effective in building reading comprehension. This conclusion has been supported by a succession of large-scale experiments and research syntheses over the last half century. This research points to the importance of code-emphasis reading programs involving daily reading of books and daily writing, directed by skillful teachers. The decoding ability taught by systematic, explicit phonics programs enables children to make sight words independently for improved reading comprehension.

How Beginners Develop the Ability to Read Words

The blind-men-and-the-elephant phenomenon in reading, explained in Chapter 1, occurs all too frequently in passionate arguments about how to teach beginning readers. A basic way people go wrong in thinking about reading is to ignore its developmental progression. For example, if we visualize reading as leading to animated talk about *Frog and Toad Are Friends* (Lobel, 1970) in a literature discussion group among fluent readers, the imposition of phonics instruction seems downright stultifying. On the other hand, if we picture another reading group given *Frog and Toad*, but stuttering and stumbling through the words, suddenly phonics seems veritably merciful. We perceive these situations differently because we intuitively understand that these two groups are operating at very different developmental levels. Students already reading with fluency and enjoyment don't need decoding instruction, but students struggling to recognize words need strategies for analyzing spellings and generating pronunciations.

CHALL'S STAGES

Jeanne Chall (1996) provided a broad developmental view of reading as proceeding through six developmental stages, outlined in Figure 1. The typical grades should be thought of as averages. In practice, most schools have readers at several stages in a single classroom. Some kindergartners avidly read chapter books, and some high school beginners struggle to identify simple words. Today's teachers must be prepared to teach readers at a wide range of developmental stages.

Stage	Typical Grades	Achievements	Challenges
Emergent Literacy Chall: Prereading	P-K	Learns to recognize letters and phonemes. Learns concepts about print and story structure.	Word-reading accuracy.
Beginning Reading Chall: Initial Reading/Decoding	1-2	Recognizes words from spellings. Gains ability to learn sight words efficiently.	Reads word by word. Needs automaticity.
Growing Independence and Fluency Chall: Confirmation, Fluency, Ungluing From Print	2-3	Improves accuracy, rate, and expression. Reads many words automatically.	Needs vocabulary and comprehension strategies for reading expository text.
Reading to Learn	4-8	Acquires facts and concepts by reading.	Restricted to single point of view. Needs critical reading.
Multiple Viewpoints	High School	Reconciles different points of view to learn from multiple texts.	Needs coherent worldview.
Construction and Reconstruction: A World View	College	Reads selectively and critically to formulate coherent ideas based on best evidence.	Needs to continue to expand vocabulary and critical reading throughout life.

FIGURE 1: Chall's stages of reading development

This book will cover the broad stages of emergent literacy, beginning reading, and growing independence and fluency, with a glance at the stage of reading to learn. As the subtitle indicates, we are looking at how children learn to make sight words as they progress from phoneme awareness (in the stage of emergent literacy) to decoding (beginning reading) to fluency (growing independence and fluency).

In emergent literacy, children acquire the building blocks of phoneme awareness and letter recognition so that they can begin using the alphabetic code to read words. Note that Chall's preferred terms, e.g., prereading, have in some cases been overruled by more popular terminology, e.g., emergent literacy. Despite the misleading suggestion of emergent literacy that literacy emerges naturally, I here adopt the more general usage in reading education. Children are ready to move beyond emergent literacy when they have learned to recognize consonant phonemes and their graphemes so that they can partially decode words.

In beginning reading, children develop the ability to make sight words. Making sight words depends on decoding, crosschecking, and mental marking to store complete or near complete spellings in memory. Decoding requires a toolkit of vowel and digraph correspondences and the skills of blending and crosschecking. Because decoding is a slow, strategic, attention-draining process, beginning reading tends to be laborious, akin to solving a page of arithmetic problems. However, in solving words by decoding, readers begin to build the sight vocabulary that makes reading easy.

With growing independence and fluency, young readers build a significant sight vocabulary, which pays tangible dividends in new reading abilities. They capitalize on their growing sight vocabularies to pick up speed, add smoothness and vocal expression, and read silently. Most importantly, relying on sight vocabulary, rather than decoding, frees up resources for thinking about the message of texts — thus improving reading comprehension.

In reading to learn, readers who have gained fluency turn their attention to acquiring the vocabulary, concepts, and strategies that improve their learning ability. Now that they have learned to read, they can read to learn. At first they read uncritically, absorbing information that represents a single of view. However, in the stage of multiple viewpoints, they learn to reconcile distinctive viewpoints by critical reading. In the stage of construction and reconstruction, they develop coherent models of knowledge by selective, critical reading of a wide array of texts and learn to transform text information into coherent, plausible, and evidence-based conclusions.

The stage of construction and reconstruction lasts a lifetime. We who are working at understanding how young readers make sight words must be selective, critical readers seeking credible evidence on which to base our teaching practice. Many of the ideas in this book may strike readers as unconventional and outside the mainstream views of reading education. I hope that does not deter your quest for coherent ideas based on the best evidence. If after careful consideration, you determine that the evidence is unconvincing for the proposals in this book, you have at least expanded your repertoire of ideas. However, in the meantime, I hope you will keep an open mind as we examine research and research-based theory to illuminate how children learn to read.

EHRI AND THE PROBLEM OF ACCESS

Probably the single most illuminating theory of how readers learn to make sight words was formulated by Linnea Ehri (1998). Ehri's insights are revolutionizing our understanding of sight word acquisition. Her theory is basic to choosing valid assessments, interpreting assessment data, setting appropriate instructional goals, and planning effective instruction. Ehri's ideas will serve as the basic "currency" of this book, to be used continually in constructing and reconstructing our understanding of learning to read.

Figure 2 introduces the idea of the lexicon and the problem of lexical access for beginning readers. The *lexicon* is the store of words held in memory, a sort of mental dictionary. Its adjective form is *lexical*, related to this personal store of words. In the lexicon, we maintain a vast amount of interconnected information. Each entry includes a pronunciation, a web of meaning, usage information, and optional spelling data. All this information is linked in a network like a webpage with pop-ups, so that if we access anything about a word, everything else pops up. For example, if we hear the word *giraffe*, we immediately have at our disposal words and images of a tall animal with brown spots, directions on how to use the word *giraffe* in a sentence, and spelling information ranging from nothing to the complete spelling.

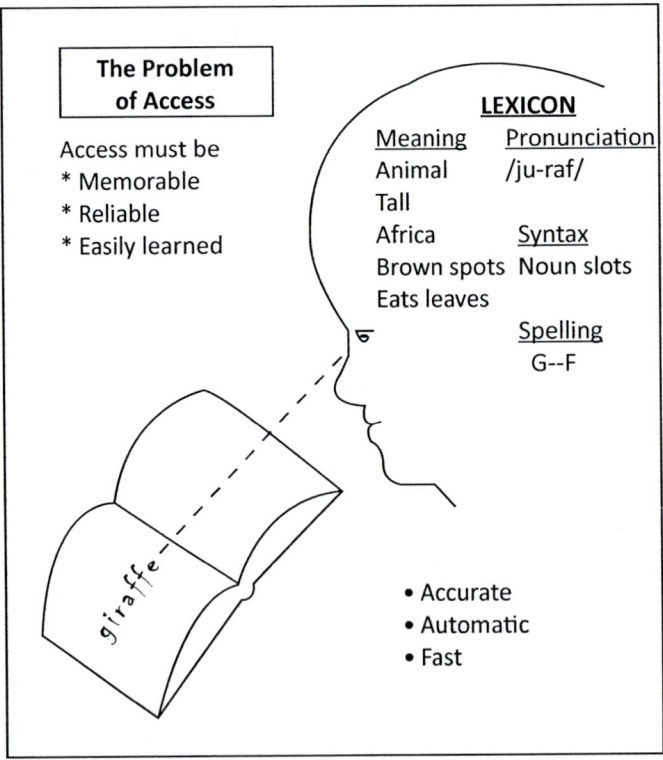

FIGURE 2: The problem of lexical access

The problem for beginning readers is to access the lexicon, i.e., to get at all this stored information in memory. Lexical access is not a problem in spoken language; the pronunciation automatically triggers the *giraffe* entry and we get the works. The beginning reader's problem is to access the lexicon from the spelling *giraffe*. For beginners, often nothing pops up.

For reliable word recognition, we need systematic access to the lexicon, methodical routines that always work for word recognition. Systematic access routes are memorable, reliable, and easily learned. A memorable access route allows us to access the word easily and effortlessly. We don't have to work it out; it just pops up. A reliable access route allows us to get the same word every time we see its spelling. When we see *giraffe*, we never access information about a garage or a girlfriend. An easily learned access route is one that can be acquired in just a few strategic trials. It does not require arduous effort, hundreds of exposures, or dull drill.

Suppose you are an emergent reader with no clue about how spellings map out the pronunciations of words. Learning a word would require matching an arbitrary and meaningless sequence of letter symbols with a spoken word. For example, imagine the words you tried to learn made no more sense than TGR for buffalo, ZBR for lion, NTP for snake, LFT for ostrich, and GRF for monkey. How could you remember such spellings? Perhaps you could simply memorize them, but that would take a lot of trials. You might be able to devise some arbitrary clues, such as visualizing the G in GRF as the monkey's long, curling tail, wrapped over a branch. Still, it would be hard to learn even the five words, and your temporary mnemonics would likely prove unreliable the next day.

But suppose you learned about letters and phonemes so that you could use consonants to begin to decode. In this case, learning a word would be easier because you would have systematic access via the consonants. For example, you might learn TGR for tiger, ZBR for zebra, NTP for antelope, LFT for elephant, and GRF for giraffe. Learning to read such spellings would be dramatically easier. The consonants you could sound out would serve as alphabetic keys to unlock the lexicon and get to the pronunciations and meanings. Knowing how alphabets work would make spellings much more memorable and easy to learn. (You might still have lingering problems with reliability with NTP and LFT, but that's a consequence of using partial spellings.)

Our thought experiment shows that decoding creates systematic access routes that are immediately memorable, reliable, and easy to learn. Such access routes allow accurate word identification. However, accurate lexical access is not good enough to support efficient reading comprehension. To optimize reading comprehension, we need fast, automatic access to words, which is to say, sight word access. Sight word access is effortless and involuntary, leaving the maximum of resources available for reading comprehension.

To experience what automatic word recognition means, try the Stroop test in Figure 3, developed by Ehri (1987). Your task is to name the pictures on the page. Work your way across each row as quickly as possible.

How did you do? Most people find it devilishly hard to name the pictures because we get interference from the words printed on the pictures. Why can't we just ignore the pictures? The reason is that automatic word recognition is not just effortless, but also involuntary. We can't stop ourselves from reading the words. They leap off the page and grab us by the mental lapels.

FIGURE 3: Stroop test (Ehri, 1987) demonstrating automatic word recognition

The Stroop test is unusual: It is the only known task where automatic word recognition poses a problem. First graders would likely perform better than adults because they would not get interference from sight word recognition. This means that difficulty with the Stroop test is a good sign because automatic word recognition is crucial for reading success. Although sight-word knowledge interferes with picture-naming on the Stroop test, in reading, instant, involuntary word recognition frees up resources for comprehension. Beginning readers need to develop a wide sight vocabulary to be able to devote their full attention to getting the message of texts.

THE DUAL ROUTE THEORY

Until recently, reading teachers and researchers assumed a dual route theory. They thought that there are two ways to recognize words—by sight or by decoding. Both ways were thought to be equally effective. Baron and his colleagues

(Baron & Strawson, 1976) called sight word readers "Chinese" (because Chinese writing features whole-word symbols) and decoders "Phoenicians" (because the Phoenicians were the first to write in alphabetic code). Everyone was thought to be either a Chinese or a Phoenician reader.

However, there are problems with the dual-route theory. The word "sight word" is used in two different ways: as a method and as a process. The sight-word method (which I will here call the whole-word method to avoid confusion) asks children to memorize whole words, especially common words, without analysis. The sight-word process, on the other hand, uses decoding to understand and store any word as a pronunciation map in memory. For example, you can read *metamorphosis* without sounding out and blending, but you learned to read it by decoding. If skillful readers use decoding methods to acquire sight vocabulary, then we have only one route to sight-word knowledge, and the dual-route theory breaks down. In this book, the term sight word will refer to words learned by decoding whose spellings have been stored in memory for instant matching to spellings detected in print. In this sense, *magnesium, theocracy,* and *allegorical* are all sight words we can recognize instantly without analysis because we have stored their spellings in our lexicons.

We know readers can decode if they can generate accurate pronunciations for pseudowords, i.e., nonsense words with regular spelling patterns but no meaning. For example, if you can read the pseudoword *bletch*, you must be decoding because you could not have memorized a word you've never seen before.

The dual-route theory says that we read words either by sight or by decoding. However, I'm guessing that you had no trouble reading *metamorphosis* by sight and reading *bletch* by decoding. If so, you are typical of skilled readers, who know a huge number of sight words, far too many to memorize, and who can also decode any legal pseudoword. Skilled readers take both routes, not one or the other. We read by sight and by decoding.

But another kind of evidence falsifies the dual-route theory: Skilled readers use more than two routes to identify words. We see at least two additional routes in the ways skilled readers pronounce the pseudowords PEDNESDAY, RASTEN, and LESIPE. Some readers use pronounceable word parts, recognizing chunks like *ped, nes,* and *day* and quickly assembling them into a three-syllable word, *pednesday*. Similarly, they may read RASTEN as "rass-ten" and LESIPE as "lee-sipe." This is a common versatile method of reading unfamiliar words. I predict you would use this method to read the unfamiliar word *electroluminescence*. Did you find the chunks *electro, lumin,* and *escence* to put together the word?

Other readers analogize to read PEDNESDAY to rhyme with *Wednesday* as a two-syllable word. Following this logic, they might read RASTEN to rhyme with *fasten* and LESIPE to rhyme with *recipe*. To analogize is to think of a word with a similarly spelled ending and to make the unfamiliar word rhyme with this word. This is another useful and sophisticated way to read unfamiliar words. When I saw a truck on the highway with the word *FAVA* printed across its side, I guessed it might be read to rhyme with *lava* or *java*. Notice that analogizing requires a well-spelled sight word in memory. Thus, if you didn't know the spelling of *Wednesday*, you couldn't have drawn an analogy from *pednesday* to *Wednesday*. This puts analogizing out of reach for young readers without extensive sight vocabulary.

One other access route is possible—contextual guessing. We can sometimes use the rest of the sentence to guess an unfamiliar word. For example, in the sentence, "Santa's sleigh was pulled by eight _____," we can guess the missing word reindeer. However, contextual guessing is not reliable with most contexts. In the sentence, "At home we have a new _____," we have little useful information for contextual guessing. Beginners have even less chance of guessing correctly than skilled readers because they have to read the words in the context accurately, without context. They can read context words like *home* and *new* by sight, by decoding, by analogy, or by pronounceable word parts, but they can't guess the unknown word without verbal clues. For these reasons, contextual guessing is rarely used by skilled readers. It is an unreliable strategy for beginners who lack decoding ability and sight vocabulary.

Thus, rather than dual routes, we have five access routes: sight, decoding, pronounceable word parts, analogizing, and contextual guessing. But these strategies are not equally efficient. Figure 4 provides a summary and examples.

Sight: Instant recognition without decoding.
    Example: *flamboyant*

Decoding: Using the graphemes in the spelling to generate a pronunciation.
    Example: *squip*

Pronounceable word parts: Merging sight chunks for rapid decoding.
    Example: *velociraptor*

Analogizing: Pronouncing a new word to rhyme with a known word.
    Example: *chambeau*

Contextual guessing: Using meaning clues in other words in the sentence to figure out an unknown word.
    Example: *The hostess served a plate of hors d'oeuvres*

FIGURE 4: Five access routes to lexical access

By far, the most efficient access route to the lexicon is sight. Sight word recognition is effortless and involuntary, maximizing resources for reading comprehension. Ideally, readers will accumulate a massive store of sight words, allowing them to work full-time at getting the message of text. Pronounceable word parts comes in second; it is the most versatile decoding strategy, available for disentangling nearly any polysyllabic English word. Analogizing is third; it is quite efficient, but in many cases, we don't have a good analogy. Decoding using grapheme-phoneme correspondences works well with most single-syllable words. The least efficient access route is contextual guessing, which is tough and unreliable.

Ehri's phases of recognizing words

How do children develop the expert ability to read words as sight words? Ehri (1998) formulated the single most useful theory for understanding the development of word recognition in her phases of recognizing words. Figure 5 provides a ready reference and guide for understanding the four phases of word recognition.

Prealphabetic, or logographic, or visual cue reading.
  Reader selects a visual cue and links it directly to meaning
    (e. g., letter, feature, illustration, bent corner, or smudge).
  Examples: *look* has eyes; *dog* has a tail; *television* has knobs.
  Benefit: Enjoyable early reading by cued recitation.
  Problem: Words are very hard to remember
    (e.g., *book*, *room*, and *boot* all have eyes).

Partial alphabetic, or phonetic cue reading.
  Reader sounds out the first consonant for a pronunciation clue.
  May use several letters or boundary letters.
  Benefit: Some word learning, accurate finger-pointing.
  Problem: Words not reliably recognized.
    (e.g., *cab*, *car*, and *can* begin alike).

Full alphabetic
  Reader uses the entire spelling to generate a pronunciation.
  Sequential: Sound out and blend phonemes in sequence.
  Hierarchical: Recognizes conditions and signals
    (e.g., that silent *e* signals long vowel).
  Benefit: Rapid growth of sight vocabulary.
  Problem: Word recognition is slow and attention-draining.

Consolidated alphabetic, or orthographic.
  Use sight chunks to rapidly assemble unfamiliar words.
  Analogizing strategy becomes available.
  Benefit: Reading rate increases comprehension enhanced as word
    recognition becomes automatic.

FIGURE 5: Ehri's phases of recognizing words

In explaining these phases, Ehri (1998) carefully avoids using the word *stages*, which suggests a mandatory progression. At least one phase, the prealphabetic phase, might be skipped altogether with early, explicit instruction. The phases suggest a succession of strategies readers learn to employ. Unlike fixed stages, readers can adopt strategies fluently in response to text challenges. For example, a reader who uses full alphabetic decoding in simple decodable text might switch to partial alphabetic decoding in a text like *Frog and Toad Are Friends*, where the words are not restricted to monosyllables with known vowels.

Notice that all four phases are "alphabetic." Each phase captures a strategic attempt to deal with alphabetic mappings. Notice, too, that there is a trend across stages. In progressing from prealphabetic to full alphabetic, readers use more of the alphabetic mapping in spellings, from none, to some, to all. In moving from full alphabetic to consolidated, they use spellings much more efficiently.

Briefly, prealphabetic readers waste the alphabetic map, using the default strategy of looking for visual cues to meaning. Partial alphabetic readers use only consonants in the alphabetic map to generate phonetic cues. Full alphabetic readers use the entire alphabetic map, but very strategically and inefficiently. Consolidated alphabetic readers quickly size up the alphabetic map using pronounceable word parts or analogizing.

The miscues, or reading mistakes, made by children are often good indicators of their Ehri phase. A prealphabetic reader might say "freezing" for *cold*. His or her miscues would make no use of the alphabetic map. A partial alphabetic reader might say "cool" for *cold*, using the beginning letter *c* to get the first consonant. A full alphabetic reader might say "called" for *cold* by sounding out and blending each letter. A consolidated alphabetic reader would likely arrive quickly at *cold* (if it is unknown) by using the pronounceable word part *old*. Consolidated alphabetic readers might also recognize *cold* in analogous words like *scold* and in multi-syllable words like *coldhearted*.

The Prealphabetic Phase

Before children learn to use the alphabet, their word reading strategies are prealphabetic. They try to remember a word from some visual cue, just as they would cue on a noticeable feature of a face, picture, or object. The particular cue they choose is idiosyncratic and arbitrary; it is unlikely that another prealphabetic reader would use the same cue. For example, one prealphabetic reader might notice the "bent fishing pole" at the beginning of *fish*, where another might associate the *s* with a worm as bait. Because visual cues are arbitrary, they must be continually reinvented. Rather than having a methodical access route that always works, prealphabetic readers have to invent a new access route for each word. Again, the visual cue is typically just part of the word rather than a unified perception of the whole word. It may be a letter or letters (e.g., the "eyes" in *look*) or a letter feature (e.g., the "tail" on *dog*). The cue may even be outside the word, such as a bent corner on a flash card or the illustration in a storybook.

The prealphabetic reader links his visual cue to the meaning of the word and not to the pronunciation. As a result, the more meaningful and concrete the word (such as *fish*, *look*, or *dog*), the easier it is to remember. However, teachers often ask children to use a whole-word (i.e., prealphabetic) method to learn high frequency words like *to* and *for*. Most high frequency words have minimal meaning; they function as syntactic glue to construct sentences with content words. For this reason, they are extraordinarily difficult to remember using prealphabetic strategies.

Gough's Thumbprint Study

Phil Gough (Gough, Juel, & Griffith, 1992) asked prealphabetic readers to learn a group of words, such as *fix, rub, rat,* and *dog*, by the whole-word method. One of the flash cards used to present a word featured an "inadvertent" thumbprint, as in Figure 6:

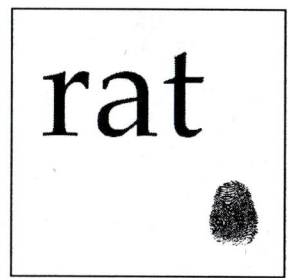

FIGURE 6: Flash card with an "inadvertent" thumbprint

With a useful visual cue, prealphabetic readers learned Gough's thumbprinted word quickly. However, when *leg* appeared with a thumbprint, it was read as "rat," and when *rat* appeared without a thumbprint, children could no longer read it. However, a card containing only a thumbprint was read as "rat"! The lesson here is that the arbitrary visual cues selected by prealphabetic readers do not help them access the word in the future. Because the same cues recur in other words, they do not serve as reliable guides to word identification.

The Red Herring of Reading Environmental Print

Children's successes in recognizing environmental print are often cited as a reason to encourage prealphabetic reading. We have probably all known preschool experts at identifying product labels for Coke, Pepsi, McDonald's, and Nike. Emergent literacy theorists (e.g., Harste, Burke, & Woodward, 1982) have proposed that children "decontextualize" environmental print. In other words, they see words on a printed sign such as a stop sign in their environment, and they gradually come to recognize the words out of context, when they are written in plain print. Following this theory, some teachers and parents try to immerse children in print. They may paper homes and classrooms with environmental print, labeling the fishbowl, the refrigerator, and the coat closet, hoping that children will decontextualize these labels and learn to read the words independently of their environmental context.

Do children learn to read words by decontextualizing environmental print? To find out, Ehri and her colleagues (Masonheimer, Drum, & Ehri, 1984) carried out an educational experiment. They found 102 prereaders who were experts at reading environmental print, able to identify 8 out of 10 of the most common product logos. They tested the hypothesis that these environmental print experts would be able to read many of the logo words without the logo. However, when the logos were removed, hardly any of the children were able to read any logo words. To further test the decontextualization theory, they altered the logos and asked if there was anything different about them. Figure 7 shows an example of an altered Pepsi label:

FIGURE 7: Pepsi label altered to read Xepsi

Even placed side by side with the original labels, most prereaders did not notice any changes in the images.

Steve Stahl and I (Stahl & Murray, 1993) replicated the Masonheimer et al. (1984) study with a group of kindergarteners and first graders. Prealphabetic kindergarteners performed much differently from full alphabetic first graders. One finding was particularly striking. Figure 8 shows a scan of the print on a McDonald's hamburger wrapper:

FIGURE 8: A one-item reading test

The word HAMBURGER is approximately 18 times larger than the word McDonald's. Nevertheless, our prealphabetic readers invariably read this environmental print as "McDonald's." Only children who could successfully read a preprimer word list, indicating movement beyond the prealphabetic phase, ever said "hamburger." We called this wrapper a one-item reading test. Only children who say "hamburger" are readers.

Perhaps prealphabetic readers have not had enough encounters with environmental print to successfully decontextualize the print. However, a simple demonstration suggests that even adults do not decontextualize the print seen in the environment. For example, see if you can read the common environmental print in Figure 9:

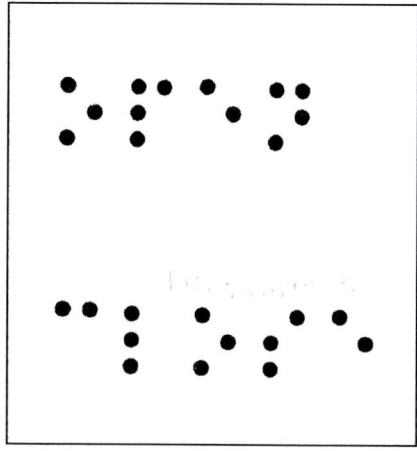

FIGURE 9: An environmental print decontextualization test for adults

You probably recognize that this text is in Braille, but can you read the words? You have probably seen these Braille words many times. Perhaps it would be helpful to show you more of the context in Figure 10:

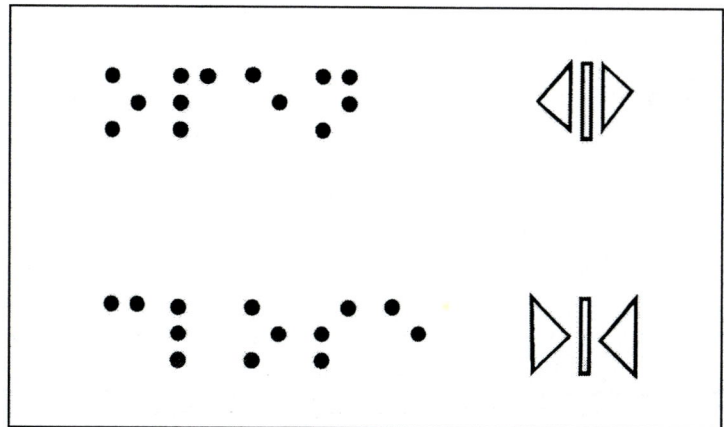

FIGURE 10: Full context for the Braille text

The logographic symbols to the right may help you identify the Braille words as *open* and *close*. However, as often as we have encountered this common environmental print, we have not learned the coded words in Braille. Most of us have neither studied the formation of the Braille alphabet nor experienced the "press" to interpret the Braille words independently of their logographic symbols.

Both experiments with children and our own experience with environmental print show that identifying environmental print is a kind of picture recognition unrelated to learning the alphabetic code. Teachers and parents who label the fishbowl, refrigerator, and coat closet do nothing to help prealphabetic children decontextualize print from the environment. The easy visual identification of fishbowls, refrigerators, and coat closets obviates any need to work out the arcane coded symbols placed on these familiar objects.

The False Hope of Natural Learning

Maybe if teachers deliberately called attention to words using a whole-word method, children would figure out that letters map the pronunciation of words and begin to make use of the alphabetic code. Byrne and Fielding-Barnsley (1989) taught prealphabetic readers the words *mat* and *sat* using the whole-word method to a criterion of six correct readings for the pair of words in succession. Having mastered the two words, the researchers asked children to transfer their knowledge to read similar words, asking, e.g., Does this [MAD] say "mad" or "sad"? Not one of their prealphabetic readers could reliably use the beginning letter to distinguish the new words. Without explicit instruction, they couldn't crack the alphabetic code. The alphabetic code is simply too complex. It depends on learning abstract letter symbols for the flowing vocal gestures of speech.

The inescapable conclusion is that prealphabetic readers use the default method of visual cue reading unless they are taught to use the alphabetic code in reading. In the absence of instruction, they try to read words as they learn a face, picture, or object, by selecting visual cues to meaning. Children do not discover how to use the technology of the alphabet to decipher the pronunciations of printed words. They need a teacher to introduce them to the mysteries of the alphabetic code.

What do readers need to become partial alphabetic—to begin to use consonant letters in decoding? They need to recognize letters and phonemes, the essential building blocks of the alphabetic code. Letter recognition is the second strongest predictor of success in beginning reading. Phoneme awareness is the strongest predictor. Once beginners become aware of phonemes, letters take on meaning, directing the assembly of phonemes in decoding a printed word.

THE PARTIAL ALPHABETIC PHASE

Partial alphabetic readers access words by sounding out consonants to identify words that are active in the lexicon. They switch from the visual cues of the prealphabetic phase to phonetic cues, i.e., the mouth moves signaled by consonants. For this reason, we sometimes call children in the partial alphabetic phase "phonetic cue readers." Because these readers use some, but not all, of the letters in decoding, they are partial rather than full alphabetic. Partial alphabetic readers waste most of the spelling map. They only decode consonants, and at first, only the initial consonant. Later they may use the boundary consonants, but they rarely make use of vowels. By ignoring the vowels, they miss the coded information at the heart of every syllable. Only the part of the spelling they decode can be stored in the lexicon for future use. As a result, partial alphabetic readers store incomplete spellings. Because sight-word recognition matches stored spellings with spellings encountered in print, partial alphabetic readers read few if any words automatically as sight words.

How can you decide if a reader is prealphabetic or partial alphabetic? The best ordinary indicator is to look at the reader's miscues, or reading mistakes. Only the miscues of partial alphabetic readers preserve the initial consonant of the text word. For example, if the reader reads "cat" for *kitten*, he or she probably used the *k* from *kitten* as a phonetic cue, along with context or pictures, to access *cat*. Whenever a miscue begins with a correct or related letter from the text word, the reader is probably partial alphabetic, sounding out part of the spelling to guess the word.

Advantages of the Partial Alphabetic Phase

Partial alphabetic readers are more accurate than prealphabetic readers because they have a systematic access route to the lexicon, i.e., a methodical routine to unlock part of the pronunciation. For example, a reader who could sound out *z* in *zebra* would have systematic access to the word. In contrast, a prealphabetic reader, unable to use *z* as a phonetic cue, might use an illustration to guess "horse" for *zebra*. Such arbitrary visual cues are not memorable, reliable, or easy to learn.

Partial alphabetic readers have an advantage in learning to read the common words like *to* and *for* that teachers present by the whole-word method. For prealphabetic readers, *to* and *for* are arbitrary letter sequences to memorize, and because they try to link visual cues to meaning, meaningless function words are especially hard to learn. However, partial alphabetic readers can use initial letters as phonetic cues, giving these readers a better chance to access function words.

Disadvantages of the Partial Alphabetic Phase

For partial alphabetic readers, lexical access remains unreliable because many words begin with the same letter. For example, the words *too, toe, tie,* and *tea* will be hard to distinguish for partial alphabetic readers because they all begin with the same phonetic cue. Partial alphabetic readers will often read a word correctly on one page, and then miss the same word on the next page. This is exactly what we'd expect to happen when readers are only processing phonetic cues rather than decoding and storing the entire spelling in memory.

The reading deck is stacked against partial alphabetic readers. Without vowels for decoding unfamiliar words, they are forced to use consonants for contextual guessing, which drains the cognitive resources that would otherwise help with reading comprehension. Partial alphabetic decoding only stores fragments of spellings in memory. This thwarts the development of sight vocabulary, which depends on storing well-spelled representations of words for instantaneous matching between the lexicon and spellings in texts. Thus, partial alphabetic readers bring an impoverished sight vocabulary to reading, and they have to laboriously invent spellings when they write.

To escape the limitations of phonetic cue reading, partial alphabetic readers need to learn the vowel correspondences that will enable them to understand complete alphabetic mappings. To this end, they need phonics instruction to acquire the vowel correspondences that will enable full alphabetic decoding and sight-word learning.

Learning Disability

The phonetic cue reading strategy may persist with older poor readers and cause a long-term drag on their reading comprehension. We call older readers with persistent problems in word recognition *reading disabled* (formerly dyslexic) or *learning disabled* (LD). Readers with LD have normal or even bright intelligence, but unusual difficulties recognizing words. Research indicates that they have specific difficulties with decoding, so that they are slowed down or stumped by the challenge of reading unfamiliar words and pseudowords (Stanovich, 1986). Ehri's (1998) explanation of the phases of development in word recognition shows the problem: Readers with LD are stuck in the partial alphabetic phase. Because they are not fully decoding words to store their complete spellings in memory, they are forced to expend valuable resources on contextual guessing. Disabled readers' good intelligence allows them to hide their word reading problems for a time by contextual guessing and memorization, but these strategies work less and less well as text difficulty increases. Unlike their peers, they cannot develop an extensive sight vocabulary without fully decoding words. With only fragments of spellings in memory, they cannot work full time at reading comprehension because they must continually expend resources on word identification. However, this analysis also suggests that readers with LD can be helped to learn full alphabetic decoding, allowing them to build sight vocabulary, with explicit, systematic phoneme awareness and phonics instruction, especially if their problems are caught early.

FULL ALPHABETIC READERS

Full alphabetic readers access words from their spellings alone, without any need for context. They learn words using decoding strategies that lead them to examine every letter in the spelling, so that the spelling comes to fully map out the pronunciation of the word—a process that enables making sight words.

Recognizing the Full Alphabetic Reader

An examination of the miscues (reading mistakes) of full alphabetic readers can help us recognize their decoding strategies. For example, a full alphabetic reader might say "own" for *one* because he is using the *o_e* vowel to choose the phoneme /O/, which with most words would be accurate. The full alphabetic reader can read pseudowords, representing words never seen before, by decoding. For example, most full alphabetic readers can read *smork*, showing that they can generate accurate pronunciations from the spelling alone. A reader who can pronounce even one pseudoword (e.g., *lat*, *sep*, or *fim*) without instruction has reached the full alphabetic phase.

Full alphabetic decoding begins as a slow, awkward strategy, but later becomes a smooth skill executed automatically. Early full alphabetic readers work sequentially from left to right through a word, sounding out and blending letter by letter. Thus, such a reader might or might not succeed with a word like *thumb*, with a consonant digraph at the beginning and a silent letter at the end. Later, full alphabetic readers begin to detect vowel and consonant digraphs (vowel or consonant "teams"), at which point we might hear, "Let's see, /th/, /u/, /m/, /b/, thumbuh? Oh, *thumb*."

The strategy of examining a pronunciation in search of a known sound-alike word that makes sense in context is called *crosschecking*. Ehri's research indicates that crosschecking is crucial for storing complete spellings for sight-word recognition. This implies that full alphabetic readers learn partly irregular words like *thumb* as sight words in essentially the same way they learn pseudowords like *spork*. In both cases, they decode all the letters in the spelling to arrive at the pronunciation. With irregular words, an additional step of crosschecking is required to mentally mark anything odd or silent, such as the *b* in *thumb*. Research indicates a moderately strong correlation between reading pseudowords and irregular words (Stanovich, 2000, p. 270). In other words, the same students who can read the most pseudowords can also read the most irregular words. This implies that we read pseudowords and irregular words by the same process, built on full alphabetic decoding.

Advantages of Full Alphabetic Decoding

Reading using full alphabetic strategies can be discouraging for young readers. It may be the toughest time in learning to read because most words are unfamiliar, and they must be solved one by one, in a slow, attention-draining struggle. Yet the advantages of full alphabetic reading over partial alphabetic reading are dramatic. Full alphabetic readers can learn new words independently, without the help of a teacher. They have a self-teaching device for learning new words (Share, 1999). Full alphabetic readers can identify words from spellings alone; they don't need pictures or contextual guessing. Because they use the complete spelling in word identification, they have reliable access to the lexicon—they nearly always get the right word. And most importantly, full alphabetic readers can acquire sight words easily by internalizing their complete spellings.

Ehri's most important insight is how children learn sight words in the full alphabetic phase by the process of decoding, crosschecking, and mental marking. We used to think children learned sight words by a whole-word method requiring dozens of exposures. This is why the best-selling basal of the 1950s and 1960s featured stories with relentless repetition of words, such as the story "See Sally Work" from *We Work and Play* (Gray, Monroe, Artley, & Arbuthnot, 1956):

Work, work, work. Sally can work. See Sally work.

Oh, Dick. Oh, Jane. See, see. Sally can work.

Oh, Sally. Funny, funny Sally. Oh, oh, oh.

The authors were applying research in writing stories with such dull, repetitive wording. Gates (1931) determined that the average reader using the standard whole-word method required 35 trials to memorize each spelling. However, more recent research has determined that far fewer trials are needed to learn words by full alphabetic decoding. Reitsma (1983) determined that full alphabetic readers can learn sight words by decoding in as few as 4 learning trials. The reduction in trials from 35 to 4 dramatically reduces the work of learning to recognize words. For average ability readers, decoding is 8.75 times easier (35 ÷ 4) for learning sight words than the whole-word method. Thus, with equal effort, the full alphabetic reader can learn nearly 9 sight words for each word memorized by the whole-word method.

Learning Sight Words by Decoding

Sight words can be learned in only four trials, but learning sight words requires decoding, not mere exposure. Figure 11 illustrates the connections full alphabetic readers make between graphemes and phonemes. To acquire a complete spelling for sight-word recognition, the full alphabetic reader must mentally connect each letter in the spelling to a phoneme in the pronunciation—or mentally mark that letter as silent or irregular. Simple words like *stop* are learned by sequentially sounding out the letters to learn the alphabetic mapping. With *check*, the digraphs *ch* and *ck* must be linked to their phonemes, requiring a more sophisticated hierarchical analysis. With *sign* and *island*, the reader's initial decoding will require crosschecking to correct a near miss in the pronunciation, followed by mental marking to remember the silent letters in storing the spelling. In each case, readers build connections using their correspondence knowledge. With irregular words, they take the additional step of mental marking to secure the unpredictable elements. In this way, the complete spelling is stored in memory for sight-word recognition when the spelling is encountered in print.

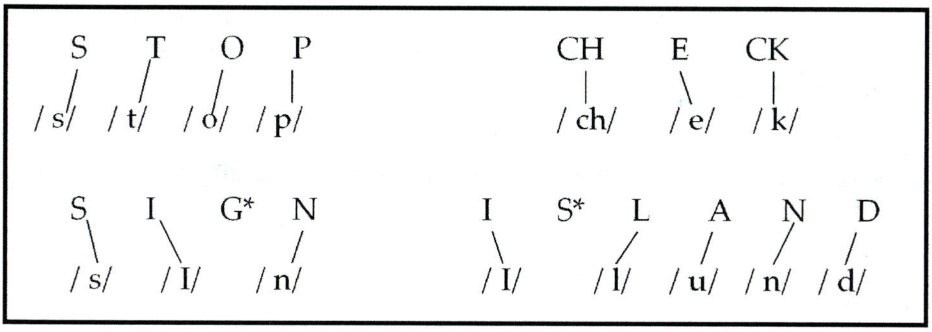

```
S   T   O   P              CH    E    CK
|   |   |   |              |     \    |
/s/ /t/ /o/ /p/           /ch/  /e/  /k/

S   I   G*  N              I    S*   L   A   N   D
\   \   /   /              \    /    /   /   /   /
/s/ /I/    /n/            /I/  /l/ /u/ /n/ /d/
```

FIGURE 11: Grapheme-phoneme connections made by full alphabetic readers

Once systematic access routes have been established, the correspondence rules use to build connections drop out. After about four learning trials, readers no longer have to sound out and blend to understand the spelling as a pronunciation map. Instead, the spelling has been stored in memory as a meaningful map of the spoken word. The spelling begins to "look like" the spoken word. In Ehri's (1991) terms, we store an "alphabetic phonological representation" of the word in memory. This means we remember the spelling as an alphabetic map of the spoken word, easy to remember because it makes sense. When we see the stored spelling in print, we can make a quick, effortless match to access the word.

How do we get beginning readers to the full alphabetic phase? We give them decoding instruction, i.e., phonics. Phonics teaches the vowel correspondences partial alphabetic readers need to complete their grapheme-phoneme connections. It is rarely necessary to teach partial alphabetic readers consonants. In the partial alphabetic phase, they already use consonants to close in on words. They need vowel correspondences to make sight words.

THE CONSOLIDATED ALPHABETIC PHASE

The consolidated alphabetic phase is the expert phase for learning sight words. Consolidated alphabetic readers take a shortcut to lexical access by remembering sight chunks of words for rapid assembly of representations of unfamiliar words. Sight chunks are pronounceable word parts like *un* and *able* recognized effortlessly and automatically in learning words like *unimaginable*. Consolidated readers can also use sight words as analogies to identify unfamiliar words. For example, I bet you have no difficulty recognizing the word *digamy* using the analogy word *bigamy*.

Advantages of Consolidated Alphabetic Decoding

Learning sight words and sight chunks confers enormous advantages in sight-word reading efficiency. Consolidated readers can rapidly decode polysyllabic words like *prefabricated* by stringing together familiar parts. With access to polysyllabic words, virtually all texts become accessible; readers are limited only by their knowledge of meaning vocabulary. Consolidated readers can quickly amass new sight vocabulary because it is easy to learn new sight words by recognizing and assembling sight chunks.

How do we learn sight chunks, such as the ubiquitous syllable *-ing*? We learn sight chunks by the same processes as we learn sight words, beginning with decoding. For example, after learning about the digraph *ng*, readers can decode the syllable *ing* en route to words like *sing* or *ring*. With *-ing* as a sight chunk, readers can quickly decode unfamiliar words like *sling*.

Analogizing

Analogizing is a strategy of the consolidated alphabetic phase. To analogize, we need a well-spelled sight word in memory with a similar spelling pattern to an unfamiliar word. We decode to acquire well-spelled sight words for analogizing. Thus, readers must gain the full alphabetic phase to learn sight words that can be used to analogize. Try analogizing to recognize the unfamiliar word *dressage*. If you thought of *message* as your analog, try again, using *massage, barrage,* or *collage*. Analogizing is not foolproof, and it is not quite as versatile as using pronounceable word parts, but it is a valuable decoding tool only available to consolidated alphabetic readers like you.

There is great interest in teaching learning-disabled readers to analogize, but efforts to do so have met with little success. Ehri's theory shows why. Students with learning disabilities tend to be poor spellers with gaps in their spellings. They don't have a large sight vocabulary of well-spelled words to analogize from. Why haven't they learned many sight words? The reason is their reliance on partial alphabetic strategies of phonetic cue reading and contextual guessing. Partial alphabetic reading only allows them to store partial spellings, which are not sufficient for sight word reading. They are missing the vowel correspondences they need to understand and remember complete alphabetic mappings.

How can we help struggling older readers in the partial alphabetic phase learn sight words, sight chunks, and skill with analogizing? They must master the full alphabetic phase, where these achievements become possible. They need effective phonics instruction to learn the vowel correspondences they need to make sight words. Some people will argue that phonics hasn't worked for older struggling readers. However, we would never say that arithmetic hasn't worked for older struggling math students. The problem is not in the subject matter, which in both cases is essential. The problem involves the teaching methods and materials.

Expert decoding skill is mandatory for learning sight words. However, we need effective teachers who can manage behaviors learned after years of frustration using methods and materials that do not look babyish, including the letterbox lesson and wordmapping, explained in Practical Chapters 3 and 8.

Moving Full Alphabetic Readers into the Consolidated Alphabetic Phase

What about full alphabetic readers, plodding through text, solving unfamiliar words with all the alacrity of solving a page of math problems? How can we help them adopt consolidated alphabetic strategies for rapid and efficient sight word learning? Because there are tens of thousands of words they need to learn as sight words for analogizing, and thousands of sight chunks they need for pronounceable word parts, full alphabetic readers must read voraciously. They need guidance in selecting and scaffolding their reading in independent level text (for independent reading) or instructional level text (when a teacher's help is available), so that frustrations are minimized. Repeated reading of the same text is important to get the four learning trials per word needed for making sight vocabulary. Coverups (uncovering difficult words chunk by chunk) are valuable for learning polysyllabic words like *interesting*. Instruction in mental marking is important for learning irregular words like *Wednesday*.

Figure 12: shows how readers at various phases might try to read the word *geode*.

Prealphabetic phase: Student guesses a word that makes sense.
    lamb
    geode   Mary had a little **lamb**.

Partial alphabetic phase: Student thinks of a word that makes sense and begins with /g/.
    girl
    geode   Mary had a little **girl**.

Full alphabetic phase: Student sounds out and blends.
    ghee-ode
    geode   Mary had a little **ghee-ode**.

Consolidated alphabetic phase: Student recognizes the chunks *geo* and *ode*.
                        Mary had a little **geode**.

FIGURE 12: Access routes for attempting to read geode across the phases of recognizing words

Suppose we ask readers of each phase to read the text, "Mary had a little geode." Suppose we scaffold by providing the beginning of the sentence, so that our readers only have to access the final word. A prealphabetic reader will waste the alphabetic map *geode*, leaving contextual guessing as a strategy to come up with "lamb." A partial alphabetic reader might use the first letter *g* to narrow the range of contextual guessing and come up with *girl*. A full alphabetic reader would use each letter in the spelling to generate a pronunciation like "ghee-ode," which he might crosscheck to get *geode*. A consolidated alphabetic reader would quickly assemble the sight chunks *geo* and *ode* to read *geode*.

Should our goal for beginning readers be to remember words by sight or to decode? Both are important: To make progress, beginners must learn to decode and to read words by sight. But decoding must come first because sight word reading depends on decoding.

SUMMARY

Many arguments about reading occur because disputants fail to recognize that there is a developmental sequence in learning to read, so that beginners do not use the processes and strategies of skilled readers. Chall (1976) described developmental stages in learning to read, including (1) a stage of emergent literacy in which children learn the elements of phoneme awareness and letter recognition; (2) a stage of beginning reading in which children learn to decode words; (3) a stage of growing independence and fluency, in which readers acquire a large sight vocabulary, enabling them to read fluently; and (4) a stage of reading to learn, in which children capitalize on fluent reading to focus on the message of texts, acquire meaning vocabulary, and learn comprehension strategies.

Ehri (1998) developed a phase theory of word recognition with special relevance for how children learn to make sight words. She described reading as a problem of lexical access, i.e., unlocking meaning information in memory from the printed word. Children learn to access the lexicon in ways that are memorable, reliable, and easily learned. Ideally, lexical access is not just accurate, but also fast and automatic, so that the sight of a printed word triggers a word representation in memory effortlessly and involuntarily, allowing maximal resources for thinking about the message of a text.

Most researchers have assumed that there are dual routes to reading words—sight and decoding. The term *sight word*, however, has been used equivocally to mean a method (here called the whole-word method) or a process of coming to understand a printed word as a phoneme map, allowing the storage of the complete spelling in memory for instant access when seeing the word in print. In addition, there are other routes besides sight or decoding. A reader can analogize by thinking of a word with a similar spelling and making the unfamiliar word rhyme with the analogy word. Alternatively, the reader can recognize pronounceable word parts and string them together for word recognition, e.g., identifying *un*, *for*, *give*, and *able* to read *unforgiveable*. Readers can also guess words from context, although contextual guessing is mainly used by younger and less skilled readers who lack a large sight vocabulary and efficient decoding, analogizing, or pronounceable word parts strategies. The most efficient access route for word recognition is sight word access because it requires no conscious strategizing that would distract from getting the message of text.

Ehri (1998) described four phases in learning to recognize words. In the prealphabetic phase, children attempt to find visual cues to meaning, e.g., using the *o's* in *look* to signal the act of looking. Visual cues can be found within or outside a word, but they rarely include the whole word. In a study by Gough et al. (1992), the visual cue was a thumbprint; children were unable to recognize the word without a thumbprint, and misread other words when they were thumbprinted. The common ability to read environmental print is a prealphabetic strategy that uses the images in logos as visual cues to meaning. Accordingly, well-meaning attempts to help children learn to read words by immersing them in a print-rich environment in which they can "decontextualize" the print have not been successful in helping children learn to read words. Because English words are encoded using an alphabetic technology, beginners must master use of the alphabetic code for efficient word reading.

The first step in learning the alphabetic code takes place in the partial alphabetic phase when readers become aware of the consonant phonemes in spoken words. With letter recognition and phoneme awareness, children begin to decode consonants. This allows them to increase their word reading accuracy, but they remain unable to make sight words for effortless word recognition. The shortcomings of the partial alphabetic phase illuminate the problems of children with reading disability, who face similar limits on building sight vocabulary because they rely on partial decoding and contextual guessing.

A milestone in learning to read is attaining the full alphabetic phase, when readers fully analyze spellings by sounding out and blending to recognize words. Crosschecking, or testing a pronunciation in context, becomes a critical strategy because it allows full alphabetic readers to mentally mark silent or irregular graphemes for a full understanding of word spellings. Spellings that are understood as pronunciation maps can be stored in memory for a quick and automatic match when these words are encountered in print; this is the mechanism for making sight words. Where whole-word memorization takes an average 35 trials, storing a complete or nearly complete spelling in memory for sight recognition takes only about 4 trials, a ninefold gain in word-learning efficiency. Because spellings are understood by matching graphemes to phonemes and mentally marking irregularities, the knowledge of reliable grapheme-phoneme correspondences taught in phonics is vital to making sight words.

With a growing body of stored sight words and sight chunks, readers enter the consolidated alphabetic phase. Consolidated alphabetic readers use the strategies of pronounceable word parts and analogizing, both of which depend on storing a body of sight vocabulary, and both of which rapidly increase sight vocabulary. Recognizing pronounceable parts allows the reader to quickly string together multisyllable words for sight word learning. Analogizing to words with similar spelling patterns allows for word recognition leaps that bypass letter-by-letter decoding. To gain this expert phase, partial alphabetic readers, including readers with learning disabilities, must first master the full alphabetic phase to establish the correspondence knowledge for making sight words and sight chunks. To gain the consolidated alphabetic phase, full alphabetic readers need rich practice opportunities for making sight words with teacher-guided readings in instructional level text. In addition, the method of repeated readings, explained in Practical Chapter 7, has been shown to produce rapid sight word gains.

The Language Processing System of Skilled Readers

This chapter is about us. As skilled readers, you would think we would be experts in how skilled reading works. In fact, however, most people have serious misconceptions about skilled reading, accepted uncritically from popular sources. It is quite difficult to think critically about these misconceptions because when we are actively engaged in reading, we can rarely observe ourselves. However, reading scientists have devised clever experiments to get at the truth. Try this true-false pretest about skilled readers like us:

1. Skilled readers rely on the overall shapes of words to recognize words.
2. Skilled readers typically pronounce the words to themselves as they read.
3. Skilled readers sample the words in a text to confirm their predictions.
4. Skilled readers take in the spelling of each word as they read.
5. Skilled readers use context to anticipate upcoming words as they read.

I'll give you the answers shortly, but I hope you'll keep these popular ideas in mind as you read the chapter and look for evidence for or against each statement.

You may be wondering: "Why are we reading about skilled readers in a book about how children learn to make sight words?" My answer is that we have gone astray in thinking about *beginning* reading because of false analogies to *adult reading*. We saw how Horace Mann urged teachers to skip the arduous decoding struggle and begin immediately with the adult processes of recognizing whole words by sight. As you will see, adult reading is extraordinarily complex and expert, and its success depends completely on mastering a large corpus of sight vocabulary. However, learning sight words depends on the more pedestrian work of decoding, crosschecking, and mental marking. Jeanne Chall (1996, p. 307) cited this false analogy in her conclusion:

The research from 1912 to 1965 indicates that a code-emphasis method—i.e., one that views *beginning reading as essentially different from mature reading* and emphasizes learning of the printed code for the spoken language—produces better results, at least up to the point where sufficient evidence seems to be available, the end of the third grade. [emphasis added]

TOP-DOWN AND BOTTOM-UP

This chapter will present Marilyn Adams's (1990) model of how skilled reading (like ours) works. Some models of skilled reading are "top-down," and others are "bottom-up." At the bottom are the printed words of the text, and at the top is our background knowledge about the topic of the text. Figure 1 illustrates these parts of the top-down and bottom-up models.

FIGURE 1: Top-down and bottom up models of skilled reading

In top-down models, skilled readers anticipate the message using background knowledge, and then sample the text to confirm their predictions. Skilled reading, according to these models, is driven from the top. However, context is not strong enough to predict the words in a text, and skilled readers do not rely on context. Instead we use spellings for sight recognition, instantly and automatically accessing meaning. Only poor readers guess from context.

THE LANGUAGE PROCESSING SYSTEM OF SKILLED READERS

In bottom-up models, in contrast, skilled readers begin at the bottom (the printed words) and work upward toward the message. They collect the features of letters into letters, letters into words, words into sentences, and sentences into messages. While it is true that glancing at letters starts the reading process, reading is far too fast for the assembly process suggested by bottom-up models. For example, skilled readers can read whole words as fast as they can name letters—in about 1/4 of a second!

ADAMS'S INTERACTIVE MODEL

Figure 2 represents Adams's (1990) interactive model of skilled reading. In interactive models, skilled readers simultaneously use top-down and bottom-up processes to determine the message of texts.

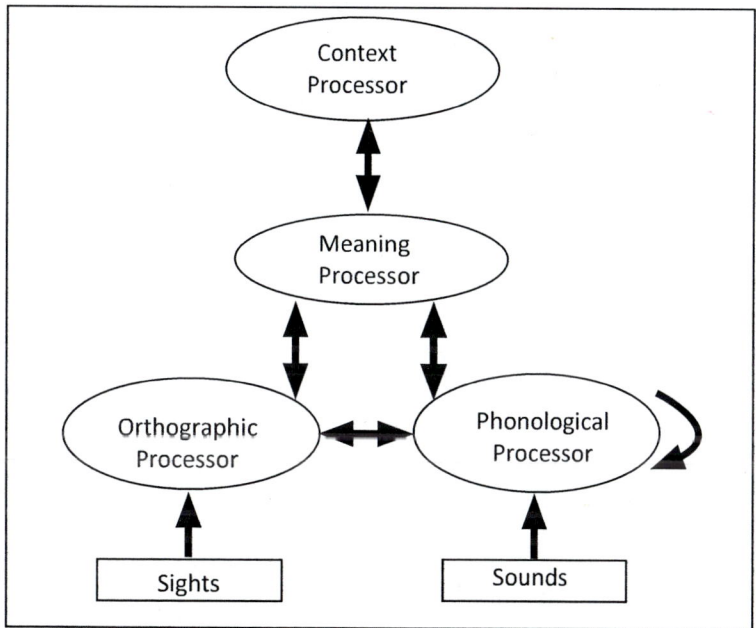

FIGURE 2: Adams's interactive model of skilled reading

We'll examine Adams's model in some depth, but briefly, there are four processors all working simultaneously to get the message of a text. The phonological processor analyzes the sounds detected in the outside world and asks, "Is it speech?" If the phonological processors recognizes sounds as speech, or what Liberman and Liberman (1992) call phonological structures, i.e., sound constructed of phonemes and linked to meanings, it activates the meaning processor for additional action. For example, the speech might be detected as /jon/ /luvz/ /mer'-E/.

The meaning processor examines speech and asks, "What are the words and morphemes (meaningful word parts), if any, in this speech?" In response, the meaning processor activates all the possible meanings for the words, including all known but irrelevant meanings. For example, activated words might include *John* or *Jon* (person, male, specific individuals, bathroom), *love* (charitable, romantic, platonic, erotic), *-s* (plural or grammatically inflected), *Mary* (person, female, specific individuals), *merry* (joyful), and *marry* (to wed, Shakespearean expletive).

The context processor selects the appropriate meanings by detecting the overlapping fields of meaning and asks, "What is the message?" In this case, the context processor might default to "John (generic male) loves (romantic) Mary (generic female)." With minimal effort, the language system has detected speech, activated a range of possible meanings, and located an overlapping set of meanings to arrive at a message about romantic love.

Note that all this took place without reading, and for nonreaders, the phonological, meaning, and context processors are all functional. But with the achievement of learning to read, there is another way into the system via the orthographic processor. The orthographic processor detects in the visual field the printed words "John loves Mary," a sequence of alphabetic characters grouped into three units. All three are sight words, allowing instant export to the meaning processor for expedited access to our set of meanings, in turn allowing rapid construction in the context processor of the likely message.

Answers to the true-false pretest. Let's return to the true-false quiz to take a critical look at the evidence about popular ideas of skilled reading. First, do skilled readers rely on the overall shapes of words in word identification? The answer is *no*, and to see why, look at Figure 3, showing the same words written in various cases and fonts.

left	next	hard	open	both
LEFT	NEXT	HARD	OPEN	BOTH
lEfT	nExT	hArD	oPeN	bOtH
lEfT	nExT	hArD	oPeN	bOtH

FIGURE 3: Mixed cases and fonts

The first row shows a typical shape for the words *next, hard, open,* and *both,* all of which have letter features extending above or below the main plane of the words. Does changing the shape to all capitals, as in the second row, slow your word recognition? Even though the words are all roughly rectangles, you didn't have any trouble reading them. What about mixing upper and lower case, as in the third row? That may slow you a little because the lowercase *l* is the same shape as the capital *I* in a sans-serif font, causing a slight processing difficulty. However, I'm betting that you have no problem recognizing the words in the last row, which uses the mixed cases and fonts of a ransom note.

If the shapes of words don't matter, what *does* matter? The answer is that we look at spellings, not shapes. The word lEfT takes an extra beat to read because the spelling becomes ambiguous—*ieft* or *left*? We need additional information to resolve the ambiguity. Eye-movement studies (explained below) show that we are sensitive to the slightest misspelling in text. We can read "feild" accurately, but it takes extra effort. In reading, spellings are important. We have a much different view of a person who is ingenious (unusually clever) than a person who is ingenuous (naïve).

Second, do skilled readers like us pronounce words to ourselves as we read? Yes, we do. The technical term for pronouncing words quietly or silently to yourself is subvocalizing. Subvocalization is a normal and useful strategy that helps comprehension by keeping words active in memory. If we didn't subvocalize in reading, the visual images of words would decay too rapidly to activate all their meanings and assemble them with the context processor. We would forget words before we reached the end of a sentence. The auditory memories of subvocalized words decay more slowly than visual memories, allowing us to assemble the message of fairly long sentences during reading. In fact, it can be helpful to vocalize (read aloud) in situations where comprehension is compromised, e.g., when reading during a catchy song or interesting TV show. Reading aloud may be necessary to maintain your train of thought.

We can informally experiment with subvocalization by trying to read some difficult sentences while repeating "double, double, double" to disrupt subvocalization. Try reading these clever puns while chanting "double, double, double . . . .":

Shotgun wedding: A case of wife or death.

Those who jump off a bridge in Paris must be in Seine.

A hangover is the wrath of grapes.

Reading while sunbathing makes you well red.

Time flies like an arrow. Fruit flies like a banana.

Disrupting your subvocalization by chanting while reading can seriously disrupt your comprehension. Such reading difficulties demonstrate the importance of pronouncing words subvocally as you read. Some well-meaning practitioners have tried to persuade readers to stop subvocalizing and use a pure sight-word method to improve reading speed. It doesn't work. Without subvocalization, our comprehension is much worse.

What about issue 3: Do skilled readers sample the printed text, or do we take in every word? Perhaps we should use the Evelyn Wood speed-reading method to take in entire pages at a glance, reading a text as rapidly as we can flip the pages. Scientists have developed sophisticated means of studying eye movements that refute such claims. Figure 4 shows a young woman using an eye tracker.

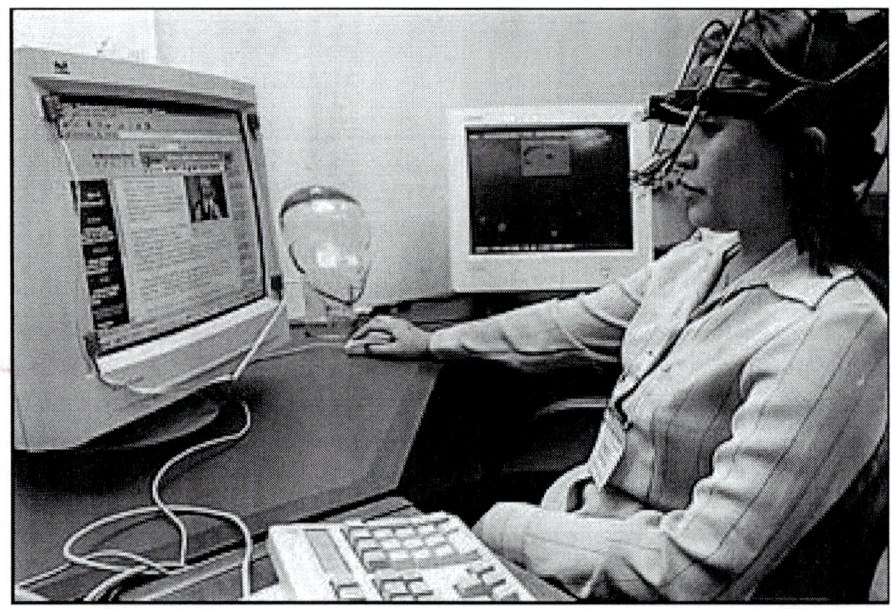

FIGURE 4: Eye tracker

Source: http://internetmarketingcoach.wordpress.com/2010/02/11/how-to-improve-website-design-with-eye-tracking-technology/

The eye tracker measures the precise gaze location and duration to provide empirical data about eye movements in reading. Eye-movement research using eye trackers has led to three key findings about skilled reading (Just & Carpenter, 1987). First, the eyes move by *fixation* and *saccade* during reading, rather than a smooth, continuous sweep. We fixate our gaze on a word for about ¼ of a second, and then we leap to the next word in a saccade in about 1/70 of a second. Contrary to popular belief, our eyes flit from word to word. Second, the evidence suggests that we ordinarily look at *every* word. We fixate on at least 80% of the content words (the words that carry meaning), and we even fixate on on 40% of the small function words like *the*, *a*, *of*, and *is*. In addition, we look at neighboring words not fixated, taking them in with adjacent words in a single fixation. There is no evidence of skipping words, sampling text, or taking in whole pages at a glance. The reason is that the word is the unit of reading. Our reading comprehension suffers unless we read each word in the text.

A third major finding of eye movement research helps us resolve the issue of whether skilled readers take in the spelling of each word as we read. The answer is *yes*, supported by two key pieces of evidence: [i] The time of fixation depends on

THE LANGUAGE PROCESSING SYSTEM OF SKILLED READERS

the number of letters in the word; we spend a few extra milliseconds with longer words and a fewer milliseconds with shorter words. [ii] Misspellings slow us down. We might spend a long half-second with a misspelled word like "porblem," showing that misspellings are problematic for reading comprehension. They may not defeat us, but they cause us to lose precious time in getting a message from text.

A final issue is whether skilled readers use context to anticipate upcoming words. Do we use context to predict words? The answer is *no*, and research suggests the probability of predicting upcoming words is as low as 20% (Gough, 1983). Try an experiment yourself with a cloze assessment, i.e., a passage with every fifth word deleted. Without looking beyond each blank, try to predict the upcoming word in this interesting passage from educational commentator Max Rafferty (1968, p. 59). Since we are testing whether we predict upcoming words, you should cover each successive line until you have made a guess about the previous blank.

This may come as a shock to mothers, but
Junior does not always tell the [1]_____;
especially about what goes [2]_____
at school. He will [3]_____
often come home and [4]_____
lie. It's just that [5]_____
he and the school [6]_____
operating on different wave [7]_____.
He functions within one [8]_____
of reference, and teacher [9]_____
working on quite another [10]_____.

Here is the complete passage you can use to check your answers: "This may come as a shock to mothers, but Junior does not always tell the [1]truth; especially about what goes [2]on at school. He will [3]not often come home and [4]deliberately lie. It's just that [5]frequently he and the school [6]are operating on different wave [7]lengths. He functions within one [8]frame of reference, and teacher [9]is working on quite another [10]one."

The difficulty of this task shows that predicting upcoming words is not a reasonable option for skilled readers. Context does not provide enough information for prediction. At best we can use it to work backwards, but backtracking slows reading down, and the effort to predict drains resources that should go to reading comprehension. Thus, for normal reading, prediction is slow, unreliable, and too much work. It is much easier to access words by reading them.

ADAMS'S MODEL REVISITED

A model is a visual representation of a theory. We often think of theories as dry abstractions that have little or nothing to do with the practical issues of teaching, but valid scientific theories organize a wide range of facts to explain cause and effect. For this reason, as Keith Stanovich (2010, p. 109) points out, "There is nothing so practical as a general and accurate theory."

To understand Adams's theory, we need the concept of *automatic spreading activation* from cognitive psychology. All our ideas are linked together in our lexicons, but most of them are dormant, or asleep. We need to activate ideas to put them to use by rousing them out of their sleep and closer to conscious attention (though not necessarily all the way; there are degrees of activation). The good news is that activation spreads automatically to other words related by meaning, pronunciation, or spelling. For example, hearing the pronunciation /tI'-ger/ may activate an animal, a golfer, or a university team; it may activate similar sounding words like *tigress* or the Milne character Tigger; and for skilled readers, it will activate the spelling *tiger*. Automatic spreading activation allows us to effortlessly and involuntarily summon ideas for rapid and coordinated understanding.

Processor	Input	Output
Phonological (natural route)	Sounds, spellings, and subvocalizations	Speech, as spoken words, syllables, or phonemes
Orthographic (learned route)	Sights	Print, as letters, spelling chunks, and word spellings
Meaning	Speech or print	Words, morphemes, and all related meanings
Context	Words, morphemes, and all related meanings	Messages

FIGURE 5: Adams's model of skilled reading

Figure 5 portrays the theory in Adams's model of skilled reading as a table. In the explanations that follow, we will be revisiting the visual model in Figure 2 to supply a deeper understanding of skilled reading. Bookmarking Figure 2 will help you follow the interactivity of the Adams model. To review, Adams's model is neither a top-down nor a bottom-up theory. Rather, it is an interactive theory that recognizes that all sorts of processing are going on at once. The processors are continually exchanging information, with the goal of making sense of the information in text. We get the message of text fastest when there is unanimity among the information from all processors. If there is a conflict, reading comprehension is slowed, and the system becomes compensatory. In other words, if a processor is weak, the other processors compensate to keep the system running. For beginning readers, the weak processor is the orthographic processor, with the responsibility of interpreting print. A weak orthographic processor has few sight words to activate and is slow to process spellings because decoding ability is limited. The processor most likely to jump in to resolve problems is the context processor, using contextual guessing. However, intervention by the context processor comes at a price: Context can't do its own job of putting together the message. As a result, we get slow, laborious reading.

THE CONTEXT PROCESSOR

The job of the context processor is to figure out the message of a text, creating an ongoing interpretation of text ideas. Its input consists of all the meanings activated by the meaning processor, whether they are appropriate or not. Most words have multiple meanings (which is why dictionaries number their definitions). For example, the word *hot* may mean at a high temperature, angry, performing at the peak of one's skill, or attractive. The context processor works to select the meaning that fits through a process of semantic overlap. To illustrate, the word *slap* most strongly activates the physical act of striking the face with an open hand. But overlapping with "Chipper Jones" and "ball," we get the message of striking a baseball sharply with a bat. Substitute "Lebron James," and the message becomes swatting a basketball, perhaps to block a shot. In each case, the overlapping fields of meaning activate specialized meanings of *slap*, leading to an accurate reading.

Thus, one way skilled readers use context is to select the correct meaning of a word that fits with related words in a message, using semantic overlap. When we ordinarily think of *sing*, we imagine melodic vocalizing. However, when *sing* overlaps with *criminal*, we get a much different message. In the context, "Given the plea bargain, the accomplice decided to sing," we arrive at the specialized meaning, "to confess a crime to implicate a criminal boss."

On the other hand, skilled readers do not use context to recognize words. As we learned in the attempt to predict upcoming words in the Max Rafferty passage, predicting words squanders resources needed for reading comprehension. The crucial information for identifying words is not in the context, but in the spelling. To make us use context to identify words, we would have to interfere with sight word recognition by degrading the print, which has the effect of making us artificial poor readers by taking out the orthographic processor. We become artificial poor readers with dim lighting, bad handwriting, a fuzzy copy, or lost glasses. With clear, legible print, skilled readers recognize spellings by sight, without context. Figure 6 shows an example of how illegible handwriting forces us to use context to resolve word recognition difficulties.

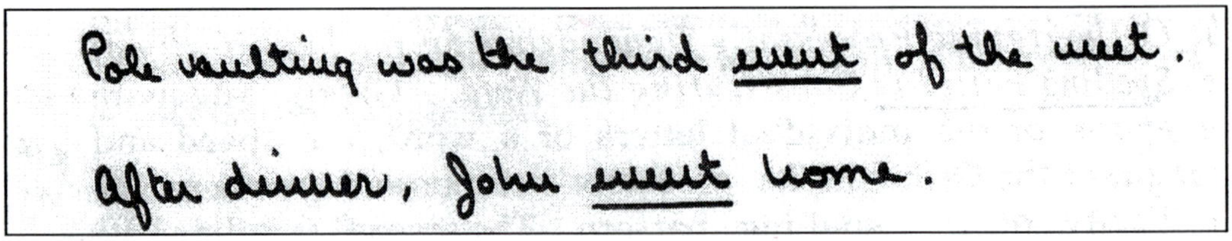

FIGURE 6: Illegible handwriting requires contextual processing (Adams, 1990, p. 164) Physically, the words *event* and *went* are indistinguishable, which forces us to use context to resolve their identities.

Contextual processing is so slow that it ordinarily does not function until after word reading; it corrects, rather than predicts word identification. Like an ancient bookkeeper reviewing accounts, context is slow, persistent, and faithful, e.g., "Her fake is red and mad? Oh, her *face* is red and mad." This points to another important function of context: We use context to monitor word recognition to watch for incongruities that we can fix by crosschecking. This is vital in learning irregular words because it helps us understand and store the irregular elements along with the predictable correspondences, so that we store the entire spelling for sight word recognition.

THE MEANING PROCESSOR

The work of the meaning processor is to activate all semantic information (i.e., meanings) linked to its speech and print input. Semantic information is stored not only in words, but in *morphemes*. Morphemes are the meaning units of a language. They can be free morphemes, or words, but they can also be bound morphemes, including prefixes, roots, suffixes, and even inflectional endings, such as the plural *-s* or the past-tense marker *-ed*. The word *undecipherable* is built of four bound morphemes: a root, *cipher* (meaning code), the prefixes *un* (not) and *de* (out of), and the suffix *able*. The collective meaning is "not able to get out of the code"—a possible danger of the illegible writing in Figure 6.

If no meaning is activated by speech or print, the context processor tries to create a new meaning entry from information gleaned from the context. For example, you probably haven't associated any meaning with the word *lambative*. However, as a skilled reader, you can skillfully deduce part of the meaning from this context: "Serious side effects of the lambative have been noted, resulting in a call for the restriction of its use." Did you pick up contextual information suggesting that a lambative is some kind of medicine? This is the basic way we glean word meanings during reading. Deriving meanings from context is the usual way we expand our vocabularies.

Thus, skilled readers use context several ways: To select the correct meanings for ambiguous words; to crosscheck words we've misread; and to derive the meanings of unfamiliar words. All these actions by skilled readers follow after word recognition. For skilled readers, word recognition takes place in a blinding quarter second, but using context takes time. Reading researchers of the past reasoned that because skilled readers are so good at using context, we probably use context to recognize words. However, context is too slow, too unreliable, and too much work for recognizing words. We have much faster ways to access words. By far the fastest is sight word recognition, followed by two runners up, pronounceable word parts and analogizing.

I received a university-wide mailing inviting me to a *theriogenology* conference. I had no idea what theriogenology is, but I had no difficulty generating the correct pronunciation using the pronounceable word parts *therio*, *gen*, and *ology*. Context was useless in leading me to the pronunciation of *theriogenology*, but it proved very useful in picking up clues about its meaning. The conference was to be held at the College of Veterinary Medicine, and the sessions included "Ultrasound in Female Bovine Reproduction," "Estrus Synchronization Programs," and "Update on Seminal Vesiculitis in Bulls." Clearly, theriogenology has something to do with reproduction in domesticated animals.

After children learn to decode, vocabulary becomes the major reading goal to help students understand challenging text. While children learn an impressive 5000-6000 words before entering school, they acquire an astounding 3000 words per year after entering school (Nagy, Herman, & Anderson, 1985). This works out to 8 new words per day, or 17 per day if vocabulary learning is restricted to school days. Almost no teacher asks students to learn 17 words per day, which implies that most words are gleaned from oral or written context.

To understand how many words children are learning, it is important to make the distinction between *running* words and *different* words. Running words include all the words in a text, no matter how often they are repeated. To count different words, we only count a word the first time it is used. Most running words in a text tend to be high frequency words. One large-scale study analyzed over 5 million running words taken from schoolbooks from grades 3-8 (Carroll, Davies, & Richman, 1971). Half of the running words consisted of 109 very common words, and just 8 words (*the*, *a*, *of*, *is*, *that*, *to*, *and*, and *in*) were used so frequently as to make up about 25% of all the words in running text. Note that such words are function words, rather than content words; they act as syntactic glue to bind content words together, but they have little meaning on their own.

In contrast, Carroll et al. (1971) found nearly 87,000 different words, most of which are relatively rare in print. About 94% of the different words occur less than one in 100,000 running words. These uncommon words provide the meaningful content of reading. Knowing "SAT" words like *acquisitive*, *emulate*, *insatiable*, and *taciturn* is the hallmark of an educated reader. SAT vocabulary is mainly found in books; valuable vocabulary words are quite rare in conversation. Two large-scale studies of vocabulary used in oral language never heard adult speakers using valuable words like *participation*, *luxury*, *maneuver*, *provoke*, *reluctantly*, *display*, *literal*, and *infinite* (Cunningham & Stanovich, 1998). Such words must ordinarily be learned by reading. Even children's books are richer sources for learning vocabulary than television shows geared to adults.

As important as context—and especially written context—is to learning vocabulary, context can be stingy in revealing what words mean. Beck, McKeown, and Kukan (2002, p. 4) give an example where context not only doesn't help, but actually misdirects the reader:

> Sandra had won the dance contest, and the audience's cheers brought her to the stage for an encore. "Every step she takes is so perfect and graceful," Ginny said grudgingly as she watched Sandra dance.

A naïve reader might guess that *grudgingly* means "with admiration." Readers have to know what *grudgingly* means in order to understand that Ginny is jealous of Sandra. Because writers don't want to waste words, they expect readers to come to their texts with most of the vocabulary needed for comprehension.

For this reason, an important duty for reading teachers is to teach children what words mean. The most effective vocabulary teachers use explicit instruction to explain words in simple language, to model how to use the words with examples and nonexamples, to guide students in using the words, to extricate words from their initial contexts, and to encourage students to generate new contexts for words. We will return to a discussion of how to teach meaning vocabulary in Chapter 11, on teaching vocabulary and comprehension strategies.

THE ORTHOGRAPHIC PROCESSOR

The work of the orthographic processor is to detect print in the visual field. Print in alphabetic languages is made of letters, but the orthographic processor may also detect sight words and sight chunks, which are shortcuts to word identification. For example, we might detect the common chunk *-tion* in reading a word like *redaction*. As explained in Chapter 3, we learn sight words and sight chunks by a sight word process of decoding, crosschecking, and mental marking, enabling us to store a chunk like *-tion* as a well-spelled alphabetic map in memory.

The orthographic processor is the only part of the language system acquired by learning. It does not develop naturally, like the phonological, meaning, and context processors. For beginning readers, the orthographic processor is typically quite weak because readers have not stored many sight words or sight chunks; even letter recognition can be a challenge for some, particularly with confusable letters like *b* and *d*. With a weak orthographic processor, beginners may compensate by leaning on the context processor for help in recognizing words, but only at a price. If the context processor is diverted to help identify words, it can't do its own job of getting the message of text.

Earlier in this chapter, we looked at findings of eye-movement research, relevant to understanding the work of the orthographic processor. Our eyes don't move smoothly: They fixate briefly on a word, and then make a rapid saccade to the next word. In reading, we ordinarily look at *every* word without skipping or sampling. We fixate 80% of the content words and take in most of the remaining words within the gaze periphery. The evidence suggests we take in the spellings of words: The time of fixation depends on the number of letters, and misspellings slow us down. We can read "thier" successfully, but it takes us an extra beat.

A few years ago, a claim went viral on the e-mail rounds, suggesting that accurate spellings are not necessary in reading. This message read as follows:

> Aoccdrnig to a rscheearch at an Elingsh uinervtisy, it deosn't mttaer in waht oredr the ltteers in a wrod are, the olny iprmoetnt tihng is taht frist and lsat ltteer is at the rghit pclae. The rset can be a toatl mses and you can sitll raed it wouthit porbelm. Tihs is bcuseae we do not raed ervey lteter by it slef but the wrod as a wlohe.

We can read this message successfully, but not without a problem. The misspellings clearly slow us down. A close examination of the spellings show that they are not thoroughly mixed within the word. For example, the spelling "aoccdrnig" happens to get the two *c*'s together, the *d* in the middle, and the *n* near its partner *g*. Using a random number generator, I thoroughly mixed the interior letters in a different passage, with the result that it becomes quite difficult (though not impossible) to decipher:

> The paicuty of dsosiucisn in the lraetruite of theacer rceresah that itnegaorters the use and vluae of dffneriet kdins of cgahne jsteoapuxd wtih the piretssnet epsmhias in the lutrertaie aobut teehcar rerasceh sggetsus the need for onneipg up cnrveitonsaos wiihtn and aorcss cnmmiuetois and ascors the two ltetrueirs aobut what this wrok is for and aubot and how it is rrenesepetd.

I'll include the translation at the end of the chapter in case you want to check your work.

Suppose I asked you to glance at the spelling *fsasyaof* and then copy it onto a sheet of paper. Most people have difficulty with this task because we can't make sense of an illegal spelling like *fsasyaof* as a pronunciation map. We are reduced to rote recall of an arbitrary sequence, much as readers with learning disabilities (LD) attempt to copy a spelling. Readers with LD have no problem with visual perception, but they have serious difficulties making sense out of unfamiliar alphabetic mappings. In contrast, I predict you would have a much easier time glancing at and copying the spelling *renackeration*, although it is equally meaningless. Using our rich knowledge of sight chunks, we can quickly process such a legal spelling as a pronunciation map and recreate it on paper.

Phonics programs of the past often attempted to train students in dictionary syllabication. However, we don't need precise syllable boundaries to read multisyllable words; we need only recognize sight chunks and assemble them into a word. Whether a beginner chunks a word as *be-fore* or *bef-ore*, he will still recognize *before* in the sentence, "We ate before the game." Readers don't need syllabication rules for recognition of longer words; they just need to assemble word chunks and crosscheck.

THE PHONOLOGICAL PROCESSOR

The work of the phonological processor is to detect speech from among all the auditory input we encounter. As the arrows in the Adams model (Figure 2) show, input may come from the sounds in the outside world; from attempts to "sound out" (decode) spellings delivered by the orthographic processor; from meanings activated by the meaning processor; or from subvocalized speech, or words we say to ourselves. Silent self-talk is common during reading; it helps us maintain words in memory as we process other words in search of the message of text. In addition, we subvocalize whenever we use language to think.

The phonological processor detects phonological structures; that is, sounds made of coarticulated phonemes. We may detect a single phoneme (e.g., /s/), a word chunk (/un/), or a complete word (*sun*). In turn, as spoken words and word parts are detected, they activate spelling information in the orthographic processor or meaning information in the meaning processor.

Some who disparage phonics say that decoding instruction produces word callers who pronounce words but fail to get the message of text—they read without comprehension. However, the Adams model predicts automatic spreading activation among the language processors. When a word is pronounced accurately, it must activate meaning information, provided the meaning is known. For example, if a reader knows what a rhinoceros is and decodes the word accurately, he must be able to access meaning information about a rhinoceros. On the other hand, he will not access the meaning of *rhinoceros* unless he generates a reasonably accurate pronunciation. If he comes up with "rinkerus," he probably won't think of a large armored animal with a horn on its nose. Thus, the Adams model explains word calling as the result of a weak orthographic processor that does not contain a well-spelled sight word for rhinoceros, nor can it assemble rhinoceros from sight chunks (*rhino, ceros*). In addition, the weak orthographic processor may be leaning on the context processor to compensate for poor decoding, with the result that the context processor is diverted from its own job of constructing the message of the text.

This analysis suggests that a word caller has not had too much phonics, but too little. The goal of phonics is to help beginners make sense of spellings as meaningful word maps, enabling them to arrive at pronunciations close enough to be corrected by crosschecking and then stored, with minimal effort, as well-spelled sight words. A student who generates "rinkerus" needs further instruction, scaffolding, and practice in using the complete spelling in decoding.

Do skilled readers usually decode? No, we recognize most words by sight, obviating the need to decode. Do we ever decode? Yes, decoding is a useful backup system for dealing with unfamiliar words like *redaction, exothermic,* or *theriogenology*. However, we don't sound out such words letter by letter; rather, we rapidly piece them together by recognizing pronounceable word parts or by analogizing, using the sophisticated consolidated-alphabetic decoding strategies of skilled readers.

Reading, even for the most skilled readers, can be demanding cognitive work. It may require us to remember facts presented chapters earlier, as in a mystery novel; it may require us to draw inferences by thinking through background information from a high school course; it may require us to draw back from inflammatory language and ask whether a claim is true; it may require us to imagine applications of facts for future use, including how to teach students to read. To manage such tasks, we need to marshal all available contextual resources without diverting them to lower level tasks. Sight word recognition save resources for reading comprehension, allowing us to think full time about the messages of text.

SUMMARY

Most models of skilled reading have visualized reading as either a top-down process, relying mostly on background knowledge, or as a bottom-up process, building information from letters to pronunciations to ideas. The interactive model developed by Adams (1990) better explains the complex and simultaneous interactions of reading processes in getting the message of a text. In Adams's model, the phonological processor detects sounds and recognizes the phonological structures of speech. The orthographic processor, which is acquired in learning how to read, detects print in the visual field and recognizes graphemes, and with increasing sophistication, word chunks and sight words. Speech and print information activates meaning information in the meaning processor, where words and morphemes (meaning units) are aroused, along with all connected semantic information, whether relevant or not. Where semantic information overlaps, the context processor activates messages in an ongoing interpretation of text.

Spellings, rather than word shapes, are used in word identification. Subvocalization, pronouncing words quietly or silently, is important in maintaining words in active memory. Eye-tracker research shows that skilled readers look at all the words in a text in order to pick up spelling information needed to get the message of the text; misspellings slow us down. While context is useful for disambiguating messages, crosschecking when we make a near miss in decoding, or gleaning the meaning of unfamiliar words, it is not used to generate the pronunciations of words. For this purpose, context is too slow, effortful, and inaccurate.

The Adams model reflects current thinking in cognitive psychology that understands reading processes as involving automatic spreading activation of information throughout the language processing system. Context, meaning, orthographic, and phonological processors are interconnected, allowing information to move through the system effortlessly and involuntarily. Beyond the interactivity of the reading system, the system is compensatory in allowing higher level processes involving context to resolve lower level processes involving words recognition. However, there is a price to pay in compensatory processing because higher level processing is less efficient when distracted from its own work.

Context processing uses semantic overlap to find meanings that are consistent with other meanings in deriving a coherent message. A wide range of meanings is briefly activated by the meaning processor, both relevant and irrelevant to the message of a text. In some cases, speech or print activates no meanings at all, in which case, context is enlisted to glean meaning information; this is the usual way we learn new meaning vocabulary. Vocabulary is learned rapidly; especially with the stimulus of reading texts, which feature much richer vocabulary than oral language. While texts are disproportionately composed of very common function words, relatively rare content words carry most of the message of text. Learning their meanings usually requires explicit instruction by teachers.

The orthographic processors of skilled readers focus on spellings during rapid-fire fixations that usually take in each of the words of a text, either directly or in the periphery. Misspellings slow this perception of spellings, forcing us to redirect the context processor to resolve lower level word-recognition frustrations. Unimpeded by such distractions, skilled readers rapidly parse unfamiliar words into sight chunks for rapid assembly and pronunciation. To generate an accurate pronunciation requires skillful decoding. The accusation that phonics, or decoding instruction, is somehow detrimental to comprehension fails to take into account that effective phonics instruction coordinates the interplay of the orthographic and phonological processors, allowing the generation of accurate phonological structures for easy access to meaning. Skilled readers use the expert processes of pronounceable word parts and analogizing to generate pronunciations of unfamiliar words. By making sight words, the well-coordinated processes of skilled readers conserve cognitive resources for the demanding mental work of reading comprehension with challenging texts.

Translation of the scrambled passage, from Lytle (2000, p. 704):

The paucity of discussion in the literature of teacher research that interrogates the use and value of different kinds of change juxtaposed with the persistent emphasis in the literature about teacher research suggests the need for opening up conversations within and across communities and across the two literatures about what this work is for and about and how it is represented.

CHAPTER 5

Preparing Students to Learn to Read

Parents and teachers of young children usually want to do everything in their power to help children build a successful foundation for learning to read. In the last 60 years, we have seen two major views of early literacy come and go: reading readiness and emergent literacy. Each view identifies key developments, makes assumptions, and suggests what teachers should do and what they should *not* do. Figure 1 compares and contrasts the reading readiness and emergent literacy views of early literacy.

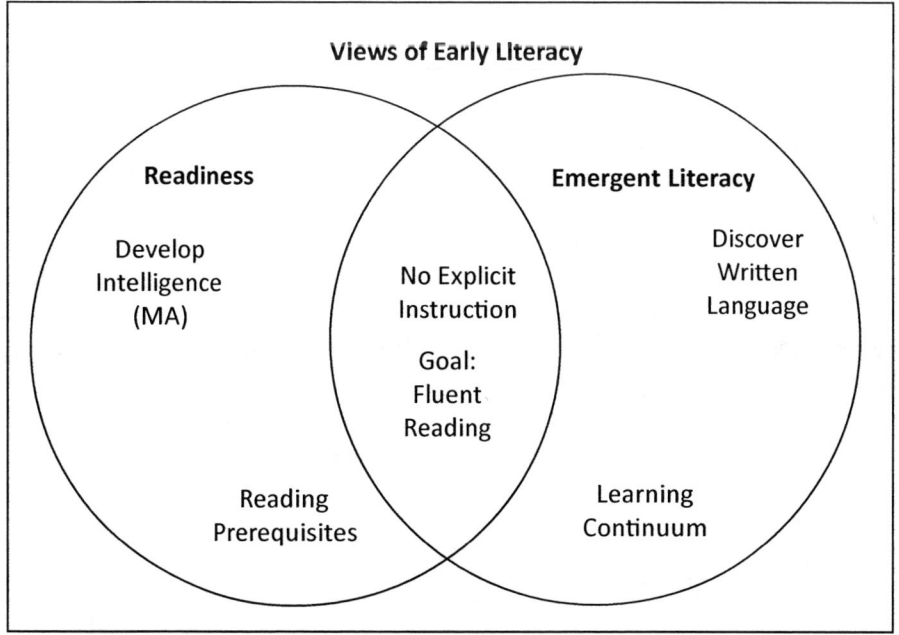

FIGURE 1: Reading readiness and emergent literacy

THE READING READINESS VIEW

The reading readiness view was dominant from the 1950s to the 1970s. According to this view, the key development for learning to read is developing the intelligence necessary for reading. Reading readiness advocates said children need maturation time before they are ready to learn to read. They assumed children must develop prerequisites for reading ability, especially perceptual skills and a mental age commensurate with the demands of reading. Without these prerequisites, children would be unprepared for reading and frustrated by reading instruction.

Accordingly, reading readiness advocates urged teachers to wait for the ripening of intelligence (which is mostly fixed) before teaching them to read. Teachers were to delay any formal reading instruction until children reached the mental age of 6.5 and to delay phonics until children reached the mental age of 7. This might require teachers to "red-shirt" kindergartners who are not yet ready to learn to read—to retain them for a second year in kindergarten. At best, according to this view, teachers can stimulate the growth of intelligence by enriching the classroom climate; e.g., by reading aloud, introducing an aquarium and terrarium, bringing in special visitors, and making field trips. However, teachers should not teach reading explicitly. Extreme readiness advocates thought explicit instruction to be positively harmful because it "hurries" a child who is not yet ready to read. According to the reading readiness view, children need time to develop readiness, and explicit teaching interferes with the natural maturation of intelligence that makes them ready.

THE EMERGENT LITERACY VIEW

In the 1980s and 1990s, the emergent literacy view came to supplant reading readiness as the dominant theory of early literacy. For the proponents of emergent literacy, the key development in learning to read is the discovery of written language. Theorists like Ken and Yetta Goodman (Goodman & Goodman, 1979) argued that children can learn literacy as easily and naturally as they learn to speak. Just as they need no formal lessons in how to talk and listen, neither do they need formal instruction in reading. Emergent literacy theorists assumed a continuum in literacy development without any prerequisites, with much important learning taking place before independent reading. Thus, there is no cause for alarm if first graders are unable to read words at the end of first grade—according to emergent literacy proponents, they are still discovering written language.

The work of teachers, in the emergent literacy view, is to immerse children in a print-rich environment where they can decontextualize printed words. Teachers are to surround children with print and involve them in authentic literacy tasks, such as organizing a play restaurant where some can pretend to read menus and others can pretend to write down their orders. Extreme advocates argued that under no circumstances should teachers teach reading explicitly; explicit instruction was thought to interfere with the natural discovery of written language. As with the reading readiness view, explicit instruction was deemed positively harmful, turning children off to reading.

As the overlapping circles in Figure 1 illustrate, there is much commonality between the reading readiness and emergent literacy views. Both views put faith in natural growth, either by the maturation of intelligence or by discovery learning. Both views reject explicit teaching as interfering with the natural growth of literacy.

More recently, however, reading theorists have questioned this opposition to explicit teaching, seeing early literacy instruction as beneficial rather than harmful. For example, anthropologist Lisa Delpit (1988) studied education in places like Papua New Guinea and in native Alaskan villages. Delpit wrote:

> I have found it unquestionably easier—psychologically and pragmatically—when some kind soul has directly *informed* me about such matters as appropriate dress, interactional styles, embedded meanings, and taboo words or actions.... Unless one has the leisure of a lifetime of "immersion" to learn them, explicit presentation makes learning immeasurably easier. (p. 283)

As an outsider during her anthropological expeditions, Delpit was grateful for any kind of explicit help she could get in negotiating the pitfalls of an unfamiliar culture. She argued that minority children in schools may similarly be newcomers to a culture of formal literacy. Because their introduction to literacy is delayed, there is no time for the luxury of immersion. Outsiders to the culture of literacy need explicit instruction to supply the knowledge and strategies that other children acquire in years of preschool immersion. If left to discover literacy on their own, they often find themselves frustrated for lack of explicit help and fall even further behind.

THE EARLY INTERVENTION VIEW

The growing interest in early and explicit teaching has led to a new view of beginning literacy, focused on early intervention. Figure 2 shows the overlap of the early intervention view with the reading readiness and emergent literacy views.

From the perspective of the early intervention view of the 2000s, the key development in learning to read is to learn the component abilities for alphabetic literacy, especially letter recognition and phoneme awareness. Advocates of the early intervention view assume that learners make better progress with explicit teaching in virtually any area. For example, those of us who have grappled with arcane subjects like statistics are grateful for professors who provide explicit instruction rather than expecting us to learn by natural growth or discovery learning.

Thus, the task of the teacher of beginning readers is to use explicit, systematic methods to teach letter recognition, phoneme awareness, and decoding. *Explicit* means instruction with clear explanations, teacher modeling, and carefully guided practice. *Systematic* means that children learn in a planned program where crucial information is built up in small increments in a planned order. For the early intervention view, teachers should not wait for maturation or discovery. The alphabetic code is a technology for representing speech. Knowledge of a technology does not mature naturally, and it is too complex to discover. Without careful teaching of component knowledge and strategies, many children will fall behind and never fully catch up.

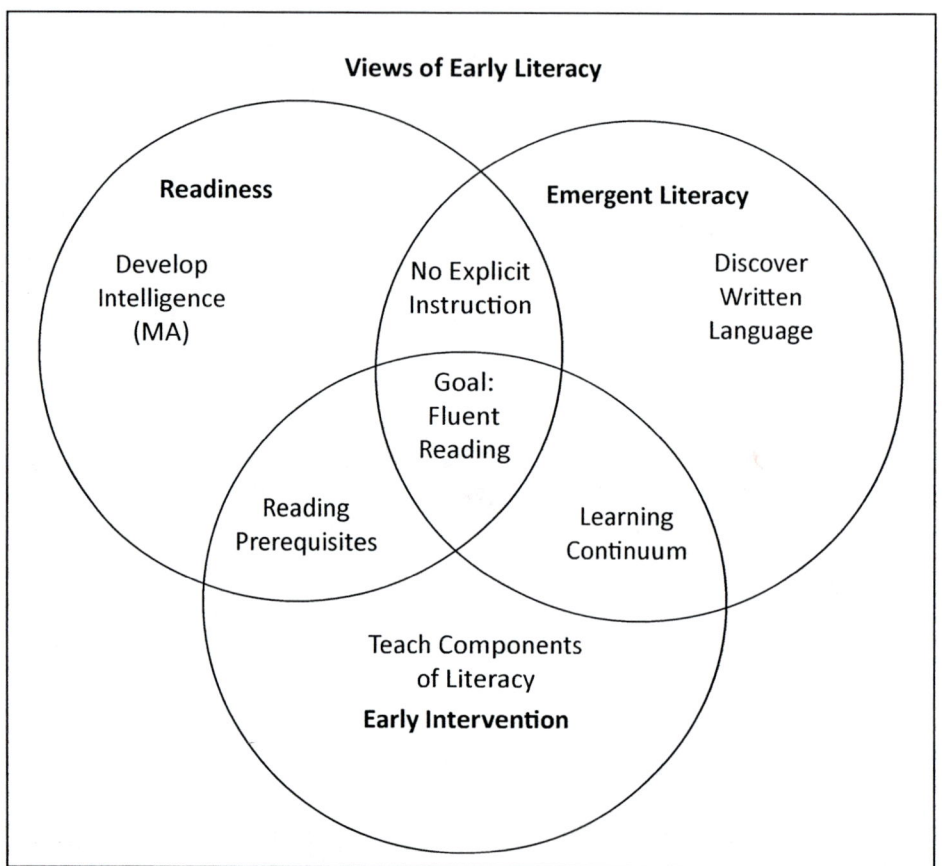

FIGURE 2: Reading readiness, emergent literacy, and early intervention

The early intervention view overlaps with previous views. With emergent literacy, the intervention view shares the idea of a continuum of literacy development. There are 26 letters to recognize in two cases, 42 phonemes, and about 80 major correspondences needed for word reading. Learning voluminous information cannot be an overnight achievement for which anyone is suddenly "ready." The intervention and readiness views share the idea of reading prerequisites. Children who lack the basics are at risk; however, the intervention view recognizes different prerequisites. Research points to phoneme awareness and letter recognition as the building blocks for success in beginning reading.

The unique implication of the early intervention view is that early, explicit, systematic instruction is vital to a successful start in reading. Explicit teaching leading to a steady diet of success, as opposed to permissive supervision in a literate environment, far from discouraging children, is a "turn on." It empowers children by equipping them with the tools of literacy, allowing them to unlock otherwise inaccessible messages. Explicit teaching eases children rapidly into the fun of literacy and allows them to reap its rewards. As Delpit (1988) warned, the literacy environment can be a foreign culture, and explicit teaching heads off frustration, making learning dramatically easier.

PROBLEMS WITH THE READING READINESS VIEW

To further understand the inadequacies of the reading readiness view, which remains influential in schools, it is useful to examine the evidence for its claims. The reading readiness view posits two prerequisites for learning to read: perceptual skills and mental age. We will examine the actual importance of these two prerequisites in learning to read, in order to shed light on some continuing issues in understanding beginning reading.

Perceptual Skills

Perceptual skill is the ability to interpret sensory data, especially from our eyes and ears, in order to detect patterns and recognize sounds. In the heyday of reading readiness, copying shapes, finding visual patterns, and listening to differences in sounds were typically important kindergarten activities toward the goal of developing perceptual skill. However, there is no evidence that such activities led to any special progress in learning to read. Training perceptual or motor skills does not work to improve early reading.

The reason perceptual training doesn't work is that reading does not require any special perceptual skill. Despite the popular idea that struggling readers with learning disabilities see things backwards, reading problems are not perceptual problems. Those with reading disabilities see and hear the world just as everyone else does; their only problems are in learning the alphabetic code. Brown (1982, pp. 63-64) explains:

> Although the perceptual centers in the brain invert the scene reported to it by the optic nerve, they cannot invert some small portion of that scene. If, for example, a person looks out the window onto a beautiful panorama of mountains, trees, and greenery, it is not possible for him to see one tree in an inverted position while all the rest of the landscape is right side up .... The perceptual center cannot interpret all of a page as right side up but leave one small word such as *was* or *saw* upside down and backward.

Why do people think students with learning disabilities see things backwards? The only evidence is that they may form letters backward, misread words like *saw* and *was*, and misspell words (e.g., "We sow sell daots on the laek"). However, evidence indicates that older poor readers and younger normal readers make the same kinds of mistakes (Stanovich, 1986). They reverse letters like *b* and *d* because they have not learned the sequence of features in forming letters. They confuse letter order in spellings because as partial alphabetic readers, they don't fully analyze spellings, especially vowels. It is easy to mix up letters when they are not recognized as parts of a meaningful alphabetic map, just as it is easy to mix up the digits in a phone number. However, difficulties with the alphabetic code are not perceptual. Normal or corrected vision and hearing are adequate for learning to read, without any special perceptual training.

Auditory Discrimination

One puzzling fact seemed to give legitimacy to the view that struggling readers have perceptual difficulties: They tended to score lower on tests of auditory discrimination. Auditory discrimination is the ability to perceive differences in spoken words such as *lake* and *rake*. Wallach and Wallach (1979) cleared up this discrepancy in a study comparing first graders in inner city and suburban schools. They tested auditory discrimination by showing pictures of, for example, a lake and a rake, and asking children to point to, e.g., the lake. Nearly every child got a perfect score because children with normal hearing have no difficulty in hearing differences in words. However, they also gave the children a phoneme awareness test in which they were asked, e.g., "Do you hear /r/ in *lake* or *rake*?" This time there were marked differences in phoneme awareness between the suburban children (93% successful) and the inner city children (12% successful). As it turns out, the auditory discrimination tests that showed deficits for readers at risk were misnamed; they actually assessed phoneme awareness rather than perceptual skill.

Learning Styles

The theory of learning styles is a popular explanation of learning problems based on claims about perception. Advocates such as Marie Carbo (1988) argue that children learn better when we match instruction to their learning style, usually described in terms of perceptual strength. According to the theory of learning styles, we perceive a task using our dominant perceptual modality, typically either auditory or visual. This implies that we should get better learning with an aptitude-treatment interaction, i.e., when instruction (the treatment) is matched to a student's preferred sensory modality (his aptitude). Accordingly, auditory learners should do better when taught with auditory methods like phonics, and visual learners should do better when taught with visual methods like the whole-word method. Figure 3 portrays this hypothesis.

		Aptitude: Learning style	
		Visual	Auditory
Treatment:	Visual (whole-word method)	X	
Teaching method	Auditory (phonics)		X

FIGURE 3: An aptitude-treatment interaction

Better learning in boxes marked with an X would show that teaching to students' learning styles improves achievement. However, eight major reviews of research have failed to find evidence of any aptitude-treatment interaction (Stahl, 1988). Some methods (e.g., explicit phonics) work well for all children, and others (e.g., the whole-word method) fail. Despite the popularity of the learning-styles hypothesis, it has been largely falsified by research. There is no magic combination of teaching methods fitted to learning styles that makes learning to read easier. Visual learners learn by the same effective methods as do auditory learners. The First-Grade Studies (Bond & Dykstra, 1967) showed that the two factors that actually make a significant difference in reading achievement are teaching method and teacher skill. Skillful teachers working with research-tested methods tend to get the best results.

Mental Age

The reading readiness view claimed that children must develop their intelligence before they are ready to learn to read. They used the index of mental age, which is derived from measures of IQ and age, using this formula:

$$MA = \frac{IQ \times CA}{100}$$

The reading readiness claim was that children need a mental age of 6.5 for formal reading instruction and a mental age of 7 for phonics. Thus, assuming a 7-year-old second grader with an IQ of 90, well within the normal range, we would compute a mental age of 6.3, leading to the bizarre conclusion that a normal second grader is still not ready for formal reading instruction, much less phonics.

The mental age of 7 claim is based on a single flawed study carried out during the Great Depression (Dolch & Bloomster, 1937). In this study, students below a mental age of 7 couldn't decode isolated words. However, children in the 1930s were not taught with explicit phonics, but rather with analytic phonics. As explained in Chapter 2, in explicit phonics, the teacher models how to sound out and blend, whereas in analytic phonics, children are expected to learn whole words and analyze them without pronouncing phonemes. For example, the teacher using analytic phonics might say, "The sound in the middle of *sit* is the same as the sound in the middle of *him*. This sound is spelled with the letter *i*." Such instruction presumes that children are aware of vowel phonemes (and short vowels are especially difficult) and fails to provide any sounding and blending model. In contrast, a teacher using explicit phonics might say, "Letter *i* looks like it's dripping, and it makes the sound we say when we put our hands in sticky, drippy stuff, /i/. Let me show you how to sound out this word [*sit*]: We can start with sticky, drippy /i/. Let's get the beginning, /s/, /i/, /si/. This much [*si*-] says /si/. Now let's put /si/ with the ending, /si/, /t/, /sit/. Oh, *sit*, like you sit in a chair. Now you try this word" [*him*]. When decoding is made plain with repeated explicit modeling, IQ is no barrier to learning to read words.

IQ and Reading

General intelligence, whether measured in mental age or IQ, is not especially important in reading acquisition, though it becomes important later when vocabulary and background knowledge play a larger role in reading comprehension. Children don't need a high IQ to learn how to read. In the First Grade Studies (Bond & Dykstra, 1967), high and low IQ students made similar gains when taught phonics. In contrast, phoneme awareness is an important predictor of success in beginning reading. The success of a predictor is measured by a correlation, which is an index varying from 0 to 1 (or -1) showing how closely two variables are related. Correlations near 0 indicate no relationship and correlations near 1 (or -1) indicate a very close predictive relationship. Figure 4 compares the correlations of IQ and phoneme awareness (PA) with success in beginning reading.

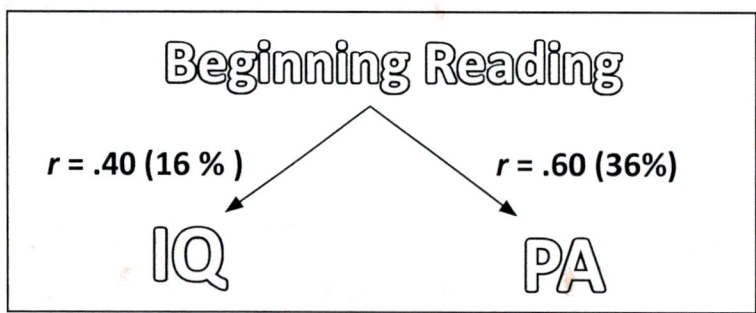

FIGURE 4: Correlations with beginning reading

The correlation between PA and beginning reading is about .60, which is somewhat higher than the correlation of IQ with beginning reading at about .40. However, that's not the whole story. The square of the correlation estimates how much variation is explained by a factor. PA explains more than twice as much variation in success in beginning reading as does IQ (36% versus 16%). By implication, children don't need a high IQ to learn to read words; in fact, children with IQs in the 60s have learned to decode successfully. In contrast, phoneme awareness is vital in learning to read words. Moreover, we know how to improve PA through explicit instruction, but we know little about how to improve intelligence. Even if we could somehow raise a beginner's IQ, it would have a small effect on his reading success.

Low readiness for reading presents a practical problem for teachers: What do we do with children who are not ready? Do we simply wait for maturation? Do we retain them in kindergarten until they show reading readiness? Knowledge of the alphabetic code does not mature. Like all technologies, it must be taught, and it is the work of primary teachers to initiate children into the mysteries of the alphabet. To summarize, the notion of a mental age of 7 for phonics instruction is a misinterpretation of a flawed experiment. The National Reading Panel Report (NRP, 2000) showed that explicit phonics is as effective with kindergartners as it is with first graders, despite the differences in mental age.

Postmortem on Reading Readiness

Recall the message from a reader with learning disabilities: "We sow sell daots on the laek." Can we infer that the reader has poor visual perception? No, there is no difference in perceptual ability between good and poor readers. Could it be that the reader has a visual learning style but has received auditory instruction with phonics? No, there is no evidence of reading gains by matching instruction to learning styles. Is it possible that the reader was hurried into phonics instruction before reading the mental age of 7? No, early explicit phonics instruction is an *advantage* in learning to read. Virtually all the claims of the reading readiness view have been falsified.

PREDICTORS OF SUCCESS IN BEGINNING READING

We've seen that mental age is a poor predictor of reading success, but that phoneme awareness offers over twice the predictive power. Letter recognition is the second strongest predictor of success in reading acquisition. If PA and letter recognition are the building blocks of reading words, fused in every correspondence and linked by the reader in understanding each new word, it should hardly be surprising that both are strong predictors of success in early reading. Adams (1990, p. 304) talks about the "special magic of learning letters and their sounds together," suggesting that it is the linkage of letters and phonemes that makes each learnable and useful.

Let's consider why letters and phonemes work together with such synergy. We know that letter recognition makes it easier to learn phoneme identities because letters serve as permanent visible symbols for phonemes. They will be used to evoke phonemes for the rest of the reader's life. In addition, most letter names feature phonemes prominently, e.g., *m* ("em"), which means most letter names are useful approximations of the isolated phoneme. We can also reasonably speculate that phoneme awareness makes learning letters easier because the phoneme is the meaning of the letter. Without PA, letters are meaningless, and any symbol without a meaning is hard to remember. Suppose I asked you to learn this symbol:

If you didn't know what the symbol meant, it would be like trying to remember some odd hieroglyphic. However, if I told you it is called a fermata, and that in music, it tells you to hold onto a note longer than usual, and if we practiced holding out notes whenever we saw a fermata, it would be much easier to learn. Similarly, imagine the problem in trying to remember the letter *w* when it is a meaningless symbol with a strange name, *double-u*. However, once *w* comes to mean the wishy-washy phoneme we detect as our lips open with "We wipe out on wild waves," then *w* is easier to remember because it is meaningful.

Assessing Letter Recognition and Phoneme Awareness

Assessing letter recognition is straightforward: We give students a page of assorted letters and ask them to name them. Information on accuracy (the number correct) and the naming time (the time in seconds to identify the letters) is informative. Ideally, by late kindergarten, children should be able to accurately name all the upper and lowercase letters in less than a minute.

Assessing phoneme awareness presents a greater challenge. We are looking for a basic level of PA *before* children learn to read and spell rather than a sophisticated level of PA that come as a result of reading and spelling ability. In *segmentation* tests, children report all the phonemes in a word. Try segmenting *tramp*. Usually this is easy for us because we know how to spell *tramp* and we can use the spelling to report the phonemes. Segmentation is much tougher for beginners without a well-spelled vocabulary of sight words. To segment all the phonemes, they have to detect each of the phonemes in turn. Detecting phonemes cannot be a mechanical task because phonemes are coarticulated into a seamless whole. For example, we purse our lips for the /r/ in *drive* even before saying /d/. In addition, phonemes pour out of the speech stream in a cascade of 10 to 20 phonemes per second (Liberman & Liberman, 1992, p. 350). Without slowing the speech stream and getting explicit help in learning phoneme identities, children cannot identify and segment the torrent of rapid, coarticulated phonemes.

In *blending* tests, children smooth together isolated phonemes to identify a word. Blending is a basic manipulation and a component of decoding, but there is reason to believe that it also relies on spelling ability. Try blending /s/, /t/, /r/, /A/, /t/. I'm guessing this is quite easy for you, given your knowledge of the spelling of *straight*. However, holding a sequence of phonemes in mind to assemble them into a word is much harder without spelling knowledge.

In *manipulation* tasks, we ask children to reverse or delete phonemes to make new words, a game-like task. For example, what would happen if we reversed the phonemes in *eat*? /E/t/ reversed is /t/E/, *tea*. That's easy using spelling knowledge. However, suppose I asked you to reverse the phonemes in *on*? Would you give the answer *no*? If so, you used spelling knowledge to arrive at the wrong answer! The solution is to segment /aw/n/, reverse the phonemes /n/aw/, and answer *gnaw*. Deletion tasks follow a similar logic. No doubt you can say *crime* without the /k/ and get *rhyme*. But can you say *think* without the /k/? If you said *thin*, you used your spelling ability rather than your phoneme awareness. The solution is to segment /th/i/ng/k/, and after deleting /k/, to reassemble /th/i/ng/, *thing*. Our resort to spelling information with items where spelling misleads us shows us that success with phoneme manipulation tasks ordinarily depends on abilities prealphabetic readers lack.

Most phoneme awareness tests pick up a level of PA that is a result of learning to read and spell words rather than an earlier, prealphabetic level of PA. If we need spelling ability to succeed with PA tests, they are not the best predictors for children who don't know how to read and spell, including those who are at risk for reading failure. If we hope to predict who is going to have trouble learning to read, we need tests that do not depend on spelling ability. My Test of Phoneme Identities, with both pretest and posttest versions in Appendix A of Practical Chapter 5, is designed as a repeating game. Children are asked to repeat a sentence, pronounce a phoneme, and then search two rhyming words for that phoneme. For example, say, "We'll see the moon soon." Now say /s/. Do you hear /s/ in *moon* or *soon*? Experimental results with prealphabetic readers found that the Test of Phoneme Identities yielded better predictive information on success in an early decoding task than a segmentation test and a standardized test of PA (Murray, Smith, & Murray, 2000).

How do most children become aware of phonemes? Alphabet books help, particularly when they give several alliterative words for a phoneme to help children identify the common vocal gesture (Brabham, Murray, & Hudson, 2006). For example, *Dr. Seuss's ABC* (Geisel, 1963, p. 46) helps children understand "what begins with *T*" by showing them an illustration of "ten tired turtles on a tuttle-tuttle tree." Invented spelling is helpful because it leads children to identify phonemes and transcribe them with related letters. A British study found that PA may begin with knowledge of nursery rhymes (Maclean, Bradley, & Bryant, 1987). Knowledge of five nursery rhymes at age 3 (see if you can recite them from these partial titles: Baa Baa, Hickory, Humpty, Jack, and Twinkle) predicted PA and decoding success at age 6. Nursery rhymes may help by calling attention to rhyme and alliteration to help children focus on sound as well as sense.

Marilyn Adams's (1990) observations of her own son John suggest the immense advantages conferred to children in stable, professional, literate homes through preschool experiences. John could recite the alphabet at age 2 and recognize capital letters by age 3. By the time he entered school, he could print his name (though he sometimes reversed letters, which is normal). He could make up rhymes and tell jokes relying on sound-alike words (Where do sheep get a haircut? At the baa-baa shop).

He could invent spellings and figure out the first letters in people's names. How did John develop all these literate abilities? Adams estimates that John enjoyed some 3000 hours of early literacy experiences, including 1000 hours of read-alouds, 1000 hours of shows like Sesame Street, and 1000 hours of various other kinds of language play, such as writing with invented spelling, making up rhymes, putting together alphabet puzzles, and computer games. This level of informal literacy instruction and play is typical in literate families. In such homes, literacy seems to emerge naturally, but in fact, children have a huge head start.

A strong consensus exists among literacy researchers that the single most important activity for eventual success in reading is reading aloud to children. Read-alouds allow children to experience the pleasure of reading, a vital motivator for learning to read. Read alouds introduce children to the language of books, which has a much different register than oral language (e.g., "Around the corner came the little old man"). They are an especially rich source of vocabulary, featuring a more opulent diet of unusual words than adult conversation or television (Cunningham & Stanovich, 1998). Children also acquire valuable culture literacy in learning about David and Goliath, the Hare and the Tortoise, and the Boy Who Cried Wolf.

Jim Trelease (2006) makes some useful suggestions in his *Read-Aloud Handbook* on the "do's and don't's of reading aloud." Trelease urges readers to provide plenty of time for conversation during and after reading, to allow children to try on the language of the book. He provides excellent ideas about the pace of reading:

> The most common mistake in reading aloud—whether the reader is a 7-year-old or a 40-year-old—is reading too fast. Read slowly enough for the child to build mental pictures of what he just heard you read. Slow down enough for the children to see the pictures in the book without feeling hurried. Reading quickly allows no time for the reader to use vocal expression.

Some mistakenly claim that children learn to read by having books read aloud to them. However, children don't learn to decode words from read-alouds. The effects of reading aloud are long-term, introducing book language, story structure, vocabulary, and background knowledge for *eventual* success in reading. Learning to read words requires acquiring a complex alphabetic technology involving letters, phonemes, and correspondences. Children can't crack the alphabetic code by listening to stories and looking at pictures.

The rich introduction to literacy John enjoyed is not universal. In one poor neighborhood, the typical child experienced only about 4 hours of reading aloud per year, or only about 20 hours of read-alouds before entering first grade (Teale, 1986). John's 1000 hours of read-alouds was roughly 50 times greater. However, the difference becomes even starker when John's read-aloud advantage is converted into years. If 1000 hours of reading aloud represent 5 years, we can estimate that read-alouds are enjoyed in literate homes for about 200 hours per year. But if 200 hours represents a year of reading aloud, then 20 hours is less than 2 months of reading aloud. By comparison, while John and his fortunate counterparts in literate homes enjoy 5 years of reading aloud, children in poverty experience only 2 months of reading aloud. They are 4 years, 10 months behind their privileged peers.

Matthew effects in reading

Nothing is so practical as a good educational theory that summarizes mountains of facts to organize our knowledge, to show cause and effect, and to illuminate practical ideas for teaching and assessment. Figure 5 illustrates Keith Stanovich's (1986) theory of Matthew effects in reading. The name "Matthew effects" is based on a teaching of Jesus reported in Matthew 13:12: "Whoever has will be given more, and he will have an abundance. Whoever does not have, even what he has will be taken from him." In the Matthew effects model, small, early deficits in reading acquisition eventually pervade everything. Children who enter school without awareness of phonemes find it difficult to understand phonics instruction and are slow to develop decoding skill. As a result, they cannot make sight words, and so they don't become fluent readers. When reading is hard work, readers avoid reading, which has negative consequences for learning vocabulary, parsing the complex sentences of books, dealing with unfamiliar text structures, and acquiring new concepts by reading. In the end, even intelligence is affected by the dearth of learning tools that must be acquired through reading. This downward spiral shows why learning disability is hard to correct. As time goes on, the small problems of PA or decoding become major problems affecting motivation, success in school, and adult learning ability.

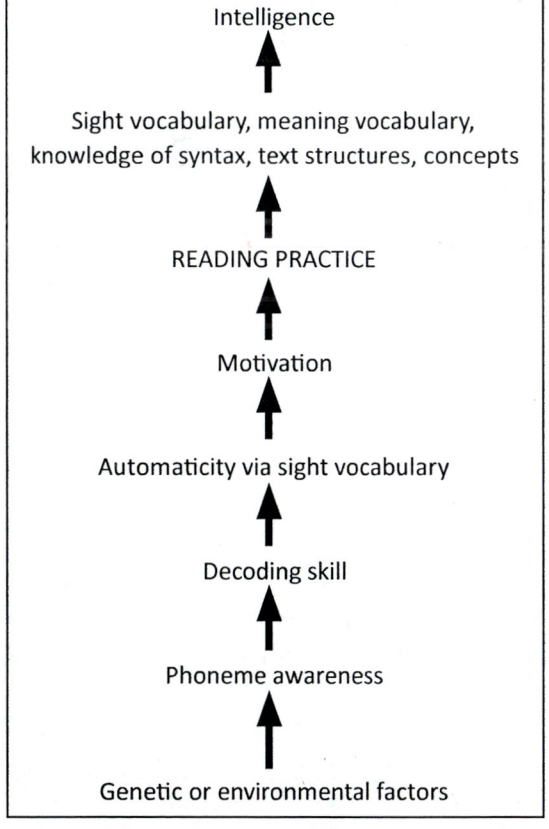

FIGURE 5: Matthew effects in reading

On the other hand, children entering school aware of phonemes tend to catch on quickly to decoding, amass sight vocabulary rapidly for fluency gains, and read voraciously because it is easy and rewarding. Through vast reading practice, they acquire the vocabulary and knowledge that enhance intelligence. Thus, early achievements in learning to read can have powerful bootstrapping effects that eventually open doorways to learning and career success. This fact led Stanovich (1986) to call for a "surgical strike" of early intervention directed at phoneme awareness to initiate a chain of positive Matthew effects. With early, explicit instruction in PA, letter recognition, and phonics, we can stop a chain reaction of negative Matthew effects and initiate productive, positive growth in reading.

INSIGHTS ON LEARNING DISABILITY

Before leaving the topic of preparing children to read, I want to leave three footnotes. First, we now have a stronger basis for understanding learning disability in reading. LD readers are bright students who are specifically delayed in learning to decode to make sight words, but doing well in other areas. Research suggests that nearly all LD readers have problems learning to read words, rooted in poor phoneme awareness. There is some reason to believe that problems with phoneme awareness have a hereditary component, analogous to tone deafness in music (Olson, 2004) as well as environmental influences.

According to the Matthew effects model, LD readers are *gifted* poor readers who are resistant to negative Matthew effects. Even though they are poor at decoding, they do not experience immediate harm to their meaning vocabulary, background knowledge, or language ability. However, because IQ has negligible effects on reading acquisition, their intellectual gifts will not help them learn to read words without explicit PA, phonics, and fluency instruction by capable teachers. If anything, their language ability may allow them to *disguise* their reading problems by memorization and contextual guessing, which means that they may mask their decoding weakness until their peers have moved on to sophisticated consolidated-alphabetic strategies that allow rapid growth in sight vocabulary—at which point PA and decoding instruction may no longer be available. Thus, LD readers need special early help breaking the alphabetic code before negative Matthew effects take their toll.

The simple view of reading (Hoover & Gough, 1990) explains reading as the product of decoding ability and language comprehension (RC = D X LC). This simple theory has strong scientific support; if we measure decoding with pseudoword reading and language comprehension with a vocabulary test, we can make an excellent prediction of reading comprehension accounting for most of the variation. The simple view predicts that reading disability has a good prognosis if caught early. The reason for this good prognosis is that language comprehension is unaffected in reading disability, so that early, intensive instruction in decoding can allow a full recovery of reading comprehension. The strong language comprehension that is intact for the LD reader can be harnessed for reading success if the decoding deficit can be remediated.

Garden-Variety Poor Readers

Second, there is another group of struggling readers often called "garden-variety" poor readers (GVs). Unlike LDs, the reading problems of GVs are not specific to decoding. They struggle in all school areas, including vocabulary. In the simple view, both decoding and language comprehension are areas of weakness. Usually, the reading problems of garden-variety poor readers begin with limited preschool literacy experience. Unlike John Adams with 5 solid years of literacy enrichment, they are 4 years, 10 months in arrears by the time they start school. Like LD readers, they begin with poor PA. However, as negative Matthew effects take hold, they fall behind in decoding ability, fluency, motivation, and reading practice as well as in vocabulary, knowledge of syntax and text structures, and background knowledge.

Both LD and GV poor readers need more intensive, explicit help early from the most expert teachers to stave off or reverse negative Matthew effects. In many elementary schools, the principal assigns a weak, ineffective teacher who has trouble managing behavior to remedial reading—a big mistake. LD and GV readers need expert teachers equipped with the best research-based strategies to make a difference. Struggling readers will not close the gap with more of the same activities other children are getting in regular classrooms. They won't catch up with shared readings or the language experience approach because these activities do not remediate phoneme awareness, letter recognition, or decoding to enable students to learn the alphabetic code. A brief 9-month program of literacy immersion in school will not make up for 4 years, 10 months neglect for GV readers. More-of-the-same activities will not remediate an unusual insensitivity to phonemes for LD readers. Struggling readers need more intensive, explicit instruction to direct the surgical strike of early intervention.

Finally, even successful beginners are not fixed forever. Learning to decode is just the beginning. Successful decoders need fluency instruction to minimize the work of reading words. To build an extensive store of sight words, they need guided reading in challenging books and motivated independent reading. To develop their reading comprehension, they need explicit instruction in "SAT" vocabulary, comprehension strategies, and study skills. Reading development continues for a lifetime.

SUMMARY

Earlier models of reading readiness and emergent literacy led to suboptimal instruction in preparing children to learn to read. The reading readiness view presumed that children needed to develop their intelligence and perceptual skills as prerequisites for reading, and it proscribed explicit instruction as harmful. The emergent literacy view adopted a false analogy to language learning in assuming children acquire literacy naturally in a literate environment. Similar to reading readiness, proponents of the emergent literacy view ruled out explicit instruction as interfering with natural literacy learning. More recent scholarship supports an early intervention view of early literacy, in which learning to read depends on learning the component skills of phoneme awareness and letter recognition. Explicit instruction in these foundational skills empowers literacy learning by providing the tools to unlock the messages of texts.

The reading readiness model continues to influence practice by suggesting that problems in learning to read involve inadequate perception, especially with children with learning disabilities. However, the weaknesses of children with LD in reversing letters, misspelling words, and misreading words owe to problems learning the alphabetic code rather than to general perceptual deficits. What were once thought to be difficulties with auditory perception in fact were problems detecting phonemes in spoken words. Efforts to match children's perceptual preferences as "learning styles" to instruction have not been successful: The best teaching methods work for children without regard to their assessed learning style. The tendency to withhold reading instruction until children reached a predetermined mental age was based on flawed research. IQ has been found to be a relatively weak predictor of success in learning to read, less than half as predictive as phoneme awareness. The two best predictors of learning to read are letter recognition and PA. There is a vital interaction between these two abilities: Phoneme awareness improves letter recognition by giving letters meaning, and letter recognition improves PA by giving phonemes visual symbols.

Measuring PA has been hampered by a reliance on tests that measure spelling ability rather than prealphabetic PA knowledge. Tests of segmentation (breaking words into phonemes), blending (assembling isolated phonemes into words), and manipulations, such as reversing or deleting phonemes, can be finessed with spelling knowledge. These tests pick up a level of PA that is a result of having already learned the alphabetic code. The Test of Phoneme Identities gets at an earlier prealphabetic level of phoneme awareness, and thus it is more useful for identifying children at risk of reading difficulties before their problems surface in reading failure.

Children learn PA informally by hearing alphabet books read aloud, inventing spellings, and learning nursery rhymes. Reading aloud is also productive for building the vocabulary and conceptual knowledge that eventually enhances reading success. Yet such informal literacy instruction is not universal: In low SES homes, children typically enjoy only about 2% as much time with adult read-alouds and accompanying literacy play. This places them not just slightly behind, but more than four years behind their more privileged peers. Early weaknesses in PA not successfully addressed in primary reading instruction tend to snowball into pervasive literacy difficulties with profound, lifelong consequences—a phenomenon known as negative Matthew effects. On the other hand, early intervention in learning PA can enable decoding success, which builds fluency and motivates reading practice. This in turn enables children to learn vocabulary and concepts that eventually improve verbal learning ability. By such positive Matthew effects, the early riches of PA can compound into life-enriching literacy knowledge.

The Matthew effects model has important implications for understanding learning disability. Students with LD may be thought of as gifted poor readers whose PA deficits have not yet become pervasive and debilitating. With effective early instruction before the onset of crushing negative Matthew effects, these children can shore up their PA deficits and learn to master word recognition, allowing their language comprehension abilities to flower in reading. A less promising prognosis, however, faces garden-variety poor readers, who are weak in both decoding ability and language comprehension. Both readers with LD and garden-variety poor readers stand their best chance of long-term success with early code instruction using the most effective strategies taught by the best available reading teachers. Children with excellent early instruction, despite all their advantages, still need a strong developmental reading program to fulfill their potential as skilled readers.

CHAPTER 6

Learning to Detect Phonemes in Spoken Words

When I was a graduate student at the University of Georgia, one of my responsibilities was to supervise reading tutors working with children with severe reading problems. I looked in on one lesson where the tutor was working with a third-grade boy who was not yet reading. The tutor held up cards with *d* and *ice*. "This says *duh*, and this says *ice*. You put them together," said the tutor.

"Duh ice."

"Say it faster. Put them together."

"Duh ice. Duh ice."

"What word is that?" asked the tutor.

"I don't know," said the boy, with a hint of annoyance.

This was the time for expert help. I stepped into the room and picked up a card with the letter *m*. "Let's try this," I said. "It's easier. Mmm ice."

"Mmm ice," the boy repeated.

"Smooth the sounds together," I said.

"Mmm ice. Mmm ice."

"Okay, what does that say?"

"I don't know!" So much for my expert help. Though this struggling reader knew *d* says "duh" and *m* says "mmm," he didn't detect /d/ or /m/ as articulatory elements in spoken words. In other words, he didn't have enough phoneme awareness to make sense out of the phonics instruction.

One of the greatest educational discoveries of the late 20th century was that phonics doesn't make sense without phoneme awareness (PA). Graphemes encoded in spellings do not signal phonemes until the reader can detect phonemes. For example, for beginners to understand that the spelling *knock* encodes the spoken word /nok/, they have to connect *kn* with /n/, *o* with /o[1]/, and *ck* with /k/. But before this is possible, they have to detect the phonemes /n/, /o/, and /k/ in the spoken word *knock*. Teaching children to detect phonemes in spoken words is the challenge of PA.

What are phonemes?

Though many teachers call phonemes "sounds," phonemes are better described as the basic vocal gestures of speech in a language (Liberman & Liberman, 1992). Phonemes are the interchangeable parts, like /d/, /m/, and /E/, from which we construct all spoken words. In English we have about 40 phonemes, which may be divided into consonants (articulatory gestures involving some friction) and vowels (voiced sounds made with an open, shaped mouth). The fluidity of phonemes and their variable representations with letters is the reason for the imprecise count. For example, the letter *x* represents a phoneme cluster /ks/, but it would confuse children to tell them that one letter represents two phonemes. The common spelling *qu* represents the phoneme cluster /kw/, but it is such a common partnership that it is convenient to treat /kw/ as a phoneme in teaching children how to read.

Phonemes are fluid articulatory gestures, continuous movements of the tongue, lips, and vocal apparatus that are coarticulated as we produce a spoken word. These gestures are not physically distinct; if we replayed a spoken word in super slow motion, we would find no clear demarcation between one phoneme and the next. Phonemes morph together, making subtle changes in neighboring phonemes. As you say one, your mouth already is changing to say the next. Try this: Put your mouth in position to say *dive*. Now change it into the position to say *drive*. Did you notice that your lips and tongue positioned themselves to say /r/ even though you had not yet pronounced /d/? Not only do phonemes morph, we pronounce them at the extraordinary rate of 10-20 phonemes per second. The speech stream is fraught with rapids.

The 40 English phonemes can be combined into a virtually limitless variety of words. English already has some 5 million words, and new words are continually being coined. My wife came home from teaching her high school class and told me she'd learned a new word, *crunk*, apparently a portmanteau of *crazy*

---

1. In this book I use a simplified way of representing phonemes without diacritical marks for those unfamiliar with the international phonetic alphabet. Consonants are represented with the most common English letter or digraph. Short vowels are written with lowercase letters (e.g., cat would be /kat/, and long vowels are written with capital letters (e.g., goat would be /gOt/). Other vowel digraphs (e.g., /aw/) are represented with their most familiar spellings

and *drunk*. Here's a challenge: What words could we make by using all four of these phonemes: /a/, /k/, /s/, and /t/? Note that you don't have to use the letters *a*, *k*, *s*, and *t*. For example, *asked* is made from these phonemes (/a/s/k/t/). Counting homonyms, I found 13 different words constructed from these phonemes. (See the answer at the end of the chapter.)

What is Phoneme Awareness (PA)

PA means the ability to detect phonemes in their natural habitat—the spoken word. Three decades of research in PA (e.g., Byrne & Fielding-Barnsley, 1990; Castiglioni-Spalten & Ehri, 2003; Wallach & Wallach, 1979) support the view that phonemes are learned like flowers and fish. To learn a flower, a fish, or a phoneme, children must learn its distinguishing features to detect it in its natural habitat. To identify a black-eyed Susan, we need to know about its dark center surrounded by yellow petals. To recognize a neon tetra, we need information about its bright blue sides and red tail. Detecting the phoneme /s/ in the natural habitat of a spoken word requires familiarity with the hissing sound we make by blowing air over a raised tongue. To understand how spellings map phonemes in written words, children must first detect phonemes in spoken words.

Phoneme Awareness and Phonics

PA instruction differs from phonics in that it leads children to examine spoken words rather than to decode written words. PA turns the attention spotlight on oral language to learn to identify the vocal elements of speech. PA instruction comes before phonics to detect the phonemes, mostly consonants, that recur in spoken language. We assess PA by asking children to test spoken words for phonemes, e.g., "Do you hear /z/ in *bug* or *buzz*?" In contrast, phonics is instruction in decoding written words. Children ready to decode written words already recognize most consonants and use them in partial alphabetic decoding. Phonics teaches them vowels, enabling them to work through complete spellings in full alphabetic decoding. We assess phonics knowledge by asking students to read pseudowords like *plake*, which requires them to understand a pronunciation map written in alphabetic code. In summary, PA is detecting phonemes (usually consonants) in spoken words, while phonics is decoding instruction, mostly focused on vowels.

But why do children need to learn to identify phonemes? For the answer, we must think back to the origins of our alphabetic writing system. As we have seen, the first writing was logographic. Each symbol represented the meaning of a word (e.g., *moon*) with a stylized symbol (say, ☽). Such writing is easy to understand, but it requires a vast number of symbols to account for the vocabulary of a language (English, for example, has about 5 million words). Writing changed when some unknown Phoenician genius recognized that words are *not* unique sounds. Instead, they are composed of a limited number of vocal gestures—phonemes. Spoken language recycles phonemes into countless phonological structures (e.g., *fits, sift, fist,* etc.) to generate the vast number of spoken words that compose a language. Recognizing this, our ingenious Phoenician devised symbols to map out the sequence of vocal gestures in spoken words, creating the world's first alphabet.

Figure 1 provides an example of how alphabetic writing maps out a spoken word. Because the spoken word *ship* is a sequenced blend of three phonemes, /sh/, /i/, /p/, we can map out *ship* with an ordered sequence of symbols—graphemes—that represent these phonemes (graphemes include both single letters and digraphs). To decode this alphabetic map (rows A to B to C), we first sound out the graphemes *sh*, *i*, and *p* into their partner phonemes, /sh/, /i/, and /p/, and then blend the phoneme sequence into an approximation of the spoken word, close enough to recognize the familiar spoken word *ship*. To encode (i.e., spell) an alphabetic map (rows C to B to A), we segment the spoken word *ship* into phonemes /sh/, /i/, /p/, and then represent the phoneme sequence with grapheme symbols, *ship*. Phonics is instruction in decoding alphabetic maps to identify spoken words. Typically, phonics has focused on the relationships of letters and phonemes, rows A and B in the figure. To decode *ship*, for example, it would be important to learn how *i* represents the vowel /i/. But we have underestimated the importance of connecting rows B and C, that is, phoneme awareness. Learning how *i* represents /i/ only makes sense if you understand /i/ as a component of spoken words like *ship*.

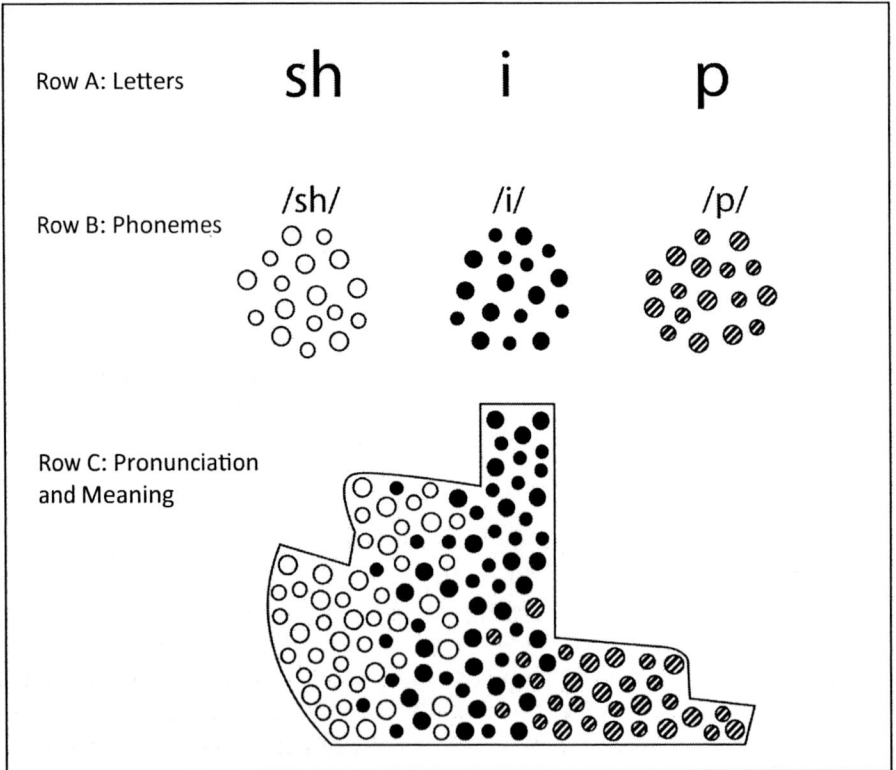

FIGURE 1: How alphabetic writing maps the spoken word *ship*

Many children raised in literate homes have little difficulty learning to detect phonemes in spoken words because they have many learning opportunities in early childhood to familiarize themselves with phonemes. Their parents typically read them alphabet books with prominent letter symbols for phonemes and a variety of example words. For example, *Dr. Seuss's ABC* (Geisel, 1963), asks, "What begins with *j*? Jerry Jordan's jelly jar and jam begin that way." Meanwhile, they learn the nursery rhyme "Jack and Jill," with alliteration that further sensitizes them to phoneme /j/. Children may additionally receive informal PA instruction when they invent spellings. For example, a child might ask, "How do you write *jump*?" and be told, "Well, /j/, /j/, *jump* starts with j, just like your sister's name, *Jessica*." Children who stretch the pronunciations of words, feel and hear their tongues and lips moving through the phoneme sequence, and then represent their mouth moves with letters, are practicing PA.

But not all children grow up in rich literacy environments, and even some with all the advantages have trouble catching on to PA. Researchers Michael and Lise Wallach (1979) compared the PA of inner city and suburban children entering first grade in the Chicago area. They showed the children pictures, e.g., of a man and a house, and asked, "Does *man* or *house* start with /m/? There were 15 such items, and children who scored at least 12 right were not guessing—they were aware of phonemes. As displayed in Figure 2, the contrast in the inner city and suburban results was dramatic.

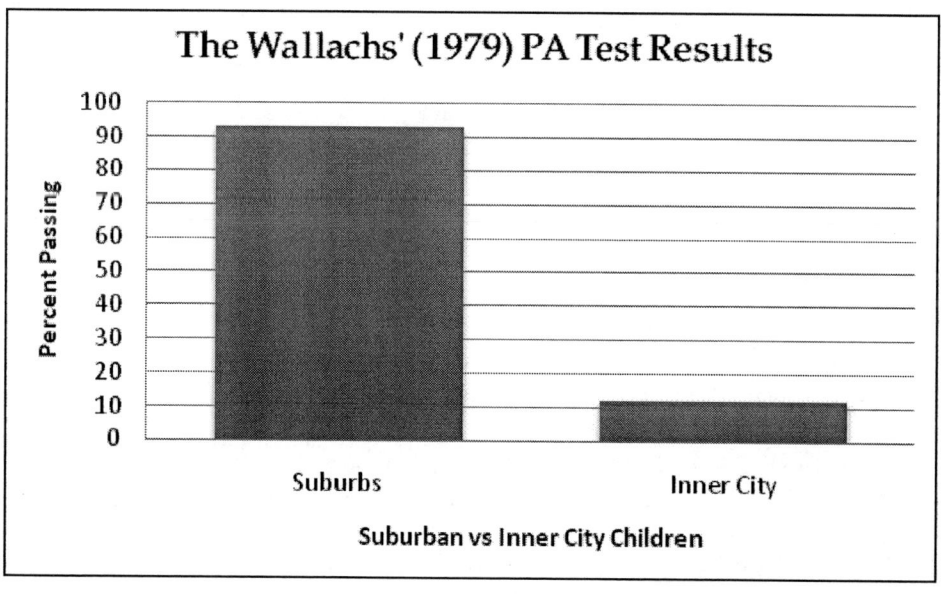

FIGURE 2: Suburban and inner city achievement in PA on entering first grade

As the chart shows, 93% of children from the suburbs passed the test, showing that they detected the phonemes to be mapped with alphabetic writing. However, only 12% of the inner-city kindergartners passed. This means 88% of the inner-city children entered first grade lacking the foundation for understanding the alphabetic code.

A longitudinal study by Connie Juel (Juel, Griffith, & Gough, 1986) showed what happens to children who start behind in PA. Juel tracked the decoding progress of children with high and low PA at the end of kindergarten (the high group averaged about 22 and the low group about 4). As Figure 3 indicates, children low in PA never caught up in decoding ability. Children entering first grade low in PA had not reached the first-grade reading level at the end of first grade, and achieved less than a year's growth each year during the four-year study. By the end of fourth grade, the children who entered first grade low in PA had not equaled the decoding scores of high PA children in second grade. These reading differences show a widening gap between "haves" and "have nots." The "have nots" fell further and further behind their peers who had the advantage of high PA entering first grade.

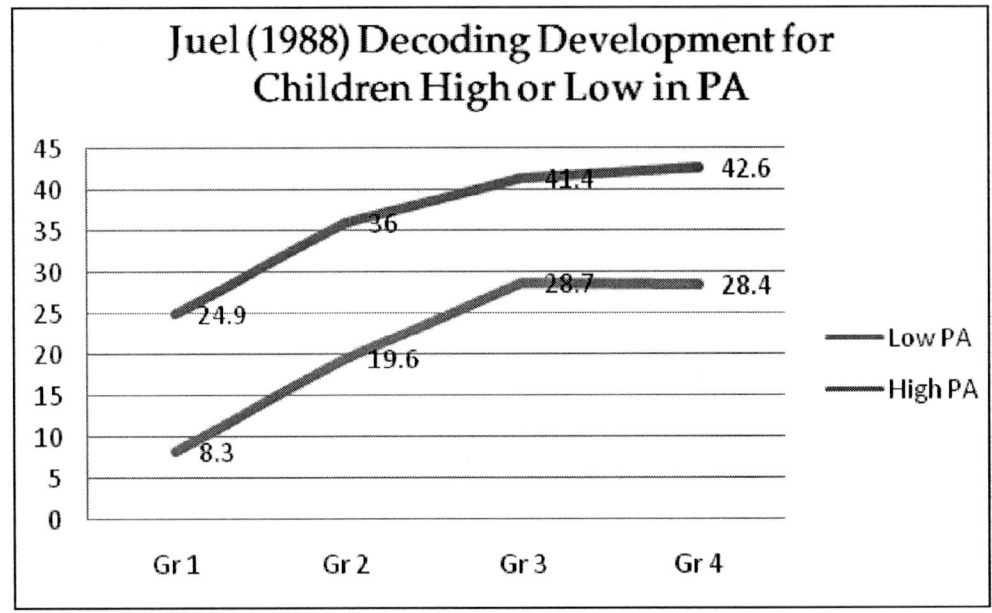

FIGURE 3: Progress in decoding through grades 1-4 for children high and low in phoneme awareness

Though these data are correlational, there is strong evidence from experimental research that PA can be taught, and that teaching PA helps children learn to read (NRP, 2000). Conversely, poor PA lies at the beginning of a causal chain that leads to poor reading (Stanovich, 1986). Children who don't have PA will struggle to learn to read words. Given ordinary instruction, they tend to muddle through beginning reading, to gain reading ability slowly, and to comprise a permanent literacy underclass in schools. On the other hand, if we could teach these children to detect phonemes in kindergarten, we could move them onto the fast track of reading achievement with their phoneme-sensitive peers. If we can address their weakness in PA early, we can get them on track to succeed in reading. In the words of Keith Stanovich (1986), it will take a "surgical strike" at the root of reading disability before the early weakness in PA develops into poor decoding, frustration with grade-level texts, a dearth of reading practice, and negative attitudes about reading that can sink a student's educational career.

Phonological Awareness

At this point, there may be some confusion about the similar terms phonological awareness and phoneme awareness. *Phonological* awareness is the ability to identify any speech unit in the spoken word. It includes phoneme awareness—the ability to detect phonemes in spoken words—but also the ability to detect syllables, onsets, rimes, bodies, and codas. For example, if we asked kindergartners to tell us the first sound in *sweetener*, they might correctly say *sweet* (the first syllable), /sw/ (the onset), or /s/ (the initial phoneme). We might picture phoneme awareness using a Venn diagram (see Figure 4). We can see that phonological awareness is the overarching concept that includes awareness of syllables, onsets and rimes, bodies and codas, and phonemes. Each of these subsyllabic parts will be examined in this chapter.

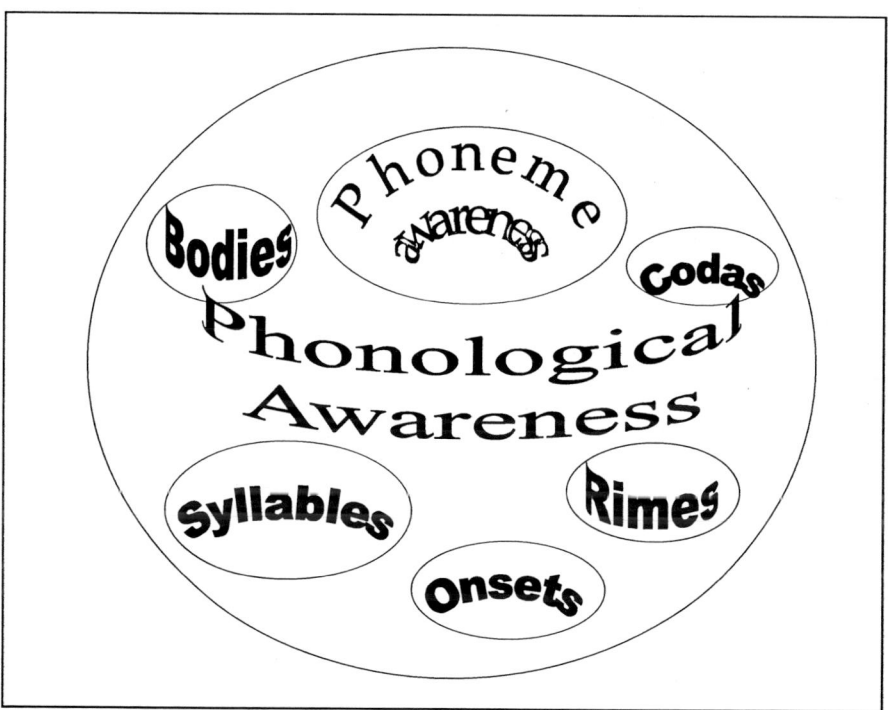

FIGURE 4: Venn diagram of phonological awareness

THE DEPTH CHART MODEL

A popular view of how to teach phoneme awareness could be called the depth chart model (see Figure 5). This plausible model suggests that becoming aware of phonemes is a matter of developing sensitivity to smaller and less meaningful units of language. Specifically, it suggests children begin by recognizing large, distinct meaningful units (messages) and then progress to recognizing smaller, distinct meaning units (words), to distinct but meaningless units (syllables), to indistinct and meaningless units (onsets and rimes), until they reach the ultimately subtle units, phonemes. The assumption in the depth chart model is that sensitivity grows automatically to all units at each level. For example, grasping the entire message, "Gymnastics is fun," comes first. Next, according to the depth-chart model, children learn to identify the words *gymnastics*, *is*, and *fun*. As they progress in sensitivity, they recognize the syllables *gym*, *nas*, and *tics*. Later, they learn the natural syllable break into onset and rime and detect /j/ and /im/, /n/ and /as/, /t/ and /iks/. On reaching the phoneme level, according to the model, children can detect the full sequence of /j/, /i/, /m/, /n/, /a/, /s/, /t/, /i/, /k/, /s/.

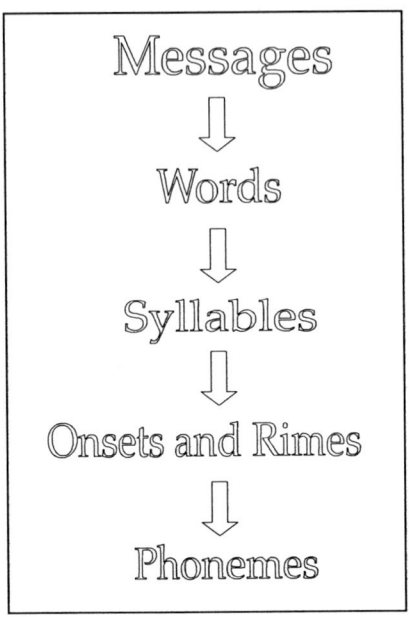

FIGURE 5: The depth-chart model of phoneme awareness

However, on closer examination, the depth-chart model breaks down. An immediate problem is how children can become aware of words. Words are not separated in speech by pauses. They flow together in normal language exactly like syllables. For example, just as there is no temporal space separating the syllables in *gymnastics*, there is no temporal space separating the words "Gymnastics is fun." Here's an experiment to try on someone who doesn't speak Spanish. Ask how many words are in the sentence, /bI-los-cOn-mE-gO/, which means "Dance with me" in Spanish. Usually answers will range from three to five. The answer is just two. You have to see it written in Spanish—"Bailas conmigo" to count the number of words. Spoken words in a sentence sound like strings of syllables. Disagreements are even common in English about the number of words in *all right*, *a lot*, *workbook*, and *time line*. The only way to resolve our differences is to see the word in print and look at the spacing. This implies that word awareness is off the depth chart—it is a *result* of learning to read.

The other major problem with the depth chart is the assumption that when young learners reach a level, they immediately gain sensitivity to all the units at that level. This does seem to be true of syllables. Once children learn to attend to the loud sound of the vowel at the core of each syllable, they can usually count syllables in *asparagus, latitude, pulchritudinous,* or any other word. Once they have the concept of loud beats in a word, they can recognize any spoken syllable. Syllables are loud speech sounds, and if they can count loud hand claps, they should be able to count syllables.

We have already seen that we can't apply any such simple insight into counting words, and the same is true for phonemes. Phonemes are coarticulated vocal gestures that flow together into words at the rate of 10-20 phonemes per second. Unless someone slows down the flow and calls attention to phonemes, we'd never learn to recognize them. Even with instruction, some phonemes are more salient—noticeable—than others. Phonemes that make a clear sound, like /s/, or phonemes produced visibly, like /p/, tend to be more salient than phonemes like /r/ or /w/, which make indistinct sounds and are not easily observed. To learn phonemes, we need to learn about the individual features of each phoneme and to learn its vocal boundaries (e.g., /t/ sounds a little different in *time* and *train*, but it is the same phoneme).

In summary, we can't expect a natural climb down the depth chart to become aware of phonemes in spoken words. We have to eliminate words from the depth chart because word awareness comes as a result of learning to read words when we attend to their spacing. We have to eliminate syllables from the depth chart because syllable awareness is a simple insight, unlike PA, which requires learning individual vocal gestures one at a time. In one respect, however, learning phonemes has an element of insight. Work by Byrne and Fielding-Barnsley (1991) suggests that when children learn a basic collection of 12-15 phonemes, the remaining 25 or so phonemes become increasingly easy to detect, probably because children have acquired some skill in examining their mouth moves to identify phonemes.

TEACHING CHILDREN TO DETECT PHONEMES

Researchers have carried out many teaching studies to improve children's phoneme awareness (Ehri, Nunes, Stahl, & Willows, 2001), but not all PA training has been equally effective. My own meta-analysis of the effectiveness of PA training (Murray, 1995) suggests that programs that teach PA effectively have four crucial components. First, they introduce a limited group of phonemes one at a time rather than expecting children to develop a general sensitivity to phonemes. Second, they make each selected phoneme memorable to children and help them learn its vocal boundaries. Third, they arrange phoneme-finding practice so that children can learn to detect the phoneme in spoken-word contexts. Finally, they apply phoneme knowledge to partial-alphabetic decoding, showing students how to parlay PA into success with reading words.

FOCUS ON INDIVIDUAL PHONEMES

Phoneme awareness is big news these days, and there are many commercial programs on the market. However, most programs to teach children to recognize phonemes are based on the depth-chart model of PA as a generalized skill in phoneme manipulations. The depth-chart model has misled teachers to work on segmenting and blending *any* word into *whatever* phonemes in contains. Such programs leave many children mystified, as illustrated in a report by McGee and Ukrainetz (2009). This dialogue shows what happens when children are asked to detect a phoneme without providing any clear means of identification:

> Mrs. Pollard: Everyone say *tub*.
>
> Children: Tub
>
> Mrs. Pollard: What's the first sound in *tub*? Jermeshia?
>
> Jermeshia: [looks at teacher]
>
> Mrs. Pollard: Listen, *tub* [emphasis on the first sound, /t/]. What's the first sound you hear in *tub*?
>
> Jermeshia: [no response]
>
> Mrs. Pollard: Cedrean. What's the first sound in *tub*?
>
> Cedrian: /t/
>
> Mrs. Pollard: Good. . . . Destiny? What's the first sound in *toes*?
>
> Destiny: [very quietly] Toes
>
> Mrs. Pollard: That's the word. What's the first sound in *toes*? *Toes*. It starts like *tub*.
>
> Destiny: [silence, looks down]
>
> Mrs. Pollard: /t/ is the first sound.

A likely reason for the uneven success of PA teaching programs is that they expect children to develop sensitivity to all the phonemes at once, which requires them to identify phonemes they've never learned about. In Mrs. Pollard's reading group, children have no information for detecting the phoneme /t/. We would hardly expect novice Scouts to learn to identify all the edible wild plants at once, or novice birdwatchers to emerge in recognition of all the songbirds at once, or preschool children to learn to identify all the letters at once. Just as beginners need to learn the critical features of edible plants, songbirds, and letters, novice readers need to get a feel for *each phoneme* they will use in reading and spelling words. This implies that PA instruction must deal with phonemes one by one.

The Phoneme-Direct Model

In the phoneme-direct model, in contrast to the depth-chart model, the teacher teaches the defining features of each phoneme, one by one. As Figure 6 illustrates, the teacher might present a picture of a ticking clock to represent the phoneme /t/. The clock image helps draw an analogy to a real-life experience of a ticking sound similar to the phoneme /t/. The image is supported by its name ("ticking *t"*), a hand gesture (a wagging finger), and its letter *t*, which will become the permanent visual symbol for /t/, a constant for a letter whose sound may vary from /t/ to /ch/ (compare /t/ in *tick* and *trick*). Children experience some of the variable sound for /t/ by stretching and breaking /t/ from the words of a tongue tickler, e.g., "Tom tricked Tim and took his train off the track." They test spoken words for /t/ ("Do you hear /t/ in *give* or *take*?"), and they begin to use the letter *T* in distinguishing rhyming words by phonetic cue reading (e.g., "Is this word [TELL] *tell* or *sell*?").

FIGURE 6: Ticking *t* illustration for phoneme-direct teaching of /t/

> **Develop a phoneme awareness lesson.**
>
> As you read through the procedures for research-based phoneme awareness instruction, you will profit most by designing and teaching your own phoneme awareness lesson. I'm going to lead you through this process in stages. Each time you run into one of these boxed texts, I'd like you to add another piece to your phoneme awareness lesson design. Your first task is to choose a phoneme to teach. Consonants are easiest to work with and typical of phoneme awareness instruction. I recommend you choose one consonant and write it at the top of your lesson-planning page in slash marks. Whenever you see this notation, think of the phoneme, not the letter name. For a list of English phonemes with spellings and sound analogies, See Appendix A.

Make the phoneme memorable

Cognitive psychologists tell us that remembering is a matter of building retrieval paths from the new experience to previous experiences, thus connecting new concepts with prior knowledge. With beginners, we want to introduce each phoneme by making connections with its letter and a sound analogy, supported by a name, an illustration, and a hand gesture. A sound analogy is a real-world sound similar to the sound made by the phoneme, as in Figure 7. To introduce the phoneme /s/, the teacher might say, "Silly, sneaky snake looks like the letter *S*, and he makes a hissing sound like what we say when we hold the end of the name *ess*, /s/. Let's make our hands slither as we make a sound like a silly, sneaky snake."

FIGURE 7: Illustrations for the sound analogies "silly, sneaky snake" and "Mmm-m."

This brief introduction initiates several retrieval paths. First, the letter *S* becomes a visual symbol of the phoneme /s/, making it easier to remember. Research has demonstrated that knowing letters helps beginners remember phonemes (Hohn & Ehri, 1983). Not only does a letter or digraph help the novice reader "see" the phoneme, it serves as a lifelong referent in written words. Second, a sound analogy of a hissing snake relates the phoneme to a familiar experience in the world. Third, the sound analogy is supported by a name ("silly, sneaky snake"), an illustration, and a hand gesture to make it vivid and accessible to young children. The gesture should act out the sound analogy in some way. A phoneme gesture like "slithering" the hand and arm for /s/ becomes a ready way for children to practice with the phoneme and to signal that they have detected it. Whether the child is in the classroom or at home, a phoneme gesture is literally always at his fingertips.

The purpose of the sound analogy is to evoke a real-world sound with some similarity to the phoneme, such as a snake's hiss. Other analogies for /s/ are possible, such as the sound of a leaky ball, a spray can, or sizzling sausage. Parents and teachers might not immediately understand the sound analogy, but the prominent display of the letter will help them make the connection. In addition, children may need instruction in vocabulary or background knowledge to understand the sound analogy. Such instruction enriches children's understanding of how the world works, and tangible experiences with sound analogies may be readily available as You Tube videos. The authors of the Open Court reading program have developed many creative associations for phonemes across a variety of editions. I have borrowed freely from Open Court materials to make the catalog of phonemes, spellings, and sound analogies in Appendix A. Teachers and students may come up with original sound analogies, which may turn out to be even more memorable for your students.

The sound analogy is not typically an alphabet example word, such as *sun*, *sock*, or *sky* (although in this case, *snake* does double duty). Traditionally, children have been introduced to phonemes in a more opaque way, with alphabet example words such as "M is for moon." However, giving alphabet example words for phonemes presumes that children already have sufficient PA to detect the phoneme in the spoken word. To understand that /m/ is for *moon* presumes precisely what we are trying to teach. In contrast, a sound analogy like "Mmm-m," as in Figure 7, captures an experience of a sound similar to the isolated phoneme. Recent Open Court materials give both illustrated sound analogies and traditional example words. For example, C is for *camera*, but it also sounds like the /k/ the shutter makes when taking a picture; F is for *fan*, but it also evokes the sound of a fan, /f/.

Tongue Ticklers

A phoneme is a concept, and to learn a phoneme concept requires experiencing the phoneme as the same mouth move across many different words. This sameness is the *identity* of a phoneme, from the Latin *idem*, meaning "the same." The central goal of PA instruction is for children to recognize phonemes as the same wherever they appear in the natural context of spoken words, despite minor variations in sound. To learn any concept, students need lots of examples to pull out the consistent idea.

A tongue tickler provides experiences with a phoneme in an alliteration that repeats the phoneme several times at the beginning of words. Researchers Michael and Lise Wallach (Wallach & Wallach, 1976) composed a useful set of alliterations they called "tongue twisters" for a noteworthy PA teaching experiment. For example, children learned to identify the phoneme /n/ by saying, "Nobody was nice to Nancy's neighbor Nick, but he was never nasty." I prefer the term "tickler" for these alliterations because the purpose is not to twist the tongue and cause scrambled speech, but to tickle it with sensation as children experience the common phoneme. The Wallachs' tongue ticklers may be a bit long for young children. Teachers can devise shorter ticklers, such as "Mom's muffins melt in my mouth." I have included the Wallachs' tongue ticklers along with a collection of vowel ticklers in Appendix B.

Tongue ticklers should be alliterations so that the target phoneme appears at the beginning of several words. Alliterations are difficult with vowel phonemes, and teachers should resist the temptation to use the vowel in the interior of words, where it requires PA to identify. Brief ticklers with four or five example words are plenty. Ticklers need not have consistent spellings because PA instruction is chiefly an oral language activity, and printed ticklers need not be displayed. A brief tickler like "Caring cats kiss crying kittens" works well despite the variant spellings of /k/ as *c* and *k*. Whenever possible, include words like *crying* where the target phoneme is part of a consonant cluster. This provides a challenge to detect the phoneme where it is less accessible and may involve a variant articulation because of the proximity of the neighboring phoneme (with *crying*, the lips are pursed for /r/ even as we are pronouncing /k/). To help children remember the tickler, it helps to tell a story; for example, this story to introduce a tongue tickler for the phoneme /m/:

> When he got home from school, Mike was very hungry. There was a wonderful smell coming from the kitchen, where Mom was baking muffins. Mom gave Mike a warm muffin fresh out of the oven. "Mmm," said Mike. "Mom's muffins melt in my mouth!" And that's our tongue tickler: Mom's muffins melt in my mouth.

Practicing with Ticklers

There are two ways to practice with the tongue tickler: stretching the target phoneme and splitting off the phoneme from words. If a phoneme is stretchable, a good progression is first to stretch the target phoneme while making the hand gesture (e.g., "Mmmany mmmice mmmake mmmusic"). As a follow-up, have students split off the target phoneme ("Mmm-any mmm-ice mmm-ake mmm-usic"). By stretching and then splitting off the phoneme, students experience the articulatory gesture, both as part of the word and in isolation. With stop phonemes like /t/, only splitting is possible. Wallach and Wallach (1979) considered splitting off the phoneme in alliterations their most effective activity for learning PA.

Using Alphabet Books

A good alphabet book offers a ready source of alliterations. For example, *Dr. Seuss's ABC* (Geisel, 1963), answers the question, "What begins with F?" with an alliteration, "Four fluffy feathers on a Fiffer-feffer-feff." However, many alphabet books are designed to teach concepts or to present an illustrator's work rather than to help young children identify the phonemes represented by letters. For example, Chris Van Allsburg's popular alphabet book *The Z Was Zapped* (Van Allsburg, 1987) gives a single example word for each letter (e.g., "The *E* was evaporating") and uses vocabulary beyond the range of many young children. For purposes of PA instruction, teachers need alphabet books with multiple examples of familiar words.

In two experiments using alphabet books to teach PA (Brabham, Murray, & Hudson, 2006; Murray, Stahl, & Ivey, 1996), we've picked up a couple of insights. One insight is that children learn phonemes better when teachers make letter-phoneme connections explicit. For example, we asked teachers to teach PA explicitly by saying, "*F* tells your mouth to say /f/. Watch my mouth: Fffour. Fffeathers." After reading about "Four fluffy feathers on a Fiffer-feffer-feff" (Geisel, 1963), teachers asked children questions such as: "When you see this letter, what's your mouth move? What's a word with /f/?" Children made the best gains in PA when teachers emphasized phonemes in this way, provided that they practiced with books on tape or with an adult reader. When they practiced with an animated computer program, the music and animations proved so distracting that the children lost their focus on phonemes.

The other insight teachers drove home to us in both experiments is that alphabet books when read from cover to cover are terribly boring. Children like books that tell stories, especially stories with problems or goals worked out during the course of the plot. Alphabet books rarely if ever have any coherent story structure. For this reason, I suggest reading alphabet books a page or two at a time. Rather than straining children's patience by reading the whole book at once, work only with the pages featuring your target phoneme and its example words.

Exploring Articulation

Phoneme awareness is one realm where discovery learning can be very effective because most children already know how to produce phonemes—they simply lack conscious awareness of phoneme identities. Teachers can ask children to be "scientists" and figure out how a phoneme is made. For example, the teacher might say, "Today we are studying the sound we make when something really tastes good, mmm-m. Say /m/. Now pretend you're a scientist and teach me how to say /m/. How *do* you say /m/?" Give children time to feel the position of their lips, find out where air is coming out, and discover the source of the sound they are producing. Some promising PA research has used mouth pictures and mirrors to help children detect the articulatory gestures that are the essential features of the phoneme (Castiglioni-Spalten & Ehri, 2003).

Spelling

The most important memory route for any phoneme is its principal letter or digraph (i.e., the *grapheme*) that alphabetically represents that phoneme in written words. The grapheme serves as a visible symbol of phoneme, and it will remain the symbol for life. Displaying letters and learning letter names has been shown to be valuable in acquiring PA (Hohn & Ehri, 1983). The letter name usually features the phoneme prominently, e.g., *em* and *ess*, making most letter names reasonably good phoneme approximations. Once children recognize a grapheme as a phoneme symbol, teachers should encourage them to write daily with invented spellings. We have good evidence (Clarke, 1988) that inventing spellings, far from confusing children about the spelling system, improves both spelling and word identification in young children who have not achieved PA. The likely mechanism for this improvement is that inventing spellings is excellent practice with PA. Children gain familiarity with phonemes as they stretch pronunciations, identify phonemes, and transcribe them with letters. As a practical matter, the teacher who would encourage invented spelling must not provide standard spellings to beginning writers. This means that in a nice way, the teacher must refuse to supply spellings prior to the development of PA (after which there is no harm in supplying spellings). If a beginner asks for a spelling, the teacher could help the student stretch out the spoken word to detect what our mouths are doing as we say the word, and write down letters for each phoneme identified.

The letterbox lesson (Murray & Lesniak, 1999) provides explicit help with alphabetic mapping (see Practical Chapter 3). Each lesson teaches a new correspondence and practices it by spelling and reading regular, one-syllable, non-rhyming example words. After teacher modeling, the student spells each word in connected squares ("letterboxes") that show the number of phonemes in the word. Guiding spelling in letterboxes helps beginners identify each word's complete phoneme sequence. After spelling all the example words, the student reads them—thus transferring letter-phoneme connections from spelling to reading. Very simple letterbox lessons (e.g., spelling and reading *it, in, sit, fin,* and *sit*) provide excellent practice for young children beginning to learn the alphabetic code.

MAKE YOUR PHONEME MEMORABLE FOR CHILDREN

Make your phoneme memorable with a sound analogy, gesture, and illustration. Help children explore articulation with an alliterative tongue tickler, stretching and splitting off the phoneme from spoken words. You can have students explore the mouth move with mirrors, use letters to invent spellings, or develop spellings explicitly with letter box lessons. You may think of other developmentally appropriate activities to make phonemes memorable to young children.

For example, to teach the phoneme /m/, you could introduce the tongue tickler "Mom's muffins melt in my mouth," explaining to children that the letter M tells us to say "mmm" at the beginning of each word. You could ask children to stretch and split off /m/ at the beginning of each word as they say the tickler, and then have them explore how they are making /m/: "Where are your lips? Where is the sound coming from? How does the air get out?" For additional practice, you might have students work in pairs to count how many times we say /m/ in "Mom's muffins melt in my mouth." The correct answer is 6.

FIND THE PHONEME IN SPOKEN WORDS

Phoneme awareness means the ability to recognize phonemes in their natural habitat, spoken words. Children are not aware of phonemes until they can recognize them in words. It takes no PA to recite a correspondence like "*T* says tuh." Children have

PA when they can tell you that /t/ is in *table*, but not in *chair*. My Test of Phoneme Identities (Murray, Smith, & Murray, 2000) assesses PA in this way. The child plays a "repeating game" and then decides which of two spoken words contains the target phoneme. For example, the examiner says, "Say: 'We'll see the moon soon.' Now say /s/. Do you hear /s/ in *moon* or *soon*?" Pretest and posttest versions of the Test of Phoneme Identities may be found in Appendix A of Practical Chapter 5.

Modeling PA

Teacher-effectiveness research has found that modeling is an important ingredient of good teaching (Rosenshine, 1995). Teachers model when they work problems for students and explain the steps in solving the problems aloud. To model PA, the teacher stretches words, talks about the clue that reveals the target phoneme, and decides aloud whether or not the phoneme is there. For example, the teacher might say, "I'm going to hunt for the "Mmm-m" sound in the word *pump*. I'll know it's there if my lips come together and hum. Pu-u-u-mp. Hold it: P u-u-u-*mmm* . . . There! In the middle my lips came together and made a humming sound. That was /m/. There is /m/ in *pump*." It is important to test nonexamples, too; for example: "Let me see if I can detect "Mmm-m" in nest. I'm going to stretch it out—nnn-e-e-e-sss-t. Nope, my lips never came together to hum. There's no /m/ in *nest*."

Phoneme-Detection Activities

The easiest place to find a phoneme is at the beginning of words, and that's a good place to begin practicing. The teacher can have children listen for a phoneme and respond in a way that will help them remember. For example, the teacher could say, "Listen for 'Mmm-m." Touch the corner of your mouth with a pretend napkin to show me when you hear it. Do you hear /m/ in *mop*? *rake*? *motor*?" Later have them search elsewhere in the word, not the beginning; for example, to check for /m/ in *broom, dump,* or *nut*. Group activities work best when every student responds at once with a silent signal such as the phoneme gesture rather than allowing the leaders to call out an answer for others to echo.

Some children have trouble moving from seeing through words to their meaning to examining the words themselves. The switch from meaning to the form of language is a metalinguistic shift, which literally means "standing beside language." The need for a metalinguistic shift was apparent in Steve Stahl's experience testing a struggling first-grader named Heather (Stahl, 1992, p. 621):

> I gave Heather a task involving removing a phoneme from a spoken word. For example, I had Heather say *meat* and then repeat it without saying the /m/ sound (*eat*). When Heather said *chicken* after some hesitation, I was taken aback. When I had her say *coat* with the /k/ sound, she said *jacket*. Looking over the tasks we did together, it appeared that she viewed words only in terms of their meaning. For her, a little less than *meat* was *chicken*, a little less than *coat* was *jacket*.

It is useful to challenge children's focus on phonemes in phoneme-finding activities by using words related in meaning. For example, the teacher could ask, "Do you hear /m/ in *boy* or *man*? Is /m/ in *more* or *less*? In *sun* or *moon*?" Using related words requires children to focus on phonemes as well as meaning, i.e., to make a metalinguistic shift from the meanings of words to their forms.

Creative Phoneme-Detection Activities

The imaginative teacher will think of many creative ways to give children practice finding phonemes in spoken word contexts. The essential idea is to devise problems where children must search spoken words for a target phoneme. There is no reason for these activities to be dull drill. Children can respond orally or make the phoneme gesture they have learned. For example, "We know we've spotted /z/ if our tongue comes up to hiss, but we also turn our voices on, /z/. Tell me which words in this sentence have /z/: "Buzz and Ozzie zipped through the zoo."

Here is a phoneme-detection activity for /s/: "We're looking for silly, sneaky snake, /s/. I'll name some clothes. If they have /s/ in them, I want you to slither your hand like a silly, sneaky snake. If they don't have /s/, I want you to cross your arms. Ready? Socks. Shoes (careful!). Pants. Dress. Shirt (careful again!). Scarf. Hat. Vest." Pulling away from their natural focus on the meaning of these clothing items to a search for the phoneme /s/ challenges children's ability to switch metalinguistically from meaning to form, which is a PA essential.

Children must also detect phonemes when they construct alliterative tongue ticklers or find alphabet example words for a written project, such as a class alphabet book. To devise a tickler like "Hank heard a horrible howl and hooting from his hammock" requires not only generating words that begin with /h/, but also weeding out those that do not.

> **ADD A PHONEME-DETECTION ACTIVITY TO YOUR LESSON**
>
> First, provide a modeling script to show how you would test words for your target phoneme. Include an example word and a nonexample. Then have children test some words. Include pairs of words related in meaning, to challenge their ability to make a metalinguistic shift from meaning to form. Begin with words with the target phoneme at the beginning, but then try words where the target phoneme is at the end or in the middle of the word. Then get creative, e.g., by asking children to find words with your phoneme in a sentence, test a semantic group of words, or make tongue ticklers for the phoneme. Begin with the science of reading education, but develop creative activities that engage children's imaginations.

APPLYING PA TO READING WORDS

If PA instruction leads to rollicking fun and games, but it is never applied to reading words, then we will not have improved children's foundational skills in learning to read. Unfortunately, many researchers who have developed creative and developmentally appropriate PA lessons stopped short of showing children how PA plays out in reading words. A notable exception is Anne Cunningham (1990), who found larger effects on reading when she showed children how to apply PA in reading.

Blending

Because decoding written words requires sounding out (pronouncing isolated phonemes signaled by graphemes) and blending (smoothing phonemes together into a recognizable approximation of a word), blending is an important component strategy in learning to read. In blending, we combine phonemes we've identified into phonological structures close enough to a spoken word to identify the word. To arrange optimal blending practice, it is important to remember that effective PA instruction addresses one phoneme at a time. Most blending practice programs expect children to deal with a variety of phonemes they've never learned to identify and to blend these sounds, not yet recognized as phonemes, into words. Effective programs for teaching PA begin by blending a newly learned phoneme to the chunks of spoken words.

Blending a new phoneme to the end of a word is easier than blending it to the beginning (Murray, Brabham, Villaume, & Veal, 2008). The easiest blending procedures take advantage of the "stickiness" of the body and coda segments of syllables. The *body* is composed of any initial consonants with the vowel, and the *coda* includes any consonants that follow the vowel. For example, the word *thick* could be segmented into /thi/ (the body) and /k/ (the coda). Body-coda blending is easier than onset-rime blending because it joins the syllable at its "stickiest" point after the vowel, rather than at its most fragile point, before the vowel. For more information on body-coda blending, see Practical Chapter 4. We can help children take the first steps in blending by having them orally blend body-coda, e.g., "What am I saying: *roo-m*? *Crea-m*? *Sli-me*?" To respond they need only deal with a now-familiar vocal gesture in spoken words, and add this gesture to the linguistically "stickiest" spot in the syllable. When they've achieved this milestone, they can move on to the slightly more difficult task of onset-rime blending, assembling, e.g., *m-oon* and *m-ess*. Finally, they can begin to orally blend fully segmented words, a component skill in full alphabetic decoding.

Phonetic Cue Reading

The most basic level of decoding is using beginning consonant letters to distinguish between activated words, which is called phonetic cue reading or partial-alphabetic decoding (Ehri, 1998). Children who have learned to identify the phonemes /s/ and /m/, and who recognize the letters S and M, should be able to distinguish SAT and MAT, SEND and MEND, or SOON and MOON (capitals may be preferred at this point to minimize problems with letter recognition). They need only decode the first letters of words to make these distinctions. To bridge the gap from PA to decoding, we can teach them how to read phonetic cues. For example, the teacher can display *SAY* and explain, "Let me show you how to decide if this word is *say* or *may*. It begins with letter *S*, which sounds like silly, sneaky snake, /s/. So this word must be *ssssay*." After the teacher has modeled several words, children can apply the PA knowledge to decide whether *MAT* is *sat* or *mat*, whether *SEND* is *send* or *men*, and whether *MOON* is *soon* or *moon*. As children develop facility with phonetic cue reading, they can practice by fingerpointing the words in predictable texts. Touching the right words while reciting a predictable text requires using the initial letters to cue the words, i.e., partial alphabetic decoding (Ehri & Sweet, 1991).

> **COMPLETE YOUR PA LESSON BY APPLYING PA TO READ WORDS**
> Include instruction and practice with oral blending, beginning with body-coda blending (with the target phoneme at the ends of words) and progressing to onset-rime blending (with the target phoneme at the beginning) and finally to blending fully segmented words. Then model how to use beginning consonants to distinguish between rhyming words, and provide practice with phonetic cue reading.

THE QUESTION OF RETENTION

If phoneme awareness can make or break a child's success in learning to read, what do we do about a child who completes kindergarten with no ability to detect phonemes? Do we send that child on to first grade anyway, or do we hold him back for another year in kindergarten? We know children need phoneme awareness to make sense of the alphabetic code and succeed in learning to read. If we send a child to first grade without phoneme awareness, we may be setting him up for failure by placing him where he lacks the skills to succeed. Stanovich's (1986), theory of Matthew effects shows how early reading failure can pervade everything. A disastrous experience in first-grade reading may dispose a child to an educational setback with lifelong consequences.

On the other hand, retention is certainly no foolproof solution. Phoneme awareness does not simply mature; it must be taught. If the kindergarten teacher had no effect during a year of instruction, putting the child back for a second year with the same teacher will likely get the same result. An excellent first-grade teacher who reviews phonemes thoroughly in an explicit phonics program seems a better bet for a breakthrough into decoding. Thus, the crucial question is *where* PA will be taught. If a gifted kindergarten teacher has an effective phoneme-direct teaching program, retention might be the best shot at reversing powerful negative Matthew effects. However, a strong first-grade teacher whose instruction features PA review, explicit phonics, and decodable text might be preferable. As Stanovich (1986) emphasizes, what is needed is a "surgical strike" at the root of the problem, and the root of the problem is learning to detect the phonemes that will be mapped in alphabetic writing.

CONCLUSIONS ON TEACHING CHILDREN TO DETECT PHONEMES

Discoveries about phoneme awareness are revolutionizing instruction in beginning reading. However, in our zeal for leading children to this vital ability, teachers have sometimes encouraged games and phoneme manipulations that have little to do with learning to read. The PA children need to learn to read requires recognizing phonemes in their natural habitat, the spoken word (Murray, 1998). To teach PA, teachers should focus on one phoneme at a time, make it memorable, give children practice finding that phoneme in spoken words, and help them apply their knowledge in reading words.

In preschool and early kindergarten, teachers should introduce phonemes with a variety of developmentally appropriate activities, along the lines of the examples in this chapter. This early work is typically with consonants, and the emphasis is on detecting the phoneme in *spoken* words. As in learning to identify flowers or fish, children need ways to remember the phoneme they need to identify. Detecting the phoneme in spoken word contexts is at the heart of PA.

By late kindergarten, in first grade, and with older poor readers, teachers should review phonemes to introduce phonics and spelling lessons. By this time, children should be able to use consonant letters in partial-alphabetic decoding. However, many of them lack the vowels to decode the complete alphabetic mapping in spellings. Vowel phonemes, especially short vowels, tend to be among the most difficult phonemes to detect in spoken words. Thus, a PA review is an excellent introduction to a phonics lesson teaching beginning readers to use vowel correspondences to decode and spell *written* words.

Answer to the phoneme puzzle about words with / a / k / s / t /: *cast, caste, tacks, tax, sacked, task. scat, skat, stack, asked, axed, acts, cats.*

SUMMARY

Phoneme awareness is the ability to detect phonemes, especially consonants, in their natural habitat, the spoken word. PA precedes phonics, which is instruction in decoding written words. Before children can understand spellings as alphabetic maps of spoken words, they must detect the phonemes to be mapped. Though we may refer casually to phonemes as sounds, phonemes are defined by their characteristic articulatory gestures. Just as recognizing a flower or a fish requires learning to identify its colors and features, learning to detect a phoneme requires learning to recognize its articulatory gesture in the natural habitat of a spoken word. Accordingly, effective PA instruction introduces phonemes one at a time, rather than expecting a general sensitivity to develop to all phonemes. Children usually need explicit teaching to learn an initial group of perhaps a dozen phonemes, after which acquiring additional phonemes gets much easier.

To introduce a phoneme, teachers need to make the phoneme memorable by connecting it with a sound analogy; e.g., that the phoneme /z/ is like the sound of zipping up a jacket, /z/. An illustration of this sound analogy that includes the principal letter helps children remember the analogy, and a hand gesture becomes a useful recognition signal. Because many phonemes vary somewhat in word contexts, practice with an alliterative "tongue tickler" helps children sample the articulatory gesture across words. Stretching and splitting off the phoneme in the tickler words helps children see the identity of the phoneme in and out of words. Studying articulation with mirrors and self-examination helps children learn more about the articulatory gesture that defines a phoneme. Inventing spellings gives valuable practice detecting and transcribing the phoneme. Teachers can use simple letterbox lessons to guide children to detect phonemes in simple, regularly spelled words and to represent them in accurate spellings.

As the phoneme becomes memorable, children need practice finding it in spoken words. Any novel strategy is better learned with modeling. To learn to detect a phoneme in spoken words, the teacher models how to test spoken example words (and nonexamples) for the phoneme. Children can then practice by testing other words for the phoneme, including words in which the target phoneme is not as salient because it is clustered with another consonant or tucked away in the middle or end of a word. If the words tested are related in meaning, children are challenged to make a metalinguistic shift from meaning to form. Teachers can design a wide variety of creative activities to practice detecting phonemes. The final phase of PA instruction is to show children how to apply PA to take the first steps in reading words. Guiding practice with oral blending helps children learn a key component strategy in decoding. Showing children how to use beginning consonants in phonetic cue reading builds a direct bridge from detecting phonemes in spoken words to using alphabetic mappings to read words.

Appendix A: English Phonemes, Spellings, Example Words, and Sound Analogies

Phoneme	Spelling(s) and Example Words	Sound Analogies
/A/	a (table), a_e (bake), ai (rain), ay (say)	Long A; Fonzie's greeting
/a/	a (flat)	Crying baby; baby lamb; home alone
/b/	b (ball)	Beating heart; drum; basketball
/k/	c (cake), k (key), ck (back)	Nutcracker; golf shot; camera
/d/	d (door) e (pet), ea (head)	Knocking; dribbling ball; drum; dinosaur
/E/	e (me), ee (feet), ea (leap), y (baby)	Long E; shriek
/e/	e (pet), ea (head)	Rocking chair; creaky door; hard of hearing
/f/	f (fix), ph (phone)	Mad cat; clothes brush; electric fan; soda fizz
/g/	g (gas)	Croaking frog, gulping soda
/h/	h (hot)	Out of breath; warm breath; tired dog
/I/	i (I), i_e (bite), igh (light), y (sky)	Long I, "Aye, aye, Captain"
/i/	i (sit)	Crying puppy; icky sticky; baby pig
/j/	j (jet), dge (edge), g[e, i, y] (gem)	Scrub brush; wood rasp; jump rope
/l/	l (lamp)	Flying saucer; mixer; lapping water
/m/	m (my)	Mmm-m; hummingbird
/n/	n (no), kn (knock)	Mosquito; motorboat
/O/	o (go), o_e (bone), oa (soap), ow (low)	Long O; Oh, I see
/o/	o (hot)	Say ah; doctor sound; cool drink; yawn
/p/	p (pie)	Popcorn; drip; skipping stone; soap bubbles
/kw/)	qu (quick)	Coffee pot; typewriter; quacking duck
/r/	r (road), wr (wrong), er (her), ir (sir), ur (fur)	Chain saw; angry lion; robot; growling dog
/s/	s (say), c[e, i, y] (cent)	Snake; leaky ball; hair spray; sizzling bacon
/t/	t (time)	Ticking clock; timer; automatic sprinkler
/U/	u (future), u_e (use), ew (few)	Long U
/u/	u (gum), a (about), e (open), o (wagon)	Cave man; mother bear; punch; foghorn
/v/	v (voice)	Electric shaver; airplane; vacuum
/w/	w (wash)	Lariat; fly rod; washing machine; helicopter
/ks/ /gz/	x (box, exam)	Pop top soda can; grease gun
/y/	y (yes)	Sticky mess
/z/	z (zoo), s (nose)	Buzzing bee; arc welder; zipper
/OO/	oo (boo), u (rumor), u_e (use), ew (new)	Ghost; howling wolf; owl
/oo/	oo (book), u (put)	Lifting weights; chin-up bar
/oi/	oi (soil), oy (toy)	Seal; squeaky gate; spring
/ow/	ou (out), ow (cow)	Inoculation; sting; pinch
/aw/	aw (saw), au (caught), a[l] (tall)	Poor thing; crow
/ar/	ar (car)	Spinning tire; grinding gears; gargle; pirate
/sh/	sh (ship), ti (nation), ci (special)	Be quiet; watering the lawn; rain
/hw/	wh (white)	Blow out the candle
/ch/	ch (chest), tch (catch)	Old train; antique car; chipmunk
/th/	th (thick, this)	Peeling tape; angry goose; wet shoes

APPENDIX B: THE WALLACHS' (1976) TONGUE TICKLERS WITH ADDITIONAL VOWEL TICKLERS

Andrew and Alice asked if Annie's active animals were angry.

Bill and Betty baked brown bread for Barbara's baby.

Carol and Claire can cook carrots, corn, cabbage, and candy.

David's daddy's dog didn't dig dirt in the dark.

Everybody saw Eddie and the Eskimo enter the elevator on the elephant.

The funny furry fly flew far to the flowers.

Gary was glad to play games in grandmother's green garden.

Harry had a horrible headache and hated to hear Henry howl.

The important Indian was ill with injuries inside the igloo.

John got juice and jelly on his jacket when Judy jumped on him.

Kenny wasn't kind in kindergarten when he kicked Kate in the kitchen.

Lisa lost the large lemon for the lizard Lenny loved.

On Mondays Michael's mother Mary mostly mopped.

Nobody was nice to Nancy's neighbor Nick, but he was never nasty.

Oliver had an operation in October, and Oscar gave him an octopus.

Peter Piper picked a peck of pickled peppers.

"Be quiet," said the queen quickly, "or I'll quarrel with your question!"

Ruth and Rachel ran after Richard's rabbit in the rain.

Sam said he was sorry he put salt in Sally's sandwich.

Tommy tricked Tim and took his train off the track.

Uncle was upset because he was unable to put his umbrella up.

Virginia visited Vicky and gave her violets and vegetables with vitamins.

When the weather is warm we will walk with William in the wild woods.

The excited experts explained that the extra X-rays were excellent.

Yesterday you yelled in the yard for a yellow yo-yo.

The zebra zoomed zigzag in the zoo.

Long Vowel and Other Vowel Tongue Ticklers

Abe the ape ate Amy's acorn.

Eagles eat electric eels easily.

Ike's ivy island is icy.

Opie owns an old oak oboe.

Ulysses usually uses union U-boats.

Our owl in the outfield is an outcast.

Austin is an awful author in Australia.

Oodles of oolong oozed from the oomiak. (An oomiak is an Eskimo boat like a canoe.)

Orba ordered orange orchids for the orchestra.

Arnie and Arthur are army archers.

Ernie had an early urge to irk Irving.

How to Teach Phonics for Sight Word Learning

Phonics has been alternately vilified and glorified in the reading wars as everything from a poison to a panacea. In reality, phonics is simply decoding instruction. In alphabetic writing, the sequence of letters in a written word maps out the sequence of phonemes in a spoken word—the alphabetic principle. Learning to read in an alphabetic language requires learning to decode words represented as alphabetic maps. For this reason, decoding is not optional in learning to read: It is mandatory. With some 100,000 words to learn between kindergarten and high school, no one can learn enough words by the whole-word method. There are far too many words to memorize. Good readers must be expert decoders because we make sight words by a sight-word process powered by decoding.

Ehri's theory of the development of word-reading ability (explained in Chapter 3) has corrected the popular idea that we learn sight words by continual exposure or repetitive drill. Instead, we can learn sight words in as few as four learning trials by decoding, crosschecking, and mental marking. For example, in learning to read the word *island*, full alphabetic beginners would probably first decode it as "iz-land." Finishing the sentence "There was an island in the lake" would provide strong contextual support for crosschecking to correct "iz-land" to *island*. Learning *island* as a sight word would require a reexamination of the spelling to mentally mark the *i* as /I/ and the *s* as silent. Finally, our full-alphabetic beginners would need to reread the sentence to secure the annotated spelling in memory.

Understanding the sight-word processes of decoding, crosschecking, and mental marking helps us put aside the canard that English is too irregular for phonics instruction. Even with irregular words like *island* or *sword*, most of the spelling can be understood using reliable grapheme-phoneme correspondences, phonics rules, and regular spelling patterns. Silent or unpredictable letters can nearly always be managed in context by crosschecking and mental marking. Accordingly, very few words in English are impenetrable by decoding, and effective phonics teaching builds the decoding expertise to enable sight-word learning.

Phonics in Reading Development

Ehri's developmental theory of word recognition is important for identifying students who can benefit from phonics. Prealphabetic readers do not use letters as symbols for the phonemes in spoken words. They may lack phoneme awareness, letter recognition, or knowledge of basic consonant correspondences—all of which are required for phonics. Partial alphabetic readers, on the other hand, understand that letters in spellings map out phonemes in spoken words, and they can use consonants as phonetic cues for word identification. With developing phoneme awareness, letter recognition, and knowledge of consonants, they are ready for phonics. Full alphabetic readers have begun to decode and are thus ideal candidates for phonics. Consolidated alphabetic readers can recognize many sight words and sight chunks for rapid identification of unfamiliar words, but they may have gaps in their knowledge of correspondences. Teachers should assess their decoding knowledge carefully to identify missing correspondences for instruction. Practical Chapter 5 provides tests and procedures for identifying correspondence gaps, including the First Names Test.

Making sight words requires full alphabetic decoding. Prealphabetic and partial-alphabetic readers cannot build any significant sight vocabulary. The problem is that these readers do not fully process spellings. Prealphabetic readers waste the entire spelling map in search of visual cues to meaning, and partial alphabetic readers only sound out consonants, leaving gaps that make word recognition ambiguous. Readers relying only on consonant cues confuse similarly spelled words like *cloud* and *could*. In contrast, full alphabetic readers make complete connections between letters and phonemes by decoding, crosschecking, and mental marking, enabling them to store the complete spellings of *cloud* and *could* as alphabetic mappings in memory. With well-spelled sight words in memory, they can make an instant match when they encounter these spellings in print for automatic word recognition.

THE CONTENT OF PHONICS

Full alphabetic decoding depends on learning vowel correspondences because vowels are the yet unanalyzed elements for partial-alphabetic readers. Two elements correspond in a *correspondence*: a grapheme (e.g., *au*) and a phoneme (/aw/). A *grapheme* is either a letter or a digraph (a 2- or 3-letter combination). A *phoneme* is an elemental vocal gesture, either a consonant (which creates some sort of friction in the vocal channel) or a vowel (a vocalization made with an open, shaped mouth). For convenience, correspondences can be written as an equation; e.g., *au* = /aw/, read "*a-u* says /aw/."

Short and Long Vowels

Short vowels and long vowels pose different challenges. Short vowels are more common in English syllables, and they have easy spellings, usually a single letter. However, the short vowels are among the most elusive phonemes, with only slight differences in sound and in mouth movements. A good way to remember the short vowels is to attend to the beginnings of the words in the sentence, "Ask Ed if odd's up" (imagine Ed is the referee, and we don't remember whose turn it is). Notice that the mouth opens widest for /o/ and narrowest for /i/. For this reason, children can make a productive contrast between /i/ and /o/ in learning short vowels. Unfortunately, by the bad luck of alphabetical order, they must first deal with the very similar short vowels /a/, /e/, and /i/. A strong phoneme-awareness review is necessary to help children identify the phonemes they will be decoding in alphabetic mappings.

Long vowels in English, /A/, /E/, /I/, /O/, and /U/ or /OO/, make the sounds of their letter names. The complication with long vowels and other vowels (e.g., /ow/ and /oy/) is that their spellings are nearly always digraphs in one-syllable words. For example, we spell /A/ with *a_e*, *ai*, or *ay*. (The grapheme *a_e*, read "*a* blank *e*," represents a divided digraph in which a consonant intervenes between the vowel and the silent *e*.) Some programs try to simplify the complexities of spelling with long vowels by using diacritical marks; e.g., marking /A/ with a horizontal line called a macron (ā) and /a/ with a curved mark called a breve (ă). The problem with this approach is that young readers need to attend to spelling signals rather than extraneous marks to understand vowels. For example, when *a* is alone, beginners should think of /a/, and when *a* is followed by a single consonant and silent *e*, they should think of /A/. Diacritical marks will not be found in most texts; as a result, they are extraneous and unreliable signals for beginning readers.

Correspondences Worth Teaching

Phonics instruction is usually included as part of a basal reading program—the reading textbook series. The basal includes an anthology of stories, expository articles, plays, and poems, and the teacher's manual provides ideas and activities. A variety of other materials is sold with the program, including workbooks, worksheets, tests, and sometimes texts intended to be decodable. In the lesson plans from the teacher's manual, new correspondences are presented anywhere from one every two weeks (the slowest pace) to two correspondences a week (the fastest pace). Because there are some 211 correspondences in primary grade reading materials (Berdiansky, Cronnell, & Koehler, 1969), even the fastest presentation pace will not cover so many correspondences in a reasonable window of time. Teaching two correspondences per week will only cover about 70 correspondences per year, a pace that would require three years of instruction for decoding mastery.

The solution is not to teach every correspondence, but only those that are reliable. Most of the correspondences used in primary texts are irregular or unreliable. One of the most glaring examples is the pattern *-ough*, for which there are at least eight pronunciations:

> A rough (/uf/), dough (/O/)-faced, thoughtful (/aw/) ploughman (/ow/) strode through /OO/ the streets of Scarborough (/u/). After falling into a slough (/OO/ or /ow/), he coughed (/awf/) and hiccoughed (/up/).

Irregularities can be solved with crosschecking and mental marking, but we don't want to mislead children by teaching them unreliable correspondences. If we eliminate irregular graphemes like *-ough* and exclude the teaching of consonant clusters, we arrive at a more manageable number of about 80 consonant and vowel correspondences to teach in the primary grades. If we begin with consonants and short vowels in kindergarten and introduce long vowels and other vowels in first grade at a pace of about two correspondences per week, we should be able to cover most of the essential content of phonics by the end of first grade and complete remediation for most struggling readers by midyear in second grade.

To maintain an efficient pace of teaching phonics, it is vital to stick with the regular and reliable correspondences and not be waylayed by irregularities. Once when I was giving a workshop in the classroom of a reading coach, I was dismayed to see a sign that announced, "The combination *wo* says /OO/, as in *two*." There is no other word in English in which *wo* says /OO/! We don't want to burden beginning readers with useless or misleading information. The regular correspondences for /OO/ are *u_e*, *oo*, and *ew*. Saddling children with irregular correspondences that rarely work amounts to educational malpractice. Irregular words are learned by following up decoding with crosschecking and mental marking, but phonics teaches the regularities that allow the reader to notice the unusual.

Systematic Phonics

Most programs follow a sequence of correspondences beginning with short vowels and proceeding to long vowels and other vowels. Systematic phonics teaches all useful correspondences in a planned order. With partial alphabetic readers who are not using any vowel correspondences, or with a group of full alphabetic readers with limited correspondence knowledge, we do well to teach correspondences systematically. This allows us to follow up phonics lessons by having students read decodable text; i.e., text using content words limited to students' current vowel knowledge (along with the high-frequency function words necessary to write any coherent text). Well-designed decodable text series accumulate correspondences so that with each new correspondence, the vocabulary of the books is enriched with a wider pool of words. Thus, where the first decodable book might be restricted to words with *a* = /a/, a later book following up a lesson on *oa* = /O/ could include any short vowel, any long vowel correspondences for /A/, /E/, and /I/, and the correspondences *o_e*, *oa*, and *ow* = /O/. Gaining access to a larger pool of words provides more engaging stories.

To maintain the decodability of practice texts, I recommend introducing the five short vowel correspondences first, in alphabetical order. Short vowels are more frequent in English and they typically use simple one-letter spellings. However, short-vowel phonemes are difficult to detect because they differ only slightly in mouth shape (compare /i/ and /e/). When followed by the nasal /n/, the differences disappear in some dialects (compare *pin* and *pen*). Basic consonant digraphs can be introduced along with the short vowels. Simple digraphs like *ck* or *ss* demonstrate that two letters can be used to spell one phoneme, and they should be included in very early phonics lessons (note that the combination represents the same phoneme as either constituent letter). Other digraphs (*ch, sh, th, ng*) may be interspersed among the short vowels. For example, after learning *i* = /i/, the beginner is ready to use the correspondence *sh* = /sh/ to review short vowels in words like *ash, dish, shed*, and *ship*.

Next, each long vowel should be introduced, first in silent-*e* patterns. Silent-*e* patterns, such as *a_e* = /A/, are divided digraphs with a consonant between the vowel and the silent *e*. Follow up each silent-*e* pattern with its digraph partners; e.g., *ai* and *ay* = /A/. If students are catching on to new correspondences readily, digraph pairs like *ai* and *ay* can be introduced in a single lesson, with the explanation that *ai* is used in the middle of words and *ay* at the end. Other pairs that might be combined are *ee* and *ea* = /E/, *igh* and *y* = /I/, *oa* and *ow* = /O/, and *oo* and *ew* = /U/. After all five long vowels are taught in their various patterns, we complete basic phonics instruction by teaching the other vowels, which are neither long nor short. These include *oo* = /oo/ (as in *book*), *oi* and *oy* = /oy/, *ou* and *ow* = /ow/, and *au* and *aw* = /aw/. With this group I would include two basic *r*-controlled vowels: *ar* = /ar/ and *er, ir*, and *ur* = /er/.

The Appendix of this chapter presents the major grapheme-phoneme correspondences to be taught in phonics programs. A close examination reveals some useful patterns. The digraphs *ck, dge*, and *tch* only follow short vowels. Three common silent-letter digraphs are *-mb, kn-*, and *wr-*. The most common grapheme for /z/ is *s*. The first phoneme in *Xenon* is /z/. The most common grapheme for /sh/ is *ti*, thanks to the ubiquitous syllable *-tion*. The letter *x* actually represents a consonant cluster, /ks/. The vowels *a, e, i*, and *o* in unaccented syllables take the schwa sound /u/. The main graphemes for for /A/ in one-syllable words are *a_e, ai*, and *ay*; for /E/ are *ee* and *ea*; for /I/ are *i_e, y*, and *igh*; for /O/ are *o_e, oa*, and *ow*; and for /U/ are *u_e, ew*, and *oo*. This kind of knowledge is part of the expertise required of those who teach phonics and spelling. As is evident in these example, reading instruction takes some "rocket science."

LANDMARKS AND PITFALLS IN PHONICS

We don't have a roadmap for teaching phonics, but research points to landmarks to aim for and pitfalls to avoid. The landmarks are teaching activities shown to work in experiments or consistent with research-based theory, such as explicit phonics;

the pitfalls are teaching activities that sow confusion or delay reading progress, such as letting the workbook teach. In this section, we will examine some issues to locate the landmarks and avoid the pitfalls.

The ambiguous consonants *c* and *g* pose problems in decoding. Figure 1 shows how *c* and *g* each map two different phonemes in spellings. A careful examination of these example words reveals a pattern: The "soft" correspondences *c* = /s/ and *g* = /j/ are cued by the letters *e*, *i*, or *y* following the consonant. If any other letter follows, the "hard" correspondences *c* = /k/ and *g* = /g/ are indicated. This pattern is highly reliable for *c* and usually works for *g*, though not always reliably (exceptions include *gimlet* and *giddy*).

Letter	Hard	Soft
c	/k/	/s/
	card	cent
	crush	cider
	curb	lacy
g	/g/	/j/
	gum	gem
	mug	engine
	grab	cagy

FIGURE 1: How *c and g* map phonemes in spellings

Here's what we know about teaching correspondences for *c* and *g*. First, we don't teach both at the same time. We establish the more common hard correspondences first, and later add the less common soft correspondences. Once both correspondences have been introduced, teach a "best-bet" strategy: Try the hard phoneme first (the best bet), and if that doesn't work, try the soft phoneme. For example, in sounding out the unfamiliar word *cyst*, first try /kist/, and if that doesn't make sense, try /sist/. Finally, teach full alphabetic readers to look for the signals *e*, *i*, and *y*: Whenever *e*, *i*, or *y* follows *c* or *g*, try the soft phoneme. Otherwise, go with the hard phoneme. This is the expert strategy, and it verifies that *cyst* is correctly pronounced /sist/.

Figure 2 displays the reliability of vowel spellings from Johnston's (2001) analysis of the 3000 most frequent English words. Recognizing the frequency of vowel spellings is helpful in applying the "best-bet" strategy. For example, the best-bet phoneme for the grapheme *ow* is /O/, which is twice as likely as /ow/. Again, we see that some detailed knowledge is required for expert instruction in phonics and spelling. The best-bet pronunciation for *ea* is /E/; for *ei* is /A/; for *ie* is

/E/; and for *oo* is /OO/. The most likely spelling for /aw/ is *o* as in *dog*; for /oo/ is *u* as in *put*; for /ow/ is *ou* as in *round*; and for /oy/ is *oi* as in *boil*.

Correspondence	Phoneme, example word, and percent of reliability
a_e	/A/ (cake) 78%
ai	/A/ (rain) 75%
ay	/A/ (play) 96%
e_e	/E/ (these) 17%
ee	/E/ (feet) 96%
ea	/E/ (seat) 64%; /e/ (head) 17%
ei	/A/ (rein) 50%; /E/ (either) 25%
ey	/E/ (monkey) 77%
ie	/E/ (field) 49%; /I/ (tied) 27%
i_e	/I/ (five) 74%
o_e	/O/ (stove) 58%
oa	/O/ (coat) 95%
ow	/O/ (snow) 68%; /ow/ (how) 32%
oe	/O/ (toe) 44%; /OO/ (shoe) 33%; /u/ (does) 22%
ou	/ow/ (out) 43%; /u/ (touch) 18%; /U/ (your) 7%
u_e	/OO/ or /U/ (rule, refuse) 77%
oo	/OO/ (boot) 50%; /oo/ (book) 40%
ew	/OO/ (blew) 88%; /U/ (few) 19%
ui	/i/ (build) 53%; /U/ (fruit) 24%
au	/aw/ (cause) 79%
aw	/aw/ (saw) 100%
oi	/oy/ (join) 100%
oy	/oy/ (boy) 100%
ia	/E/a/ (piano) 54%; /u/ (Asia) 46%
y (unaccented)	/E/ (lucky) 100%

FIGURE 2: Reliability of vowel spellings

Phonics Rules

Ehri's (1998) phase theory of recognizing words identifies two subphases during the full alphabetic phase. The sequential subphase is letter-by-letter decoding, which works well to identify words like *map*, where the reader need only sound out and blend in a left-to-right sequence. In contrast, in the *hierarchical* subphase, the reader uses conditional rules to select likely phonemes to sound out and blend. For many words (e.g., *page, face,* and *night*), sequential decoding doesn't work. These words require hierarchical decoding to make use of conditions, e.g., that silent *e* is part of the divided digraph *a_e* and signals the soft phonemes for *g* in *page* and *c* in *face*. Hierarchical decoding is also needed to recognize digraph teams like *igh* in *night*.

A generalization stating the conditions for deciding which phoneme is cued by a grapheme is a phonics *rule*. A phonics rule could be thought of as a correspondence with a condition attached. For example, the grapheme *y* doesn't always say /y/. At the beginning of a syllable, *y* says /y/ (*yes*), but as a vowel in the middle of the syllable, *y* usually says /i/ (*gym*). At the end of an accented syllable, *y* says /I/ (*fly*), but if the syllable is unaccented, *y* says /E/ (*penny*).

Sometimes rules work well, sometimes not. Consider the following phonics rules:

GRAPHEME	CONDITION	PHONEME
vowel	followed by consonant and silent *e*	long vowel

The silent-*e* rule works well, with an overall estimated reliability of 63%, and with about 75% reliability for the specific vowels *a_e, i_e,* and *u_e* (Johnston, 2001).

GRAPHEME	CONDITION	PHONEME
vowel	single letter	short vowel

Informally, we can say "Single vowels are short." The single-vowel rule, "When a vowel letter is in the middle of a one-syllable word, the vowel is short," is similar to the silent-*e* rule in reliability, with an estimated reliability of 62% (Clymer, 1963).

GRAPHEME	CONDITION	PHONEME
vowel	followed by vowel	long vowel

This popular rule is vivid and memorable: "When two vowels go walking, the first one does the talking and the second one is silent." However, with a reliability of only 45%, the "two vowels" rule works less than half the time (Clymer, 1963). It is not hard to think of words where it applies, such as *peace* and *tail*, but we overlook the even greater number of words were it does *not* apply, such as *piece, bread, cause, giant, oil,* and *sound*. A minimal standard for phonics rules is that they work at least half the time, but "two vowels go walking" fails most of the time. "Two vowels" fails because it is an overgeneralization. With vowel digraphs, we need specific rules, e.g., *ew* usually says /OO/. (See Figure 2 for additional useful and specific rules).

How to Think about Phonics Rules

Phonics is often criticized because the rules don't always work. But would it be reasonable to only teach rules with no exceptions? That would eliminate virtually all useful rules because almost all rules have exceptions. Phonics rules that lead to more right answers than wrong answers are useful. It is important to keep in mind that phonics rules are designed to get beginners close enough to crosscheck and correct nonsense readings. For example, in decoding *wash*, the single-vowel rule suggests a short-vowel pronunciation. However, in the context, "Did you wash the dishes in the sink?" that pronunciation can easily be corrected. A good phonics rule doesn't have to generate a perfect pronunciation; it only has to get the reader close. If reading words were a game of golf, we need phonics to drive the ball onto the green, but we need crosschecking to putt the ball for par. Both a driver and a putter are necessary: The reader needs the driving power of decoding to get in position to use the finishing stroke of crosschecking.

Because the goal of phonics is to get an approximate pronunciation, the best phonics rules are stated simply. Phonics rules are *heuristics*—temporary models to establish a word identification strategy, to be discarded with the development of word recognition skill. Simple rules are more memorable than complicated rules. With phonics rules, there is a trade-off between accuracy and practicality. The more exact we make a rule to fit every possible circumstance, the less useful the rule is in decoding. Adams (1990, p. 251) gives an egregious example of an unusable rule found in a basal manual:

> Refer to the CVC pattern and explain that when the vowel letter *i* is between two consonant letters, the corresponding vowel sound is usually unglided.

Such teaching would fly over the heads of primary grade students, and on consideration, it isn't all that clear to adults. The jargon CVC refers to a consonant-vowel-consonant pattern, as in *bad* or *mud*. By extension, CVCC is the pattern in *risk*. However, what pattern is in *rich*: Is it CVC or CVCC? The CC or VV terminology is inherently ambiguous with any digraph. A much simpler, more understandable, and more memorable rule is "Single vowels are short." It doesn't always work, e.g., with *hold* or *mind*. However, in context ("Hold onto the rail; mind your step") the rule generates pronunciations easily corrected by crosschecking.

As we'll see in Chapter 10, phonics rules are easier than spelling rules. Phonics rules begin with a grapheme that under some condition cues a phoneme, for example, that the digraph *oa* says /O/. Spelling rules begin with a phoneme that under some condition specifies a spelling, e.g., that the phoneme /O/ can be spelled *o*, *oa*, *o_e*, or *ow*. Such rules are much more variable because there are nearly always more ways to spell a phoneme than to sound out a grapheme.

Given our many spelling options in English, spelling is much more complex than phonics, and it is usually taught throughout the elementary grades. In contrast, the limited set of useful phonics rules can ordinarily be mastered by the middle of second grade.

Workbook Phonics

Correspondences may be taught with a workbook, a bound collection of written exercises, or worksheets, an unbound collection. These written exercises may come with a basal program, with an adjunct (add-on) phonics program such as Saxon Phonics, or as independent materials. Teachers should assign written exercises cautiously. Many workbook phonics pages are busy-work exercises such as word searches that do not require any reading and squander precious instructional time. However, a few may require word reading, e.g., to select pictures that match printed words. Because workbook pages and worksheets are written exercises, their selection and use should depend on the quality of the exercise. Written exercises may work for independent decoding practice or provide informal assessments to check on student learning. Accordingly, effective teachers use workbooks selectively, in contrast to teachers who serve a steady diet of workbook pages and worksheets.

Teacher effectiveness research has found that overreliance on workbooks and worksheets is associated with low reading achievement (Rosenshine & Stevens, 2002). The problem with letting the workbook teach is that seatwork is not very engaging. A live teacher is usually needed to motivate students to take an interest in instruction. In addition, practice alone does not teach. At best, workbooks and worksheets could follow up live modeling and guided practice led by the teacher. Workbooks and worksheets in phonics mostly provide practice in reading isolated words; rarely do students read any sort of connected text, which is not only more engaging, but more productive for crosschecking, mental marking, and sight-word learning. Recently, many teachers have turned to computer programs for teaching phonics with exercises similar to those in workbooks. Such e-workbooks tend to focus on spelling rather than reading, and they are fraught with the same kinds of problems found in paper workbooks.

Decodable Text

The most effective reading practice to follow up phonics lessons is reading decodable text. Decodable text is engineered for decoding success by restricting the content words to the vowels learned to date. For example, the book *Bud the Sub* (Cushman, 1990) tells a simple story using only the five short vowels in one-syllable content words. Reading decodable texts require reading more words than workbooks with more engagement under a natural time pressure that encourages making sight words. By restricting content words to correspondences children have learned, reading decodable text encourages beginning readers to stay with decoding strategies because they work to unlock the words in the story (Juel & Roper/Schneider, 1985). Without restricting words for decodability with learned correspondences, early decoding attempts will not be consistently successful, and readers will fall back on phonetic cue reading and contextual guessing.

Explicit Phonics

Explicit phonics is a well-researched landmark in reading education (Adams, 1990). In explicit phonics, the teacher models how to sound out and blend—how to pronounce the phonemes cued by graphemes and blend them into a recognizable word. While explicit phonics has been on the rise in the last decade, traditional basal manuals recommended analytic phonics, in which children were asked to memorize words by a whole-word method and only later analyze them into phonemes, under strict instructions not to pronounce phonemes in isolation. During the late 1990s, decisions by Texas and California to require primary-grade basal readers to present explicit phonics with decodable text had a strong influence on basal publishers. Texas and California are the two largest educational markets in the US. Most major publishers responded to the financial exigencies to sell books in these states by reforming their programs to incorporate at least some measure of explicit phonics and decodable text.

Analytic phonics does not work well for beginning readers. Beginners find it difficult to memorize arbitrary spellings of whole words, which requires about 35 learning trials for the average reader (Gates, 1931). To learn 10 words at 35 trials per word would take an exhausting 350 repetitions, analogous to memorizing 10 phone numbers. In contrast, making sight words by decoding requires only about four trials per word (Reitsma, 1983), only about 1/9 the effort of memorization. In addition, analytic phonics does not allow the teacher to model how to sound out and blend, for modeling would mean pronouncing phonemes in isolation, which may cause mild distortion. Instead of modeling, analytic phonics uses complicated explanations. MacGinitie (1976, p. 372) provides an example:

> The teacher is instructed to write the word *girls* on the board. The teacher then says, "You can find out what this word is. With what consonant does it begin? With what consonant does it end? You know the sounds that *g* and *r* and *l* and *s* stand for. I am going to say something and leave out this word at the end. When I stop, think of a word that begins with a sound *g* stands for, ends with the sounds *r* and *l* and *s* stand for, and makes sense with what I said."

This is an extraordinarily complex set of instructions for 6-year-olds to grasp. Of course, with a very strong context ("In this class there are many boys and . . . ?), children will get the answer *girls*. However, their response has nothing to do with the intricate instructions of analytic phonics.

The memorization urged by analytic phonics programs is actually a bad habit in learning to read, a counterproductive strategy used by poor readers. Decoding is far more efficient for learning words. Thus, an explicit phonics program would model how to sound out *girls* by showing students how to sound out and blend phonemes:

> The teacher is instructed to write the word *girls* on the board. The teacher then says, "The letters *ir* work together to make a sound like a rooster crowing, 'ir-ir-ir-ir-ir.' If this much [*ir*] says /er/, we can put that together with the beginning, /g/ /er/, /ger/. Now we'll add the ending, /ger/ /l/ /z/, /gerlz/. Oh, *girls*, as in 'This class has many boys and girls.'"

Such explicit instruction is far more understandable for beginning readers in first grade.

Pronouncing Phonemes in Isolation

Until recently, most basal readers used the clunky methods of analytic phonics because their consultants were linguists, who stress that phonemes are coarticulated in normal speech and always distorted when pronounced in isolation. This was interpreted in the basal manuals as a prohibition against isolating phonemes during phonics instruction, which left the alternative of memorizing whole words and analyzing them in the abstract. However, the dangers of isolating phonemes were exaggerated. For example, in the sentence, "I have a fat bag," we can certainly isolate the single-phoneme words *I* and *a* without distortion. The vowel /a/ can be pronounced with little or no distortion, as can continuant consonants like /f/. Unvoiced stops like /t/ present no serious distortion problems except in the consonant cluster *tr*, where narrowing the tongue and lips for /r/ changes /t/ to something closer to /ch/. Only voiced stops like /b/ and /g/ get markedly distorted when pronounced in isolation. The reason voiced stops are distorted in isolation is that they are pronounced with the voice "on," so that the vowel is part of the production. If a voiced stop like /b/ in *bag* is pried away from its vowel /a/, we have to add a substitute schwa vowel, which makes /b/ in isolation sound like "buh." However, the schwa vowel acts as a sort of plain brown wrapper that children can easily remove in blending. Adding schwa to isolated consonants actually increases children's success in blending, perhaps by making spoken phonemes easier to hear (Murray, Brabham, Villaume, & Veal, 2008). With crosschecking, children correct near-miss pronunciations in context, to access words accurately.

There are good reasons for teachers to pronounce phonemes in isolation during phonics instruction. We have voluminous scientific evidence that explicit phonics, which isolates phonemes to model how to sound out and blend, is more effective than analytic phonics (Adams, 1990). Teachers tend to ignore the prohibitions in basal manuals against pronouncing phonemes in isolation (Durkin, 1984); probably because they recognize that their students need modeling, and modeling decoding requires isolating phonemes for blending. Pronouncing phonemes in isolation in phonics makes phonemes easier to hear, and the minor distortions of phonemes when pronounced in isolation cause little or no harm because they can be corrected with crosschecking. For these reasons, pronouncing phonemes in isolation is not only reasonable but necessary for optimal instruction.

Linguistic Readers

The linguistic readers of the 1960s offered an alternative to the Dick and Jane readers by providing decodable text, such as "The pan is on the van. The cat can bat the pan. Dan can pat the cat." It is easy to discount the value of simple decodable texts, which are anything but children's literature. Adams (1990, p. 322) commented, "Even when read silently by skillful readers, such texts produce the disruptiveness on tongue twisters." However, this is an early decodable text in which all the content words can be read using short *a*. Decodable texts are not written for skillful readers, but for beginners learning to apply the alphabetic code. They provide connected text children can read successfully by applying decoding knowledge. In decodable text, the early stories never rise to the level of children's literature because the pool of available words is tightly restricted. However, later stories improve as more correspondences accumulate.

The hidden problem in linguistic readers is not apparent without reading the teacher's manuals. Linguistic programs were developed by linguists who feared that phonemes would be distorted with explicit phonics, which models and guides practice in sounding out isolated phonemes for blending. With this in mind, linguistic programs mandated analytic phonics, where students were asked to memorize whole words and later analyze them without isolating phonemes. In analytic programs, teachers are barred from modeling how to decode because such modeling isolates phonemes to sound out and blend. As the analysis above indicates, the problems of phoneme distortion were exaggerated, and the minor mispronunciations that result from decoding are easily corrected with crosschecking.

The linguistic programs assumed that students would discover correspondences given their repetition in decodable text. Decodable text is excellent for practicing new correspondences in story contexts, but not for revealing correspondences by discovery learning. It is not that powerful. Thus, there were two strikes against linguistic readers: The early decodable stories were dull, and the analytic phonics approach left children at sea, unable to understand the decoding strategies that teachers were forbidden to model. With some justification, the linguistic readers disappeared into the dustbin of history, while leaving a residual bad taste for decodable text. This is unfortunate, because use of decodable text was the one good thing about the linguistic readers.

Dictionary Syllabication

Phonics programs often provide extensive instruction for dividing words into syllables, under the supposition that accurate syllable division will help readers decode unfamiliar words. They may, for example, teach readers about open syllables, which end with a vowel that leaves the breath channel open (e.g., *ba-con*), and closed syllables, which end in a consonant that closes off the breath channel (e.g., *rad-ish*). When readers can recognize open and closed syllables, they may be able to apply a phonics generalization that open syllables have long vowels and closed syllables short vowels. This seems useful, e.g., in dividing and pronouncing known words like *va-por* and *rap-id*.

Unfamiliar words, however, are not so easily unlocked. Consider the unfamiliar words *sapid* and *sapor*. Is it *sa-pid* or *sap-id*, *sa-por* or *sap-or*? The rule on open and closed syllables is a classic example of a "catch 22," a frustrating situation in which one is trapped by contradictory regulations or conditions. We have to know how to divide a word into syllables to know how to pronounce it, but we have to know how to pronounce it in order to divide it into syllables! In contrast, the analogy strategy actually works to decode these words. If you know the words *rapid* and *vapor* as sight words, you can analogize to find accurate pronunciations for *sapid* and *sapor*.

While analogizing is often helpful, the most useful strategies for decoding multisyllable words are coverups and crosschecking. To use coverups, the reader covers the word and then reveals each chunk one by one, using vowels as syllable markers. A craft stick decorated with eyes is a helpful tool for coverups; we call them "coverup critters." To use crosschecking, the reader tests the pronunciation in a sentence context, looking for a sound-alike word whenever no meaning is accessed. Using these strategies, the dictionary syllabication boundaries become superfluous. For example, whether a reader divides *be-gin* or *beg-in*, either attempt will produce an approximation of *begin* adequate to access the word in the context, "We will begin to eat."

Correspondences or Phonograms?

Many teachers are concerned about the variability of vowel correspondences. For example, the grapheme *a* represents different phonemes in the words *cat, bacon, father, ball,* and *again*. Some teachers throw up their hands and conclude that phonics is useless because English is hopelessly unpredictable. Others, however, say the solution is to teach larger units called phonograms, in which vowels are more stable. Both of these conclusions are problematic.

A *phonogram* is the spelling of a rime, e.g., *ail* or *ale*. A *rime* is the spoken part of a syllable beginning with the vowel, e.g., /Al/. A *word family* is a group of words that rhyme and share a phonogram, e.g., *pail, rail, mail, sail,* and *trail*. The payoff for teaching phonograms is that vowel spellings tend to be regular within word families. For example, *ail* is nearly always pronounced /Al/, where *ai* may represent other phonemes in *again, aisle,* or *haiku*. Figure 3 displays a set of 37 basic phonograms that will unlock nearly 500 words (Wylie & Durrell, 1970). Note, however, there are approximately 100,000 words in printed school English (Nagy & Anderson, 1984). A mere 500 words is just 0.5% of the words readers need—a drop in the bucket.

-ack	-ame	-at	-ell	-ight	-ink	-op	-ump
-ail	-an	-ate	-est	-ill	-ip	-ore	-unk
-ain	-ank	-aw	-ice	-in	-it	-ot	
-ake	-ap	-ay	-ick	-ine	-ock	-uck	
-ale	-ash	-eat	-ide	-ing	-oke	-ug	

FIGURE 3: Basic English phonograms

Benchmark School near Philadelphia serves readers with learning disabilities, i.e., bright students who have found decoding difficult. The phonogram approach is an attempt to circumvent decoding problems. The Benchmark word-identification program (Gaskins, 1988) teaches children to analogize from key words representing common phonograms. For example, students learn the words *ten*, *tell*, and *hope* to represent the *-en*, *-ell*, and *-ope* phonograms, along with more than 100 other key words, using a whole-word method. These key words are displayed on a "word wall," where they gradually accumulate over the course of first grade. The program teaches students to analogize from the key words when they have trouble reading or spelling words. For example, to read the unfamiliar word *envelope*, the student would use *ten* to read *en*, *tell* to read *vel*, and *hope* to read *lope*, and then test the word in context ("I put everything in an envelope for Jean"). Research at Benchmark, however, determined that children were unable to remember the key words to use as analogies (Gaskins, Ehri, Cress, O'Hara, & Donnelly, 1996-1997). As a result, they had to search the word wall for analogies. When students rely on words posted on classroom walls rather than storing them in memory as sight words, analogy words are not available outside of class. The whole-word method proved unsuccessful in learning the key words as sight words, and the word walls probably delayed sight-word learning by providing a substitute way to access words.

Problems with Phonogram Instruction

There are clear disadvantages in substituting phonogram learning in place of acquiring vowel correspondences. Phonograms are word chunks, and word chunks are learned in the consolidated alphabetic phase when they become useful as pronounceable word parts (see Chapter 3). Sight chunks are learned by the same decoding, crosschecking, and mental-marking process as sight words. As with sight words, young readers need knowledge of vowel correspondences to learn sight chunks. Thus, it would not be possible to skip instruction in vowel correspondences in preference for learning phonograms. Without decoding, phonogram chunks would have to be memorized. Memorizing phonogram chunks is even less efficient than memorizing whole words (an average of 35 trials per word) because phonogram chunks like *-ade* and *-ake* are meaningless. At 4 trials per word, decoding is about 9 times easier for learning sight chunks.

Using decoding, it is easy to build on a vowel correspondence such as *a_e* = /A/ to acquire a sight chunk like *ade*; acquisition requires only a simple body-coda blend. Thus, rather than requiring tedious lessons memorizing *-ade, -ake, -ale, -ame, -ane, -ape,* and *-ate,* a reader with knowledge of the *a_e* correspondence could easily generate all the *a_e* phonograms. In addition, there are many more phonograms (nearly 300 in primary texts) than vowel correspondences (about 40), so that the phonogram approach increases the content of phonics more than sevenfold. Finally, phonograms, while more regular than vowel correspondences, are still not perfectly regular (compare *hear* and *bear, beat* and *great*).

For these reasons, revising phonics instruction from vowel correspondences to phonograms would make learning to read more difficult. Nevertheless, there are a few phonograms worth teaching, such as *-all, -old,* and *-ind*. In these common phonogram patterns, the single vowels *a, o,* and *i* do not represent the expected short vowels. Late-primary phonics or spelling lessons revealing such patterns would be useful in learning some of the fine points of the alphabetic code.

BLENDING

Besides knowledge of correspondences and phonics rules, phonics instruction teaches the strategy of blending. To understand blending, it is helpful to learn some terminology for the parts of a syllable. Figure 4 gives examples to understand the terms onset, rime, body, and coda.

Onset and Rime

The *onset* is the spoken part of the syllable before the vowel. It could be a single consonant or a consonant cluster, but the onset is optional—a word could begin with a vowel, in which case no onset would exist. The *rime* is everything else: the vowel with any consonants that follow. The rime is mandatory because it includes the vowel. To review, the spelling of a rime is a phonogram. For example, the spoken word part /At/ is a rime that could be spelled with the phonograms *-ate, -ait,* or *-eight*.

Breaking up a syllable into onset and rime is easy. There seems to be a natural break point in a syllable between onset and rime. As evidence, it is easier for preschool and kindergarten children to identify entire onsets and rimes than phonemes within onsets or rimes. For example, if we asked young children to tell the beginning sound in *swing*, many would say /sw/, the onset. If we asked them to find the phoneme /m/ in *warm* and in *match*, more children would be successful with *match*, where /m/ is the entire onset, than with *warm*, where /m/ is part of the rime. Again, children find it easier to identify /t/ in *time*, where /t/ is the whole onset, than in *train*, where /t/ is only part of the onset. Because of the natural onset-rime break point in syllables, children are better able to segment syllables into onset and rime than into other subword parts (Treiman, 1985).

Body and Coda

Onset and rime are the easiest subsyllabic parts to segment, but because the onset-time break-point is the most fragile place in the syllable, it is a difficult place to blend. To make blending easier, we can divide the syllable at its stickiest point, where the body joins the coda. The *body* is the spoken syllable through the vowel. Like the rime, the body contains the vowel and is mandatory. The *coda* consists of any consonants that follow the vowel, and like the onset, it is optional. It may be helpful to think of a coda as in a musical piece—a pleasing finish but not a composing requirement.

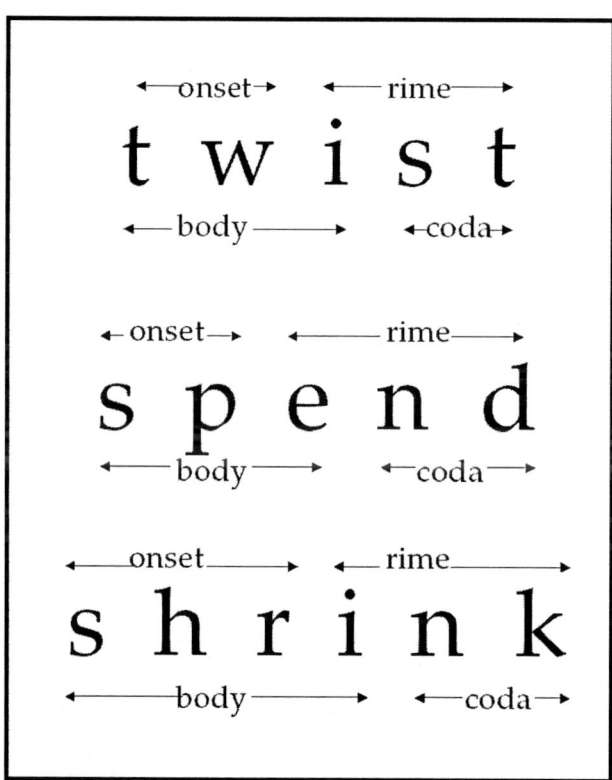

FIGURE 4: Onsets, rimes, bodies, and codas of syllables

The payoff for analyzing words into body and coda is that body-coda blending is easier than onset-rime blending (Murray et al., 2008). The body-coda break point just after the vowel is the stickiest place in the syllable. For this reason, it is the hardest place to segment (something we wouldn't ask children to do), but it is the easiest place to blend. For example, /d-Is/ is a tough blend for *dice*, but /dI-s/ is an easy blend. A useful sequence for teaching blending is to begin with body-coda chunks, e.g., *swee-t*. After children are blending body-coda, they can move to onset-rime blending (*sw-eet*), which has the advantage of only holding two chunks in memory. Later, children can graduate to phoneme blending (*s-w-ee-t*), which can vary from 2-6 chunks. Our initial work at each linguistic level might be with pictures or with riddles, e.g., "I'm thinking of what Little Bo Peep lost: It was a *shee-p*." When transitioning to blending phonemes rather than body-coda chunks, children will need letters to hold the phoneme sequence in memory. Letter tiles are ideal for guiding blending because we can separate and join letters, to signal the steps in blending words.

A minor issue in teaching blending is whether to pronounce letter names during instruction in sounding out and blending. Some letter names mislead students about phonemes; for example, the oral spelling *h-o-g* does a poor job of cuing the phonemes /h/, /aw/, /g/. In reading, we want printed letters to signal phonemes rather than letter names. Thus, a better strategy than pronouncing letter names is to uncover letters or move letter tiles in a vowel-first, body-coda sequence: /o/; /h/ /o/, /ho/; /ho/ /g/, /hog/? Oh, *hog*. Note that the initial /o/ pronunciation is easily corrected to /aw/ by crosschecking.

Two Body-Coda Approaches to Blending

There are two basic approaches for body-coda blending: vowel-first blending and successive left-to-right blending. Both take advantage of the stickiness of the body-coda chunks. In the vowel-first approach, blending begins with the vowel. For example, in modeling how to blend *beat*, we would first isolate *ea* for sounding it out as /E/. Next we would blend the onset /b/ to the vowel /E/ to get the body, /bE/. It it vital to put each chunk together before proceeding, in order to consolidate it, rather than asking the beginner to hold on to multiple phonemes in working memory. Next we blend the body /bE/ to the coda /t/; taking advantage of the stickiness of the body-coda break-point. Finally, we crosscheck to make sure we have a word: "Oh, *beat*, like beat a drum."

Later we can fade the scaffold of beginning with the vowel in preference for successive blending, which maintains the natural left-to-right directionality of alphabetic writing. To model with *beat*, we would sound out *b* and *ea* to make the body, /bE/, and then blend body-coda, /bE/ /t/, /bEt/: "Oh, *beat*, like you beat your sister in checkers." Again, it is important to use letter tiles to guide the blending steps and to form chunks, en route to the final blend. Both of these measures ease the burden on a child's working memory.

An engaging method for teaching blending uses a blending slide and letter tiles, illustrated in Figure 5. The teacher scaffolds blending with the blending slide by telling a story about letters on the playground while moving letters for body-coda blending. For example, to show students how to blend *sock*, the teacher could introduce the character *s*, *o*, and *ck*: "The letters *s*, *o*, *c*, and *k* were playing on the playground. Letters *c* and *k* were such good friends who were always together that they were called /k/. Letters s and o were new friends. They decided to make a team /so/. The /so/ friends began to climb the slide together, /so/, /so/, /so/. But when they got to the top of the slide and saw how high they were, they called to /k/, 'Come catch us!' When the group /k/ came to the end of the slide to catch them, down came the /so/ friends, like this /so-o-o-o-o-o/ until they ran into /k/, /so-o-o-o-o-o/ /k/, /sok/. 'Let's all be friends,' they said. 'You can call our team *sock*!'"

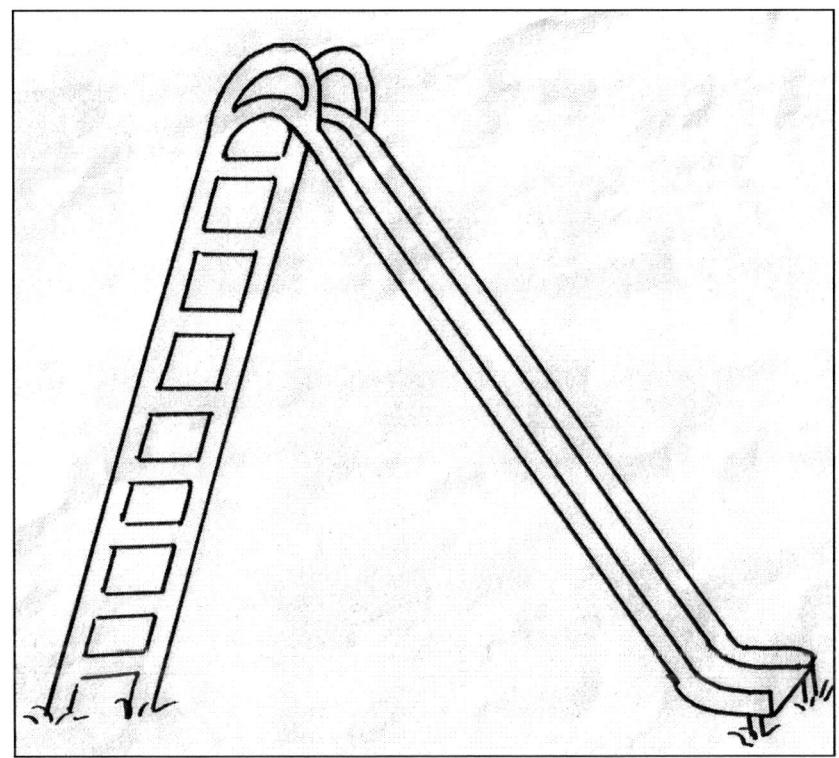

FIGURE 5: The blending slide

SUMMARY

Phonics is decoding instruction. Because English maps the phoneme sequence of spoken words, phonics teaches children to decode spellings to access their pronunciations. Decoding is essential in making sight words. Readers use correspondence knowledge in decoding to generate approximate pronunciations to be corrected by crosschecking and mentally annotated for storage as sight words. The growing skill with decoding in the full alphabetic phase heralds a rapid growth of sight vocabulary.

Phonics teaches vowel correspondences, showing how vowel graphemes (either single letters or digraph) signal vowel phonemes. Phonics begins with short vowels, which usually have easy, one-letter spellings. However, because short vowels like /a/, /e/, and /i/ are similar in sound and mouth shape, they challenge children's phoneme awareness. In contrast, long vowels and other vowels are easier phonemes to manage, but they are spelled with digraphs; for example, /O/ may be spelled *o_e*, *oa*, or *ow* in one-syllable words. Recognizing these vowels from spelling patterns is more reliable than marking them with diacritical marks. Fast-paced basal programs teach about two correspondences per week, which appears inadequate to teach the 211 correspondences found in primary grade materials. However, teachers should not teach irregular graphemes such as *ough*; only about 40 vowel correspondences are required for decoding expertise. Correspondences worth teaching are listed in the Appendix of this chapter. Studying them affords opportunities for learning some of the "rocket science" needed for explicit, systematic instruction in reading words.

Research helps us deal with some of the issues in teaching phonics by pointing to counterproductive pitfalls and well-established landmarks for teaching success. One landmark is to teach a two-phase strategy for dealing with the ambiguous consonants *c* and *g*. We teach the "hard" phoneme /k/ and /g/ for *c* and *g* first because it is more frequent in words, and then follow with the soft phonemes /s/ and /j/. The "best bet" strategy directs beginners to try the hard phoneme first; if it doesn't work, to try the soft phoneme. The more sophisticated "signals" strategy says to use the hard phoneme unless *c* or *g* is followed by the signals *e*, *i*, or *y*; in which case, to try the soft phoneme first. The best bet strategy can be applied with many vowels; for example, *ow* is twice as likely to say /O/ as to say /ow/.

A correspondence with conditions attached is a phonics rule. Some rules are useful guides in decoding; for example, silent *e* signals the long vowel, or single-vowels are short. Others, however, like "two vowels go walking," fail more often than they succeed. Effective rules work most of the time, and they are stated in simple, memorable language. Even when phonics rules don't deliver an accurate pronunciation, they usually come close enough to correct by crosschecking.

Workbooks and worksheets provide written exercises with phonics. A steady diet of seatwork is associated with low achievement in learning to read, but some written exercises are valuable as independent practice and for assessment. A highly productive practice to follow up phonics instruction is reading decodable text, which restricts content words to those with learned vowel correspondences. With decodable text, phonics works to decode words, and children are more likely to stick with decoding strategies in preference to memorization or guessing.

Explicit phonics features modeling by the teacher showing how to sound out and blend to decode words. Research has found explicit phonics to be more successful than analytic phonics, which requires memorizing whole words and analyzing them without pronouncing phonemes in isolation. The danger of pronouncing phonemes in isolation has been exaggerated. Most phonemes can be isolated accurately, and the minor distortions in blending voiced stops can be corrected by crosschecking. Linguistic programs provided decodable text in hopes that children would induce spelling patterns without explicit instruction in sounding out in blending, which requires pronouncing phonemes in isolation. However, the alphabetic code is too complex for young children to figure out without explicit teaching.

Although young readers must soon deal with multisyllable words, dictionary syllabication is unnecessary to locating syllables. With crosschecking, readers can use vowels to identify rough syllable boundaries sufficient for word identification. Some authorities advocate teaching phonogram units (rime spellings) instead of vowel correspondences because their regular pronunciations. However, phonograms are word chunks best learned by decoding, and decoding requires knowledge of vowel correspondences. Revising phonics to replace the focus on correspondences with a focus on phonograms would be much less efficient for learning to read.

Phonics not only teaches correspondences and phonics rules, but also strategies for blending. Syllables break easily into onset and rime units, where the onset includes any consonants before the vowel, and the rime includes the remainder of the syllable. However, the most effective blending instruction takes advantage of the body and coda segments of spoken words. The body includes everything through the vowel, and the optional coda includes any remaining consonants. Initial blending work might productively use pictures or riddles, but blending phonemes for learning words works best with letter manipulatives. A minor blending issue is whether to use letter names in blending instruction. Because letter names do not consistently signal the correct phonemes, teachers usually do better to pronounce phonemes while moving letter tiles without reference to letter names. An effective initial approach for blending phonemes is vowel-first blending. Vowel-first blending helps children sound out the vowel before forming the body chunk, and then joins body to coda to recognize a word. Later, successive blending is more efficient because it maintains a left-to-right progression, blending correspondences in sequence to form the body chunk and then joining it to the coda for word recognition. A blending slide might be used to introduce blending strategies with an engaging narrative.

Appendix: Major Grapheme-Phoneme Correspondences with Example Words

Phoneme	Single letter graphemes	Digraphs
Consonants		
/b/	b (back, rob, best)	
/d/	d (dog, pad, doll)	
/f/	f (fix, leaf, food)	ph (phone, graph, phonics)
/g/	g (girl, frog, game)	
/h/	h (hop, hand, help)	
/j/	j (jam, jump, job) g (gym, huge, gem)	dge (fudge, edge, bridge)
/k/	c (cat, clam, cow) k (kiss, keep, kite)	ck (brick, sack, luck)
/l/	l (leg, pal, left)	
/m/	m (map, jam, must)	mb (limb, thumb, jamb)
/n/	n (no, run, nut)	kn (knee, knit, know)
/p/	p (pot, hop, pail)	
/r/	r (rat, rock, red)	wr (wrap, write, wring)
/s/	s (sack, bats, see) c (cell, face, cent)	
/t/	t (tie, rat, toe)	
/v/	v (van, save, vex)	
/w/	w (weed, will, wave)	
/y/	y (yarn, yell, yes)	
/z/	s (was, has, dogs) z (zone, zip, zoo) x (xerox, xylophone, Xavier)	
/ch/		ch (chair, each, chop) tch (catch, witch, notch)
/sh/		sh (shop, ash, shy) ti (action, station, caution)
/th/ /<u>th</u>/		th (thin, path, <u>th</u>is)
/zh/	s (measure, pleasure, treasure)	
/ng/	n (bank, sink, honk)	ng (sing, bang, wrong)
Consonant clusters treated as consonants		
/hw/		wh (which, where, why)
/kw/		qu (quit, quiet, quote)
/ks/	x (box, e_x_it, ax)	

\<tr>	Vowels	
	Short vowels	
/a/	*a* (act, ham, tag)	
/e/	*e* (end, egg, hen)	*ea* (head, bread, deaf)
/i/	*i* (it, him, did)	
/o/	*o* (odd, hot, box)	
/u/ schwa	*u* (up, gum, bus), *a* (about), *o* (potato), *e* (enough), *i* (continent)	
	Long vowels	
/A/	*a* (April, agent, bacon)	*a_e* (ace, rate, plane) *ai* (aim, raid, pain) *ay* (say, play, day)
/E/	*e* (even, equal, Eden) *y* (baby, penny, happy)	*ee* (eel, beet, see) *ea* (eat, dream, team)
/I/	*i* (I, item, ivy) *y* (cry, dry, fly)	*i_e* (ice, ripe, time) *igh* (high, night, sigh)
/O/	*o* (open, over, hotel)	*o_e* (vote, pole, code) *oa* (oak, boat, foam) *ow* (snow, show, low)
/U/ /OO/	*u* (human, usual, unite)	*u_e* (use, rule, tube) *ew* (few, new, flew) *oo* (tool, boot, soon)
	Other vowels	
/aw/	*o* (off, dog, log)	*au* (auto, Auburn, fault) *aw* (awful, raw, saw)
/oy/		*oi* (oil, soil, avoid) *oy* (boy, toy, annoy)
/oo/	*u* (push, put, sugar)	*oo* (cook, good, look)
/ow/		*ou* (out, count, loud) *ow* (how, brown, cow)
	R-controlled vowels	
/ar/		*ar* (art, bard, barn)
/er/		*er* (her, under, herd) *ir* (sir, girl, dirt) *ur* (fur, burn, surf)

Choosing Texts for Reading Instruction

Creating effective beginning reading instruction requires striking a balance between a meaning emphasis and a code emphasis (Chall, 1967). In a meaning-emphasis program, teachers introduce students to the riches of children's literature. In a code-emphasis program, teachers explicitly teach children the alphabetic code. Obviously, both are important, but deciding which to emphasize for beginning readers forces us to make decisions on which texts we want beginners to read, especially in late kindergarten and early first grade: Should they read decodable text or children's literature? Like many decisions, the choice of texts involves a tradeoff. Either children read decodable text for rapid growth in decoding ability at the expense of a rich literary experience; or they read stories with well-rounded characters in interesting situations, but with a word-learning burden that may delay learning to decode.

WHAT MAKES A TEXT DECODABLE?

Decodable text matches the content words in the text with readers' current vowel knowledge. The content words are the nouns, action verbs, adjectives, adverbs, and longer prepositions that carry meaning, as opposed to function words, which are the linking verbs, articles, pronouns, smaller prepositions, and conjunctions that show the relations between content words. For example, consider this text from *Frog and Toad Are Friends* (Lobel, 1970, p. 28):

> Toad and Frog went for a long walk. They walked across a large meadow. They walked in the woods. They walked along the river. At last they went back home to Toad's house.

Toad, Frog, went, long, walk, walked, across, large, meadow, woods, along, woods, river, last, back, home, Toad's, and *house* are content words. In contrast, *and, for, a, they, in, the, at,* and *to* are function words. Because function words serve mainly as semantic glue to organize the content words, some teachers call them glue words, a terminology more concrete for young learners. Function or glue words are high frequency words that appear constantly in text. In fact, the top 109 function words account for about half of all running words in text (see Chapter 4). Because these words are so common, children need a reading vocabulary of glue words to read any text. Accordingly, these words must be taught very early, and whole-word methods may be necessary for initial instruction until children learn to decode them. Glue words "don't count" in assessing the decodablity of a text. Only content words should be assessed for decodability.

Some people argue that English is hopelessly irregular so that reading by decoding is virtually impossible. However, these fears are exaggerated. Every English spelling maps the phonological structure of the spoken word it represents. Even a word as irregular as *of* (/uv/) has a degree of decodability; the *o* represents the schwa /u/ sound typical in unaccented syllables (see Chapter 7), and the *f* maps the same mouth move as /v/, omitting only the voicing. Irregular words like *island* are mostly regular; after crosschecking, readers learn that the *i* is long and the *s* is silent. By mentally marking these elements, adept decoders can quickly add the spelling *island* as sight vocabulary.

Regular and Irregular Words

Spelling regularity seems to be a continuum that depends on the size of a word's word family. To review, a word family consists of all that words that rhyme and share a phonogram, such as *light, sight, tight, slight,* and *bright*. The phonogram *ight* is a spelling of the spoken rime /It/. Regular words have large word families, and irregular words either have small families or no families at all. Thus, *bay* is regular because it has a large word family. *Shout* has a medium-sized family, and *could* is irregular because it has a very small family with only two siblings, *would* and *should*. Words like *was, of, said, are, the, what,* and *were* are clearly irregular because they are orphans. These words have no families—none has a rhyming word sharing the same phonogram. Figure 1 shows the top 50 most common words in English in alphabetical order; note how many of these common words are irregular. However, because glue words are indispensible for composing even the simplest stories, such words may be used freely in composing decodable text.

TEACHING GLUE WORDS

Because glue words are essential for reading any text, they must be taught. However, *how* we teach glue words depends on children's developmental Ehri phase (see Chapter 3). Prealphabetic and partial alphabetic readers must learn glue words by memorizing their spellings; this requires spelling drill. However, spelling drill need not be tedious. For example, to learn the word *was*, teachers can lead students in clapping the spellings, or snapping their fingers, marching, or doing the twist to each letter.

a	but	have	it	that	was	you
all	by	he	not	the	we	your
an	can	his	of	their	were	
and	do	how	on	there	what	
are	each	I	one	they	when	
as	for	if	or	this	which	
at	from	in	said	to	with	
be	had	is	she	use	word	

FIGURE 1: Top 50 most common words in English

Full alphabetic readers learn irregular glue words by decoding, crosschecking, and mental marking. These strategies are not only easier but much more reliable than memorization. For example, a full alphabetic reader might decode *could* as /kowld/, but on crosschecking, would correct the attempt and mentally mark the *l* as silent and the *ou* as /oo/. After a few trials, the reader would store the annotated spelling *could* in memory for sight word recognition. As evidence for this view, there is a high correlation between reading pseudowords and reading irregular words (see Chapter 3). The same readers succeed in reading both pseudowords and irregular words because each of these achievements depends on decoding skill. Full alphabetic readers learn irregular words as sight words by decoding with the additional steps of crosschecking to access the word and mental marking to note the silent or irregular letters. With a complete and meaningful alphabetic map in memory, readers can instantly match spellings they perceive in print with spellings stored in memory for automatic word recognition.

For this reason, teachers should help students reconfigure glue words they have memorized into sight words relearned by decoding, crosschecking, and mental marking. For example, teachers can guide students to decode *was* as "wass" and then crosscheck to recover the correct pronunciation /wuz/, to be re-examined to annotate *a* as the schwa /u/ and *s* as /z/. This might be done in a spelling lesson with other words in which *s* represents /z/, such as *is*, *has*, and *does*. The word *were* might be decoded as "weer," crosschecked to the correct pronunciation /wer/, and then mentally marked with an instruction to ignore the silent *e*. Note that this process depends on a fairly sophisticated knowledge of the alphabetic code (e.g., that the most common spelling for /z/ is *s*, that silent *e* marks a long vowel, and that *er* says /er/). This implies that code knowledge is an essential foundation for sight word learning rather than an impediment.

Comparing Basal Programs

Figure 2 contrasts the typical meaning-emphasis programs for beginning readers that emphasize reading children's literature with the unusual code emphasis programs that have children read decodable text. In actual programs, meaning and code emphases are mixed, and there has been a decided shift in major programs toward including greater code emphasis. Nevertheless, typical programs today tend to emphasize meaning over code. This figure elaborates the information in Chapter 2 by noting differences in texts in meaning and code emphasis programs. In meaning emphasis programs, there is a mismatch between phonics instruction and the words used in texts. Because content words in meaning-emphasis texts are not restricted to vowels students have learned to decode, children can rarely use what they have learned in phonics lessons to read the words in their texts. Phonics works in the workbook, but not in the real book.

TYPICAL PROGRAM: Meaning Emphasis	UNUSUAL PROGRAM: Code Emphasis
Incidental: Teaches correspondences as needed; or systematic program with spotty correspondence coverage.	**Systematic**: The program covers all major correspondences in a planned order.
Analytic: Students memorize whole words, which they later analyze. Teacher never pronounces phonemes in isolation.	**Explicit**: Teacher pronounces phonemes in isolation to model how to sound out and blend.
Extensive: Phonics lessons continue sporadically throughout the elementary grades.	**Intensive**: Children learn about two correspondences per week and complete the program by mid-second grade.
Mismatched: No attempt is made to match the phonics lesson with the words used in stories. Consequently, phonics rarely works when reading stories.	**Integrated**: Students read stories in which most words are decodable using correspondences taught in phonics lessons.

FIGURE 2: Typical and unusual reading programs

In code-emphasis programs, phonics instruction is integrated with the words in texts. This means that decoding strategies work to unlock the words in code-emphasis texts. When decoding works, readers stick with decoding rather than phonetic cue reading, contextual guessing, memorization, and other suboptimal strategies. Early texts must be specially engineered to achieve this integration between phonics instruction and reading practice by carefully restricting content words to those with vowels learned to date. Thus, program developers face a trade-off: Either children read decodable text, in which they can succeed in reading the words of stories with little inherent interest, or they read children's literature, with much richer stories but with content words beyond the reach of their early decoding skills.

ATTEMPTS TO SOLVE THE FRUSTRATION PROBLEM

Reading readiness and emergent literacy programs (see Chapter 5) historically tried to resolve this dilemma in different ways. The Scott-Foresman reader *Fun With Dick and Jane* (Gray & Arbuthnot, 1946) used word repetition and engaging pictures to help children over the hurdle of learning words that were not selected for decodability. Figure 3 shows the results. This is not decodable text because the content words are not restricted to learned vowel patterns. The publishers commissioned illustrations of cute characters in amusing situations to keep children engaged in the difficult task of whole-word learning, and excessive repetition allowed children opportunities to memorize the words. However, like the worst decodable texts, the selectivity of words led to stilted, unnatural language.

FIGURE 3: Text from the Scott-Foresman reader Fun With Dick and Jane

Later emergent-literature programs tried to solve the word frustration problem by using predictable texts. A favorite text was *Brown Bear, Brown Bear, What Do You See?* (Martin & Carle, 1967):

Brown Bear, Brown Bear, what do you see?

I see a red bird looking at me.

Red Bird, Red Bird, what do you see?

I see a yellow duck looking at me.

Again, these words are not selected for decodability. However, the text invites the reader to use the illustrations to identify the new content on each page (e.g., Brown Bear, Red Bird) and to plug this content into a rhyming, rhythmic pattern ("... what do you see? I see a ...."). With such texts, most prealphabetic readers can experience almost immediate success with a book, becoming enthusiastic "readers" on day one. However, children's success with predictable books depends on cued recitation rather than reading words; it is a kind of pretend reading that can be accomplished by attending to the illustrations without even looking at the words. Such texts are fun to read and provide an engaging introduction to book language, but they do not teach children to read words.

After an enjoyable experience with predictable books, children graduate to reading rich children's literature, such as Arnold Lobel's (1978) *Mouse Tales*, where they encounter text like this:

> Once there was a very tall mouse and a very short mouse who were good friends. When they met Very Tall Mouse would say, "Hello, Very Short Mouse." And Very Short Mouse would say, "Hello, Very Tall Mouse."

Lobel writes delightful children's literature, with well-developed characters in humorous situations. But how do beginners read the words? Without the repetition of *Dick and Jane*, and without the predictable patterns of *Brown Bear*, children are faced with a very tough word-reading challenge. The jump from the fun of reciting predictable books to the frustration of reading children's literature is, for many, a first-grade crisis.

Other professional writers have fared no better in writing children's literature with decodable words. Even the brilliant Dr. Seuss had trouble writing interesting children's books with words beginners could read. We may mistake books like *The Cat in the Hat* (Geisel, 1957) for decodable text, but not a single page is composed using only short-vowel content words. Early books written to be decodable, such *The Indian Book* (Dickson, 1973) featured amateurish illustrations and such charmless text as this:

> Jim is six. Jim is six and big. Jim *is* big. Dad can tell Jim is big. Jim will get as big as his Dad.

When decodable texts offer such low quality fare, we can understand why they are scorned. However, more recent texts, such as Sheila Cushman's (1990) *Tin Man Fix-It*, manage to tell structured stories with problems to solve:

> The tin man is Tim. Jim is the fix-it man. Sid is a big kid. Sid zips in. Sid zigs and zags. The big kid hits Tim.

Granted that we have no contender for the Caldecott Medal (awarded to the best illustrated children's book of the year), the story of the tin man's accident engages children's interest, and the professional illustrations help them make sense of the spare text. In addition, the progression of books in the Phonics Readers series (from Educational Insights) accumulates vowel correspondences, allowing more interesting stories. For example, when students have mastered short vowels and several long vowel correspondences, they can successfully read *Kite Day at Pine Lake* (Cushman & Kornblum, 1990):

> Jeff's kite is wide. It is a big size. Jeff's kite is fun to fly. Fay's kite dives down. It dives by Ike's kite. Ike's kite is red with dots. Jan's kite is fine. It has five sides. It is a nice kite.
>
> Bob sees the kites. He is sad. Bob has no kite to fly.

Each new correspondence learned as children progress through the Educational Insights Phonics Readers expands the vocabulary pool, giving the writer opportunities to create more engaging stories.

More advanced readers can tackle their first chapter books constructed with decodable text in the creative works of Matt Sims, written for High Noon Books. For example, the six-chapter book *The Tug* (Sims, 1999) tells a suspenseful tale of a young man working for a tug boat captain who doesn't like his dog Sam. It begins:

> It was six. Bob was in bed. The sun was not up yet. But Bob had to get up. He had to get to his job. Bob had a job on a tug. Bob got up out of bed. He fed his dog Sam.

Later, when work on the tug is imperiled by a thick, unexpected fog, Sam's barking helps the crew locate the dock for a successful mooring. Young readers who navigate through the decodable words to the satisfying conclusion feel justifiable pride in conquering their first chapter book.

Trade-Offs with Beginning Texts

Writing an engaging decodable text offers a very different challenge than writing a work of children's literature because in each case, the writer must cope with tradeoffs. Imagine you have just won the Caldecott Medal, given for the best illustrated children's book of the year, and your telephone is ringing nonstop with offers to write for basal readers and other children's publications. You pick up the phone, and an editor asks you to write for a meaning-emphasis basal reader. Not clear about the jargon, you ask her to fax you the kind of story they are looking for, and she sends an episode from *Mouse Tales* (Lobel, 1978). Scanning the story, you realize the editor is looking for stories with rounded characters in interesting situations. You ask if there are any restrictions on the words you can use in the story. She says, "We'd appreciate it if you can keep the words to one or two syllables and the sentences short." That leaves a wide pool of words available to tell an interesting story that will engage children's interest.

Suppose the moment you hang up, the phone rings again with an offer to write for a code-emphasis basal. Realizing the value of an example, you ask for a fax and receive a copy of *Kite Day at Pine Lake* (Cushman & Kornblum, 1990). The editor explains that they are looking for a story for children who have just learned the *ee* and *ea* long vowel correspondences. When you ask what the word restrictions are, the editor says, "I'm afraid the restrictions are very tight. You can use any high frequency function word, but for the content words, you can only use regular, one-syllable words with the vowel correspondences children have learned so far. In this case, they will have learned all the short vowels and the correspondences for long *A* and *E*. For example, you could write about a dream team on the way to a game with the Eels team on the beach near Fleet Street." That rules out most of the words you could use with the previous publisher, including irregular words, words with more advanced vowels, and words with two syllables.

With a drastically reduced word pool, creating a work of children's literature is not a realistic goal. At best, you can make a reasonably engaging story under severe vocabulary limits. Fortunately, most children are not that critical about the literary qualities of beginning reading texts. Success is their biggest motivator. If they expect success in reading the words, they are willing to tackle the reading. In contrast, they won't enjoy the world's greatest stories if they have to struggle inordinately to figure out the words.

Writing Decodable Text

One strategy teachers can use to create a decodable text that tells an engaging story is to begin by writing (or appropriating) an engaging story, initially without concern for decodability. For example, the Aesop's fable of The Boy Who Cried Wolf is a memorable work, but the words are not decodable:

> There once was a shepherd boy who was bored as he sat on the hillside watching the village sheep. To amuse himself he took a great breath and sang out, "Wolf! Wolf! The Wolf is chasing the sheep!"

By using a thesaurus program such as Thesaurus.com to find decodable synonyms, it is possible to replace long words, irregular words, and words with untaught vowels with decodable words; in this case, geared toward students who have only learned short vowels:

> There was a lad that felt sick and dull as he sat on the hill. His job was to tend the lambs from a mad dog that wished to hunt and kill the lambs. For fun, he yelled, "Mad dog! Mad dog! A mad dog hunts the lambs!"

Using this method, it is possible to compose engaging stories and then translate them into decodable text rather than to attempt to compose within the suffocating strictures of a tightly controlled vocabulary. Children still get productive decoding practice, and they encounter rich characters and engaging situations, albeit without the precise word choice that marks genuine literature.

An Experiment with Decodable Text

To get the best start in reading, do children need a code-emphasis basal featuring decodable text? Or can they have the best of both worlds: An adjunct (add-on) phonics program and a meaning-emphasis reader featuring children's literature? The best evidence for answering these questions comes from a landmark experiment designed by Juel and Roper/Schneider (1985). The researchers discovered an ideal research site, a school district that taught every first grader for 30 minutes daily with the same adjunct phonics program, but allowed teachers to choose either a meaning-emphasis basal (Houghton-Mifflin, the then best seller) or a code-emphasis basal (Economy). The district afforded a natural research opportunity to compare the effect of the practice texts (children's literature with engaging stories versus decodable text) in a situation where phonics instruction was the same for both groups. Juel and Roper/Schneider tested first graders' reading at midyear with two key tests: pseudowords (regularly spelled nonwords) and "switch words" (words appearing only in the other basal that the children had not read). Pseudoword reading is a pure measure of decoding ability because it simulates an encounter with a word never seen before that can only be accessed by decoding. Reading switch words tested whether children could read untaught real words.

The results showed that children who read decodable text in the code-emphasis basal did better on both these tests than children who had read early literature in the meaning-emphasis basal. Code-emphasis readers' advantage with pseudowords showed that they were better at decoding. Their advantage with switch words showed that they were more independent readers, able to learn new words without the help of the teacher. Surprisingly, children reading the code-emphasis basal were better able to read words with long vowels, even though their phonics program had only taught them short vowels. These results suggest that children who read decodable texts, where a decoding strategy works, stick with decoding strategies when they encounter unfamiliar words. They pick up decoding skills, sight word knowledge, and sight-chunk knowledge that helps them tackle unfamiliar words. Their blending and cross-checking skills enable them to work out pronunciations of new words with correspondences not yet taught in phonics class and to use correspondences and patterns (such as the silent-*e* rule) only mentioned by a parent or teacher.

Juel and Roper/Schneider (1985) showed that while teaching phonics is important, giving decodable text determines whether students will actually use decoding strategies. Phonics doesn't "take" without decodable text. Children given literary texts before they have mastered word reading soon learn that the phonics they've been taught doesn't work to unlock the words of their stories. This not only leads to frustration when reading stories, but also it diminishes children's motivation to study phonics. Why take it seriously if it doesn't work? They muddle through with phonetic cue reading, contextual guessing, and memorization.

In contrast, children given decodable texts stay with decoding strategies because they work. For example, when they learn that *oa* says /O/ and can apply this knowledge to read *The Boat Made of Soap*, phonics knowledge is functional. Each story becomes a signpost of success, allowing readers to see their headway in learning to read. Success reading stories, in turn, motivates their work with phonics by showing them that learning how to decode enables them to read stories. Teachers, too, are motivated to teach phonics thoroughly and explicitly because they see how explicit teaching helps their students succeed with reading. With an expanding group of vowels, both teachers and students enjoy better stories with more natural vocabulary (compare the excerpts from *Tin Man Fix-It* and *Kite Day at Pine Lake* to sample the gains in language quality within the Educational Insights series). Juel and Roper/Schneider concluded that the decodability of the words in children's practice texts is as important as their method of instruction for making progress in reading. Explicit phonics is not enough: Beginners need decodable text to practice the decoding strategies learned in phonics to turn strategies into skills.

Typical Practices in Primary Reading Instruction

While there has been a trend toward more explicit phonics instruction in American schools since 2000, most programs emphasize meaning over code. Virtually all programs teach phonics, but instruction is rarely thorough and explicit. Phonics instruction is systematic in the sense that it covers correspondences in a planned order, but coverage of major correspondences is incomplete, omitting such useful correspondences as *-dge* and *-tch* after short vowels, the *e*, *i*, and *y* signals for soft *c* and *g*, and the /O/ and /ow/ phonemes for *ow*. Lessons are wasted teaching dozens of consonant clusters rather than teaching blending strategies with any consonants. Some decodable texts are presented as adjunct materials, but they are rarely fully decodable; irregular words are mixed in with decodable words. Phonics practice materials are often worksheets. Basal manuals invite some modeling, relaxing the counterproductive counsel against pronouncing phonemes in isolation, but most instruction is presented as minilessons, i.e., brief explanations with demonstrations, omitting the guided practice, text application, assessment, and reteaching needed for mastery. Such minilessons amount to barely more than mentioning, and they are often in the context of a workshop approach with independent reading and writing activities carried out in learning centers. By substituting minilessons for thorough, explicit instruction, phonics in today's primary classrooms is usually sketchy and inadequate.

We can speculate about some of the reasons phonics has been played down into minilessons. We are only recently emerging from the great reading wars of the twentieth century, and few teachers know why or how to teach phonics explicitly and thoroughly. The logistics of working with reading groups invites teachers to relegate phonics practice to seatwork or to unsupervised learning centers. Most live teaching in reading groups is devoted to supervised practice in oral reading, and assigning phonics exercises as seatwork keeps other students busy and frees teacher time to scaffold children's reading aloud. However, the principal reason for downplaying phonics relates to the dearth of decodable text. Meaning-emphasis programs leave a mismatch between phonics instruction and reading, so that phonics doesn't work with the stories children read. If the content words in their texts are irregular or feature untaught correspondences, phonics seems pointless for reading basal stories. Students are not motivated to study phonics lessons that don't pay off in reading, and teachers are not motivated to teach phonics thoroughly and explicitly when such instruction will do little to help children progress through their basal readers.

If a shortage of decodable texts accounts for the inadequacies of phonics instruction in today's primary classrooms, the solution is obvious: Teachers working with beginning readers need texts engineered for decodability to make phonics pay off in reading. With decodable series that carefully limit content words to words with learned vowel patterns, students see that phonics works and take instruction seriously. Learning new correspondences allows young readers to read their texts more successfully and independently, and as they accumulate a growing correspondence toolkit, they move into more engaging stories with more natural language. With a well-stocked toolkit of correspondences and crosschecking ability, students can graduate into children's literature not restricted for decodability, where the rewards of reading multiply. Because teachers want their students to make progress through their basals, they will teach phonics more thoroughly and systematically when students read decodable text.

Round-Robin Reading

Observation studies suggest that most live reading instructional time in primary grades is devoted to supervised oral reading, and a distressing number of classrooms arrange round-robin reading. In round-robin reading, each child reads aloud a paragraph or page of a text in a planned order, working around the reading table. (When the order of readers is not planned, this arrangement is called "popcorn" reading.)

Round-robin reading has a number of negative consequences. It works against listening comprehension because readers have not practiced reading their assigned parts. As a result, their reading is rarely fluent, and word-by-word reading is difficult for listeners to understand. Round-robin reading violates a venerable guideline for reading instruction: Never ask students to read aloud materials that they have not had a chance to read silently. Of course, some students are practicing the paragraphs they are slated to read, which also works against their listening comprehension with the rest of the text. Round-robin reading also impedes reading comprehension. Able readers may enjoy the spotlight, but less successful readers may be anxious or embarrassed when their efforts are put on display, especially if they must endure corrections from the teacher or classmates. For all these reasons, arranging round-robin should be recognized as a default method of amateur teachers that should rarely if ever be imposed on young readers.

Although I have had harsh criticism for round-robin reading, it may be possible to arrange round-robin *repeated* reading to overcome its limitations. With this variation, three readers read each page, and then they follow along silently as others read the same page. The order of readers alternates so that a different reader starts each page, and the teacher intersperses questions after each reading to keep the group involved. Round-robin repeated reading solves the inattention and embarrassment problems of round-robin reading by creating opportunities for reading or reading along with the same texts multiple times. As a method of repeated reading, it allows young readers to learn sight words and improve their fluency.

Silent Reading

Oral reading locks in a slow, methodical pace that militates against reading comprehension. It is akin to getting stuck in a crawling lineup of cars after an accident on the interstate. Good readers figuratively switch gears as they read; they change speed according to the type of text, the purpose for reading, and the kinds of problems they encounter. They may even stop to reread a passage to repair their comprehension or to savor the delights of a well-turned passage.

To facilitate the gear-shifting of skilled reading, students should read silently for most purposes by the time they reach the first-grade instructional level. (Note that first-grade level is independent of grade placement; advanced kindergartners may be ready for silent reading, and reading-delayed second graders may not have attained a first-grade reading level.) Silent reading allows readers to stop, reread, check a reference, or ask a question; it allows readers to speed through less important material or to read slowly to relish details. In addition, silent reading is about twice as fast as oral reading, which means a transition to silent reading can potentially double the amount of instructional reading practice for first-grade level readers.

DR-TA

One of the best alternatives to round-robin reading is the directed reading-thinking activity, usually known by its acronym DR-TA (Stauffer, 1969). The DR-TA features silent reading, with all its speed-shifting benefits. Its effectiveness comes from student predictions during reading. To prepare a DR-TA, the teacher chooses a narrative text, preferably one with a surprise ending. Expository texts do not work for DR-TA because predictions usually require story structure. The teacher divides the narrative into manageable sections so that students read to stopping points for discussion and consolidation.

The discussion in DR-TA follows a simple three-step routine: Students (1) predict what will happen, (2) read to test their predictions, and then (3) review their predictions to confirm or revise them. The teacher asks two key questions to elicit predictions: "What do you think will happen?" and "Why do you think so?" These questions are motivating because there are no wrong answers, and because the act of making a prediction encourages students to read to verify their accuracy. In explaining why they made their predictions, students model their inferences in ways that benefit other readers; they reveal textual cues that helped them infer suspected facts not made explicit by the writer. To follow up on these predictions later, it is important for the teacher to jot down predictions and to record the names of students who made each prediction. Then, students read to the next predetermined stopping point. Those who finish early may jot down predictions to share while others catch up. Writing predictions and recording the evidence for those predictions engages the "thinking" in the directed reading-thinking activity. To review the predictions from the previous round, the teacher asks each student prognosticator, "What did you find out?" At this point, DR-TA cycles back for more predictions ("Now what do you think will happen? Why do you think so?"), and the reading proceeds.

The DR-TA is effective for reading comprehension for at least three reasons. First, it supports less-skilled readers by dividing the reading into manageable units. This makes the reading assignment much less daunting than assigning an entire story or chapter. Second, asking for predictions creates interest. Because there are no right answers and everyone's speculations are important, students build confidence in drawing inferences. Third, the DR-TA scaffolds active reading guided by self-questioning and evokes the expert processes of drawing inferences from text cues to suspected facts. Good readers model their inferences for others, explaining how they picked up their ideas for insightful predictions.

Appropriate Reading Levels

A crucial move for leading young readers to make progress is guiding reading at their instructional levels. Reading researchers have long recognized that reading with low error rates of about 2-5%—the instructional level—is optimal for reading progress (Betts, 1946). An error rate of 0-1%—the independent level—offers insufficient challenge for rapid growth in sight vocabulary. An error rate beyond 6%—the frustration level—is detrimental to reading comprehension, and leads children to forgo crosschecking. Without crosschecking, readers are unable to make sight words, which depends on crosschecking and mental marking to supplement decoding. The independent, instructional, and frustration levels are often described by their success rates in word recognition. Readers at the independent level read with 99-100% success. Independent-level reading is important whenever no teacher is present to scaffold, as when students are reading library books at home. Readers are at their instructional level when they read with 95-98% success. As the name suggests, the instructional level is important for optimal progress during reading instruction because instructional-level texts are too difficult to read independently. Readers achieving success rates from 0-94% are reading at their frustration levels. Frustrated readers make little or no progress in learning sight vocabulary, experience dismal levels of reading comprehension, and develop negative attitudes toward reading.

The best way to remember all these numbers is to memorize the 95-98% success rates at the instructional level. Any success rate below 95% indicates frustration-level reading, and any success rate above 98% indicates the independent level. The reciprocals of these figures indicate the error rates at the independent (0-1% errors), instructional (2-5% errors), and frustration levels (6-100% errors). Computations for error and success rates are based on error counts that recognize only uncorrected reading miscues as scorable. Some confusion has been created by authorities who recommend a 90-95% success rate for instructional level reading. This lower success benchmark counts any deviation from text as a scorable miscue. Using normal miscue counting that excludes self-corrections but using the 90-95% benchmarks would place children in frustration-level texts, a very serious teaching error. Placing children in frustration-level is detrimental to learning effective reading strategies and positive attitudes; it is educational malpractice.

SEATWORK WITH READING GROUPS

Small-group instruction may cause behavior management problems when children not currently working with the teacher must be kept busy with independent work, either as seatwork or at a learning center. Teacher-effectiveness research looks for correlations between teaching practices and student achievement, and regimens of inordinate seatwork are associated with poor reading achievement (Rosenshine & Stevens, 2002). As explained in Chapter 7, this likely owes to a reliance on low-grade written exercises in workbooks and worksheets, many of which amount to little more than busywork. Accordingly, teachers need to look for more productive kinds of independent practice for students not involved in the live instruction of reading groups.

There are many positive alternatives to busywork for independent reading and writing. Some written exercises, including worksheets, provide useful independent practice or assessment to determine whether students have mastered new concepts and strategies. In particular, reading guides have been found to help both good and poor readers remain focused during reading, especially with expository text (Armstrong, Patberg, & Dewitz, 1988). Teachers may have children read silently at their seats or in centers, to take advantage of the gear-shifting gains in reading comprehension of silent reading. Students who read more rapidly can respond to open-ended writing prompts (e.g., "What surprised you when you were reading this story?") in written journals while slower readers catch up. Partners may reread stories quietly to one another. Assisted reading, or reading along with a peer or with a recorded reading, can help beginners gain reading fluency.

ORGANIZING READING GROUPS

An ongoing controversy has been whether to organize homogeneous achievement groups for reading instruction. *Homogeneous* achievement groups group children working at similar reading levels together for focused instruction. One important reason for achievement grouping is to have students read at an instructional level where they can make maximum progress. Rather than reading text that is too easy or too hard, we want students reading at a high level of successful challenge. Placing children at a frustration level is especially deleterious. When pushed to read at a frustration level, children easily get off task and lose instructional time. Even with successful behavior management, they tend to forgo self-correction: They do not add sight vocabulary, which requires decoding, crosschecking, and mental marking to store spellings in the lexicon. Instead, they focus on sounding out words rather than getting the message of the text. As a result, they miss the humor, suspense, and lovable characters in children's literature—in short, everything that makes reading fun.

In addition, homogeneous grouping allows teachers to address the specific needs of students, which vary according to their developmental level (see Chapter 3). Prealphabetic readers need phoneme awareness to enable partial alphabetic decoding; no books are decodable for them. They can only succeed with predictable books, in which they can be helped to fingerpoint the words to attend to phonetic cues (Ehri & Sweet, 1991). Partial alphabetic readers need all vowel correspondences, beginning with short vowels, to enable full-alphabetic decoding. They are ready to read short-vowel decodable books to apply their new phonics knowledge in reading connected text. Full alphabetic readers need to extend their vowel knowledge and build sight word and sight chunk entries in their lexicons. They need to read more advanced decodable texts and instructional level children's literature accessible with decoding and crosschecking. Consolidated alphabetic readers need to gain fluency, improve their meaning vocabulary, and learn comprehension strategies. They need to read literature and expository text at their instructional levels. The diverse needs of readers at very different instructional levels argue powerfully for differentiated instruction in homogeneous achievement groups.

The chief argument against homogeneous grouping is that children in the lower groups lose status and self-esteem. However, placing them in heterogeneous groups will not raise their status or improve their self-esteem. Their reading problems become painfully obvious in a mixed group of readers where they cannot compete with peers. Self-esteem problems are actually ameliorated with homogeneous grouping because in the company of peers reading at similar achievement levels, they can hold their own, especially when they are placed in instructional level texts.

However, there is a more serious disadvantage with homogeneous grouping: Children in the low groups tend to fall further and further behind their more successful peers. One reason the gap increases is that teachers pace their lessons more slowly with struggling readers. They look for fluent oral reading in their basal stories as an indicator that students are ready to move on to new stories. As a result, nonfluent students in low groups tend to spend more time on each story than students in high groups. This means that over the course of a school year, struggling readers read fewer stories. In addition, they learn fewer new correspondences and strategies because these lessons are presented along with each story in the teacher's manual and adjunct materials.

One way to ease the sting of being placed in a low status group is to organize other groups for many instructional purposes and to flexibly group and regroup students for instruction (Opitz, 1999). In some cases, heterogeneous grouping works well, e.g., for cooperative learning. In cooperative learning, high achievers try to earn group rewards under conditions of individual accountability (Slavin, 1980). In order to win free time or computer privileges for the group, able students may be willing to tutor struggling peers to help their group succeed. Grouping students by interest, talent, subject knowledge, or student choice can place students in a wide variety of different groups so that placement in a homogeneous reading group becomes simply another of many such groupings.

Cross-Class Grouping

One good idea for efficient instructional grouping is cross-class grouping (Fry, 1977, p. 281):

> There are several varieties of cross-class grouping in which two or more teachers combine their good or poor readers. For example, at 10:00 AM every morning all the good readers in the third grade from two different teachers' classes meet together with one of the teachers, while the poor readers go to the other teacher's room. Occasionally, cross-class grouping becomes cross-grade grouping so that the best readers of grades 3, 4, and 5 all go to one room, etc. The aim in this regrouping for reading is to get more homogeneous grouping; this means grouping where the pupils tend to be alike.

This type of grouping is often called by different names in different areas. Cross-grade grouping may be called the Joplin plan, redeployment, or the platoon system. There might be fine differences in these various plans or systems, but they are all some type of cross-class or cross-grade homogeneous grouping.

Cross-grade grouping creates the advantages of homogeneous achievement groups—getting children into instructional level texts and arranging work on the critical achievements for developmental progress. As a bonus, cross-grade grouping solves the problem of seatwork. When a whole class of students is working at similar achievement levels and reading instructional texts, there is no need to organize seat work for other students.

Regrouping

Within homogeneous groups, it is vital to assess achievement frequently to determine when students are ready to move to new groups. For example, children in a prealphabetic group reading predictable texts should be tested for phonetic cue reading to determine whether they can make better progress in a partial alphabetic group reading decodable text (see Practical Chapter 5). For full alphabetic readers, the STAR tests from Renaissance Learning provide quick, painless estimates of children's instructional reading levels. STAR uses cloze tests—tests in which readers must supply a missing word—administered on classroom computers. For example, a young reader might be asked to find the best word to complete this item, where each choice works grammatically:

> The dog _____ through the yard.
> barked   ran   dug   fell

The novel aspect of STAR is that the program adjusts the difficulty of the items in response to students' success during the test. This avoids frustration with difficult items, which often leads students to stop trying, leading to invalid scores. When a child misses several items, STAR switches to an easier level, allowing a reading level estimate within about 15 minutes of testing.

MATTHEW EFFECTS REVISITED

The theory of Matthew effects in reading (Stanovich, 1986), introduced in Chapter 5, helps us understand the drastic consequences of early reading failure and the promise of successful early reading intervention. Students who fall behind in phoneme awareness struggle to learn how to decode. Children who can't decode are unable to make sight words, and so they face persistent struggles reading words rather than building the sight vocabulary that enables fluent, automatic reading. The struggle to read words dampens motivation for reading, which means students read little. Without voluminous reading practice, readers are delayed in learning meaning vocabulary, knowledge of sentence and text structures, and the concepts learned through reading. Without these achievements, students do not develop the thinking skills for coping in the competitive worlds of school and society.

Children who detect phonemes early are ready to move into decoding as a natural next step. Skillful decoding enables readers to amass sight vocabulary; this lets them make the transition from decoding to fluency. Easy, fluent reading contributes to the motivation to read widely, and with avid reading, readers gain meaning vocabulary, sentence and text structure knowledge, and conceptual riches only accessible through reading. Unlocking these riches provides the intellectual capital for enhancing intelligence and conferring advantages in both academic and economic spheres. As Matthew 13:12 predicts, "Whoever has will be given more, and he will have an abundance. Whoever does not have, even what he has will be taken from him."

SOLUTIONS FOR STRUGGLING READERS

Stanovich (1986) pointed out the most far-reaching solution to the dilemma of struggling readers: Intervene early to make a "surgical strike" at the root of the problem of poor reading. The critical intervention is a high quality phoneme-awareness program in late preschool and early kindergarten. As described in Chapter 6, the best evidence supports a phoneme-direct model in which teachers begin with the most salient phonemes and present them in memorable ways, including meaningful illustrations, sound analogies, hand gestures, and tongue ticklers. In the phoneme-direct model, teachers give children practice finding phonemes in spoken words, and they apply their phoneme awareness to achieve partial alphabetic decoding. By second semester kindergarten and in first grade, they build on this foundation with explicit phonics instruction (Chapter 7), and they include spelling routes to understanding alphabetic mappings with techniques like the letterbox lesson (Practical Chapter 3). With phonics and spelling instruction, children make sight words by decoding, crosschecking, and mental marking, and with avid reading, gain the ease and fluency that allow them to learn by reading.

Struggling readers need special instruction to close the gap with their more successful peers. Programs like Reading Recovery (Clay, 1993) provide intensive, one-on-one instruction from expert teachers to regain lost ground. In their reading groups, struggling readers benefit from low-frills instruction, i.e., basic instruction in phoneme awareness, phonics, and fluency, with practice in decodable text. More able readers may branch off into entertaining enrichment activities, such as painting a mural of a coral reef, but struggling readers, years behind in reading development, can't afford these luxuries. Motivating the hard work needed to catch up obviously requires some opportunities for participation ("If you can make 60 words per minute and answer my question, you get to paint a tropical fish on the coral reef"), but the chief need of readers at risk is for more explicit strategy instruction and more reading in instructional level text. It may be valuable to arrange "two-a-days," which by analogy with competitive sports, arrange two sessions each day for struggling readers. Meeting a second time provide another opportunity for live instruction with the teacher.

Probably the single most powerful reform for delayed beginning readers today is putting them into a well-written series of decodable texts. They need a match, rather than a mismatch, between the phonics instruction that precedes reading practice and the content words they must reckon with during reading. When students can bring vowel correspondence knowledge and decoding strategies to bear in identifying words, they make rapid gains in acquiring decoding skill and sight vocabulary. With an expanding decoding toolkit, stories get more interesting, motivating learning. In response to student success, teachers see the payoff in teaching phonics thoroughly, explicitly, and systematically. With students engaged in productive practice reading decodable text, teachers recognize that teaching phonics well is crucial to building sight vocabulary, gaining fluency, and proceeding expeditiously through basal readers.

SUMMARY

Effective reading teachers strike a balance between a rich experience of children's literature and explicit instruction in acquiring the alphabetic code. To apply decoding knowledge learned in phonics lessons, children need initial practice in specially engineered decodable text, so that the content words in the text can be decoded using vowel correspondences learned to date. Maintaining decodability requires that the content words in beginning texts (not the function or "glue" words) be restricted to regular, one-syllable words with known vowels. Regular words have large word families, with many other words that rhyme and share common phonograms (rime spellings). Irregular words have few or no rhyming words that share the same phonogram pattern. Since many of the most common words in English are irregular, a small body of such words must initially be memorized via whole-word drills. Memorized words, however, must later be relearned through decoding, crosschecking, and mental marking for reliable sight word recognition.

Typical basal reading programs emphasize meaning over learning the alphabetic code, and they thus create a mismatch between the vowel correspondences taught in phonics and the content words in stories. Code emphasis programs integrate phonics instruction with the content words in texts by providing carefully engineered decodable text where content words are restricted to taught spelling patterns. Historically, basal readers used heavy word repetition or predictable text patterns to enable beginners to read words. This kind of practice proved unhelpful in the transition to children's literature, where word repetition is rare and singsong patterned language disappears.

High quality decodable text remains uncommon. Writers of decodable texts face a trade-off between the goal of creating a memorable story, which requires a very wide pool of words, and the goal of restricting the vocabulary to regular, one-syllable words with known vowels, which necessitates a relatively small pool of words. One possible solution is to compose the story using an unrestricted vocabulary and then replace content words with decodable synonyms by using a thesaurus program.

In a district where all children studied the same phonics program, a groundbreaking experiment compared word-reading progress with groups reading either early children's literature or decodable text. Children who could apply phonics instruction by reading decodable text were better at reading words by midyear. This study suggests that children are less likely to derive the full benefits of phonics instruction without early reading practice in decodable texts. In practice, however, typical programs downplay phonics instruction because texts are not decodable using learned correspondences. These facts suggest that an important reform in beginning reading instruction would be to restrict texts for decodability when children are learning basic short and long vowel correspondences. As a result, success with phonics would link to success in reading stories, motivating both students and teachers to take phonics seriously.

Typically, teachers devote most live reading time to the practice of round-robin reading, which militates against reading and listening comprehension. A possible reform is to use round-robin repeated reading to overcome the inattention and embarrassment problems of round-robin reading. Readers who reach the first-grade level would benefit by a switch to silent reading, which enhances comprehension by allowing a flexible range of reading speeds and increases overall reading practice. DR-TA capitalizes on the flexibility of silent reading and motivates reading by asking students to predict what might happen in each new section of text. Students justify their predictions by reference to text clues, thus modeling for peers how to draw inferences from the words of text to suspected but unstated facts.

A vital responsibility for reading teachers to make sure readers are working with instructional level text, defined as text in which they are 95-98% successful in reading words. For reading on their own, their texts should be at their independent levels, where their word reading is 99-100% successful, and under no circumstances should they be expected to read at their frustration levels, where their word reading is 0-94% successful. Students pushed to read at the high error rates of the frustration level stop crosschecking and self-correcting, stop making sight words, read with little comprehension, and develop negative attitudes toward reading. Children not working directly with the teacher during reading instructional time typically are assigned seatwork, often with low quality exercises or time-wasting busywork. More productive uses of instructional downtime include reading guides, silent reading with writing in response to open-ended prompts, partner reading, and assisted reading.

Homogeneous achievement grouping is usually necessary to keep children reading at their instructional levels and to teach them the concepts and strategies they need to move ahead in reading. The counterargument that homogeneous reading groups harm the self-esteem of those placed in low groups fails to consider that struggling readers face even greater self-esteem problems when competing with able readers in heterogeneous groups. The more serious problem is that poor readers tend to make slower progress through their basals than good readers, which means they read less text and learn fewer strategies. This reading differential causes a growing gap between good and poor readers. To counteract potential negative effects of achievement grouping, teachers should group readers flexibly for many purposes, including the use of heterogeneous groups for cooperative learning. Cross-class grouping can solve the seatwork problem by creating homogeneous achievement groups using readers from multiple classrooms so that entire classes are working on similar strategies with instructional level texts. Whenever grouping is used, it is important to regroup students periodically by administering informal tests or brief STAR assessments.

The far-reaching effects of different levels of reading practice are central to the Matthew effects model. Matthew effects can be negative or positive. Early deficits in phoneme awareness delay learning to decode, which in turn impedes the ability to make sight words and gain reading fluency. When reading is hard and unrewarding, children do not get sufficient practice to learn vocabulary and concepts through reading, which eventually has negative effects on intelligence. On the other hand, early success with phoneme awareness propels success in decoding, leading to rapid sight-word gains and early fluency. When reading is easy and enjoyable, children are more willing to undertake the voluminous practice needed to build meaning vocabulary and conceptual knowledge for enhanced learning ability. The Matthew effects model implies that early intervention is of critical importance in getting children on the road to reading success. Children who fall behind in beginning reading need specialized, intensive instruction with expert teachers, such as offered by the Reading Recovery program, to recover lost ground. Low-frills instruction and two-a-days in reading instruction will help them focus on learning missing strategies, and working with a high quality series of decodable text will maximize motivation and learning during the crucial breakthrough period of beginning reading.

CHAPTER 9

Moving from Decoding to Fluency

We all feel for the child struggling to sound out words, backtracking to correct mistakes, fighting his way through a text to the point of exhaustion, and missing out on the pleasure of reading. For skilled adult readers, there is no barrier between the printed words of a text and their meanings. But for a beginning reader, the barrier is formidable. How can we help the children who, in the words of Jeanne Chall (1996), are "glued to print"?

WHAT IS FLUENCY?

Full alphabetic readers who are glued to print need reading fluency. *Fluency* means reading with automatic word recognition. In practical terms, a fluent reading takes place when most or all words in a text are in the reader's sight vocabulary. A reader has *specific* fluency with mastery of the words in a particular text. Specific fluency can usually be gained over several rereadings of an instructional level text. However, we would not say that a young reader who has mastered a single text is a fluent reader. Most children reading at a third grade level are fluent with easy texts such as "I Can Read" books, but not fluent with challenging texts such as science textbooks.

To the extent that a reader has a sight vocabulary sufficiently large to read the words in a wide range of literature and expository text effortlessly, we recognize that reader as a fluent reader—a reader who has achieved *general* reading fluency. General fluency accrues slowly, analogously to developing a large meaning vocabulary. Learning only a few words may establish fluency with a specific text, but gaining general fluency requires making tens of thousands of words into sight words.

Gaining general fluency yields enormous advantages to a reader. Rather than plodding through text, solving each word one at a time, the fluent reader can recognize words effortlessly and automatically—speeding up reading dramatically. With fluent reading, he can work full time at getting the message of the text, which allows significant improvements in reading comprehension. When reading aloud with automatic word recognition and enhanced comprehension, he can supply the prosodic elements of pitch, pause, and emphasis that provide dramatic interpretation to the reading. If a fluent reader learns about good books and good authors, the ease of reading fluency will likely help him develop the habits of avid reading. Automatic word recognition is an important cause of all these good results.

If fluency is reading with automatic word recognition, the basic path to building sight words explained in this book, accelerated by avid reading, will lead to general reading fluency. We make sight words by decoding (either grapheme by grapheme or by recognizing pronounceable word parts for quick assembly of word chunks), by crosschecking to correct any near misses in decoding, and by mentally marking any odd or irregular elements in the spelling, as discussed in Chapter 3. Understanding the alphabetic mapping allows the reader to store the annotated spelling in memory, by rereading the word across a few learning trials. When we can match a stored spelling with a printed word, word recognition is automatic.

A Misunderstanding about Fluency

There is a popular misunderstanding that fluency *is* fast reading, or that fluency *is* reading with expression. Speed and expression are happy results when most or all the words in a text are accessible as sight vocabulary. Where this misunderstanding becomes detrimental is when teachers focus on trying to get results without taking effective means to reach these results. For example, if you want to get a high score on the GRE test, you have to study the concepts and strategies that will be tested, such as vocabulary. Simply taking the test over and over again is going to be frustrating and expensive without making an appreciable improvement in scores.

The misunderstanding of fluency as fast reading has led to much educational malpractice in recent years. Rather than teaching beginners a rich and thorough body of correspondences for decoding, teachers have subjected them to a regimen of daily speed-reading practice.

Practicing reading passages under testing conditions does not improve reading fluency because testing does not allow the word learning necessary to build sight vocabulary. The impetus for this treatment has been the DIBELS Oral Reading Fluency Test (Good & Kaminski, 2002). DIBELS provides a poorly designed measure of fluency that has children read unpracticed passages aloud for one minute and counts the number of words read accurately without checking for comprehension. Reading a cold passage under speed pressure, students can guess or skip unfamiliar words, and because there is no check for reading comprehension, skipping words is actually a good strategy to reach prescribed "benchmarks." Without a comprehension requirement, the DIBELS does not accurately measure reading fluency, but simply speed of word naming (Samuels, 2007). Actual fluency is marked by the capacity to multitask: to read words and to comprehend the message of text simultaneously, which depends on making word recognition automatic.

Sight Word Vocabulary Underlies Fluency

Rashotte and Torgesen (1985) provided experimental evidence that automaticity of word recognition is the defining feature of fluency. They studied struggling readers under three reading conditions: repeated readings of stories with word overlap (i.e., many of the same content words were repeated across passages), repeated readings of stories with minimal word overlap, and an equivalent amount of reading in different stories (not repeated reading). They found that readers *only* made measurable fluency gains in repeated readings of passages with word overlap. Readers did not gain fluency by repeated readings using passages without word overlap or by reading different stories.

The finding that fluency gains come from repeated readings of passages with word overlap suggests that fluency gains come by making the words in the passages into sight words. Reitsma (1983) found that full alphabetic readers could add new words to sight vocabulary in as few as four trials, a number commensurate with the typical number of word encounters in the method of repeated reading. In a replication with normal readers using the method of repeated reading, we found that children who read six chapters in a single book, where there was a natural word overlap across chapters, read the final chapter in that book an average 20 words per minute faster than a control group reading six single chapters from six other books by the same author at the same level of readability (Murray, 2009).

DO WHOLE WORD METHODS OR CONTEXTUAL GUESSING BUILD FLUENCY?

Children struggling with text, solving words one by one, are plodding through texts, and their laborious reading pays poor dividends in learning. Historically, two popular methods have been advanced for helping readers gain fluency. One solution was to teach children words by a visual whole-word method, an idea that goes back to Horace Mann (Adams, 1990). Mann's idea for reading reform was to eliminate phonics for beginning readers in favor of learning whole, meaningful words. He believed learning whole words would allow beginners to read like adults. Thus, according to Mann's theory, learning words by a whole-word, visual method would help students become fluent faster.

The other solution, notably advanced by Ken Goodman (1967), was to teach young readers to use context clues in a "psycholinguistic guessing game" to replace decoding. Goodman thought beginners should use semantic context (meaning information from the story or from background knowledge) and syntactic context (the grammar of the sentence) to identify unfamiliar words. As a last resort, the reader might use "graphophonic cues" by decoding initial consonants as supplementary information for word identification (see Figure 1). According to Goodman, better contextual guessing would make reading easier and more fluent. Thus, we have two claims about the way young readers build reading fluency. Would learning words by a whole-word method make reading easier? Or would learning to predict words from context help students become fluent faster? We will examine these two claims to determine whether either way would provide a clear path to reading fluency.

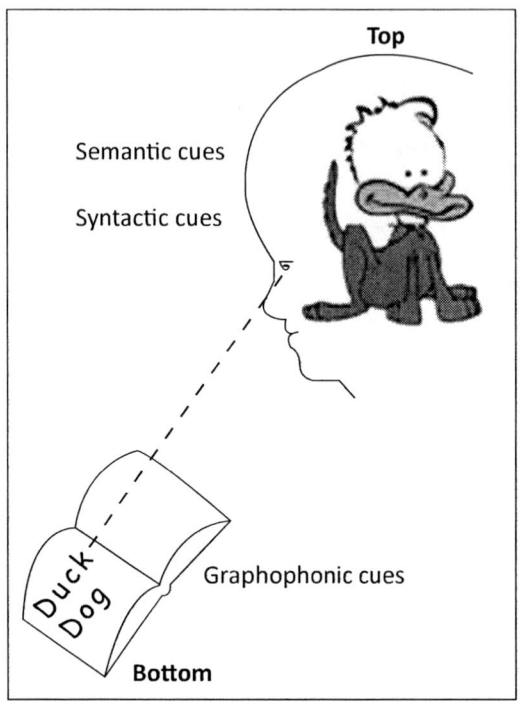

FIGURE 1: Reading as a psycholinguistic guessing game

THE WHOLE-WORD METHOD

First, let's consider Horace Mann's claim that learning words by a whole-word method would improve reading fluency. It is certainly true that gaining an extensive sight-word vocabulary is vital in skilled reading. Decoding word by word crowds out capacity so that the reader quickly runs out of working memory and stops comprehending. Skilled readers rarely decode words; probably 99.9% of the words we read as skilled adults are sight words, including rare words like *hyperventilate* and *colloquialism*. When word recognition is effortless and automatic, we can devote all our cognitive resources to getting the message of text. Unquestionably, we want beginners to stop decoding most words and switch over to sight recognition. Skilled readers develop a sight vocabulary in the range of 100,000 words—a rough estimate of the number of different words read through elementary and secondary school (Nagy & Anderson, 1984).

Mann's ideas become implausible in considering *how* we acquire such a vast sight vocabulary. Can we acquire any sizable number of sight words by whole-word methods, i.e., by learning words as visual shapes or as memorized letter strings? Figure 2 presents a text as it might look to a novice learner without decoding ability. We can use such an image to simulate the process of learning to read using a whole word method. Could you learn to read this text by reading?

$$¢¿\# \ \$ \ \pm\wedge \ +?$$
$$\#¿\infty\$\sqrt{?} \ ¢\}\approx\%, \ ''*¿¿\&, \ *¿¿\&.$$
$$¢\sqrt{\sqrt{}} \ \infty\$\approx¢.''$$
$$''¿\$, \ ¿\$,'' \ ¢\}\approx\% \ ¢\}**\neq.$$
$$''\approx\infty \ \approx¢ \ +?\sqrt{}\infty\infty\infty\neq.''$$

FIGURE 2: Text for simulating learning to read

Could you learn to read it by having it read aloud to you? Most likely, it would require tedious drill with dozens of trials to remember each word. For example, the word *¿¿& is *look*, and the word ¢}≈% is *said*[11]. Imagine the toil of remembering each of these strange shapes without knowledge of the alphabetic code that makes spellings into meaningful pronunciation maps. The whole word method poses an enormous memory burden to young children who have not learned the alphabetic code. As Gates (1931) recognized, learning each word would take an average of 35 trials. If the 100,000 word sight vocabulary typical of adult reading were learned by this method, the beginner would face a prohibitive 3,500,000 practice trials.

Content Words are Infrequent

Surprisingly, we rarely encounter most words 35 times in an entire year of reading. While function words such as *the, a, of, is, that, to, and,* and *in* appear with high frequency in texts, it is rare to find content words repeated even 5 times in a primary-grade text, and over a third appear only once (Jorm & Share, 1983). Many words whose meanings are quite familiar to children are relatively uncommon in print. For example, the words *arrow, mice, flour, pump, parade, noisy, choir, jazz,* and *fur* appear on average only once in 100,000 words of text (Carroll, Davies, & Richman, 1971), which is about a month of reading for the average fifth grader. Given that these words are seen only about once a month, it would take several years before

---

1   The complete text is titled "Something Pretty," and it reads, "Mother said, 'Look, look. See this.' 'Oh, oh, said Sally. 'It is pretty.'"

readers could learn these words if learning a word required 35 encounters in text. And if we engineered text to get a deliberate repetition of these words, as in *Fun With Dick and Jane*, we would be giving readers a diet of deadly dull text with stilted and unnatural language.

Efficient Word Learning

Fortunately, readers who have learned the alphabetic code don't require 35 encounters to learn a word. They can acquire new sight words in only a few trials by the sight-word processes of decoding, crosschecking, mental marking, and rereading. For example, if a full alphabetic reader decodes *listen*, he might initially come up with "liss-ten." Completing the sentence "Listen to our song" provides contextual information so that the reader can crosscheck to recognize *listen*, which in turn allows him to mentally mark the *t* as silent. Rereading the sentence begins to secure the new word in memory, which requires only about 4 practice trials (Reitsma, 1983). These sight-word processes record the annotated spelling *listen* in memory as a meaningful pronunciation map for instant recognition when *listen* is encountered in reading.

Ehri calls this sight-word process *amalgamation*, by analogy with the bonding of metals into alloys (Ehri & Soffer, 1999). To amalgamate words, readers bind each letter in the spelling to a phoneme in the pronunciation (or mentally mark it as irregular), until the spelling and pronunciation are inseparable. Once the spelling begins to "look like" the pronunciation, the reader can make an automatic match between the stored spelling and the printed word—it becomes a sight word. As evidence, Ehri (1980) asked young readers to learn to read pseudowords with ambiguous spellings. For example, one group learned a pseudoword spelled *sney* while another group learned it as *sneigh*. Later, when Ehri asked the readers to spell the pseudoword, they included the odd letters *y* or *g* in their spellings, depending on which spelling they had received. Readers had mentally marked these letters in representing the pseudoword in memory.

From Whole Words to Literature?

To be fair, Horace Mann did not envision learning whole words by drill, whether on flash cards or in stilted text. However, without repetitive practice, the problem of learning whole words without decoding, crosschecking, and mental marking defies solution. If we want children to read whole, meaningful texts, they have to read the words in those texts because texts are made of words. Reading the wonderful stories of children's literature entails frustration and drudgery for children who haven't built up a large sight vocabulary, particularly when they lack the decoding tools to make sight words. Ironically, the fastest route to enjoying children's literature is to develop decoding knowledge and skill in a code-emphasis program.

Blouke Carus was a German publisher who immigrated into the Chicago area in the 1960s. Carus began looking for a school for his children where they read children's literature like Aesop's Fables. However, every school he contacted was using the bestselling Dick and Jane readers from Scott-Foresman, which featured charming characters, beautiful illustrations, funny stories, but inane texts with tough words. Carus decided to publish his own series, which he would call Open Court. When he enlisted the help of Richard Venezky, Carl Bereiter, and other reading researchers to develop the program, they told him that getting children into literature quickly would require explicit, systematic phonics and practice in decodable texts. The original program took the unconventional step of beginning with long vowels, which for all their spelling complications, represented easy phonemes. Figure 3 provides a sample of an early Open Court text designed around long vowels. The Open Court programs never made much money, although they have survived. Principals and reading teachers looked at the high level literary texts and said, "Our children will never be able to read this in first grade." However, with a clear introduction to phoneme awareness, with explicit, systematic phonics, and with practice in decodable text, a basal series can rapidly expand the pool of words to present engaging stories as children master correspondences and build sight words and sight chunks. I found this to be true when I taught my own children at age four to read with Open Court materials.

The Two Crows and the Snail

A crow tried to open a snail to eat it. He hit it with his beak. He bit it. He kicked it. It still didn't split.

Another crow came by. She played a sly trick.

"Fly high with the snail," she said, "and open your beak. If the snail hits the road, it will split. I'll wait here to see."

The first crow flew high and opened his beak. The snail hit the road and split.

The other crow came and ate the snail.

FIGURE 3: An Aesop fable written as decodable text

GUESSING WORDS FROM CONTEXT

Ken Goodman (1967) thought he'd found a solution to gaining fluency without decoding. Goodman argued that predicting words from context in a "psycholinguistic guessing game" would help children become fluent readers faster. That idea fits well with the emergent literacy view that learning to read is easy and natural, so that we learn to read by reading. However, the facts reviewed in Chapter 5 of this book demonstrate that reading only *seems* to emerge naturally when instruction in school has been preceded by some 3000 hours of family literacy experiences ranging from daily read-alouds to informal instruction in letter recognition and phonological awareness. That kind of preschool literacy experience is rare in low SES homes.

Of course, contextual guessing sometimes works as a way to recognize words. However, guessing is more likely to work with common function words than with content words, which are much less common and harder to predict. For example, in the following sentence from *The Great Gilly Hopkins* (Paterson, 1978), the common words in boldface type are fairly easy to guess in context:

> **I am** sorry **to** bother **you with my** problems, **but as my** real mother, **I** feel **you have a** right **to** know **about your** daughter's situation.

However, those words act as semantic "glue" and supply little meaning of their own. Without the content words, they tell us little or nothing:

> I am ... to ... you with my ... but as my ... I ... you have a ... to ... about your ....

In contrast, the unpredictable content words convey quite a bit of the message, albeit in broken English:

> ... sorry ... bother ... problems ... real mother ... feel ... right ... know ... daughter's situation.

These examples demonstrate that we can guess common function words, but they don't reveal the message. They are like the glue that remains on a child's art project when all the colorful shapes have fallen off into her backpack. The rare content words are very hard to guess, and they are essential to getting the message in texts.

Because contextual guessing is unreliable and drains resources needed for comprehension, beginners who learn more reliable strategies for recognizing words—decoding, using pronounceable word parts, analogizing, and recognizing sight words—stop guessing at words. Guessing only persists with less skilled readers who use partial alphabetic strategies, sounding out consonants for phonetic cues. Full alphabetic readers encountering an unfamiliar word (e.g., *wrestle*) decode to come up with an approximate pronunciation ("wuh-ress-tul?"), finish reading the sentence to crosscheck ("The boys wuh-ress-tul at recess? Oh, *wrestle!*"), mentally mark odd letters (*wrestle*), and then reread to regain the message of the story, thereby further securing the word in memory ("The boys *wrestle* at recess").

Influence of Practice Texts

The books we give beginners to read influence whether they use guessing or decoding strategies. Predictable books like *Brown Bear, Brown Bear, What Do You*

See? (Martin & Carle, 1967) encourage guessing by providing easy sentence patterns, helpful illustrations, and words much too difficult for readers not yet adept at decoding. Predictable books are valuable for prealphabetic readers because they are the only books these children can read successfully. Reciting predictable books helps prealphabetic beginners learn the syntax and vocabulary of books as well as the delights of rhythm and rhyme. Experiences with predictable books provide opportunities for learn concepts about print, including the important vocabulary of *letters*, *words*, and *sentences*. However, reading predictable books does not help novice readers learn to read words unless teachers direct their attention to print. For example, prealphabetic readers who are taught to fingerpoint the words in a predictable text (i.e., to touch each word as it is read) learn to use letters as phonetic cues (Ehri & Sweet, 1991), a key strategy of the partial alphabetic phase.

The question of whether to use predictable books with partial alphabetic readers continues to be debated. We know children cannot learn sight words without decoding, and predictable books do not require children even to look at the words, much less decode them. Predictable books invite young readers to use a cued-recitation strategy, i.e., reciting the rhythmic and rhyming patterns by cuing on illustrations rather than by reading words. To learn to make sight words, however, partial alphabetic readers must begin to decode complete spellings, crosscheck to correct near-misses, mentally mark irregular letters, and reread to secure the annotated spelling in memory.

The best practice for developing decoding skill is to work through a series of decodable books in which the words are carefully engineered to be easy enough to decode using learned correspondences (Juel & Roper/Schneider, 1985). With decodable books, the decoding strategies learned in phonics work to unlock the words of the story. As young readers develop a well-stocked correspondence toolkit and a growing vocabulary of sight words and sight chunks, they acquire enough crosschecking and mental marking ability to allow passage into literary and informational texts at the reader's instructional level.

Reducing Predictability

Some predictable series begin with tightly patterned language fully supported with illustrations, and gradually introduce less predictable elements. For example, an early book from Dominie Press is titled *I Can Draw* (Klein, 1996):

> I have a red crayon. I can draw a red flower.
> I have a blue crayon. I can draw a blue flower.
> I have a green crayon. I can draw a green flower . . .

A later book in the series, *The Balloon* (Arrendo, 1997), requires more varied sentence completions:

> I can be fun to play with.
> I can be big. I can be small.
> I can be round. I can be different shapes.

The idea of gradually withdrawing predictability has some surface plausibility, but it increases word recognition burdens without helping children develop the decoding tools to shoulder those burdens. Easy texts for recitation become frustrating texts full of difficult words.

A better solution is to introduce very easy decodable text, such as in *A Cat Nap* (Cushman, 1990a) from Educational Insights, in which content words use only short *a*:

> Tab is a fat cat. Tab naps in a bag. Tab naps and naps.

Later books in the series, such as *Rube and the Tube* (Cushman, 1990b), use an expanding pool of words built from a much larger set of correspondences to create more interesting stories with more natural language while still maintaining decodability:

> Meet Duke. He sells tubes. Kids use the tubes at the sea.

Rather than pulling the predictability rug out from under children, it is more reasonable to expand the vocabulary of decodable words to the point at which children can be weened from engineered decodable texts and introduced to early literary and informational books—such as the Aesop's fables published by Blouke Carus in Open Court.

Evaluating Guessing Game Theory

Is reading a psycholinguistic guessing game with three cuing systems that can be improved with better guessing skill? In the era of emergent literacy, it was widely believed that skilled readers orchestrate semantic, syntactic, and graphophonic cues in order to read words. The notion of orchestrating a chorus of cues is certainly appealing. However, skilled readers do not take such a circuitous route. They recognize most words from spellings stored in memory for sight recognition. When they encounter unfamiliar words, they make them into sight words by decoding, crosschecking, mental marking, and rereading to store accurate spellings in memory. Only poor readers persist in contextual guessing—to compensate for inefficient decoding. Thus, the psycholinguistic guessing game is not tenable as a way to reading fluency. We want beginners to *know* the words they encounter, not to guess them.

FLUENCY THROUGH DECODING

Our analysis has discredited the whole-word method and contextual guessing as a solution to the problem of fluency. That leaves decoding, which begins as slow, laborious problem-solving. While decoding may seem an unlikely basis for fluency, learning to decode is the critical attainment for building sight vocabulary. As in learning any skill, developing accuracy is necessary for gaining automaticity.

It is easy to underestimate the benefits of learning to decode. The full alphabetic reader can learn words independently of teachers and parents using decoding as a self-teaching strategy. Decoding in combination with crosschecking, mental marking, and rereading brings rapid growth in sight word knowledge, which in turn frees up cognitive resources for reading comprehension. Not only does the reader gain sight words, but he also builds a growing store of sight chunks for tackling polysyllabic words. Decoding, crosschecking, and mentally marking pronounceable word parts like *pneu, mono, ultra,* and *micro* prepares the reader for reading such prodigious words as:

pneumonoultramicroscopicsilicovolcanoconiosis

If we can read this sesquipedalian name of a lung disease caused by breathing volcanic dust, we can read virtually any word, and such boundless word-reading skill ultimately depends on decoding.

In moving from the prealphabetic phase to the full alphabetic phase, does reading get easier? If we use predictable texts with prealphabic readers and decodable texts with full alphabetic readers, we have to admit that initially, reading gets harder, not easier. Beginners lose the easy recitation method that works with predictable text in taking on the challenge of decodable books. When each new word is a problem to solve, finishing a single story can be a daunting task, and there are tens of thousands of words to make into sight words by decoding, crosschecking, mental marking, and rereading before reading gets easy. To make reading easy, readers need an enormous sight vocabulary for automatic word recognition and to use in analogizing. In addition, they need a huge sight chunk vocabulary of pronounceable word parts for efficient processing of polysyllabic words.

How do we help full alphabetic word-by-word readers become fluent readers? First, we support and encourage them as they weather the difficult season of full alphabetic decoding. Decoding can be tedious, but it is a necessary step toward sight word recognition. Second, we supply novice readers with decodable texts matched to their current vowel knowledge. More advanced readers ready to move into the more natural vocabulary of literary and informational text still need instructional level text—in which they can recognize 95-98% of the words both in accurate pronunciation and in accessible meaning. Third, we guide readers to reread the sentence whenever they struggle to identify a word. Rereading sentences not only helps the reader secure a newly recognized word in memory as sight vocabulary, but also it helps him re-engage with the story. Fourth, we guide students to reread complete texts to master the material before moving on. Repeated reading of texts offers a direct route to fluency by helping readers rapidly build sight vocabulary (see Practical Chapter 7 on the best ways to arrange repeated reading practice). Finally, we encourage voluntary reading to promote the avid level of independent reading necessary to add a significant proportion of the 100,000 English words encountered from preschool to high school into sight vocabulary.

THE INDIRECT APPROACH TO FLUENCY: VOLUNTARY READING

Ultimately, readers must take an active interest in reading to undertake a volume of reading that will build a significant sight vocabulary for reading fluency. Reading voluntarily and avidly involves readers in the kind of self-teaching that enriches meaning vocabulary, builds conceptual knowledge, improves reading comprehension, and enhances verbal intelligence (Stanovich, 1986). Chapter 5 explained the Matthew effects model, which recognizes a central role for avid reading practice as the doorway to the riches of reading. Given the importance of developing enthusiastic reading practice, an important goal for reading teachers is to encourage students to read voluntarily and avidly—not just in assigned texts, but in texts they choose to read.

If students need plenty of reading practice, teachers might assign reading as homework. However, it is doubtful that under most circumstances, assigned reading would evolve into a passionate interest in reading. For this reason, we have to question the widespread recommendation that students be assigned to read for 20 minutes per day, and have parents sign off to verify this reading. Under such a regimen, students may be watching the clock instead of engaging seriously with the text, and parents can hardly be expected to serve as vigilant timekeepers—given their own evening activities.

Reading Motivation at Benchmark

It would be a mistake to categorically rule out any reading homework. At Benchmark, a private school for readers with learning disabilities, teachers assign daily reading homework, but they organize the homework around reading choices, book restrictions, and motivating activities (Pressley, Gaskins, Solic, & Collins, 2006). Students visit the school library daily to find good books and to return books when they have lost interest. Students are restricted to books they can read at an independent level of 99-100% accuracy; to this end, the books are coded with colored tape by reading level. Students check out an average of 4-5 books per day and read some 600 books per year. Readers have opportunities each day to tell classmates about what they are reading; which means they must comprehend what they are reading, to have something to say. Daily book sharing allows children to learn about good books from peers as well as teachers.

The success of Benchmark in motivating unusual reading practice for powerful positive Matthew effects shows that reading homework can be effective if it is planned well. First, effective teachers arrange for student choice—a crucial motivating factor in voluntary reading. Second, to make choice accessible, students need frequent and, if possible, daily visits to an extensive school library, supplemented by well-stocked classroom libraries. It takes time to discover the good books, and students need daily opportunities to correct their mistakes when they make poor choices. Third, children need guidance to choose easy books at their independent levels. Instructional-level texts are not appropriate for reading homework because in all likelihood, no teacher will be home for instruction. Fourth, effective teachers cultivate readers' interest with read alouds and booktalks. As explained in Practical Chapter 1, an effective booktalk introduces characters in their ordinary situation and then explains how a problem arises that sends the character in search of a solution. Booktalks that focus exclusively on the problem leave listeners curious about how or whether a solution can be found. Fifth, successful teachers arrange peer discussions to find out about good books others have discovered and to motivate engaged reading. Students in regular book discussion groups have to read in order to have something to say to peers.

Summer Reading Lists?

The practice of assigning summer reading is widespread, especially in private schools and affluent public school districts. However, given the motivational discoveries at Benchmark, the way summer reading is typically assigned tends to be ineffective. Summer reading lists often prescribe difficult instructional or frustration level texts rather than the easy books appropriate for independent reading. They assign the books that *must* be read rather than allowing student choice. Teachers rarely supply motivating booktalks to create interest in reading the books, and they impose an external reading purpose such as writing a book report or taking a test. Imposing onerous adjunct tasks for reading works against engaged, aesthetic reading.

However, there is no reason that summer reading assignments can't be redesigned to take advantage of the factors that motivate reading engagement. Summer reading lists could be composed of easy, independent-level books rather than difficult literature classics. Different lists could be distributed to students reading at different levels to ensure that every student has choices he can read successfully on his own. Students could be given choices to read; e.g., 5 books from a list of 20 choices. Teachers could give booktalks on all the choices during the closing weeks of spring semester. A highly conscientious teacher might invite students by e-mail to meet in the library on the first Saturday each month to reevaluate their choices and to find new books to replace those readers found disappointing. Although it's necessary to find some means of assessing whether books were actually read, students might give evidence of their reading success by passing a brief test on the computer. Rather than writing book reports, they could participate in book discussions that would invite further reading in response to the positive comments of their peers.

Verifying Reading

How can we find out if students have read, without piling on the burden of a book report? We can invite students to compose brief book reviews to tell others about the books they've read. Their reviews could be composed on cards with stoplight color-coding to provide an immediate overall evaluation: Green cards mean "go for it"; yellow cards mean "caution—not everyone will like this book"; red cards mean "stop, don't bother." In classrooms equipped with computer technology, students can post electronic reviews on the web. A class website might show photos of each student, so that clicking the photo would display scans of books jackets or illustrations, and clicking an illustration would open a review.

One of the most useful commercial reading programs is Accelerated Reader, which has compiled more than 140,000 brief quizzes (typically 10 questions) that assess a vast library of children's books. The quizzes are administered electronically on computer, and they provide immediate feedback on whether a passing score has been attained. In my experience, the quizzes probe an appropriate level of detail and cannot be passed using test-taking skills. I was unable to pass the quiz on *Clifford's First Christmas* (Bridwell, 1994), a book I hadn't read, despite multiple attempts. However, after reading *Dear Mr. Henshaw* (Cleary, 1983), I had no trouble answering all 10 questions correctly. My informal investigation suggests that the quizzes reliably separate those who have read with comprehension from those who have not.

Reading Incentives

Many teachers hope to influence voluntary reading by creating reading incentive programs. Students can read books to purchase items in a school store, to win an opportunity for special events such as parties or field trips, or to arrange a self-effacing challenge from the principal, e.g., to shave his head. The popular Book-It program from Pizza Hut arranges for children who read books to eat pizza. Such programs clearly ramp up reading as long as the rewards are offered. However, there is no evidence that incentive programs cause a general improvement in reading attitudes, achievement, or habits (McQuillan, 1997). In fact, tangible rewards may even discourage reading in the long run by defining reading as work rather than an end in itself. Schwartz (1982, p. 53) observed that in a classroom with tangible incentives for reading:

> The rate of book reading increased astronomically . . . . But the system had other effects. It changed the pattern of book selection (short books with large print became ideal). It also seemed to change the way children read. They were often unable to answer straightforward questions about a book, even one they had just finished reading.

Some of the negative influences of tangible incentives for reading can be reduced by making incentives intangible. Students can win recognitions, such as reading ranks, e.g, working their way from Hufflepuff, to Ravenclaw, to Slytherin, and finally to Gryffindor (Rowling, 1997). They might win a special chance to read, e.g., an invitation to a reading sleepover at school. Teachers might also recognize reading by giving books, a unique kind of tangible reward that defines reading itself as the reward for reading.

If teachers do arrange an incentive program for reading, they should think carefully about how to measure reading achievement for a fair competition. Counting the number of books would encourage students to read short books with large print.

Counting the amount of reading time would encourage clock watching rather than comprehension. We might equalize the reading of students at different levels by counting the number of pages read to discount the value of reading short books. But given the current choices, the high-tech solution offered by Accelerated Reader may be the best option. In Accelerated Reader, the number of points to be awarded depends on book difficulty, and conscientious teachers can disallow any books well below a student's reading level. Only books actually read, resulting in sufficient understanding to pass the brief, well-constructed quizzes, count toward the reward.

Sustained Silent Reading

Teachers have long believed that sustained silent reading (SSR) programs provide a useful way to promote voluntary reading. These programs may be called "drop everything and read" (DEAR) or "super quiet reading time" (SQUIRT), but the rationale is to give students a daily opportunity to read in class. SSR promoters reason that children need time to discover the pleasures of reading, and that independent reading is so important as to merit the investment of classroom time. What children read is strictly their choice: Anything that keeps them interested during the SSR period is eligible. In SSR, everyone reads, including the teacher, whose engaged reading is supposed to demonstrate avid reading for students. There are no tests, no reports, and no grades associated with SSR. When the reading time is over, students return to their regular classroom work.

One of the most newsworthy findings of the National Reading Panel Report (2000) was that SSR programs do not reliably improve fluency. The NRP examined the results of 18 experimental studies of SSR, and the general finding was that SSR had no measurable effect on reading volume, reading comprehension, or attitudes toward reading. However, one large-scale study (Manning & Manning, 1984) showed that SSR could have promising results under the right conditions. The researchers studied fourth graders in 24 classrooms randomly assigned to one of four treatments, with 6 classrooms in each treatment. One group, the control group, continued with their regular classroom work rather than participating in SSR. The other three groups participated in SSR. One group carried out SSR as described above. In another group, teachers arranged regular individual conferences with SSR readers to talk about what they were reading. In a third SSR group, teachers arranged peer discussions so that children talked about what they were reading with other students. Consistent with the dismal overall results of SSR, the standard SSR program had no better effect on reading attitudes, reading achievement, or voluntary reading than in the control group without SSR. However, both the groups that included conferences improved attitudes toward reading, and the group that arranged peer conferences also showed significant improvement in reading comprehension. These positive results suggest that the combination of SSR with peer discussions improves reading.

We can speculate why peer discussions as a supplement to SSR boosted reading where teacher conferences did not. Peer discussions were likely more motivating for voluntary reading practice than teacher conferences. With peer discussions, readers get recommendations they more readily take seriously. For example, while the teacher may recommend some classic work like *Anne of Green Gables* (Montgomery, 1908), a peer may recommend something much more accessible and tantalizing, such as a tale from the *Goosebumps* series by R.L. Stine. In addition, there is a peer-pressure factor in peer discussions. Students have to actually read to participate in book discussions. Accordingly, they have a natural incentive to read to comprehend in order to have something to say to their clasmates. Wilson (1992, p. 163) sees this peer pressure factor as critical to motivating children to read:

> Reading becomes something that students do because of friendship, because their friends read. Reading becomes part of the culture of the classroom.

A classroom where children are engaged in daily reading to participate in literary conversations with their friends is an ideal community for fostering voluntary reading.

Why doesn't the standard SSR program improve reading? When SSR remains an isolated activity, a reader has no one to share the story world found in books. Unless the reader has already developed internal motivation to read, standard SSR provides no social stimulus to read, and accordingly, no gain in voluntary reading practice. In addition, SSR costs valuable instructional time, which is a precious resource teachers can't afford to squander. Classrooms that forgo SSR retain this block of time to teach reading strategies, introduce vocabulary, or provide guided reading in instructional level texts. This suggests that teachers who provide SSR time should use it at marginal times for explicit instruction, such as "bellwork" when students are arriving at in the morning, or just after lunch for a calming interlude after hard play. They should save their instructional prime time for explicit teaching.

A recent experiment in "scaffolded silent reading" with third graders (Reutzel, Fawson, & Smith, 2008) showed the promise of another SSR variation to overcome some of the shortcomings of SSR. In scaffolded silent reading, teachers confer with students to monitor their reading progress, and they guide them into book selections at an independent level appropriate for reading on their own. In a comparison with guided repeated reading, a technique well established for improving reading fluency (see Practical Chapter 7), the students in the scaffolded silent reading group made similar gains. This suggests that guided repeated reading can be used with a SSR variant that involves teacher or peer conferences to improve reading fluency.

Book Selection

Without adult guidance, young readers typically make hasty book choices based on cover illustrations. In contrast, avid readers are quite choosy in the books they select (Wilson, 1992, p. 164). In a bookstore or library, they browse at least five books for each book chosen. They know their reading interests and favorite authors. Avid readers like me will read everything written by a favorite author; I recently read every book written by Brian Jacques, creator of the imaginary world of Redwall, where heroic animals do battle with evil vermin to save their abbey. Part of an avid reader's browsing strategy is to sample the text to decide if the book is accessible and interesting. Avid readers do not complete every book they start; they are not averse to admitting they've made a poor choice and resuming the search for a good read.

From the book selection practices of avid readers, we can develop ideas for helping young readers make better book choices. Children need introductions to books by teacher booktalks, read alouds, and peer discussions. Besides learning about good books in these ways, teachers and parents need to monitor children's book selections to make sure they are reading on an independent level. A popular benchmark for book selection is the "five-finger test," in which children raise a finger for each word they don't know; if five fingers come up within a single page, the book is too hard. However, the five-finger test miscalculates the independent level. We need a *two*-finger test for the independent level. Assuming 100 words on a page, if young readers encounter even *two* words they don't know (i.e., 2% miscues), that book is probably too difficult for independent reading.

In the effort to get children to read voluntarily, widely, and avidly, it is a mistake to urge them to read high quality children's literature on their own. The transcendent works of children's literature, if written at the instructional level of a reading group, should be read under the guidance of a teacher, with strong scaffolding before, during, and after reading. If a literary work is written beyond the reader's instructional level, it can be read aloud by the teacher, and supplemented with explanations and discussions that allow students to vicariously experience the work. For independent reading, quantity is more important than quality. Easy-access books, page-turners, and series books are ideal for promoting reading fluency. Some series I've enjoyed include the *Harry Potter* books, the Lemony Snicket *Series of Unfortunate Events*, the *Redwall* books by Brian Jacques, the *Beezus and Ramona* books by Beverly Cleary, and C. S. Lewis's *Chronicles of Narnia*. Readers who have started series like these find easy access to the next books, given that they are well acquainted with the characters and situations from previous reading.

SUMMARY

Fluent reading is reading with automatic word recognition. We can think of fluency as specific to a particular text, so that all or most of the words in that text are represented in the reader's sight vocabulary. Readers have general reading fluency when their sight vocabularys are so large as to encompass most words used across a wide range of literary and general informational text. Becoming a fluent reader speeds up reading, improves reading comprehension, allows expressive, prosodic oral reading, and removes impediments to avid reading. The critical path to achieving fluency is building sight vocabulary through the processes of decoding, crosschecking, mental marking, and rereading.

Popular views of fluency have tended to focus on the results of fluency rather than on its cause: developing an extensive sight vocabulary. The misconception of fluency as reading speed has led teachers to direct children in speed-reading practice that discounts reading comprehension. This misplaced emphasis has had negative effects on fluency and reading motivation. Assessing reading fluency must include a check for reading comprehension because getting the message of the text shows that word recognition is automatic. Fluency improves only when repeated readings recycle the same words—evidence that fluency depends on enlarging the reader's sight vocabulary.

Historically, two ineffective solutions have been advanced for improving reading fluency: teaching reading by a visual whole-word method and teaching beginners to attend more closely to semantic and syntactic context during reading. Whole word methods fail to supply an efficient means of learning the estimated 100,000 sight words need for general fluency in English. Most of the different words we need to learn are relatively uncommon in print so that we do not see them in frequencies where whole word memorization is possible. The view of sight-word learning in this book is based on Ehri's amalgamation theory, which shows that drill and repetition are unnecessary for learning sight words. In Ehri's model, we make sight words by a process that begins with decoding to bond the letters in the spelling to phonemes in the pronunciation. If decoding fails, we correct a near-miss with crosschecking, mentally mark any unexpected letters, and store the annotated spelling in memory for an instant match in reading. With explicit and systematic instruction in phoneme awareness and phonics, children acquire the tools to move rapidly through a decodable series, and with a growing correspondence toolkit and crosschecking skills, the path from simple texts to children's literature is readily negotiable.

While the claim that reading fluency depends on developing skill in a psycholinguistic guessing game has been popular, there are rarely enough clues to guess the content words in texts. For this reason, young readers developing decoding skill rarely use context to guess at words; guessing characterizes the ineffective strategies of younger and less-skilled readers. In leading beginners to more efficient word-learning strategies that depend on decoding, it is important that they receive the phonics instruction that teaches decoding and that they practice in decodable, rather than predictable text. Predictable texts allow a cued recitation strategy that circumvents the task of reading printed words. Reducing the predictability of the text cannot make a way from predictable books to children's literature because eliminating the patterned language takes away the only effective reading strategy available to novice readers. The alternative is to use a decodable series that expands the available pool of words by systematically adding vowel correspondences; this eventually allows a relaxation of decodability strictures. Readers who can supplement decoding with crosschecking can navigate successfully through early literature.

Decoding allows young readers to learn words independently by self-teaching. When readers decode, crosscheck, and mentally mark irregular letters, they rapidly build a reading vocabulary that includes sight chunks for increased efficiency in word learning. Sight chunk knowledge allows progress into reading polysyllabic words—the final frontier for word recognition. Ironically, the key development for rapid sight-word learning is decoding. Thus, effective help for struggling readers begins with encouraging their work during the frustrating full alphabetic phase and supplying them with decodable text so that their decoding efforts can be successful. Rereading is crucial for building sight vocabulary, whether at the sentence level or in repeated reading of texts. Ultimately, the development of reading fluency depends on acquiring the habits, attitudes, and interests of avid readers.

Leading readers into the voluntary practice of voracious reading is a key goal of reading instruction. Discoveries at Benchmark School indicate that reading homework can be productive if it is arranged carefully. Students must choose their own books for independent reading, and making good choices depends on frequent library visits (daily if possible), guidance choosing books at an independent level, and teacher booktalks that develop interest by highlighting the problem without revealing the plot. The motivating consequences of talking with peers about books also promote voluntary reading. While summer reading lists typically do not take advantage of these motivational arrangements, summer reading homework could be enhanced with better methods: (1) restricting selections to easy, independent-level books; (2) allowing students to choose from among recommended books; (3) giving booktalks to entice students to read; (4) arranging optional library visits for book choice corrections; (5) assessing reading using easy quizzes accessible by computer; and (6) organizing book discussions in lieu of book reports. Readers can demonstrate their successful reading with brief, color-coded book reviews, by reviews posted on websites, or with the useful technology of Accelerated Reader.

Although incentive plans are popular for inducing voluntary reading, they tend to be effective only as long as the rewards continue. Providing recognition rather than rewards, offering reading opportunities as prizes, or giving books as rewards for reading—all these moves counter the inadvertent negative incentives of giving tangible rewards. In measuring voluntary reading, teachers should consider the number of pages read or the accumulation of points with Accelerated Reader, in preference to counting the number of books read or the amount of reading time.

Sustained silent reading (SSR) has not been found to improve children's interest in voluntary reading, attitudes toward reading, or reading fluency. However, one promising study showed that SSR can be productive when coupled with peer book discussion. Peer discussions provide recommendations students take seriously, and regular discussions provide peer pressure to read to be able to participate. SSR programs that lack peer interaction do not provide such motivation to read, and they cost valuable instructional time without providing learning outcomes comparable to instruction. In lieu of peer discussion, SSR may be more productive as scaffolded silent reading, where teachers confer regularly with students and guide them in choosing independent-level books.

Teachers can capitalize on the strategies of avid readers in helping children choose books. They can help children learn about good books with booktalks, read alouds, and book discussions, and they can monitor children's selections to keep outside reading easy enough to proceed without instruction. The two-finger test, restricting book choices to books in which children can read with fewer than two unsolved words per page, is helpful in arranging successful independent reading. Book series are especially valuable for independent reading because after gaining a foothold in the first book, readers gain access to successive books with the same characters and similar situations.

Developing Word Recognition Through Spelling

Early childhood educator Maria Montesori (1966) famously said children should "write first and read later." This is sound advice because there is good evidence that early writing helps children learn to read. Children identified as preschool readers are commonly observed to invent spellings before they learn to read words. A key finding of the First Grade Studies (Bond & Dykstra, 1967) was that first-grade programs emphasizing daily writing activities lead to higher reading achievement. And how do we learn any code, e.g., Morse code? The usual procedure is to encode messages to build the knowledge for decoding them—to write first and read later.

Today, composing messages with invented spelling has become a staple kindergarten activity. Accordingly, teachers need some knowledge of how to decipher the strange-looking spellings young children may produce. One clue is that beginners treat letter names as sounds, e.g., YL for *while*, YNS for *once*, and MTN for *mitten*. Early spellings tend to lack vowels. When vowels begin to appear, long vowel phonemes, which sound like the familiar letter names, usually appear before short vowels, e.g., KAM for *came* and RAN for *rain*. To record short vowels, beginners typically choose the closest-sounding long vowel, e.g., BAD for *bed* or HET for *hit*. They omit vowels when recording the vowel-like liquids /l/ and /r/, e.g., KLR for *color* and GRL for *girl*. Nasals like /n/ and /m/ are omitted before stops, resulting in AD for *and* and WET for *went*. For a challenge, try your hand at reading the Rosie story from a beginning speller (Figure 1). Were you able to translate the wonderful invention in the last sentence, "APLEVAVTER"?

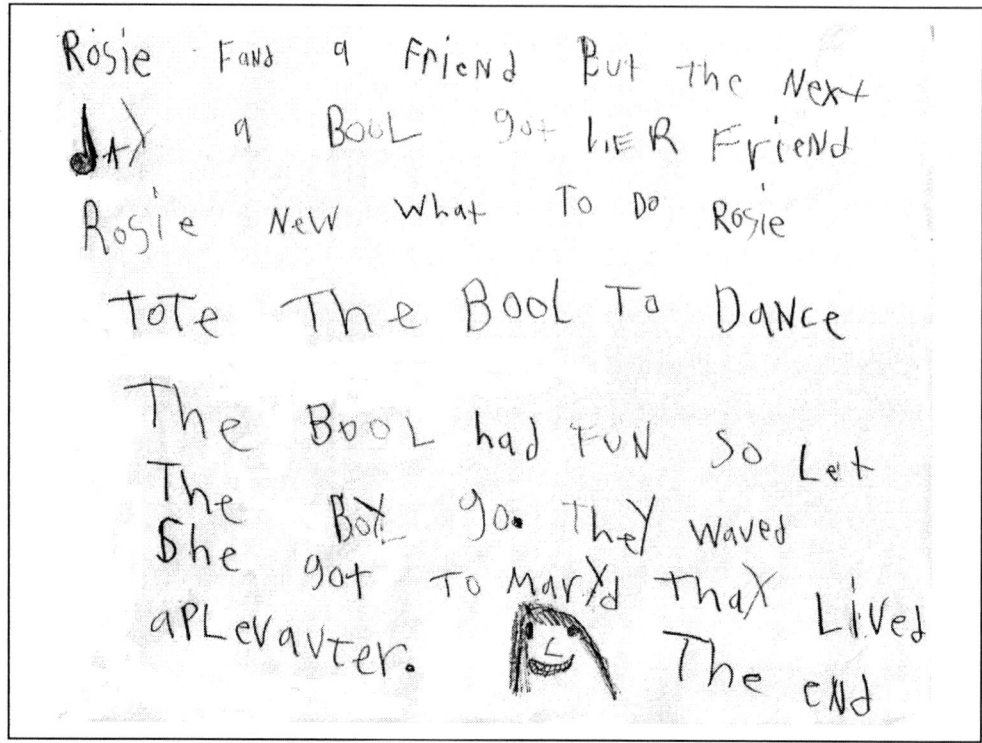

FIGURE 1: The Rosie story

SPELLING STAGES

Spelling typically develops in stages that parallel Ehri's (1998) phases of sight word learning. The most coherent scheme was formulated by Gentry and Gillet (1993), summarized in Figure 2.

In the prephonemic stage, there is no relation between the marks on the page and the phonemes in the word. Children may draw or scribble, but they don't have the idea of representing a word's pronunciation alphabetically. They show alphabetic insight in the semiphonemic stage, when they encode some phonemes, beginning with consonants. In semiphonemic spelling, children use letter names to represent sounds they detect in words, e.g., using the letter name *aitch* to approximate the /ch/ phoneme in *beach* as BH. Semiphonemic spellers often use phonetically related letters for phonemes, e.g., JV for *drive* to represent the sound of /d/ clustered with /r/. In the phonemic stage, spellers represent all the phonemes in words with actual or related letters, e.g., DRIV for *drive*. Phonemic spelling indicates well-developed phoneme awareness; the speller detects all the phonemes in spoken words and represents them with letters. Usually, the last phonemes encoded in spellings are short vowels and consonant clusters, both of which present extraordinary challenges to the development of phoneme awareness. In the transitional stage, young spellers build on their phonemic transcriptions of words by adding spelling conventions, e.g., marking long vowels with silent *e*, as in NIGTE, which also records the *g* mentally marked as silent during reading. The morpheme *ed* denoting past tense begins to appear whether it is pronounced /ud/ and in *folded,* /d/ as in *moved*, or /t/ as in *talked*. After spellers have stored so many accurate spellings that they rarely need to invent spellings—as is the case with readers of this book—they are in the standard spelling stage.

Stage	Characteristics
Prephonemic: Writers do not represent phonemes in spellings.	Scribbles, drawings, and mock letters. Random letters. Copied words and memorized spellings (MOM, DAD, I LOVE YOU).
Semi-phonemic: Writers use letters to represent some (but not all) of the phonemes in words.	Letter name spellings, e.g., YL (*while*), YNS (*once*), MTN (*mitten*). 1, 2, 3-letter spellings, usually omitting vowels, e.g., BH (*beach*). Phonetically related letters, e.g., JV (*drive*). Standard spellings for common words.
Phonemic: Writers record a letter for each phoneme in a word, omitting silent letters.	NIT (*night*), TIGR (*tiger*), THRU (*through*), DRIV (*drive*). Increased standard spellings of frequently used words.
Transitional: Writers build on phonemic spellings, adding conventions of standard spelling.	Records silent letters, e.g., NIGTE (*night*), TIGRE (*tiger*), THRUHG (*through*). Preserves morphemes, e.g., *ed* to mark past tense despite pronunciation differences as in WUNTED (*wanted*), MUVED (*moved*), TAWKED (*talked*). Most spellings still invented rather than recalled.
Standard: Writers remember most spellings rather than invent them.	More standard spellings than phonemic and transitional spellings.

FIGURE 2: Stages of spelling development (Gentry & Gillet, 1993)

Imagine the strategies a phonemic speller uses to invent a spelling, e.g., for *moose*. The first step is to stretch the word and sample the articulatory gestures in forming the spoken word. Next, the phonemic speller begins to transcribe the sequence of phonemes with related letters, perhaps *m* for /m/, *u* for /OO/, and *c* for /s/ using the letter name *cee*, producing MUC. This strategy might be termed phonemic transcription because the speller is transcribing the phonemes detected in the word.

Because invented spellers detect phonemes in spoken words and represent them with letters, invented spelling is excellent phoneme awareness practice.

CLARKE'S LANDMARK EXPERIMENT

If we look to science for public knowledge about teaching and learning, we have to be prepared to revise our preconceptions when they are refuted by contrary evidence. I thought allowing children to invent spellings would delay their understanding of the alphabetic code, and I was wrong. I changed my mind after reading about a landmark experiment by Linda Clarke (1988) in Canada. At a time when teachers were skeptical of invented spelling, Clarke persuaded two first-grade teachers to try invented spelling for the year, and compared them with two other first-grade teachers who preferred traditional spelling practices. All students wrote daily. In the experimental invented-spelling classes, the teachers nicely refused to provide spellings for children, telling them to sound out the words and print letters for the sounds they detected. In the traditional spelling classes, the teacher provided spellings by writing them down for children. Children in the traditional spelling group could also ask friends or consult word lists or picture dictionaries. Clarke collected and copied their daily writings, gave pretests and posttests of reading and spelling, and observed their writing behavior systematically, allowing accurate estimates of the percentage of time they spent writing, rereading, waiting for the teacher, talking with friends, etc.

Traditional spellers showed some advantages for their treatment. For example, they used more complex sentence structures and more sophisticated vocabulary in their writing. They could explore better language usage because they could ask and receive, which allowed them to try on new words (e.g., *locomotive*) learned in recent experiences to expand their writing vocabularies. Invented spellers, in contrast, tend to substitute simpler words (e.g., *train*) when spelling demands are formidable. A friend's son who was in a whole language class came home each day with another story about soccer. His dad was puzzled and asked him why, when he was interested in so many things, he always wrote about soccer. He said, "Dad, I know how to spell *soccer.*"

Traditional spellers made fewer spelling errors in their stories (because the teacher provided spellings), but their stories tended to be shorter than those of invented spellers. The observational data showed why: The traditional spellers spent 18% of their time—nearly 1 minute in 5—waiting for the teacher to give them spellings. They lost additional writing time searching for spellings in word lists and picture dictionaries or asking their neighbors for help.

Why Invented Spelling works

Invented spellers wrote longer stories because they quickly learned there was no point in asking the teacher for spellings. However, the more significant and surprising finding of Clarke's (1988) study was that at the end of the year, invented spellers tested higher in word recognition and spelling. The likely reason is that invented spelling practices phoneme awareness. Children who detect phonemes in spoken words are better able to encode them in spellings or to make sense of spellings in reading words.

Imagine an invented speller working on a story about riding the train at the zoo. His initial spelling for train might be HN, using the letter name *aitch* to represent the slightly distorted /t/ clustered with /r/. Later he notices the salient long vowel /A/ and revises his spelling to HAN. In a writing conference, he reads his draft (WE RD ON A HAN) to the teacher: "We rode on the train." The teacher responds, "I bet that was fun. We used to ride the train to my cousins' house in Illinois," and she writes the standard spelling *train* below HAN on the draft. On subsequent revisions, our invented speller remembers the initial letter *t* and begins to use the spelling TAN. But on rereading his work, /tAn/ doesn't sound quite right, and he alters it to TRAN. This final invented spelling captures all four phonemes in train and shows growing phoneme awareness by detecting and representing both phonemes in the *tr* cluster.

When Should Invented Spelling Stop?

The underreported result of the Clarke (1988) study was that invented spelling did not help everyone. The advantage of the experimental group came from low achieving beginners. High achieving students made equivalent gains whether spellings were provided or whether they had to invent them. If phoneme awareness gains are responsible for improved reading and spelling under a regimen of invented spelling, we can surmise that high achievers were already aware of phonemes, and thus, had nothing to gain by inventing spellings.

This helps us answer an important question: When should invented spelling stop? When are students ready to learn standard spellings rather than being pushed to invent spellings? After spellings are phonemic—that is, once children begin to represent all the phonemes in words—they have all the phoneme awareness they need to learn to read and spell words. Once their phonemic spellings indicate well-developed phoneme awareness, they are ready to learn standard spellings for words. At this point, there is no reason not to provide spellings when students ask for them. Providing spellings allows children to try on more sophisticated sentence structures, concepts, and vocabulary, allowing them to invest new language acquired in reading in their writing.

On the other hand, prephonemic and semiphonemic spellers should invent spellings rather than study standard spellings. These novice writers do not have well-developed phoneme awareness. If the teacher asks them what sound is in the middle of *cat*, they may think of a cat's purring rather than the phoneme /a/. Spellings remain meaningless without PA, and a spelling word appears as an arbitrary letter sequence that must be memorized. Given a list of spelling words to learn, they can only memorize them as adults memorize telephone numbers, by repetitive drill. Memorization is difficult and frustrating; it is a highly inefficient way to learn spellings. Invented spelling is vital for prephonemic and semiphonemic readers because developing PA helps them understand spellings and make sense of phonics. For example, if the teacher explains that the letter *a* says /a/, they can detect /a/ in *cat* and apply this decoding tool to begin to use the alphabet to read and spell words.

Maximizing the Benefits of Invented Spelling

Invented spelling is a practice opportunity for students to develop phoneme awareness and not an instructional program. For the most rapid introduction to detecting phonemes in words, children need intentional instruction in phoneme awareness, as described in detail in Chapter 6. Briefly, effective PA instruction introduces consonant phonemes one by one with a sound analogy, along with their principal graphemes; provides practice detecting each phoneme in words; and applies this knowledge in decoding the initial letters of words. For example, the teacher might introduce /p/ as "popcorn *P*," showing an illustration of popping corn. Children would learn a hand gesture of flicking their fingers out in imitation of popcorn popping. They would sample /p/ in a tongue tickler, such as "The prettiest pig picked a perfect place for a picnic." Then students would practice detecting the phoneme in words ("Is popcorn *P* in *cake* or *pie*?") and learn to use the letter *P* in phonetic cue reading ("Is this word [PAIR] *pair* or *share*?").

Meanwhile, teachers can encourage invented spelling, with all its benefits for developing PA through phonemic transcription. Rather than simply refusing to help with spellings, they can sometimes scaffold invented spellings by drawing letterboxes to show the number of phonemes in words children would like to spell. For example, the teacher could draw a sequence of four boxes to help a beginner transcribe the four phonemes in *train*. This process can be formalized in simple letterbox lessons, where the teacher guides students to spell regular, one-syllable words. Letterbox lessons are explained in detail in Practical Chapter 3.

An Invented Spelling Controversy

Some teachers have raised concerns about the practice of writing spellings directly on a student's draft to clarify their ambiguous inventions, e.g., printing *train* below the invention HAN. These teachers think that writing on a child's draft in some way violates the integrity of the child's composition. This concern seems unwarranted for several reasons. First, the teacher's annotation comes after the child's attempt, so that there is no interference with the process of phoneme detection, which is the chief value of invented spelling. Second, the annotation preserves the intended wording of the novice writer, which might otherwise be lost when the child tries to reread the message later. Third, annotating the draft allows parents to enjoy the child's message. On receiving "WE RD ON A HAN" days after the inspiration for the message has been lost, few parents would be able to appreciate what the child has written without the teacher's annotations. With the transcription, the parent can respond to the good memories of the train ride and praise the composition.

A BRIEF HISTORY OF SPELLING INSTRUCTION

If we could turn back the clock 200 years, we would see plenty of spelling work in American schools. There are several reasons that spelling work occupied a central place in the curriculum. Classrooms in the early nineteenth century were decidedly low tech. Chalk and slates were available, but one of the few books with multiple copies was Webster's *Blue Back Speller*. Most students attended one-room schools, where children of many ages and grades worked in a single classroom. Under this arrangement, spelling was an easy subject for older students to tutor younger children. Teachers had no problem with drill as a teaching method. Drill means repeated practice of a strategy toward the goal of automaticity, and it can be productive for some purposes. For activities aimed at automaticity, such as typing, shooting free throws, or acquiring vocabulary in a second language, drill is an effective method. For learning how to spell, however, drill is usually suboptimal because it stresses memorization rather than understanding. Only after spelling reaches the phonemic stage, when children begin to mentally mark the ambiguities of silent or irregular letters, does drill regain its value.

One other reason gave impetus to spelling work in schools: It helps children learn to read. Phonics aims at learning to decode printed words, but learning sight words requires a spelling analysis that goes beyond sounding out and blending. For example, a child can successfully decode *catch* by blending /k/ /a/ /t/ /ch/, but spelling instruction brings greater clarity with the rule that we spell /ch/ with *tch* after short vowels. The combination of explicit, systematic phonics with spelling instruction is highly productive for learning to read words. For example, a good phonics rule is that *ai*, *ay*, and *a_e* all represent /A/ in decoding one-syllable words. This limits to three the choices for spelling /A/ in regular words. For spelling words, students only need learn the conditions for using these graphemes: The divided digraph *a_e* is most common in one-syllable words (Hanna & Hanna, 1966). The digraph *ai* is only used in the middle of a word and *ay* only at the end.

THE CONNECTION BETWEEN WORD RECOGNITION AND SPELLING

Does learning to spell improve reading? Following the logic of Ehri's (1998) theory of the development of the ability to read words, better spelling must improve word recognition. When spellings are better understood, they are easier to remember. Readers can use well-spelled entries in the lexicon for sight-word recognition by matching the letters in printed words to stored spellings in the lexicon. This principle is illustrated in Figure 3.

FIGURE 3: A reader's encounter with the word elephant.

Imagine a young reader is trying to make sense of the printed word *elephant*. If he can connect the spelling to the pronunciation he knows, he can get all sorts of information he has stored about elephants. However, his lexical access depends variously on his ability to decode this rather long word, or on a helpful context to allow him to guess the word, or on a stored spelling that can be used for sight word recognition. Reading and spelling go hand in hand—they are two sides of the same coin. Optimal success in reading and spelling depends on having stored an accurate spelling in the lexicon. The better the stored spelling, the easier the lexical access. If the reader has stored a perfect or near-perfect spelling, he can make an automatic match when he sees the word in print. If not, he has to use more labor-intensive strategies to access the word.

Poor spellers don't understand word spellings as sensible pronunciation maps. It is hard for most people to remember arbitrary sequences they don't understand. Poor spellers store only the fragments of the spelling they can interpret, such as boundary consonants. As a result, they have to guess many words from consonant cues. Without accurate word spellings stored in the lexicon, readers have to guess from phonetic cues supported by context. However, guessing takes more resources than sight recognition, which is effortless and involuntary, and it therefore costs the reader resources that could otherwise be devoted to reading comprehension. When beginning spellers master phoneme awareness, they are ready to learn standard spellings. Learning standard spelling, in turn, will help readers make sight words and improve their reading comprehension.

Teaching standard spelling

The goal of spelling instruction is not just to learn a collection of individual words—there are far too many words to acquire one by one—but to acquire spelling power. Spelling power is the ability to learn and remember spellings efficiently. The acquisition of spelling power requires learning spelling correspondences, rules, and patterns. Trying to learn a spelling without making use of correspondences, rules, and patterns is like trying to memorize a phone number. It's a formidable task: For example, learning the spelling for *sergeant* without understanding it would require memorizing a 9-letter sequence and to remembering it without substituting or misordering the letters.

Correspondences

Spelling correspondences are more complex that phonics correspondences because there are more ways to spell a phoneme than there are ways to sound out a spelling. For example, if a reader sees the *i_e* pattern in a word, there is a 74% probability that it will be pronounced /I/ (Johnston, 2001). However, when challenged to spell the phoneme /I/, the speller must choose between *i_e* and syllable-final *i*, *y*, and *igh*, all of which have appreciable frequencies in spelling /I/ (Hanna & Hanna, 1966). For this reason, spelling is more difficult than phonics, and the spelling curriculum is usually undertaken only after phonics has been mastered.

Rules

Spelling rules can be valuable for learning spellings. For example, most of us will recall at least part of the the *i*-before-*e* rule: *i* before *e* except after *c*, or when sounded as /A/ as in *neighbor* or *weigh*. Thus, if we want to spell a low-frequency word like *wield*, the *i*-before-*e* rule helps us select the *ie* combination over the *ei* alternative. However, spelling rules are much less reliable than phonics rules, as illustrated in a spelling bee in which fourth graders went up against a computer— and won (Simon & Simon, 1973).

In this spelling bee, the computer was not preloaded with tens of thousands of accurate spellings, as is the spelling and grammar check in Microsoft Word. Instead, it was programmed with 300 spelling rules to generate spellings. Imagine how the computer might reason, given the pronunciation /fuj/. Given the rule that the phoneme /j/ is spelled *dge* after a short vowel, the computer would spell *fudge* correctly. Given /bach/, the computer could generate *batch*, using *tch* after the short vowel. But suppose the computer were given the pronunciation /aw-fun/. It would choose *o* as the most common spelling of /aw/, but then double the *f* to distance the silent *e* from the *o* (which would otherwise signal /O/, with the resulting spelling

OFFEN. Sorry, computer—you have to sit down. There is no spelling rule to cover the silent *t* in the correct spelling, *often*.

Spelling rules have too many exceptions to reliably generate accurate spellings in English. One study found that 300 spelling rules generate fewer than half of the correct spellings of the 17,000 words analyzed (Hanna & Hanna, 1966). In contrast, 166 phonics rules can generate accurate pronunciations for 90% of the one- and two-syllable words common in primary grade texts (Berdiansky, Cronnell, & Koehler, 1969). The general unreliability of spelling rules implies that they must be combined with word-specific knowledge in learning to spell. For example, the *i*-before-*e* rule must be tempered with knowledge of exception words like *either, neither, seize, weird,* and *leisure*. Thus, good spellers begin with rules, but they mentally mark silent and irregular letters, e.g., the silent *p* and hard *ch* in *psychology*, to remember spellings. They resolve ambiguities in vowels by learning which of several possible letters is standard. I recall my mother showing me how to spell *separate* on the white-erase board in our kitchen by writing it *sepArate*, pointing out that the *A* "separates" the predictable parts of the word; I have never forgotten this lesson. The exceptional parts of some words (e.g., *rendezvous*) can be learned by giving them a private pronunciation (e.g., /ren-dez-vooz/). In general, learning to spell requires applying rules and then mentally marking the odd or exceptional letters.

Patterns

Good spellers go beyond correspondences and rules to develop sensitivity to spelling patterns. For example, if I asked you to devise a spelling for a pseudoword pronounced /sE-bA-shun/, you would probably come up with either *cebation* or *sebation*, both of which conform to common spelling patterns in English. A spelling like *seebayshun* would be phonemic, but it offends our sense of English spelling patterns. In learning to spell *sergeant*, most of the spelling (s_rge_nt) can be generated using correspondences, rules, and patterns. For example, we typically use *ge* to spell /j/ within words. Learning to spell *sergeant* requires learning the *er* rulebreaker in the first syllable and noting that *a* spells the schwa vowel in the second. Armed with an arsenal of spelling correspondences, rules, and patterns, learning to spell *sergeant* requires learning only two details about the spelling rather than memorizing the nine-letter sequence. Learning spelling correspondences, rules, and patterns develops our spelling power—the ability to learn spellings easily. A systematic developmental spelling program teaches the reliable correspondences, rules, and patterns in a planned order.

EVALUATING SPELLING ACTIVITIES

Promoting avid reading, organizing spelling bees, and choosing words from students' writings are all popular ways to develop spelling ability. But do these activities promote spelling power? Reading books probably does little to improve spelling. The reason is that reading comprehension is under intense time pressure. We must quickly assemble the words we read into message units or risk losing some of the words from short-term memory. If we stop reading to invest the time and effort to learn word spellings, we are sidetracked from getting the message of the text, and we lose comprehension. For example, in reading *The Arabian Nights*, we frequently encounter the name *Scheherazade*, and we may have learned how to pronounce it. However, most of us have not taken the time to analyze the spelling by breaking it into chunks and mentally noting the irregularities of the spelling. Such an effort would be a serious distraction from our reading goal of finding out whether Scheherazade survives another Arabian night. Learning to spell a word accurately is more difficult than learning to read a word. As a result, we can usually read many more words than we can spell.

Is a spelling bee a good way to learn word spellings? The competition of a spelling bee can certainly be highly motivating for learning spellings, especially for spellers who know how to learn words efficiently by building on spelling correspondences, rules, and patterns. These spellers can learn words independently by studying before the competition rather than trying to work them out during the competition. However, the spelling bee itself is not a good environment for learning spellings. One student told me that she would never forget the word that cost her the spelling championship—*sergeant*. I asked her how to spell *sergeant*, and she began, "s-a-r . . . ." Apparently, she *did* forget. The problem with spelling bees for learning words is that a spelling is a visual map of the pronunciation; learning a visual map requires studying the visual map. Hearing a spelling recited does not help students understand its alphabetic mapping.

We could make spelling bees more productive for learning spellings if we had students visually map the words rather than spelling the words aloud. It is certainly within our present technology to have competitors work with hand-held spelling devices that would display their spellings on the hand unit. When a competitor was ready for his spelling to be evaluated, he could press a button to project this spelling onto a screen. This would not only help spectators learn the spellings of words, but also prevent the "startovers" that cannot be permitted under strict spelling bee rules.

A popular idea for organizing spelling study is to abandon spelling books and choose spelling words from the literature students are reading and from their misspelled words in their writings. While these words might have greater interest for students, this approach would be less likely to develop spelling power, which comes from acquiring spelling correspondences, rules, and patterns. An assortment of interesting words would not reveal correspondences, rules, and patterns. To learn to spell under these conditions, students would have to detect spelling correspondences, rules, and patterns without explicit instruction and without words selected to reveal these regularities.

SPELLING PROGRAMS

To learn spelling correspondences, rules, and patterns, students make optimal progress with a systematic spelling program that carefully selects words that illustrate these regularities. For example, a second-grade unit teaches students how to double final consonants with *-ed* and *-ing* after short vowels, with example words like *chopped, begged, shopping,* and *flapping*. A third-grade unit teaches students to maintain common prefixes like *pre-, pro-,* and *re-* across words, using example words like *prevent, produce,* and *review*. A fourth-grade unit shows students how to use *g* before the signals *e, i,* and *y* to spell /j/, and how some words spell /ch/ with *t*, using example words like *challenge, ginger, future,* and *fortune*. A sixth-grade unit teaches the meanings and spellings of the morphemes *graph, bio, therm, meter,* and *geo*, combining these morphemes in example words like *biographer, thermometer,* and *geography*. In these units, the words are carefully selected to reveal correspondences, rules, and patterns. Students are not just learning particular words: They are developing spelling power to learn new spellings efficiently.

Because effective spelling lessons teach spelling power, a valid spelling test should include words that students have not studied illustrating the correspondence, rule, or pattern. For example, when students are learning the *i*-before-*e* rule and studying words like *shield* and *yield*, it would be appropriate to ask students to spell *field*. This assessment could be scaffolded by making the analogy explicit: "Your spelling word is *field*, as in a field of corn. It follows the same spelling rule as *shield*." The point of asking students to spell words they haven't studied is to see if they have learned the correspondence, rule, or pattern that is the goal of the lesson. When I first proposed this kind of assessment at an inservice with intermediate grade teachers, the teachers were shocked. Asking children to spell words they hadn't studied was unheard of. But these teachers used an analogous strategy to assess learning in math. They asked students to practice adding 5 + 3 and 6 + 4, but they wouldn't hesitate to test them on problems like 5 + 4 and 6 + 3. In math, it is clear that we are teaching the ability to add, not the particular sums. Similarly, spelling instruction should teach and assess a correspondence, rule, or pattern, not just the particular example words that illustrate this pattern.

In Practical Chapter 8, I explain how to teach wordmapping, an extension of the letterbox lesson explained in Practical Chapter 3. Letterbox lessons are spelling and reading lessons restricted to regular, one-syllable words. Wordmapping lessons work with multisyllable words and irregular spellings. This versatility makes them ideal for teaching the spelling curriculum for second grade and beyond. The basic idea is to have students work carefully in analyzing the phoneme structure of words before encountering word spellings. This replaces the ineffective strategy of memorization with practical steps for understanding spellings as pronunciation maps.

SUMMARY

Invented spelling has become standard practice in primary classrooms in recognition of the fact that transcribing spellings helps children learn the alphabetic code. Children's first spellings are prephonemic, representing messages with drawings or scribbles. When children begin to understand how spellings map the pronunciations of words, they begin recording the consonants they detect in spoken words. Their semiphonemic spellings may use letter names rather than phonemes. In the phonemic stage, they begin to detect and transcribe all the phonemes in words with related letters, indicating a well-developed awareness of phonemes. Later in the transitional stage, they build on their phonemic spellings by adding silent letters and spelling conventions. The strategies of detecting phonemes in spellings and representing them with letters is excellent practice for acquiring phoneme awareness.

Clarke (1988) carried out the pioneer study for understanding the effects of invented spelling. First graders who invented spellings became more proficient at reading and spelling words than first graders for whom teachers provided spellings. The apparent mechanism for their gains was learning to detect phonemes through phonemic transcription. Until children have reached the milestone of PA mastery, they make the best progress when teachers nicely refuse to provide spellings, so that daily writing provides regular opportunities for phoneme detection. Their work practicing phoneme detection in invented spelling should be supplemented with explicit instruction in PA. When teachers annotate children's messages in invented spellings by recording their words in standard spelling, their messages are preserved for later reading, which helps parents enjoy their children's writings at home. One caveat in interpreting Clarke's study, however, is that the gains in spelling and reading words from inventing spellings came only from students low in phoneme awareness. Once students have learned to detect spellings, providing spellings gives them opportunities to benefit from writing by practicing new vocabulary, organizing ideas, and relating new concepts to background knowledge, which is to say, the benefits enjoyed by adult writers.

Historically, reading instruction in American schools featured copious spelling instruction. Older children often tutored younger children in one-room schools by helping them spell words with chalk on slates. While their drill methods were not the best, the development of spelling ability helped beginners learn to read words. As novice readers store more complete and accurate spellings in memory, they become better able to use these spellings for sight word recognition. Thus, reading and spelling are complementary processes in gaining mastery of alphabetic writing, allowing students to develop sight word knowledge to make word recognition and spelling effortless and automatic and freeing resources for reading comprehension and written composition.

Students who are ready to learn to spell need instruction aimed at developing spelling power, which is the ability to learn and remember spellings efficiently.

Spelling power depends on learning spelling correspondences, rules, and patterns. Instruction in spelling correspondences builds on phonics knowledge by teaching how phonemes are represented in various positions in words. Spelling rules are useful for generalizing correspondences across words, but their reliability is limited; applying spelling rules requires knowledge of word-specific exceptions. Learning to spell also requires developing a sense of the spelling patterns typical in English. When spellers can generate much of a spelling by applying correspondences, rules, and patterns, the work of learning spellings is reduced to learning the exceptional elements in spellings, such as ambiguous vowels and silent letters.

Several popular ideas about promoting spelling may work against learning to spell. We rarely learn accurate spellings from reading because the intense time pressure required by reading comprehension does not allow the close study of the unpredictable elements in spellings needed for accurate reproduction. Although spelling bees encourage students to invest time in word study in preparation for competitions, the competitions themselves are generally of limited value for learning words because spellings are recited rather than mapped. When teachers abandon structured spelling programs in favor of culling interesting words from literature and misspellings from student writings, they do not provide a systematic program for learning the correspondences, rules, and patterns needed to build spelling power.

To learn spelling correspondences, rules, and patterns, students need a careful selection of words for detecting spelling commonalities across words. The lessons in published spelling programs are useful to this end. Because spelling lessons aim at developing spelling power, teachers should assess spelling power with tests that include some example words not studied by students. The techniques of letterbox lessons and wordmapping are designed to teach students how spellings map out the phonological structures of words.

Looking Ahead: Teaching Vocabulary and Comprehension Strategies

Making Sight Words has been focused on teaching children how to read words, from the earliest partial alphabetic decoding to the mastery of word recognition evident in fluent reading. However, learning to read words is simply a means to an end. The end of reading is to get the messages encoded in texts, and to enjoy them, learn from them, and critically assess their validity. This chapter will look at ways fluent readers can enhance their language comprehension through reading. There are two important ways readers can build on fluent reading to improve their language comprehension. One way is to learn the meanings of the versatile vocabulary words used by skillful writers; this vocabulary is found almost exclusively in written works. The other is to learn research-supported strategies for reading comprehension that allow the reader to reduce texts to a compact gist and to weave connections between the text and the reader's background knowledge. In this chapter, we look beyond making sight words to harnessing the power of literacy to learn by reading. In other words, we shift our focus from learning to read to reading to learn.

TEACHING VOCABULARY

After a reader masters word recognition, the next great challenge for reading comprehension is to learn the meanings of the words used by great writers and thinkers in expressing their ideas. These unique, versatile, and expressive words are sometimes called "SAT" vocabulary because they are tested in college entrance examinations as indicators of advanced learning ability. Literate SAT vocabulary rarely appears in print and is even less common in speech. About 94% of the words used in English have a frequency of less than 1 in 100,000 running words of text

(Adams, 1990). This means that if an avid reader read 100,000 running words a month, putting him at the 80th percentile in reading volume, he would on average encounter most of these words less than once a month.

Two large-scale studies collected the vocabulary used in the conversations of adults (Cunningham & Stanovich, 1998). Some of the words adults were never heard to use in conversation in either study included *participation, maneuver, reluctantly, literal, luxury, provoke, display,* and *infinite*—all of which are almost certainly within the vocabularies of readers of this book. This indicates that even moderately challenging vocabulary is almost exclusively found in the enclave of books. When great novels are presented as movies, nearly all the rich wealth of vocabulary used by the authors of these books disappears. Even children's books use a more sophisticated vocabulary than adult conversations or TV geared to adult audiences.

How do we learn these rare, once-a-month words? Given that they are almost never used in conversation, we must learn most of them by reading. Yet even reading is problematic for learning words because writers are quite stingy in supplying meaning information for the words they use. For example, examine this quotation from Jane Austen's *Pride and Prejudice*:

> You may as well call it impertinence at once. It was very little less. The fact is, that you were sick of civility, of deference, of officious attention. You were disgusted with the women who were always speaking, and looking, and thinking for your approbation alone. I roused, and interested you, because I was so unlike them. Had you not been really amiable, you would have hated me for it; but in spite of the pains you took to disguise yourself, your feelings were always noble and just; and in your heart, you thoroughly despised the persons who so assiduously courted you.

Austen expects readers to know the meanings of *impertinence, civility, deference, officious, approbation, amiable,* and *assiduously*. Writers choose words carefully, and they have none to spare for redundant contextual information that would provide any strong clues to word meanings.

Ineffective Vocabulary Instruction

Accordingly, explicit instruction in vocabulary is a vital supplement to wide reading for learning vocabulary. It not only directly supplies meaning information for rare SAT vocabulary words, but also enriches the contextual information that can be used to glean word meanings from reading. Fortunately, we have excellent research directing high quality vocabulary instruction (Beck, McKeown, & Kucan, 2002). Unfortunately, the usual vocabulary "instruction" is dismal to the point of malpractice. Teachers typically assign vocabulary learning without teaching the words, often by giving students a list of words to look up in a dictionary, copy definitions, and use in sentences. That students are not prepared to use words correctly is evident from their amusing misusage:

Devious: Straying from the right course; not straightforward. "On the nature hike, we were devious and got lost."

Disrupt: Break up; split. "We disrupted the candy bar so we could all share it."

Morbid: Not healthy or normal. "I think I need to stay home from school today—I'm feeling morbid."

The typical look-it-up vocabulary assignment is ineffective because encounters with the new word are too few and too shallow, with little or no information about usage. As a result, students get mere acquaintance with new vocabulary rather than word ownership. Ownership is the goal of vocabulary instruction; it is the ability to access word meanings effortlessly and to use words in speaking and writing. Usually, ownership requires some 10-18 engaging encounters in a variety of spoken or written contexts (McKeown, Beck, Omanson, & Pople, 1985).

A Model of Vocabulary Learning

Coming to own a new vocabulary word seems to be a four-step process, as summarized in Figure 1. First, we must locate the boundaries of meaning from plain-language explanations, examples, and nonexamples. For instance, the word *disrupt* means to break up a process; loud talk in the back of the room can disrupt a class. A speaker would not disrupt the class by speaking when called on, and in informal situations, it would not be disruptive to speak without raising your hand. However, it is nearly always disruptive to shout over someone trying to speak. Second, we must learn to use the new word with other words. We can't simply "disrupt," nor can we disrupt a physical object like a candy bar. We can only disrupt an event or process, such as a meeting or a conversation.

1. **LOCATE**: Find meaning boundaries. *Locate* the critical attributes of the concept from explanations, examples, and nonexamples.

2. **RELATE**: Use the word with other words. See *relationships* between the concept and other known words—how to use the word.

3. **EXTRICATE**: Explore new contexts. See how the word is used in a variety of contexts—*extricate* the word from its original context.

4. **GENERATE**: Make new sentences. *Generate* new contexts for the learned concept—put the word to use.

FIGURE 1: Four mental operations in concept learning

Third, we most extricate the new word from its original context. Without special effort, the word *disrupt* will likely become lodged in a classroom, but many events or processes can be disrupted. For example, the lyrics of a popular song might disrupt our thoughts as we read, or an intransigent political leader might disrupt arms negotiations. Finally, we are ready to take the final exam in vocabulary learning by generating new contexts. For example, we might talk about how a terrorist attack disrupted the tourism industry in 2001, or how bank failures in 2008 disrupted the economy. The ability to generate new and appropriate contexts demonstrates word ownership. Teachers err in expecting students to use a word correctly in a sentence from a brief, shallow encounter with a dictionary definition. Usage is the final exam, not the introductory exercise.

An Exemplary Program

The McKeown et al. (1985) study with fourth-grade students exemplifies a rich vocabulary instructional program. The researchers selected words in semantic groups for study, i.e., words with common meaning elements. For example, one week they taught eight words naming types of people: *accomplice, virtuoso, rival, philanthopist, novice, hermit, tyrant,* and *miser.* Learning a word is easier with related words: They activate one another, and they allow students to compare and contrast words to see the relationships between words. Because semantic grouping is important for learning words, teachers should consider teaching a published vocabulary program presenting words in semantic groups, appropriate to the grade level. Simply collecting unfamiliar words from a story or article students will read almost guarantees that the words will not fall into a single semantic category.

In the McKeown et al. (1985) program, teachers introduced selected words with simple definitions, examples, and nonexamples, and then asked students to comment about the words. For example, they might explain that an accomplice is sort of an assistant criminal, not the mastermind. He might be paid $100 to stand guard during a bank robbery. Teachers asked students if an accomplice would squeal to the police to stay out of jail, rob a bank by himself, or enjoy babysitting. In justifying their choices, students got initial usage practice with the word; a student might respond, "I think an accomplice would squeal to the police because it isn't worth going to jail for a lousy hundred bucks." Students were asked what else an accomplice would do (e.g., drive the getaway car), and as a written followup, they had to complete a sentence using the word (e.g., The accomplice swore he would never break the law again because . . .).

The next day students were asked to try the words in pairs and see if they could go together. For example, could a philanthropist be a miser? Could an accomplice be a novice? The effort to relate words to other words generated productive discussion in which students had to exercise their knowledge of words to justify their answers. The emphasis was on understanding the words rather than getting the right answer. For example, a student might argue that a philanthopist could be a miser because he would have to hoard a lot of money before he could give it away. Note that using words with related words is only possible when words are organized into semantic groups.

McKeown et al. (1985) found that the most productive practice for gaining word ownership came from an activity they called "Word Wizards." Students looked for their vocabulary words outside of class; they could earn points by seeing a word in print, hearing it spoken, or using it themselves. The points they earned could be used to earn ranks, progressing from word apprentice, to word journeyman, to word wizard.

By collecting usage instances, students greatly increased their time thinking about word meanings. In addition, they brought new contexts to the attention of classmates. McKeown et al. (1985) found that students whose rich instructional program included Word Wizards learned words mentioned only 4 times as well as they learned words encountered 12 times. They demonstrated ownership of these words by their ability to make faster semantic decisions about them (e.g. Could a tyrant be a miser?) than could control groups who learned definitions rather than rich usage information or who studied the words in rich contexts without the extended practice of Word Wizards. Given that challenging vocabulary words are rarely used in conversation and occur less than once in 100,000 running words of text, students find that using the word themselves is the easiest option. In a similar activity, college athletes in a critical reading class practiced "word workouts" that demonstrate the productivity of extending learning beyond the classroom:

> Even though I played like a pro in high school, I felt like a *novice* on the college football field.
>
> Coach asked who the *accomplice* was since no guy could have gotten into the girl's locker room on his own.
>
> Hey, don't be such a *miser*; share that Snickers bar with me.
>
> I am a true basketball *virtuoso*, according to Coach.

TEACHING READING COMPREHENSION STRATEGIES

To read texts on their own, readers need comprehension strategies. *Strategies* are problem-solving procedures readers can use independently of the teacher; reading comprehension strategies are tactics to understand and remember key ideas in reading. We can use comprehension strategies to reduce a lengthy text into a compact and memorable gist, or to make connections between text ideas and background knowledge. Strategic reading is particularly important with *expository* text, i.e., text written to impart information to readers. We often read expository text to remember key information for later use. Because there is usually less press to remember the ideas in narrative text, and because narratives have a familiar structure that allows us to follow the progression of the story, reading comprehension strategies are less important with narratives.

Strategies contrast with scaffolds and with skills. *Scaffolds* are ways teachers support the learning of students, e.g., by preteaching vocabulary or preparing reading guides. *Skills* are learned automatic responses, e.g., automatic word recognition during reading or activating background knowledge. Teachers cannot teach skills directly, but most strategies can become skills with sufficient practice, e.g., sizing up a paragraph quickly to generate a topic sentence.

Research-Based Comprehension Strategies

Not all strategies recommended to teachers have a strong research base. For example, we often see recommendations to have students predict what they will learn from a text, but there is little evidence that making a prediction before reading enhances reading comprehension, at least with expository text. I doubt that many of us stop to consciously predict what we are about to read; instead, we simply begin reading and enjoy the automatic spreading activation from the ideas we are reading to what we already know.

To know whether a strategy is effective, the best evidence is that it has been shown to work in educational experiments. In an educational experiment, students are randomly assigned to an experimental treatment (in this case, learning a reading comprehension strategy) or to a control group, which does something interesting or useful not expected to improve reading comprehension. If the experimental group performs significantly better than controls on outcome measures, we have evidence that the treatment caused the difference. The strategies to be discussed here have been tried in experiments from middle elementary (3rd grade) to middle school (8th grade). They are teachable single strategies rather than composite strategy packages, and they can usually be taught in 10 hours of instruction or less. The five most useful strategies that fit these criteria (Pressley, Johnson, Symons, McGoldrick, & Kurity, 1989) are (1) summarization, (2) question generation (asking good questions), (3) question-answer relationships (strategies for answering questions), (4) visualization (forming representational imagery during reading), and (5) using story structure to organize the ideas in a narrative text.

READING COMPREHENSION BASICS

Before explaining the top five strategies for reading comprehension, let's consider some of the basic concepts about reading comprehension. Comprehension is essential to reading. Everything we do in reading education, including teaching phonics, is designed to enhance reading comprehension.

The Simple View

Gough and Tunmer (1986) explained the essentials of reading as a formula they called the simple view of reading (Figure 2). In the original, the formula is $R = D \times C$; I find it helpful to expand the labels to express the common element of comprehension in reading and listening. According to the simple view, reading comprehension is the product of decoding and language comprehension. Reading comprehension (RC) is simply reading, getting the message encoded in a text. To read a text, we have to translate the printed words into language (D) and comprehend the language (LC).

$$RC = D \times LC$$

RC: **Reading comprehension**; the ability to get the message of a text by reading

D: **Decoding skill**; the ability to translate printed words into language

LC: **Language comprehension**; the ability to get a message by listening

Reading is the product of decoding and comprehension.

To read, we must (a) translate print into language

and (b) understand the message.

FIGURE 2: The simple view of reading

Because the simple view proposes reading to be a product, if either of its key factors is absent (i.e., if either D or LC = 0), there is no reading (RC = 0). For example, if we attend a Shakespeare play and comprehend the language, laughing with the humor or grieving over the tragedy, but we can't decode the words in the script, we can't read Shakespeare. Similarly, if we can decode the words of *Don Quixote* in Spanish but we don't comprehend the Spanish language, we can't read Cervantes's masterpiece.

The expert level of D in the simple view is automatic word recognition, or fluency (D = 1), so that reading comprehension is limited only by language comprehension (RC = LC). With instant, automatic access to a 100,000-word sight vocabulary, we can work full time at getting the messages in texts, with no impediments in translating the printed words into language. In other words, readers can turn their full attention to language comprehension when they have mastered word recognition.

Background Knowledge and Schemata

The largest factor in language comprehension is background knowledge. The more we know about a topic, the easier it is to read and understand something new in that area. If Catholic and Jewish students read a story about a bar mitzvah, the Jewish students would have a huge advantage in background knowledge, but if the story were about First Communion, the advantage would be reversed. I once tested some precocious first graders who could read a sixth-grade word list successfully. I followed up by asking them to read a sixth-grade passage about the civil rights movement. Though they could read all the words in the passage, they had little or no comprehension because they didn't understand ideas about civil rights, discrimination, boycotts, Jim Crow laws, or suffrage. Being able to pronounce the words was not sufficient to unlock the message of the text.

Our background knowledge for any familiar event is organized into a *schema* (the plural is *schemata*). A schema is a reader's generic idea of a situation. For example, most of us have a well-developed schema for weddings, telling us how people dress and in what order they approach the officiating minister. Of course, this schema may not always be accurate, e.g., for an Elvis wedding in Las Vegas, but it usually provides enough general script that we can fill in the details. To comprehend in familiar situations, we activate the appropriate schema and fit the particular information into "slots" in the schema. This allows us to "read between the lines," i.e., to infer information not directly stated. If we read, "Joe pulled up to the pump," we are instantly equipped with a service station schema that helps us visualize what is going on. Writers don't need to tell us everything that is happening because we can draw inferences to flesh out a skeletal text with information from the relevant schema. Figure 3 illustrates some possible components of a reader's firehouse schema.

FIGURE 3: Firehouse schema (courtesy of Steven Darian).

Activating a schema is automatic. We don't need a strategy of prediction to evoke our knowledge of weddings or service stations. Activation spreads automatically among ideas in the lexicon. However, in scaffolding students' reading, we have to build background knowledge when there is no schema to activate. For example, if students are going to read about the Hopi Indians, they might need background information on adobe, pueblos, and kachinas. With poorly written text, we may have to work at getting an interpretive schema. Bransford and Johnson (1973) give an example of a text whose schema is not immediately apparent:

> The procedure is actually quite simple. First you arrange things into different groups. Of course, one pile may be sufficient, depending on how much there

is to do. If you have to go somewhere else due to lack of facilities, that is the next step; otherwise, you are pretty well set. It is important not to overdo things. That is, it is better to do few things at once than too many.

It may take some thinking to recognize that this passage is about doing the laundry. See if you experience any schema problems in reading this text from Sanford and Garrod (1981):

> John was on his way to school. He was terribly worried about the mathematics lesson. He thought he might not be able to control the class again today. He thought it was unfair of the instructor to make him supervise the class for a second time. After all, it was not a normal part of a janitor's duties.

Did you find yourself switching schemata several times as you read? Abruptly switching schemata causes a momentary discombobulation we experience as humor. Here's a report from an Australian newspaper that will give American readers some comprehension difficulties:

> A hair-raising century by Australian opener Graeme Wood on Friday set England back on its heels in the third test at the Melbourne Cricket Ground. Unfortunately, living dangerously eventually cost the Australians the match. Wood was caught out of his crease on the first over after lunch. Within ten more overs, the Australians were dismissed. Four were dismissed by dangerous running between creases. Two were dismissed when the English bowlers lifted the bails from the batsmen's wickets. The three remaining batsmen were caught by English fieldsmen. One was caught as he tried for a six. When the innings were complete, the Australians had fallen short of the runs scored by the English.

It's not that we have trouble reading the words: We don't have a schema for cricket. To understand this passage, we need instruction in how cricket is played, perhaps delivered by an instructional video designed for an audience unfamiliar with the game. A good instructional principle for such situations is to show the video before students read to build the necessary background knowledge for reading comprehension.

Problems in reading comprehension are often analogous to difficulties with the cricket passage: Readers lack a usable schema for making sense of the ideas in the text. When they are reading about algebra, arthropods, or archaeology, they may be challenged to build a new schema to manage the new information. In this case, the new schema might be called a mental model of the ideas in the text. In building a mental model, readers must comprehend the hierarchy of ideas, i.e., the organization in which some ideas are more important and central to understanding the information and other ideas that are less important or trivial. The task of reducing a voluminous text to a manageable gist is to clear away the trivia while remembering the important central ideas.

Propositions

To detect the hierarchy of ideas in an unfamiliar text, much important work goes on subliminally, below conscious attention, at the level of propositions. A *proposition* is the smallest unit of information that can be judged true or false. To be judged true or false, a proposition must have a subject and predicate, i.e., a noun and a verb. Even a simple sentence like "Mary had a little lamb" has several propositions. The basic subject-predicate or subject-predicate-object structure, stated in the present tense, is a basic proposition, i.e., "Mary has a lamb." Adjectives and adverbs are embedded propositions that can be unpacked into subject-predicate form, i.e., "The lamb is little." Verb tenses, too, embed propositions that can be made explicit; here, "Having is in the past." Thus, a sentence like "A rolling stone gathers no moss" can be analyzed into three propositions: "A stone gathers moss," "the stone is rolling," and "the moss is none." The sentence "Little Miss Muffet sat on a tuffet" expresses four propositions: "Miss Muffet sits," "Miss Muffet is little," "sitting is on a tuffet," and "sitting is in the past."

Each of these propositional ideas must be momentarily comprehended and sifted in search of important or main ideas repeated in the text and linked to other ideas. They are "linked" if they have common elements with other propositions. As we read, we are on the lookout for important, well-connected propositions that surface again and again. In Little Miss Muffet, the spider plays a central role worth noting. At the same time, we lose interest in propositions with few or no links; they are not worth remembering. For example, because there is no further mention of tuffets or curds and whey in Little Miss Muffet, we need not remember her furniture or breakfast details. The hierarchy of main ideas and important details is the *deep structure* of a text. We want to remember the ideas in the deep structure, but there is no reason to clutter our thoughts with the actual words of text, or *surface structure*. Once we have used the actual words in the surface structure to identify the deep structure, we can lose the exact words. We can also clear away the trivial propositions with few or no links to other propositions and any redundant information, such as examples. Our goal is to recognize the well-linked central hierarchy of ideas, with the main ideas, key topics, and vital details. Good comprehenders do not remember trivia, and good teachers do not assess knowledge of trivia. Rather, they probe the well-linked central hierarchy of ideas with questions beginning with *how* and *why*.

Figure 4 illustrates the work of reading comprehension, using a semantic map. The goal of reading is to construct an elaborated summary, an abbreviated mental model of the writer's message with critical connections to background knowledge. Two main transformations take place when we comprehend. We summarize a vast text into a compact hierarchy of ideas, easy to remember. The work of summarization involves apprehending the elemental propositions, organizing the important ideas into a hierarchy, and discarding trivia. At the same time, we are making connections between the ideas in a text and our background knowledge. Where our background knowledge is strong, we activate an appropriate schema to organize the information, relying on the default values to flesh out our understanding and inserting particular facts into ready-made slots in the schema. In areas where our background knowledge is weak, we build mental models of the important ideas identified through summarization, both to supply a temporary text model for the main ideas in the text we are reading but also to develop a permanent schema for more rapid comprehension of future texts.

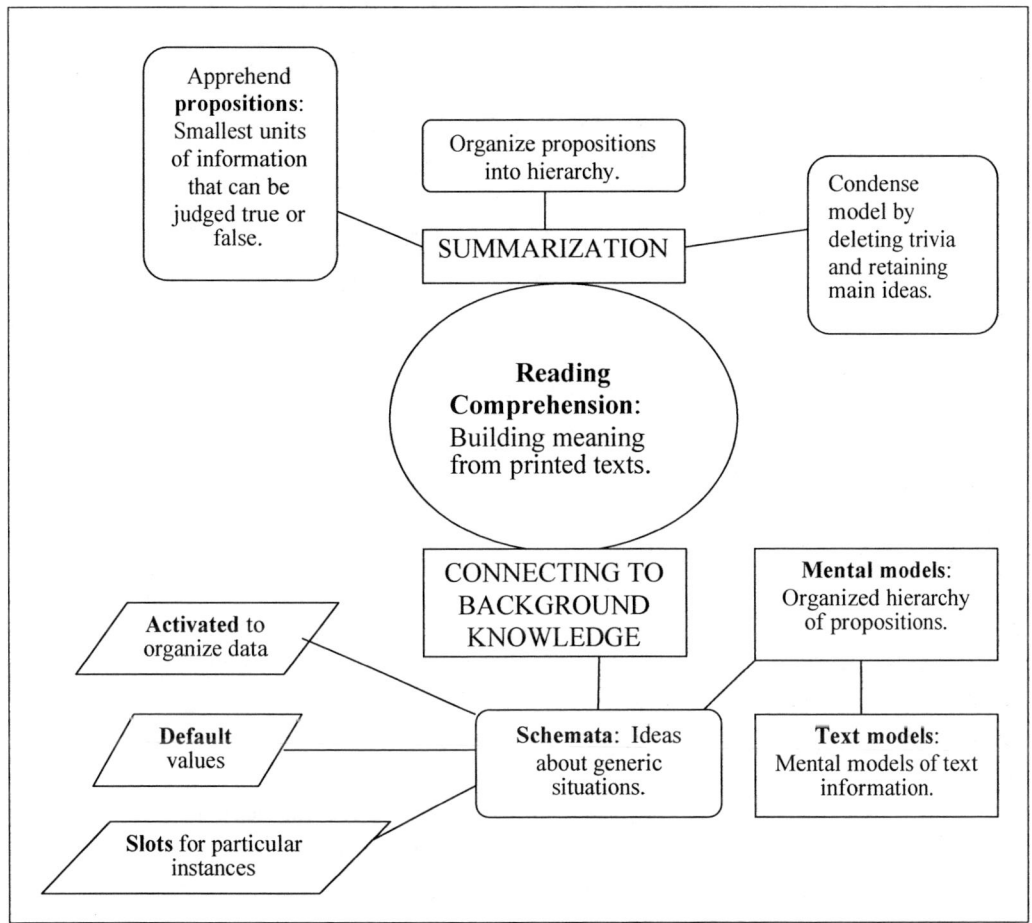

FIGURE 4: Semantic map of reading comprehension.

FIVE RESEARCH-BASED STRATEGIES FOR READING COMPREHENSION

SUMMARIZATION

In summarization, readers reduce a text that may have hundreds or thousands of words into a compact and memorable gist. Kintsch and Van Dijk (1978) explained the work of summarization as following six rules, which we can further condense into three, as in Figure 5.

> 1. Delete trivial information (stuff you know isn't important).
> 2. Delete redundant information (information repeated, e.g., examples).
> 3. Substitute superordinate terms for lists of items (use a more general term for a list of things).
> 4. Integrate a series of events with a superordinate action term (use a more general terms for a series of events).
> 5. Select a topic sentence (sentence that covers all information in text).
> 6. Invent a topic sentence.
>
> **Summary of summarization rules:**
> 1. Delete trivia and redundancies.
> 2. Superordinate items and events.
> 3. Find or compose a statement that covers everything the writer is saying about the topic.

FIGURE 5: Kintsch and Van Dijk's rules for summarization

The summarization rules suggest components of the summarization strategy that can be taught. First, the reader has to clear away the trivial and redundant information that is not worth remembering. Clearing away the trivia leaves the important ideas that are linked to many other ideas and prominent in the hierarchy of the text. Thus, the positive side of removing the trivia and redundancies is determining what's important. We know what is trivial and what is important in a couple of ways. First, we usually have some background knowledge from what we've heard or read in the past. These ideas tend to be more important. Second, we notice repeated references to the important ideas. If an idea is mentioned only once or twice in a text, and if it doesn't ring any bells in our background knowledge, it is probably not worth remembering. It may help students to literally cross out ideas that are trivial and to highlight or underline ideas that are important, as illustrated in Figure 6.

> The <u>Declaration of Independence</u> is one of the most important documents in the history of the United States. It <u>signifies the colonies' break from England</u> and the rule of ~~George III~~. The Second Continental Congress formed a committee to write the Declaration, but the Committee thought it would be better for only one man to write the document. It took <u>Thomas Jefferson</u> ~~seventeen days~~ to <u>write the Declaration</u> of Independence.

FIGURE 6: Example of underlining important ideas and striking through trivia[11]

---

1. Text from http://www.rightsofthepeople.com/education/government_for_kids/6-8/documents/declaration/index.php

Once a text has been annotated to indicate important ideas and to cross out trivia, it is a relatively easy next step to construct a topic sentence, such as "Thomas Jefferson wrote the Declaration of Independence to explain the break from England."

Next, the Kintsch and Van Dijk rules direct us to substitute superordinate terms for multiple items or events. A *superordinate* term is an umbrella term; for example, *animals* is a superordinate term for cats, dogs, mice, and birds. Golf, tennis, football, and baseball could be captured by the superordinate term *sports*. Finding more general terms for nouns is relatively easy, but identifying superordinate terms for a series of predicates is more challenging. We can summarize sentences about buying a lamp, looking for nice and affordable clothes, and eating out as *shopping*, thus gaining a major reduction in text. Reading a text slowly, rereading important parts, making notes, and reviewing the notes could be economically superordinated into *studying*. Identifying a superordinate predicate for a series of statements is at the heart of the problem of summarization.

The final step identified by Kintsch and Van Dijk is to generate a topic sentence that captures the gist of the text, covering all the major ideas in a few words. A topic sentence states the topic of a paragraph and the main point the writer is making about that topic. Usually, we must compose this sentence because the majority of paragraphs do not contain a topic sentence, even in elementary textbooks. For this reason, workbook exercises requiring students to select topic sentences are not realistic. A useful strategy for writing topic sentences is about-point (Morgan, Meeks, Schollaert, & Paul, 1986). First, write down what the paragraph is *about*, the topic. Then, generate a predicate that captures the main *point* the author is making about the topic. This will be a superordinate statement of the actions or events in the paragraph. Again, finding a superordinate term for a series of predicates is the major challenge in summarization. We can illustrate this process of superordinating predicates to compose a topic sentence by analyzing the following paragraph about the cheetah (Silverstein & Silverstein, 2003):

> The cheetah is the fastest runner in the world. It has been clocked at up to 70 miles an hour—faster than the fastest racehorse. (The fastest a human has ever run is less than 28 miles an hour.) The cheetah is a sprinter, not a long distance runner. In its home in the grasslands of Africa, its speed helps it to catch food. In the cooler parts of the day, in the early morning or just before sunset, the cheetah hunts. When it sees an antelope or gazelle, it slithers through the grass until it is less than 200 yards from its prey. Then it puts on an incredible burst of speed. Within two seconds, it goes from a standing start to a speed of 45 miles an hour.

The topic of the paragraph is obvious—it is about the cheetah. But how can we superordinate all the information in the predicates? It is the fastest runner, a sprinter rather than a long distance runner; its speed helps it catch food; when hunting, it slithers close to an antelope or gazelle; it puts on a burst of speed. The common element issuing a powerful sprinting speed to chase down prey.

Summarization solves the basic reading comprehension problem of reducing a large text made of hundreds or thousands of words into a compact and memorable deep structure made of relatively few words. Using writing while summarizing makes it possible to collect the predicate ideas for superordination. Graphic organizers are often helpful in summarizing, particularly when they reveal the text structure, e.g., Venn diagrams for comparison-contrast texts or semantic maps for enumeration-description texts. When working beyond the paragraph level, we can write a summary of our summaries. Summarization is something of an art as well as a skill that develops with expert reading. In comparisons of the effects of teaching comprehension strategies, summarization nearly always ranks first or near first in effectiveness (NRP, 2000).

QUESTION GENERATION

Besides getting the gist, the other main goal of reading comprehension is connecting text information to our background knowledge in order to understand it. The best way to make these connections is consciously, by asking good questions as we read. Questions deliberately link ideas to other ideas in a text or to the background knowledge of the reader. The ability to ask good questions makes the reader active in gethering information and reading critically. For this reason, question generation rivals summarization in effectiveness, and together they take top honors as the two most powerful reading comprehension strategies (NRP, 2000).

However, we cannot simply assign readers to ask questions because without instruction, young readers ask about trivia. Literal questions about trivia are the easiest questions to ask because all the information needed for such questions can be found in a single sentence, e.g., "What year did Columbus discover America?" The questions that lead to reading comprehension focus on important ideas in text, e.g., "Why did Columbus sail west?" Good questions integrate ideas and capture large blocks of text information. They either connect the ideas in the text to background knowledge to help us draw inferences or think critically, or they bring together information from different sentences in the text to support summarization. Teachers can teach a vital reading comprehension strategy by showing students how to ask questions that bring ideas together. But teachers, too, must learn to ask students questions that bring ideas together. Observational studies suggest that about 70% of teacher questions are literal (Guszak, 1967).

In a landmark study of question generation, Davey and McBride (1986) used explicit instruction to teach an experimental group of sixth graders how to ask good questions. The researchers explained and modeled how to ask good questions, and gave students guided practice with feedback. A key part of the training was to teach students to evaluate their questions by asking three questions about their questions: Did they cover important information? Did they bring information together? Could they answer the questions themselves? Thus, they taught students to focus on important information, to bring information from different sentences together, and to verify that the questions were neither too trivial nor too far from the text to answer. Posttests indicated that the experimental group led several different control groups in reading comprehension. The likely explanation is that they became better at connecting text information to other text ideas and to background knowledge.

QUESTION-ANSWER RELATIONSHIPS (QARs)

The first step in learning to ask good questions may be to understand the types of questions, which is the goal of learning question-answer relationships (Raphael, 1984). QARs help readers analyze questions to know where to look for the answers. Figure 7 shows the QAR taxonomy (name system) for questions.

Right there	The answer is in a single sentence in the text. The words used in the question and in the answer are usually in the same sentence.
Putting it together	The answer is in the text, but not in a single sentence. Readers need to collect information from more than one sentence and put ideas together to answer the question.
Writer and me	The answer is partly in the text. Readers need to think about what they already know and about what the text says to see how they fit together.
On my own	The answer is not in the text. Readers have to use what they already know to answer the question.

FIGURE 7: The taxonomy of questions in QARs

Right-there questions are literal: The answer is found within a single sentence. Putting-it-together questions require drawing a conclusion from stated information in at least two different sentences, i.e., summarization. The generic about-point question is a putting-it-together question: What point is the writer making about the topic? A writer-and-me question requires us to elaborate on information in the text by using our background knowledge. It often begins with *why*, e.g., "Why is it important for animals to be fast? A generic writer-and-me question might ask, "How does your background knowledge explain what the writer is saying?" On-my-own questions are open-ended questions, i.e., questions with multiple right answers. They call for information primarily in the readers' minds and not in the text. Figure 8 shows the principal types of open-ended questions.

Open-ended questions can be high or low level questions. Personal response questions may be useful to open discussions or as journal prompts, but they elicit low level thinking. Evaluation questions call for the highest level of thinking, weighing value standards to determine what is good or right. Interpretation questions draw on background knowledge; they are related to writer-and-me questions, but they go further from the text. Divergent thinking questions are good followup questions and draw on students' creativity.

Personal response—opinion, feeling, or self-report.
Examples: What would you do if you were the main character? What did you think of Robin Hood?
Unlike evaluation, personal response demands little reasoning. Personal response questions are low level questions that simply elicit emotion or opinion.

Evaluation—judging something according to some standard.
Examples: Was what this character did the right thing to do? Was Robin Hood right to steal from the rich and give to the poor? Why or why not?
Evaluation is the highest level of comprehension in Bloom's taxonomy. Evaluation questions require knowledge of objective evaluative standards.

Interpretation—a translation into different words or a connection with something familiar.
Examples: What is the message in this poem? Is Robin Hood more like a policeman or a robber? Why?
Moderately difficult—requires putting text ideas together.

Divergent thinking—imagining other possibilities.
Examples: If we ran out of fossil fuel, how would transportation change? How else could Robin help the poor?
Moderately difficult question—requires combining text ideas with background knowledge and using creativity.

Figure 8: Types of open-ended questions

One of the most useful applications of QARs is to improve the questions teachers ask. We especially want to replace literal questions with higher level questions because students tend to remember what we ask about. If we ask about trivia, they will remember trivia. If we ask them to bring important information together, they will remember unifying, important ideas.

VISUALIZATION

Visualization is a vital way to make connections between the ideas in a text and background knowledge. We want readers to generate representational images, images that represent the content of a text. Skilled readers generate mental movies as they read. Other senses are involved in these mental movies—touch, hearing, smell, and taste—which suggests visualization might better be called imagination. The texts that work best for visualization are narratives because young readers have more background knowledge for more familiar situations of narratives. Stories with rich descriptive passages are ideal.

To teach visualization, teachers should begin with single sentences and have students visualize by listening with their eyes closed. Students can describe their mental images or draw them on paper. Next, we want them to read texts, but to stop to visualize what they've read. The crucial complication is to lead them to visualize during reading. To visualize during reading, word recognition must be automatic. Only fluent readers can fully engage their imaginations during reading. Visualization is incompatible with the struggle to recognize words. You can test your visualization ability by reading the following passage:

> There is absolutely no light at the bottom of the ocean. Some fish that live at the bottom of the ocean know their food by its color.

Were you able to get the picture, or did you detect a problem? If you wondered how fish could know their food by its color with absolutely no light, you were monitoring your reading comprehension. Research suggests that children trained to visualize are better at detecting inconsistencies in texts. Thus, visualization helps us monitor our reading comprehension and take executive control of learning, which is a key feature of metacognition. We can figuratively stand beside our learning and bring learning under control.

USING STORY STRUCTURE

Practical Chapter 1 shows how to design effective booktalks by building on the characteristic structure of stories, emphasizing the problem without giving away the solution worked out in the plot episodes and resolution. Children can also use story structure in comprehension. When they understand how stories work, they can use story structure to expect key story events. For example, when a character becomes embroiled in a problem, they can expect a solution.

Children begin to learn about story structure early when they listen to stories read aloud. Story structure diagrams are useful for making story structure more explicit. Figure 9 illustrates a story map children can use to tie story events to the general story structure. Filling out a story map is a scaffold rather than a strategy. A strategy is an independent problem-solving tactic, and it isn't realistic to expect readers to stop and draw a story map when then want to understand how events are organized in a story. In an experiment (Nolte & Singer, 1985), one group of fourth and fifth graders filled out a story map during reading. Another group learned to ask story-structure questions, e.g., what is the setting? Who are the main characters? What was their goal or problem? The students who learned to ask story structure questions made bigger gains in reading comprehension. Unlike using a story map as a scaffold, self-questioning about story structure can be done anywhere, at any time, without any special materials. It is an independent strategy for learning and remembering ideas in a text.

STORY MAP for _____

SETTING
When and where does the story take place?
What is the ordinary situation?

MAIN CHARACTERS
Who is the story about?

GOAL OR PROBLEM
What does the main character want, or how do things go wrong for the main character?

RESOLUTION
What finally happens? How does it all turn out?

PLOT EVENTS
What does the main character try to do?
How does that work?

Attempts	Results

FIGURE 9: A story map

SUMMARY

Fluent readers can build on their automaticity of word recognition by reading to learn. Teachers can help them improve their reading comprehension by teaching meaning vocabulary and reading comprehension strategies.

Valuable and versatile words are rare in print and virtually absent in conversation. This implies that these words must be learned by reading challenging texts or by explicit instruction. The authentic contexts in reading are problematic because writers expect their readers to possess a vocabulary commensurate with the text. What passes for instruction in vocabulary is notorious for asking students to look up words, copy definitions, and write sentences before they understand how vocabulary words are used. Learning a word seems to involve a four-step process. First, we locate the boundaries of meaning from explanations, examples, and nonexamples. Second, we learn how to use the words with other words by examining usage examples. Third, we learn to extricate the word from its original context by seeing how it can be used in other contexts. Fourth, we are ready to generate our own contexts to use the word in original sentences. By taking these steps with words, we come to own them—we have instant access to their meanings in reading and listening, and we can use the words in writing and speaking.

Effective vocabulary instruction builds on this model. Teachers choose semantically related words that are versatile and challenging to students. They provide user-friendly definitions along with examples and nonexamples. Effective instruction carefully scaffolds student usage by asking them to complete sentences rather than to generate sentences before they have ownership. Teachers pair words for students, asking them to exercise their growing knowledge to make semantic decisions, e.g., about whether a philanthropist is a miser. Effective vocabulary instruction extends beyond the classroom by asking students to locate or use their words outside of class and to report their usage back to the class.

Besides learning vocabulary, readers improve their comprehension by learning strategies, independent problem-solving tactics for learning from text. Strategies differ from scaffolds by being independent; they differ from skills by their conscious use, but over time, strategies can become skills. The five strategies with the strongest support in educational experiments are summarization, question generation, question-answer relationships (QARs), visualization, and using story structure.

To understand why these strategies are effective, it is helpful to understand the basic processes of reading comprehension. Reading comprehension is a product of skillful word recognition (translating printed words effortlessly into language) and language comprehension. To the extent that students can build a vast sight vocabulary, they can work full time at developing their language comprehension through reading. The largest factor in language comprehension is background knowledge. The more we know about a topic, the easier it is to understand texts written about that topic. Background knowledge is organized into schemata; a schema is a reader's generic idea about a situation. We ordinarily comprehend by activating an appropriate schema and fitting situational details into "slots" in the schema. However, we often encounter topics for which we do not have well-developed schemata, in which case we need strategies for building mental models that can become schemata.

Detecting the important ideas in texts depends upon an almost subliminal process of detecting and weighing propositions. A proposition is the smallest unit of information that can be judged true or false, which requires a subject and predicate. Even simple sentences have multiple propositions. The reader's task is to recognize propositions that are prominent in the text by their connections with other propositions, and to discard propositions not well linked. This analysis leads to a recognition of the deep structure of the text while discarding the surface structure, i.e., the actual words of the text. The work of reading comprehension requires finding important ideas while reducing the words in text to a compact gist and connecting the ideas in the text to our background knowledge, organized in schemata.

Summarization and question-generation are the strongest strategies for reading comprehension. Summarization depends on learning to delete trivia and redundancies to arrive at important ideas; to generate superordinate terms for lists of particular items or events; and to compose topic sentences that make good use of superordinate predicates. This complex mental work is supported by writing and the use of graphic organizers. In question generation, readers deliberately link ideas to one another and to background knowledge. The ability to generate good questions must be taught, for by default, both teachers and students tend to produce literal questions. To teach question generation, teachers must explain and model good questioning and give students guided practice in which they evaluate the questions they ask. The key evaluative criteria are whether they are about important ideas, whether they bring ideas together, and whether the asker can answer them. An important adjunct strategy is learning question-answer relationships, or QARs. The most valuable QARs for reading comprehension are "putting it together," identifying questions aimed at summarization, and "writer and me," identifying questions aimed at connecting text information to background knowledge. QARs help students understand where to look for answers, and they can be used to guide students and teachers to ask better questions.

Two other research-based comprehension strategies are visualization and using story grammar. Visualization is like playing a mental movie during reading, and for maximum effectiveness, visualization requires fluent reading. Readers who can visualize are better able to monitor their comprehension during reading. Readers who can use story structure can anticipate story events and read more actively. The most effective use of story structure is to self-question about key story events rather than to fill in a story map.

12 CHAPTER

Epilogue: Landmarks and Pitfalls in Learning to Read

Since the early twentieth century, scholars have been using scientific methods to develop public knowledge about how teachers can most productively lead children into skilled reading. It has been a productive century, but we remain far from a GPS guidance system programed with certain knowledge about how to direct every reader in every situation, or even from a roadmap through developmental reading. Nevertheless, we have identified many landmarks of productive practice, as well as many pitfalls—practices we know to be unproductive, misleading, or dangerous. In this final chapter, we will review these landmarks and pitfalls in the light of reading research over of the last century. Teachers who expect to be successful in leading children to literacy must be energetic, resourceful, and inventive, but they must also navigate with the science of reading education, monitoring progress toward known landmarks established by research and away from dangerous pitfalls, however seductively packaged.

A NEW VIEW OF SIGHT WORDS

Teaching beginning reading must aim at the landmark of sight word knowledge but avoid the pitfall of thinking of sight words as common words, memorized by their shapes or spellings. A sight word is any word recognized instantly and automatically. Sight words are not learned by memorization, but rather by a process of sizing up spellings as meaningful maps of word pronunciations. When we understand spellings as alphabetic maps, they become easy to remember because they "look" like the pronunciation of the word.

A pitfall in thinking about beginning reading is to confuse it with the word recognition mastery of adult reading. Children use much different reading strategies than skilled adults, which necessitates a developmental perspective on reading. Beginning readers are challenged to identify words; skilled readers are engaged in a critical reading of the messages of texts. Reading teachers must move beginners toward word recognition automaticity so that they devote more resources to comprehension. Paradoxically, decoding turns out to be a necessary step in the process of making sight words, which frees up children's resources to attend to the message of texts.

A persistent pitfall in resolving conflicts about reading instruction has been our penchant for addressing issues politically rather than scientifically. Scientists propose theories to explain cause and effect and test them against other plausible theories in educational experiments. When a theory of reading survives in the arena of experimentation, we gain public knowledge about what causes reading to succeed or to fail. In contrast, when we acquiesce to persuasive rhetoric or testimonial evidence, we base our practices on opinion or claims not backed by science, to the detriment of children's progress in learning to read.

Phonics can be either a landmark or a pitfall. The term phonics simply means decoding instruction. Because readers of alphabetic writing learn words by decoding, most children benefit from effective phonics in learning to read words. The problem is that not every kind of phonics pays off. Effective phonics explicitly and systematically teaches children how spellings map out the pronunciations of words, a critical step in making sight words.

How alphabets work

Three Writing Technologies

From history we know that several technologies have been developed for recording speech. Writing developed to facilitate trade in early civilizations, but its effects were far reaching. Acquiring writing enhanced our power to remember, to communicate across distances and time, and to enhance education. The earliest writing technology was logographic, in which symbols directly represented the meanings of words. This was problematic because would-be readers had to memorize symbols by the thousands, and the system was not flexible enough to readily represent new words. A second technology, the syllabary, was developed to encode the sounds of syllables, but that too was impractical for languages like English with thousands of syllables.

The alphabet has been called the greatest social invention in history because it enabled ordinary people to enjoy the power of literacy. The insight behind the alphabetic is that words are made of a relatively small set of phonemes (the elemental articulatory gestures used in a language). Following the alphabetic principle, an alphabetic language maps out the sequence of phonemes in a spoken word with a sequence of letters. The alphabetic technology dramatically reduced the number of symbols to a manageable number (26 in English). In addition, it enabled users to read words they'd never seen by decoding, and to write any message, including nonsense, by encoding it. Thus, the alphabet is a completely versatile system. However, because alphabetic writing operates at the phoneme level, beginners must learn to detect phonemes in spoken words, i.e., to acquire phoneme awareness. This has proved difficult for some learners: Without explicit instruction in phoneme awareness, these children have trouble making sight words.

The Great American Reading War

Teachers in early American schools taught the alphabetic code with drill methods that involved spelling and reading syllables. Horace Mann ridiculed phonics methods and by persuasive rhetoric, urged teachers to adopt a meaning-emphasis approach featuring whole-word methods and analytic phonics. Analytic phonics requires children to memorize whole words and only later to make sense of their spellings. This proved to be a pitfall not only because memorization is difficult, but also because teachers were barred from modeling how to decode, which requires pronouncing phonemes in isolation. By the 1930s, Mann's influence was dominant: Most American schools taught reading by whole-word methods.

The counterattack against whole-word methods began in the 1950s with the publication of Rudolf Flesch's bestseller *Why Johnny Can't Read*. Flesch rightly argued that alphabetic writing requires decoding instruction, but he overstated his case, minimized the difficulties of phonics, and vilified opponents. The politicization of phonics posed a major pitfall by diverting the dispute about reading from science to politics. Harvard professor Jeanne Chall reset the debate by publishing an extensive analysis of the literature showing that explicit, systematic, intensive phonics—a code-emphasis approach—is more effective for teaching children to read with comprehension. Chall's book became a major landmark in reading education, both for encouraging more effective instruction and for elevating the debate from the hot rhetoric of politics to the cool deliberations of scientific methods. However, political action proved helpful when the federal government authorized a series of large-scale experiments and research syntheses in the wake of Chall's book. This research has further reinforced the landmark status of systematic, explicit phonics to help children make sight words and improve their reading comprehension. In addition, the federally sponsored studies pointed to the value of daily reading of books and daily writing, taught by skillful teachers, with early intervention for children at risk.

HOW BEGINNERS DEVELOP THE ABILITY TO READ WORDS

A pitfall in thinking about reading, exemplified by Mann's mistake, is thinking beginners use the processes and strategies of skilled readers. Chall described six developmental stages in learning to read, including (1) a stage of emergent literacy, in which children are challenged to acquire the building blocks of phoneme awareness and letter recognition; (2) a stage of beginning reading, in which children are challenged to learn to decode words; (3) a stage of growing independence and fluency, in which children are challenged to acquire a large sight vocabulary for fluent reading; and (4) a stage of reading to learn, in which children are challenged to focus on the message of expository texts to learn meaning vocabulary and acquire comprehension strategies.

Ehri's phase theory of learning to read words has special relevance for learning to make sight words. All beginners must learn to access the lexicon, i.e., to unlock meaning information stored in memory from a split-second encounter with a printed word. To learn to read words, lexical access must become memorable, reliable, and easy. To maximize resources for reading comprehension, lexical access must go beyond accuracy to become fast and automatic, so that encountering a word in print effortlessly and involuntarily triggers the word in memory, allowing the reader to focus on the message of text.

Historically, researchers in reading have fallen into the pitfall of the dual route theory—thinking we can only read words by sight or by decoding. The ascendance of meaning-emphasis methods featuring whole-word memorization made this pitfall all the more treacherous. In fact, skilled readers use a sight word process to understand spellings and store them in memory for instant access when these words are encountered in print. In addition to sight and decoding, readers can analogize, use pronounceable word parts, or guess. To analogize, we think of a word with the same spelling pattern and make the unfamiliar word rhyme with the analogy. To use pronounceable word parts, we learn sight chunks and assemble them to identify multisyllable words. To guess words from context, we think of a word that makes semantic and syntactic sense, given the surrounding words in a sentence. Of the available strategies, sight word recognition is the most efficient because it is effortless, leaving all conscious resources for getting the message of text. For this reason, methods that rapidly build sight vocabulary are landmark methods for learning to read. Contextual guessing is worst because it drains mental resources without reliably leading to accurate word identification. Accordingly, teaching contextual guessing is a pitfall that delays reading development.

Phases in Learning to Read Words

In learning to recognize words, beginning readers move through four phases. In the prealphabetic phase, beginners try to link visual features of a word to its meaning. Children's surprising mastery of environmental print depends on the prealphabetic strategy of picture recognition, e.g., associating the arches in the McDonald's logo with the restaurant. Efforts to immerse children in a print-rich environment in hopes they will "decontextualize" the print have been a pitfall in reading education. In contrast, teaching phoneme awareness and letter recognition enables children to begin decoding in the partial alphabetic phase. The first letters decoded tend to be beginning consonants, which serve as phonetic cues for word identification. Still, consonants alone are unreliable for word recognition, and partial alphabetic readers lack the decoding ability to make sight words. Children with reading disability tend to persist with partial alphabetic strategies, decoding consonants and using contextual guessing to finesse word recognition as a substitute for decoding.

Attaining the full alphabetic phase is a landmark for the developing reader. Full alphabetic readers fully analyze spellings by sounding out and blending phonemes to identify words. Because most words have irregular elements in their spellings, full alphabetic readers learn to crosscheck, i.e., to test a pronunciation in context and use a sound-alike word if an attempt doesn't "click." After crosschecking, word learning gains efficiency when readers mentally mark silent or irregular elements to understand the spelling as a meaningful alphabetic map. A mentally annotated spelling can be stored in memory for a quick and automatic match when a word is seen in print. Thus, the process we use to make sight words entails decoding, cross-checking, and mental marking. Whole-word memorization takes about 35 trials, but the process of decoding, crosschecking, and mental marking allows sight word learning in only about four trials. Mathematically, this means decoding is about nine times easier than memorization. Because the sight-word process begins with decoding, phonics is a critical instructional component in making sight words.

As young readers learn sight words and sight chunks, they further accelerate word learning in the consolidated alphabetic phase by using the strategies of pronounceable word parts and analogizing. These expert strategies are landmarks in reading development because they bypass letter-by-letter decoding. Mastery of full alphabetic decoding is prerequisite to the use of these sophisticated strategies. In addition, progress into the consolidated alphabetic phase depends on getting rich practice opportunities through teacher-guided readings in instructional level text, through repeated readings, and through avid independent reading.

THE LANGUAGE PROCESSING SYSTEM OF SKILLED READERS

An Interactive Model

Models of skilled reading portray reading either as top-down, relying mostly on background knowledge, or bottom-up, relying on decoding. The inadequacies of both models point to the need of an interactive model of skilled reading. Marilyn Adams's useful model portrays the work of four interactive processors. (1) The phonological processor analyzes sounds to detect the phonological structures of speech. (2) The orthographic processor (acquired in learning to read) analyzes print to recognize graphemes, sight words, and sight chunks. (3) The meaning processor examines speech and print to activate meaning information, arousing morphemes (meaning units), words, and all linked semantic information, including irrelevancies. (4) The context processor uses overlapping fields of meaning information to detect the message in a text.

Misconceptions about skilled reading are understandable because observing our own reading is difficult. Skilled readers use spellings rather than word shapes to recognize words. We subvocalize, pronouncing words quietly or silently, to maintain words in memory as we assemble the messages of sentences. As demonstrated in eye-tracker research, skilled readers look at all the words in text rather than merely sampling words. The fact that misspellings slow us down shows we are processing spellings as we read. We rarely use context to identify words because it drains resources needed for reading comprehension.

Four Processors at Work

Reading processes use automatic spreading activation to diffuse information throughout the language processing system. The context, meaning, orthographic, and phonological processors interact to move information through the system without conscious attention. If there is conflict in the system, the higher level context processor compensates to resolve difficulties in word recognition. When context processing is diverted in this way, however, reading comprehension suffers.

The meaning processor briefly activates a wide range of meanings, whether relevant or irrelevant to the message of a text. To detect the message in text, the context processor uses semantic overlap to activate meanings that fit with other meanings. When speech or print fails to activate any meaning at all, we use context to glean meaning information to acquire new vocabulary. As growing reading ability unlocks the rich vocabulary resources in texts, readers rapidly acquire new word meanings. Although function words are disproportionately frequent in texts, the content words that carry the message of a text tend to be relatively rare, often appearing less than once in 100,000 running words. Explicit instruction by teachers helps young readers learn the meanings of valuable but uncommon words.

The orthographic processor recognizes spellings during rapid-fire fixations. We typically look at all the words of a text, either directly or in the periphery. Because we recognize words by their spellings, misspellings interfere with word recognition. Skilled readers rapidly process unfamiliar words by identifying sight chunks as pronounceable word parts. Our expertise with word recognition depends on skillful decoding. The claim that phonics impedes comprehension is a pitfall in understanding reading education. Decoding skill coordinates the interplay of the orthographic and phonological processors, allowing not only easy access to meaning, but the manufacture of sight words through the expert processes of pronounceable word parts and analogizing. By making sight words, skilled readers save resources for the demanding mental work of comprehending challenging texts.

Preparing Students to Learn to Read

Two Mistaken Views of Early Reading

Earlier models of reading readiness and emergent literacy were pitfalls for teachers preparing children to learn to read. Reading readiness proponents thought children needed to develop their intelligence and perceptual skills as prerequisites for reading, so that explicit instruction is harmful. Emergent literacy proponents made a false analogy to language learning in arguing that children acquire literacy naturally, and they too ruled out explicit instruction. The early intervention view better captures our contemporary understanding of early literacy by recognizing the importance of learning its component skills. For early intervention proponents, explicit instruction in phoneme awareness and letter recognition provides the essential tools for learning to read.

The reading readiness view continues to mislead teachers by suggesting that problems in learning to read are perceptual, especially for readers with learning disabilities. Weaknesses in reversing letters, misspelling words, and misreading words do not come from general perceptual deficits but from difficulties learning the alphabetic code, beginning with poor phoneme awareness. Efforts to match instruction to children's perceptual preferences or "learning styles" have been unsuccessful. Effective methods work for children without regard to any assessed learning style. Claims that children can't learn to read until they reach a predetermined mental age were based on poor research. IQ is a relatively weak predictor of success in learning to read when compared to phoneme awareness. Letter recognition and PA are the two best predictors of success in learning to read, and these abilities interact: Letter recognition helps PA by making visual symbols for phonemes, and phoneme awareness helps letter recognition by giving letters meaning.

Despite the importance of PA, teachers and researchers have found PA difficult to measure because we rely on tests that inadvertently assess spelling ability. When we test segmentation (breaking words into phonemes), blending (assembling phonemes into words), or manipulations such as reversing or deleting phonemes, we are measuring spelling knowledge. These tests pick up a level of PA that is a result of having already learned some of the alphabetic code. In contrast, the Test of Phoneme Identities gets at a prealphabetic level of phoneme awareness, which means it is more useful for identifying children at risk before a PA weakness causes wider reading difficulties.

Matthew Effects in Reading

Until recently, PA instruction was almost exclusively informal through activities such as interactive read alouds with alphabet books, invented spelling, and reciting nursery rhymes. Reading aloud is the premier activity to prepare children for eventual success in reading because it builds vocabulary and conceptual knowledge. However, the extent of informal literacy instruction tends to depend on socioeconomic status. Children in poverty typically receive only about 2% as much reading aloud as children in professional homes. Comparisons of time spent in read alouds suggest low SES children are more than four years behind more affluent peers. The Matthew effects model shows that early weaknesses in PA can snowball into pervasive literacy difficulties with profound, lifelong consequences. At the same time, early intervention in PA instruction can enable decoding success, leading to fluency and motivated reading practice. Avid reading enables children to learn the meaning vocabulary and concepts that eventually improve verbal learning. Thus, early PA wealth compounds into life-enriching literacy knowledge.

The Matthew effects model is a major landmark for understanding reading disability. Students with LD are often gifted poor readers whose PA deficits have not yet affected general functioning, so that they remain bright, effective learners except in the realm of reading. Effective early instruction in PA and decoding can prevent the onset of crushing negative Matthew effects, allowing their language comprehension talents to develop through reading. Unlike readers with LD, garden-variety poor readers, who are weak in both decoding ability and language comprehension, face more daunting challenges. Either way, struggling readers stand their best chance of long-term success when reading teachers provide early PA and decoding instruction using the landmark strategies explained in this book.

Learning to detect phonemes in spoken words

Phoneme awareness is the ability to detect phonemes in their natural habitat, the spoken word. Before beginners can understand spellings and remember their alphabetic mappings, they must detect the phonemes that are mapped. Phonemes make sounds, but they are better defined as the basic articulatory gestures of a language, the elements from which we construct spoken words. Learning a phoneme requires learning to detect its gesture in spoken words. Landmark PA instruction introduces phonemes one at a time rather than trying to develop a general sensitivity to all phonemes at once. After children learn some dozen phonemes with the careful, explicit teaching of a skilled teacher, acquiring additional phonemes gets much easier.

Introducing a phoneme begins by making the phoneme memorable through a sound analogy, e.g., that the phoneme /s/ is like the sound of a sneaky snake, "Ssss." An illustration of a "sneaky snake" that includes the letter *S* helps children remember the analogy, and a hand gesture such as "slithering" the hand from side to side becomes a useful recognition signal. Because phonemes vary somewhat in word contexts, working with an alliterative "tongue tickler" helps children sample the phoneme across words. When children stretch and split off the phoneme in the tickler words, they learn the identity of the phoneme in and out of words. Children can also learn more about the articulatory gesture that defines a phoneme by studying its articulation with mirrors.

Stretching words to invent spellings gives valuable practice detecting and transcribing phonemes. Simple letterbox lessons guide children to detect phonemes in regular, one-syllable words and to represent them in accurate spellings.

Once instruction has made a phoneme memorable, children need phoneme finding practice. To show how to detect a phoneme in spoken words, the teacher models how to test spoken example words (and nonexamples) for the phoneme. Children practice PA by testing words for the phoneme, including words where the target phoneme is placed at the middle or end, or clustered with another consonant. If the words children test for the phoneme are related in meaning, they learn to make a metalinguistic shift from meaning to form. The final phase of a PA lesson leads children to apply PA to take the first steps in decoding words. Showing children how to blend the target phoneme into partial words helps them learn a key component strategy in decoding. Showing them how to use beginning consonants in phonetic cue reading builds a direct bridge from PA to decoding words.

How to Teach Phonics for Sight Word Learning

What is Phonics?

One of the key landmarks in reading research is Linnea Ehri's recognition that decoding is essential in making sight words. Despite all the controversies, phonics is simply decoding instruction. Most children need phonics to learn to decode spellings and identify words. Children's growing skill with decoding in the full alphabetic phase heralds a rapid growth of sight vocabulary.

Phonics teaches vowel correspondences, i.e., the link between vowel graphemes (which can be either single letters or digraphs) and vowel phonemes. Phonics usually begins with short vowels, which have easy, one-letter spellings. Short vowels challenge children's phoneme awareness because they are similar in sound and mouth shape. Long vowels and other vowels are clearer phonemes to detect, but their spellings usually involve digraphs. Recognizing vowels from their spelling patterns (e.g., noting that the digraph *igh* signals /I/) is more reliable than identifying them from diacritical marks. Even fast-paced basal programs only teach about two correspondences per week, but teachers need not present irregular vowel correspondences such as *ough*; children need only about 40 vowel correspondences to become decoding experts. Teachers who learn to identify the useful and reliable correspondences make good use of the "rocket science" needed for explicit, systematic phonics.

Phonics Landmarks and Pitfalls

Research has established landmarks for phonics success as well as counterproductive pitfalls. One landmark is the "best bet" strategy for dealing with the ambiguous consonants *c* and *g*. We teach their more common "hard" phonemes (/k/ and /g/) first, and then follow with their soft phonemes (/s/ and /j/). Beginners should try the hard phoneme as their best bet; if it doesn't work, they should try the soft phoneme. Ultimately, readers need a sophisticated "signals" strategy, using the soft phoneme whenever *c* or *g* is followed by the signals *e, i,* or *y*; without these signals, readers should prefer the hard phoneme. By learning vowel frequencies, teachers can help beginners apply the best-bet strategy with many vowels; for example, students should try /O/ for *ow* because that phoneme is twice as frequent as /ow/.

When a correspondence comes with conditions, we have a phonics rule. Some phonics rules are quite useful, e.g., that silent *e* signals the long vowel or that single vowels are short. However, the popular rule about "two vowels go walking" fails more often than it succeeds. There are two standards for useful rules: They have to work most of the time, and they must be stated in simple, comprehensible language. Even when phonics rules don't produce a perfect pronunciation, they are useful if they get the reader close enough to the word to correct by crosschecking.

Many teachers rely on workbooks and worksheets to teach phonics, but overreliance on such materials is an instructional pitfall associated with lagging achievement in learning to read. Teachers should use written exercises selectively; some have value for independent practice or for assessment. A landmark activity to follow up phonics instruction is practice reading decodable text. Decodable text restricts content words to those featuring learned vowel correspondences. When children read carefully selected decodable text, they find that phonics works to unlock the words, and they stay with decoding strategies rather than falling back on guessing or memorization.

When teachers model to show how to sound out and blend words, their phonics instruction is explicit. Research indicates explicit phonics is more effective than analytic phonics, which requires children to memorize whole words and analyze them. Analytic phonics has been a pitfall because it does not allow teachers and students to pronounce phonemes in isolation. This prohibition is unreasonable because most phonemes can be isolated accurately, and minor distortions are correctable with crosschecking. Linguistic programs offered children decodable text (a landmark) but expected them to induce spelling patterns by analytic phonics (a pitfall). The alphabetic code is too subtle and complex to work out without explicit instruction.

Although beginners must soon deal with multisyllable words, they do not need dictionary syllabication to locate syllables. Instead, they can use vowels to identify rough syllable boundaries and crosscheck to complete word identification. Some programs try to teach phonograms (rime spellings) instead of vowel correspondences to overcome the irregularity of vowel spellings. However, phonogram chunks are more easily learned by decoding, which requires knowledge of vowel correspondences. Teaching phonograms in place of vowels is a pitfall that unnecessarily complicates phonics.

Besides covering correspondences and phonics rules, phonics teaches blending. A landmark is to scaffold blending with the body and coda segments of spoken words. The body of a syllable includes everything through the vowel, and the optional coda includes any remaining consonants. Teachers can begin oral blending work with pictures or riddles, but they should shift expeditiously to guiding blending by moving letter tiles. In blending, it is better to pronounce phonemes than to use letter names because letter names do not consistently signal the correct phonemes. Vowel-first blending works well for beginners because it guides them to sound out the vowel (the novel element in the word) before assembling the rest of the word. They next blend any beginning letters to the vowel to make the body, and finally they join body and coda to recognize a word. With developing blending skill, readers can sound out and blend phonemes in a left-to-right progression. Using a blending slide introduces body-coda blending with an engaging narrative.

CHOOSING TEXTS FOR READING INSTRUCTION

Decodable Text

Teachers of beginning readers must strike a balance between providing rich experiences with children's literature (a meaning emphasis) and providing explicit decoding instruction (a code emphasis). To practice the decoding strategies learned in phonics lessons, children need decodable text, i.e., text specially engineered so that nearly all content words in the text (not the function or "glue" words) can be decoded using the vowel correspondences introduced to date. Because children are continually learning new vowel correspondences, decodable texts must be delivered in a reading series with an expanding pool of words reflecting the new correspondences being taught. Providing children with well-written decodable text is a landmark strategy for teaching beginning reading.

Decodable text for beginning readers features mostly regularly spelled, one-syllable words. Regular words like *mail* or *ride* can be defined as those with large word families, so that many other words rhyme and share their phonogram patterns (rime spellings). In contrast, irregular words like *was* or *of* have small families or none: Few if any rhyming words share their phonogram patterns. Since many high frequency words in English are irregular, children must memorize the spellings of some common words. However, for reliable sight word recognition, these words must be relearned later by decoding, crosschecking, and mental marking.

Alternatives to Decodable Text

Until recently, basal reading programs strongly emphasized learning whole words over acquiring the alphabetic code for an early experience of literature. This meaning emphasis dug a pitfall for beginning readers because they experienced a mismatch between the vowel correspondences taught in phonics and the content words encountered in stories. Historically, basal readers used heavy word repetition or predictable text patterns to enable beginners to manage words with irregular spellings or advanced vowel patterns. This kind of practice left children unprepared for the transition to children's literature, where word repetition is rare and singsong patterned language disappears. Code-emphasis programs better integrate phonics with the content words in practice texts by limiting the vocabulary in early texts to manageable words.

Unfortunately, there are few high quality decodable text series in print, partly because they are difficult to write. Creating a memorable story requires a very wide pool of words to achieve the precise diction of literature; restricting the vocabulary to decodable words, which is vital for learning to decode and make sight words, tightly restricts the word pool. A possible solution for writers is to first compose an engaging story and then replace the content words with decodable synonyms by using a thesaurus program.

An Experiment with Texts

The landmark experiment demonstrating the importance of decodable text was carried out in a district where all first graders studied the same phonics program, but then practiced by reading either a meaning-emphasis or code-emphasis basal series. Children who could apply phonics instruction by reading decodable text in the code-emphasis basal were better at reading words by midyear. Reading texts where phonics "works" to unlock the words of decodable texts provides congruence between instruction and practice. Most programs, however, have made phonics less useful by featuring texts not restricted for decodability. Accordingly, one of the landmarks in beginning reading education is to restrict texts to those featuring words decodable with the vowel patterns learned to date. With integration between phonics and text, children's success reading stories links to their progress in phonics, motivating both students and teachers to take phonics seriously.

Reading Practice in the Classroom

One of the pitfalls of typical classroom instruction is that teachers devote an inordinate amount of time to round-robin reading, which militates against both productive oral reading practice and listening comprehension. One possible solution would be to use round-robin repeated reading, in which a succession of children reread the same text to fluency, interspersed with conversation about story events. Round-robin repeated reading would overcome some of the inattention and embarrassment issues with round-robin reading.

By the first-grade level, most reading should be silent rather than oral. Silent reading allows readers to change reading speeds when encountering difficulties.

This enhances comprehension. In addition, silent reading roughly doubles reading speed, allowing increases in reading practice. The directed reading-thinking activity (DR-TA) makes good use of silent reading. In DR-TA, the teacher divides a narrative text into brief plot episodes and motivates reading by asking students to predict what might happen in each new section of text. When students justify their predictions by explaining the text clues leading to their predictions, they model for peers how to draw inferences as they read.

Levels of Text

A venerable landmark in reading education is to place readers for instruction in instructional level texts. The benchmarks for the instructional level are 95-98% success in reading words. For independent reading, e.g., with library books, children need texts at their independent levels, where their word reading is 99-100% successful. A grave reading pitfall occurs when readers are given texts to read at their frustration levels, where their word reading is 0-94% successful. Students pushed to read with high error rates lose comprehension, give up crosschecking, and consequently stop making sight words. In time, a diet of frustration-level text leads children to develop negative attitudes toward reading. Another common pitfall in classrooms occurs when children not working with the teacher in a reading group are assigned seatwork consisting of low quality exercises or time-wasting busywork. Reading seatwork can be more productive when children complete written guides, write about their readings in response to open-ended prompts, or read along with peers, the teacher, or a recording in assisted reading.

Grouping for Instruction

To keep children reading at their instructional levels and to help them learn the critical concepts and strategies to move ahead in reading, homogeneous achievement grouping is an instructional landmark. Though some argue that placement in a low reading group harms children's self-esteem, struggling readers face even greater self-esteem issues when competing with skilled readers in heterogeneous groups. Cross-class grouping can mitigate seatwork and motivational problems by creating whole-class achievement groups using readers from multiple classrooms, so that every student in the class is working on similar strategies with instructional level texts.

The more serious problem with homogeneous grouping is that poor readers progress more slowly through their basals. They read less text and learn fewer strategies. As a result, the gap between good and poor readers widens. To counteract these potential negative effects of achievement grouping, teachers should group readers flexibly for many purposes, including the use of heterogeneous groups for cooperative learning. Whenever grouping is used, informal assessment data should be used to regroup students to reflect new learning. In addition, low reading groups should be scheduled for extra reading times to give children in lower groups practice levels comparable to those in higher-level groups.

Matthew Effects Revisited

The Matthew effects model, showing how the rich get richer and the poor get poorer, explains the far-reaching effects of different levels of reading practice. Early deficits in phoneme awareness trigger negative Matthew effects by delaying learning to decode, which impedes children's ability to make sight words and gain reading fluency. Without fluency, reading is hard and unrewarding, and children do not willingly choose a level of reading practice that enables them to learn meaning vocabulary and concepts through reading. With vocabulary and concept growth stagnant, a struggling reader's learning ability cannot keep pace with that of avid reading peers. In contrast, early success with phoneme awareness starts a chain of positive Matthew effects. Familiarity with phonemes enables success in decoding, leading to rapid gains in sight-word knowledge and reading fluency. When reading is fluent, children are better disposed to develop habits of avid reading needed to build vocabulary and conceptual knowledge for enhanced learning ability.

The Matthew effects model points to the landmark of early intervention to get children on a trajectory for positive Matthew effects. If children can be identified early as at risk and given specialized, intensive instruction with expert teachers, they can be helped to reverse a pattern with potentially lifelong consequences. Struggling beginners need low-frills instruction and "two-a-days" for increased reading practice. They especially need a high quality series of decodable text to maximize learning and motivation during the make-or-break years of beginning reading.

MOVING FROM DECODING TO FLUENCY

What is Fluency?

Reading fluency means reading with automatic word recognition. Specific fluency is achieved in reading a text where all or most of the words in the text are in the reader's sight vocabulary. General reading fluency is characteristic of readers with a sight vocabulary large enough to encompass the vocabulary used across a wide range of literary and general informational texts. Becoming fluent increases reading speed, improves comprehension, allows for more expressive oral reading, and promotes avid reading. The critical path to fluency is learning sight words by the tens of thousands by the sight-word processes of decoding, crosschecking, mental marking, and rereading.

One of the pitfalls in thinking about fluency is to define fluency by its results, especially the result of faster reading. Misunderstanding fluency as reading speed has led teachers to direct children in speed-reading practice at the expense of reading comprehension. A valid assessment of reading fluency must check whether the reader got the message of the text because comprehension ordinarily accompanies automatic word recognition. Repeated reading is a landmark practice for increasing reading fluency. By rereading texts to a speed criterion with continual attention to comprehension, readers make sight words through repeated decoding, crosschecking, mental marking, and rereading. Repeated reading with word overlap across readings builds immediate fluency faster because the store of sight words learned in previous readings makes reading texts with the same words easier.

Two False Promises for Fluency

Two major pitfalls for promoting reading fluency have been popular historically: trying to develop fluency by whole word methods and by teaching beginners to orchestrate contextual cues during reading. Given that there are about 100,000 sight words needed for general fluency in English, whole word methods are impractical. Surprisingly, most of the different words we need to learn are too infrequent in print to learn by mere exposure. Moreover, drill and extensive repetition are not necessary for learning sight words. The landmark insights of Linnea Ehri show that we make sight words by a process that begins with decoding. Decoding bonds the letters in a spelling to the phonemes in the pronunciation. We correct near-misses by crosschecking, after which we mentally mark any unexpected letters and store the annotated spelling in memory. Sight recognition in reading is automatic because storing the spelling in memory enables an instant match on encountering the printed spelling. Thus, acquiring the ability to make sight words depends on learning to decode. With a growing correspondence toolkit and crosschecking skills, children can negotiate the path from simple texts to children's literature.

A more recent pitfall has been the claim that reading fluency depends on developing skill in a psycho linguistic guessing game. Writers rarely supply the redundant clues to guess the content words in texts. For this reason, only younger and less-skilled readers resort to guessing. Skilled readers building large stores of sight words find it much easier to look at words for instant, automatic recognition. Making sight words depends on decoding rather than guessing, which means the landmark methods for gaining fluency are best learned with explicit phonics and practice in decodable text, rather than with guessing practice in predictable text. Giving children predictable texts encourages a cued recitation strategy that short-circuits the process of making sight words. We can't lead children from predictable books to children's literature merely by reducing the predictability of the texts because eliminating the patterned language leaves novice readers lacking decoding skills adrift and unable to read the words. In contrast, students who work through a decodable series that systematically expands the available pool of words with new vowel learning eventually allows a relaxation of the decodability strictures. With crosschecking, mental marking, and repeated reading, beginners can be weaned from decodable books to early literature.

Despite the allure of whole-word methods and contextual guessing, it is decoding that creates a self-teaching device for making sight words. The sight-word processes of decoding, crosschecking, and mentally marking irregular letters rapidly builds sight words and sight chunks for increased efficiency in word learning. Sight chunk knowledge is crucial for reading polysyllabic words, the last major challenge in word recognition. Despite rhetoric to the contrary, the key skills for rapid sight-word learning come from phonics. This means we should encourage the decoding efforts of struggling readers during the full alphabetic phase and help them stick with decoding strategies by supplying decodable text. Rereading, too, is basic for making sight words, whether at the sentence level or by repeated reading of texts. Ultimately, becoming a fluent reader depends on acquiring the habits, attitudes, and interests of avid readers.

Encouraging Voluntary Reading

Effective reading teachers create a reading culture in which voluntary reading is the currency of conversation. Even reading homework can be productive if it is arranged carefully. To develop voluntary reading, students must have the freedom to choose their own library books. They need frequent library visits (daily if possible) to make and revise good book choices. Teachers can help them choose books at an independent level. They can also give daily booktalks that tease listeners by highlighting the problem without revealing the plot. Talking about books with peers is a landmark activity for promoting voluntary reading. In conversations about books, children get reading recommendations they take seriously. In addition, the mild peer pressure of a regular discussion group induces children to read so they can contribute to the discussion. Applying these same principles can improve summer reading homework. We should allow students to choose from a menu of recommended books. We should restrict selections to easy, independent-level books, and we should give booktalks to entice students to read. When children return from summer vacation, we should organize post-reading discussions in lieu of book reports. Readers can demonstrate that they have read by creating brief, color-coded book reviews, by posting reviews on a class website, or by passing the easy quizzes offered by Accelerated Reader.

Incentive plans remain popular for inducing voluntary reading, but their motivating value extends only as long as the rewards continue. They may become pitfalls by defining reading as work done for an external incentive. The negative effects of incentive plans may be ameliorated by providing recognition instead of rewards, by giving reading opportunities as prizes, or by awarding books as rewards for reading. In measuring voluntary reading for these incentives, teachers should count the number of pages read or Accelerated Reader points earned, in preference to counting the number of books read or the amount of reading time.

Research suggests that sustained silent reading (SSR) has been an instructional pitfall, with little or no effect on voluntary reading, attitudes toward reading, or reading achievement. However, SSR can be productive when coupled with regular peer book discussions that harness peer pressure to read; students read in order to participate in the discussions. SSR programs without motivating peer discussions cost valuable instructional time that could be better spent teaching vocabulary or guiding students in reading instructional-level texts. Scaffolded silent reading holds promise for developing reading fluency by arranging teacher conferences and giving help to select independent-level books.

Children left to their own devices tend to judge books by their covers. Teachers can help students make better book choices by providing regular booktalks and read alouds, and they can monitor children's choices to select independent-level books for outside reading. The popular five-finger test (allowing five unknown words per page before vetoing a book) has been a pitfall for book selection, allowing students to check out books too difficult for independent reading. Because the benchmark for independent reading is 99% success in reading words, a two-finger test can be helpful: We limit choices to books children can read with no more than one unsolved word per page. For readers needing fluency, teachers should promote "page turners" rather than the children's literature, which requires instructional guidance. Reading book series encourages voluntary reading because when readers become familiar with the characters and situations in the first book, they gain admittance to other books with the same characters and similar situations.

DEVELOPING WORD RECOGNITION THROUGH SPELLING

Spelling develops across five spelling stages. Prephonemic "spelling" represents messages with drawings or scribbles. Semiphonemic spellings begin to record consonants that beginners detect in spoken words. Phonemic spellings transcribe all the phonemes in words with accurate or related letters, indicating well-developed phoneme awareness. Transitional spellings are phonemic spellings that include silent letters and attempts at spelling conventions. Standard spellings are remembered rather than invented.

Invented Spelling

Invented spelling is a landmark in early literacy because stretching spellings to identify and transcribe phonemes helps children learn the alphabetic code. A landmark study showed the benefits of invented spelling for acquiring phoneme awareness. First graders who transcribed phonemes in invented spellings became better at reading and spelling words than first graders for whom teachers provided spellings. Until children have mastered PA, they make the best progress in phoneme awareness when teachers nicely refuse to provide spellings while arranging daily writing times with regular opportunities to practice phoneme detection. Invented spelling should be supplemented with explicit PA instruction. Annotating children's messages in invented spellings with standard spellings preserves their messages for later reading and helps parents enjoy their children's writings at home. Only students low in phoneme awareness benefit from invented spelling. Once students have learned to detect phonemes, providing spellings helps them practice new vocabulary, organize ideas, and relate new concepts to background knowledge.

Spelling Instruction

In 19th century American schools, spelling work was central to reading instruction. In one-room schools, it was convenient for older students to tutor younger children, often by helping them spell words on slates with chalk. This focus on spelling ability helped beginners learn to read words because spelling and word recognition are closely related. When readers store complete and accurate spellings in memory, they become better able to use these spellings in recognizing sight words. To the extent that word recognition and spelling become effortless and automatic, students free up resources for both reading comprehension and written composition.

Spelling instruction should aim at developing spelling power, the ability to learn and remember spellings efficiently. Acquiring spelling power requires learning spelling correspondences, rules, and patterns. Spelling correspondences are more complex than phonics correspondences because they specify how phonemes are represented in various positions in words. Spelling rules can be useful (as with the "*i* before *e*" rule), but their reliability is limited. Spelling patterns (e.g., the *-tion* suffix) are important in English because accurate spelling often relies on pattern knowledge rather than direct phoneme transcription. When students can generate spellings by using correspondences, rules, and patterns, learning to spell any particular word is reduced to learning the exceptional elements in spellings. For example, they may need only to remember which vowel to use for schwa or which letters are silent.

Several popular ideas about promoting spelling have proven to be pitfalls in spelling instruction. Reading books rarely helps us learn accurate spellings because reading is under intense time pressure, while spelling requires a close study of unpredictable elements in a spelling. Spelling bees may motivate students to invest time in word study, but students rarely learn words during the competitions because spellings are recited rather than mapped. Abandoning structured spelling programs to collect spelling words from literature or from student writings provides no systematic program for learning the correspondences, rules, and patterns needed for spelling power.

For learning spelling power, teachers should carefully select words with spelling commonalities, e.g., words that double the final consonant before adding *-ed* or *-ing*. Published spelling programs are useful for disciplined spelling study.

Because spelling lessons aim at developing spelling power, spelling tests should include words students haven't studied that exemplify the correspondence, rules, or patterns they are learning. Letterbox lessons and wordmapping activities help students understand how spellings map out the phonological structures of words.

Teaching vocabulary and comprehension strategies

Once readers have learned to read, they can build on reading fluency by reading to learn. Teachers can build their reading comprehension by explicit instruction in meaning vocabulary and in reading comprehension strategies.

Teaching Vocabulary

The valuable and versatile words used by educated readers and writers tend to be rare in print and virtually absent in conversation. Students can learn these words either by reading challenging texts or by explicit instruction. Learning words by reading is unreliable because writers do not provide redundant clues to meaning; they expect their readers to know the words they use. The typical instruction in vocabulary is a pitfall approaching malpractice. Teachers ask students to look up words, copy definitions, and write sentences before students understand how to use the words.

Landmark studies of vocabulary instruction suggest learning a word involves a four-step process. First, learning a word requires locating its boundaries of meaning by studying examples and non examples. Second, learners need usage information, with many examples to show how the word is used with other words. Third, learners must extricate the word from its original context by seeing how it can be used in other contexts. Finally, learners are ready to generate new sentence contexts for the word; this is the final step rather than something students can accomplish by reading a dictionary definition. The goal of explicit vocabulary instruction is not just acquaintance, but ownership, allowing instant access to word meanings in reading, writing, speaking, and listening.

Landmark vocabulary instruction follows the four steps of this model. Teachers should select words that are versatile and challenging to students, and they should present them in semantic groups so that students can use them together. Teachers should provide user-friendly definitions as well as generous examples and nonexamples. They should scaffold students' initial usage by asking them to complete sentences rather than to generate sentences prematurely. Teachers should challenge students to compare semantically related words by asking them to make semantic decisions, e.g., about whether a novice is a virtuoso. In addition, teachers should ask students to locate or use new words outside of class and to report their findings, thus extending learning beyond the classroom.

Teaching Comprehension

Besides learning vocabulary, readers can improve reading comprehension by learning strategies, i.e., independent problem-solving tactics for learning from text. Unlike scaffolds, strategies can be used independently of the teacher. Unlike skills, strategies are used consciously rather than automatically, although over time, strategies can become skills. Five single strategies have strong support from the science of reading education: Summarization, question generation, question answering, visualization, and using story structure. Strategies can be especially effective when used in combination.

Understanding why these strategies are effective requires some knowledge of the basic processes of reading comprehension. According to the simple view of reading, reading comprehension is a product of skillful word recognition (that is, translating printed words effortlessly into language) and language comprehension. Building an extensive sight vocabulary allows readers to turn their attention to improving their language comprehension. Background knowledge is the largest single factor in language comprehension. The more we know, from algebra to zoology, the easier it is to understand texts written about what we know. Background knowledge is organized into units called schemata. A schema is a reader's generic idea about a situation. In most situations, we can comprehend texts on familiar topics by activating an appropriate schema and assimilating details into "slots" in the schema. However, with topics for which we do not have well-developed schemata, we need strategies for building mental models that can develop into schemata.

The subliminal process of detecting and weighing propositions underlies the work of finding important ideas in texts. A proposition is the smallest unit of information that can be judged true or false, which means any proposition must have a subject and predicate. Propositions include the simple subject and predicate of a sentence, and adjectives, adverbs, and prepositional phrases function as embedded propositions. To find the important ideas, the reader must recognize propositions well linked with other propositions and discard propositions not well linked. By deleting poorly linked propositions, the reader comes to recognize the deep structure of the text while discarding the surface structure, i.e., the actual words. Finding important ideas while reducing the words in text to a compact gist is the process of summarization. Connecting these ideas to our background knowledge, organized into schemata, completes the work of reading comprehension.

Comprehension Strategy Instruction

The two strongest strategies for improving reading comprehension are summarization and question generation. Summarization follows a series of rules, directing the reader to delete trivia and redundancies to locate important ideas; to substitute more general or "superordinate" terms for lists of particular items and events; and to compose topic sentences. At the heart of summarization is the work of superordinating predicate terms that collectively explain the author's point. Thinking of summarization as "about-point" focuses attention on the central activity of determining superordinate predicates. The work of summarization can be scaffolded with graphic organizers, and efforts to articulate summaries in writing are helpful for evaluating them.

The strategy of question generation involves deliberately linking ideas with other ideas in a text and to background knowledge. By default, both teachers and students tend to produce literal questions, which are seductively easy to ask and to answer. Reliance on literal questioning is a serious pitfall in the classroom. For this reason, the strategy of asking good questions must be taught. In effective question-generation instruction, teachers explain and model how to ask good questions, guide students in asking questions about texts, and help students evaluate their questions. Students need help deciding whether their questions are about important ideas, whether they bring ideas together, and whether they know the answers. Learning question-answer relationships, or QARs, is an important first step in question generation. QARs depend on recognizing the type of question being asked, to know where to look for the answer. The most valuable question types are "putting it together," which are questions where the answer must be collected from multiple sentences, and "writer and me," which require connecting text information to background knowledge. QARs can be used to guide students and teachers to ask better questions.

The comprehension strategies of visualization and using story grammar also have a strong research base. Visualization necessitates fluent reading in order to play a mental movie during reading. Readers skilled in visualization are better able to monitor their comprehension during reading—which helps them take executive control over learning. Readers familiar with story structure can anticipate story events and read more actively. While teachers can scaffold story comprehension by having students fill in a story map, story structure becomes a strategy when students learn to question themselves about key story events during reading.

A FINAL WORD

I hope readers will remember two central lessons from *Making Sight Words*. First, you will experience your greatest success in teaching children to read by basing your instruction on the scientific evidence about what works in teaching reading. Both traditional activities and popular current activities may be at variance with the science of reading education. Aim at research-tested landmarks, such as teaching phoneme awareness to lay the groundwork for phonics. Avoid the pitfalls identified by research, such as teaching children to rely on context in a psycholinguistic guessing game.

Second, children learn best when teachers get explicit. Discovery learning may work well in suburban schools in professional neighborhoods, where children have enjoyed thousands of hours of preschool literacy experiences. It does not work well in urban or rural schools with children of poverty, where students are often years behind in learning the nuts and bolts of literacy and the language of books. Whenever children are challenged to master new ideas and strategies, they learn better with explicit instruction. They make optimal progress when teachers explain when and why to use a strategy, model how to solve problems with the strategy, and scaffold simplified practice without all the snags of real-life situations. They apply their learning most readily when teachers gradually lead them into the complications of whole texts, and when teachers continually assess their progress to revise instruction. The sequence of explicit teaching gives children their best chance to put new ideas to work and move ahead in learning to read.

PRACTICAL CHAPTERS

PRACTICAL CHAPTER

How to Introduce a New Book

An invitation to tutor

Teaching beginners how to make sight words takes practice, and the best practice activity is actually teaching a struggling reader. Actual teaching provides a chance to apply the abstract ideas of reading research in practice, an indispensable element of effective teacher-education programs.

Tutoring a single struggling beginner provides an excellent learning opportunity for reading instruction. Working with a single student avoids most problems of behavior management encountered with groups of children (though managing behavior remains an important consideration). A teacher's undivided attention is highly motivating to a single student. In addition, tutoring is inherently powerful. Tutoring maximizes individualization, allowing the tutor continual opportunities to assess and refocus teaching on deficits revealed in the assessment. Tutors can readily note problems, address confusions, and supply immediate feedback for a single student. Tutored students get all the "turns," greatly increasing their opportunities for active response. Some studies have found very large effects for tutored students over group-instructed students (Anania, 1982; Burke, 1984), although the National Reading Panel reported only a nonsignificant trend favoring tutoring over small-group and whole-class approaches for phonics instruction.

One popular and successful approach to tutoring is *Reading Recovery*, a first-grade tutoring program developed in New Zealand by Marie Clay (Clay, 1993; Pinnell, Fried, & Estice, 1990). Reading Recovery teachers see their students every day for a half-hour of individual instruction, with the aim of "recovering" grade-level reading ability in order to head off a career in remedial reading.

A Reading Recovery lesson features four basic activities. First, the student reads one or more familiar books (typically including a book introduced in the previous lesson) while the teacher keeps a running record (an informal assessment of oral reading explained in Practical Chapter 6). Next the student works with letter manipulatives, either to learn to identify letters or to construct words. Then the student writes a message or story, using invented spelling. Finally, the teacher introduces a new book and helps the student read the book aloud. Reading Recovery lessons begin and end with reading and devote about half the lesson to reading practice, a benchmark of effective remedial teaching.

Other practical chapters in this book will introduce you to teaching strategies vital to the success of tutoring in the Reading Recovery lesson format. Note that these are not official Reading Recovery activities, carried out according to program rules. Rather they are adaptations loosely structured around the Reading Recovery format, with variations designed to strengthen techniques of questionable effectiveness. For example, where Reading Recovery leaves considerable latitude for word study activities (Pinell et al., 1990), research studies have demonstrated large effects by adding explicit spelling and phonics instruction to this part of the lesson. For this reason, I have included the letterbox lesson as a specific research-based lesson for word study. Explicit instruction in encoding and decoding words enhances the efficiency of the Reading Recovery program and enables students to reach grade level reading significantly earlier (Iversen & Tunmer, 1993; Tunmer & Hoover, 1993).

BOOK INTRODUCTIONS

We begin with ideas on how to introduce a new book to students. All too often, teachers simply hand over a book to a beginning reader, with the less-than-stimulating introduction, "Here, read this book." This presumes the student is naturally interested in any story and motivated to read—a presumption we would not extend to ourselves. As enthusiastic readers, we tend to be quite choosy when browsing books and reading materials. Avid readers usually browse at least five books for each book they decide to buy or check out from a library (Wilson, 1992). We can safely assume that young readers with very limited sight vocabulary, facing the difficult struggle of reading a new and unfamiliar book, are going to be at least as reluctant to embark on a book out of the blue. They need to develop strong interest and motivation before taking on the difficult task of reading an unfamiliar book. Marie Clay of Reading Recovery lavished an entire scholarly article on the problem of how to engage young readers with a new storybook (Clay, 1991).

Making effective book instructions requires knowledge of story structure (see Figure 1). The familiar stories of western culture have a characteristic format (Mandler & Johnson, 1977). Early in the story, the author introduces the setting, which acquaints us with the main characters in their ordinary situation. For example, the folktale Rumpelstiltskin begins by telling us about a young and beautiful woman who is extraordinarily skilled at spinning fiber into yarn—her yarn is silky, strong, and flawless. Her father is very proud of his daughter, and he likes to boast that his daughter could spin straw into gold. This is the setting—the ordinary life of the characters before a problem arises.

Setting	Goal/Problem	Plot Episodes	Resolution
Characters	Initiating event leads to goal or problem	Subgoal/problem Attempt—Outcome, leading to subgoal/problem Attempt—Outcome,	End state
Location			Related events
Time	Related events	leading to subgoal/problem and so on	

FIGURE 1: Model of story structure

Stories then typically progress by describing an initiating event that takes the characters out of their ordinary life, an event that creates a problem or encourages the main character to develop a goal. In Rumpelstiltskin, the initiating event takes place when the young woman is called to the castle and ordered to spin straw into gold, with the promise to become the queen—and the countervailing threat to be put to death if she fails. Initiating events create a tension that propels the reader on a search for resolution. After developing the reader's engagement with the problem or goal, stories typically unfold a series of plot episodes in which the main character attempts to solve the problem or reach the goal. Some attempts succeed, moving the character closer to a final solution, but others fail so that the "plot thickens," leading to even thornier problems. In Rumpelstiltskin, the plot continues with the intervention of a strange creature who promises to spin the straw into gold in exchange for the woman's first-born child. This proposal solves the immediate problem but creates a new problem—to save the first-born child. In the end, the problem is usually justly resolved in a happy ending, leaving the main character satisfied and successful. However, if the character has chosen illicit means to resolve the problem (e.g., harming the innocent), we prefer the character to come to an unhappy ending. The tale of Rumpelstiltskin is resolved with the rescue of the child and the demise of the miscreant Rumpelstiltskin.

Knowing about story structure is useful in many ways. For example, teachers who understand story structure can ask about structurally important story events, such as main characters, initiating events, problems, major plot episodes, and resolutions, rather than asking about literal details and story trivia; such questions scaffold children's story comprehension. Students who learn about story structure write more interesting stories, as opposed to meandering, inconclusive narratives.

An important application of story structure for tutoring is to introduce new books with effective *booktalks*. The secret is to dramatize the problem of the story and then tell no more. First introduce the main characters in their ordinary situation. Then recount the initiating event, playing up the goal or problem confronting the main character. Then stop. Don't get into the plot, and certainly don't give away the resolution. For example, an effective booktalk on Rumpelstiltskin would introduce the wondrous spinstress, bring her before the king, but stop at the impossible dilemma of either spinning straw into gold or being put to death. This unresolved conflict engages listeners' imaginations and creates a motivation to read to find out what happens. Paradoxically, the means of motivating students to read is to tease and frustrate them with the unresolved problem of the story.

To introduce the delightful picture book *The Story About Ping* (Flack & Wiese, 1970), we might use story structure to create the following booktalk:

> Ping is a little duck with a very big family. They live on a houseboat on the Yangtze River in faraway China. Every day the houseboat stops, and all the ducks leave the boat to hunt for good tasting bugs and to fish in the river. At end of the day, the duckboy calls, "La la la lei," and all the ducks *hurry* back to the boat, because the last duck home gets a spank.
>
> But one day Ping is upside down catching a fish and doesn't hear the call. When he realizes he will be last, he doesn't want to get a spank. So he hides.
>
> And then the houseboat with all his family and friends sails away, and he is all alone on the banks of the Yangtze River. Now what will he do?

This type of booktalk focuses listeners' attention on the problem faced by the main character in the book. Its motivation derives from projecting the potential reader into the character's situation and experiencing the emotion of the problem. Here we share Ping's anguish at separation from his family, a stranger in a strange land.

GUIDELINES FOR EFFECTIVE BOOKTALKS

A booktalk is a creative work. There are many ways to make it effective, but I offer the following guidelines for maximizing motivation before reading:

1. Choose a book you like. It is hard to sell readers on a book you don't really enjoy yourself.

2. Show the pictures as you talk. Whatever the proverbs to the contrary, students *do* judge a book by its cover, and they focus on illustrations during a booktalk. The pictures hold the listeners' attention and become associated with the story in their minds. After the booktalk, leave the book where the cover is visible; it will reawaken the thoughts, emotions, and interest created by the booktalk.

3. Keep the booktalk brief, usually not more than two minutes. To keep the booktalk brief and engaging, introduce the main characters in their

ordinary situation, tell about the initiating event, and dramatize the problem. Then stop: Don't get into the plot, and especially avoid revealing the resolution.

4. Option: You may want to read aloud a brief excerpt; e.g., an introductory episode or a suspenseful part. If you do read aloud, practice first. A skillful read-aloud rarely comes naturally. If you do read a part, don't read very much. A booktalk is essentially an informal talk, not a reading.

5. Option: You may want to compare the book to similar books children know by the same author or of the same genre. In this way, children's interest in other books by the author or in the same genre can be siphoned off into the new book.

As a rule of thumb, teachers who motivate their students to read avidly give 5-10 booktalks per week. Some give a booktalk or two each day, while others reserve a special day each week to give all their booktalks. How do they find time to read all those books? First, note that you don't need to read an entire book to give an effective booktalk. You only need to read until the initiating event creates a goal or problem, because that's all that's covered in a booktalk. Once you've read that much, your own interest will likely be high, and you'll find it easy to communicate your interest in the book to your students. One important way to find time to read children's books is to initiate a program of sustained silent reading (SSR), coupled with literature discussion (see Chapter 9). The idea is to set aside a daily block of time for free reading (say, 20-30 minutes), and to model your own reading as your students read. You can make good use of SSR time by reading the beginnings of a couple books each day and making notes for your booktalks. Of course, reading the complete books is usually enjoyable in itself, and you will have ideas to contribute to the literature discussions.

DEVELOPING INTEREST IN A VARIETY OF BEGINNER BOOKS

The earliest beginners lack the decoding skill that enables making sight words. Accordingly, they often read *predictable books* with patterned language. Rhyme and verbal repetition provide an end-run around the problem of reading words. Predictable books don't have conventional story structure. For example, the predictable book *Playing* (Prince & Curtain, 1999) uses a simple rhyming text to present a narrative about a young girl who visits a park. Each page begins with the words, "I like . . . ," and the illustrations reveal what she likes. It begins as follows:

> I like to run.
>
> I like to hide.
>
> I like to jump.
>
> I like to slide.

Once children pick up the language pattern, they can use a strategy of cued recitation to pretend-read the simple text, allowing them to quickly join in on a shared reading. Because there is no inciting incident or problem to dramatize for readers, a booktalk might begin with a have-you-ever question, followed by, "Well, in this book . . . ." The have-you-ever question activates children's background knowledge and interest. The in-this-book follow-up relates listeners' experiences and interest to the characters and events in the predictable book. For example, a booktalk for *Playing* might follow this structure:

> Have you ever had a day with no jobs, a day just for play? What did you do? Well, in this book a girl goes to the park and has a wonderful time playing. Let's read to see what she likes to do.

Tying children's background knowledge and interest back to the book is a crucial step. Unless you refocus children's curiosity on the book, they will likely develop greater interest in storytelling than in story reading.

A couple of cautions are in order concerning predictable books. First, they are inherently less motivating than problem-centered books. Second, children who have made even a glimmer of progress in learning to decode, and who are using initial consonants to identify words, need books with easier words than those found in predictable books. They make better decoding progress with decodable books, which tend to have some story structure amenable to problem-centered booktalks. As long as a book has story structure, children will derive greater reading motivation from booktalks that zero in on an inciting incident and its resulting goal or problem.

Dr. Seuss's popular masterpiece *The Cat in the Hat* (Geisel, 1957) uses a simple first-grade vocabulary. It might be introduced thus:

> The *Cat in the Hat* is about two children, brother and sister, who are all alone at home on a cold, wet, rainy day. Mom is away, and they can't think of anything to do. Suddenly, a giant cat as big as a grown-up walks right into their house! He says he has a lot of good games and tricks to play. What kind of games, and what kind of tricks? Well, their fish tries to warn them: [Here read the fish's warning on page 11 and the cat's reply on page 12]. The cat's games and tricks are going to make a big mess of the house. How can they stop him? How can they clean up before Mom gets home?

A serious attempt to ameliorate the problems of struggling beginners will usually not allow you to the luxury of using children's literature. Most of your booktalks will attempt to peak beginners' interest in fairly ordinary decodable practice texts. With such books, it is almost never possible to develop distinctive characters, describe complex situations, or achieve rollicking humor. However, decodable books adapt the words of the text to children's decoding ability, allowing beginning readers to achieve success with a decoding strategy. With such books, it is important to dramatize minor problems, hyping the excitement beyond the mild situations portrayed in the books. For example, we might introduce the decodable book *A Cat Nap* (Cushman, 1990) as follows:

> This is a story about a very sleepy cat named Tab, who belongs to a man named Sam. Tab can fall asleep just about anywhere, but in this book, he falls asleep in a bag that holds Sam's baseball equipment. Sam is late for his game, and he grabs his bag and heads out the door. But where is Tab? I thought he was in the bag!

The following booktalk introduces a more advanced decodable book, *Meg and Jim's Sled Trip* (Appleton-Smith & Piontek, 1998):

> Meg and Jim get caught in a big snowstorm. When the weather finally clears, they can go sledding. The first time down the hill, they each fly down on their own sleds and have an exciting ride. The next time, they decide to double up on one sled. The sled goes faster and faster until it starts to spin out of control! Uh oh: Looks like trouble. I sure hope they're okay.

Readers familiar with this simple text may note that Meg and Jim's suffer only a minor spill into some soft snow, which gets inside their clothing. But the point is to exaggerate the danger of the tandem sledding to persuade young readers to take on the fairly arduous task of reading an unfamiliar book.

PRACTICAL CHAPTER

How to Scaffold Word Learning During Oral Reading

My wife observed a young boy trying to read an assigned story to his mother in the waiting room of a clinic. He was stuck on the word *house*, which he had read as "hog." His mother, with growing impatience, kept telling him to "sound it out." He began to squirm and kick his feet. "Sound it out. Sound it out!" Her commands became louder and sharper, but the boy struggled on, hot tears welling up in his eyes.

Helping children read is a vital teaching responsibility for teachers and parents who work with beginning readers. But some ways we *try* to help really don't help much, and we may make matters worse. We can, like the mother in the clinic, badger struggling readers into tears of frustration. Or, we can provide words immediately, short-circuiting learning by cutting off the close study needed to connect letters with phonemes and understand alphabetic mappings (Ehri, 1998). We can ask questions about letters and phonemes, try to teach a phonics lesson, or ask students to try again and again, taking them so far from the story that they lose their motivation to read—motivation we helped create with engaging booktalks.

Beginning readers need to read lots of actual books to learn to read, rather than isolated words in workbooks or on flashcards (Bond & Dykstra, 1967). Compared to reading flashcards, students read more words with much greater interest. (Have you ever seen a reader curl up in the corner with a good deck of flash cards?) In addition, words read in books are more likely to be learned as sight words because of the natural time pressure to read words fast enough to comprehend the message of text (Samuels & Flor, 1997). A good rule of thumb for reading instruction is that students should spend *half* of their instructional time in actual reading. In Reading Recovery, students begin and end each lesson reading books (Pinnell, Fried, & Estice, 1990). If a lesson finishes early and a few extra minutes are available, there is rarely a better use for this time than reading or rereading a book. Unfortunately, observational studies suggest elementary students spend as little as 7-8 minutes per day reading connected texts (Durkin, 1984).

Why don't novice readers read more? One problem is that they have not built up enough sight vocabulary to read books easily. For beginners, reading is very hard work. They need a skillful and patient adult to *scaffold* oral reading. To scaffold reading is to support students' reading slightly above the level they can read on their own by encouraging them, asking helpful questions, and guiding their efforts to maximize engagement and learning. Beginners particularly need support when reading a new book. With a familiar book, we often want to assess a student's reading, and scaffolding and assessment don't mix. Valid assessment requires the teacher not to scaffold. If the teacher helps the student read during an assessment, it is unclear whether we are measuring the student or the teacher—the results are muddied.

Where Scaffolding goes Wrong

Scaffolding can go wrong in two major directions. First, we can provide the word immediately, sparing the reader any frustration with the new word. In this case, our help short-circuits any word learning, and the reader is no closer to reading the word next time. At the other extreme, we can teach a phonics lesson. Extended instruction in decoding takes the reader too far from the story and destroys the motivation to read. Effective scaffolding must be brief and unobtrusive enough to allow the reader to stick close to the meaning of the story. Scaffolding is especially helpful if we can model a strategy that the student can learn to use independently. For example, if we ask students to reread whenever they figure out an unfamiliar word, they may well start to beat us to the punch by rereading on their own.

SELF-HELP STRATEGIES

How can novice readers most effectively help themselves learn unfamiliar words during reading? Research suggests that the three key self-help strategies are *decoding*, *crosschecking*, and *rereading*, in that order. Minor strategies that may help the beginner for a limited time include *fingerpointing* (tracking the print with a finger to keep one's place) and *coverups* (physically covering the word with a finger and revealing it bit by bit to simplify decoding).

Decoding

Decoding is the beginner's single most valuable strategy for learning unfamiliar words. By decoding, beginners match the letters they see in written words to phonemes they detect in spoken words, which helps them learn new words and add them to their sight vocabularies (Ehri, 1998). Given the importance of decoding to learn sight words, young readers should rarely if ever skip over unfamiliar words. Instead, they need to use the spelling to generate a pronunciation attempt. Even if decoding doesn't reveal the word, it at least produces a working model close enough to correct by crosschecking. Beginners can help themselves decode by using *coverups*. To use coverups, they physically cover the unknown word with a finger, card, or "coverup critter," which is a decorated Popsicle stick with googly eyes (See Figure 1). Then they slowly uncover the word from left to right, revealing the graphemes or chunks for sounding out and blending. Using coverups breaks down the word into manageable chunks to support decoding.

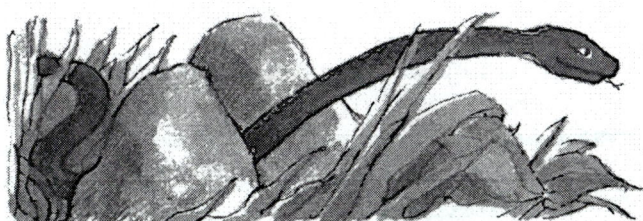

Figure 1: Using a coverup critter to simplify decoding; text and illustration from Lobel (1970).

Crosschecking

Crosschecking is the strategy of examining a pronunciation to make sure it makes sense in context. To crosscheck, a reader must finish reading the sentence to understand the context and then revise his decoding attempt as needed to make it fit the context, both in terms of meaning (semantics) and grammar (syntax). For example, if a beginner misreads *light* as "lit," but continues on to the end of the sentence, she may say, "The lit was turned off . . . oh, the *light* was turned off." Crosschecking depends on decoding, to come up with an attempt that can be self-corrected. Saying "blank" rather than generating a decoding attempt, once a common recommendation of reading authorities, will usually not provide the missing word. Context is simply not strong enough to supply an unread word from thin air. In fact, contextual guessing without decoding rarely works more than 25-30% of the time (Ehri, 1990), and readers only guess important context words that carry significant meaning information about 10% of the time (Gough & Walsh, 1991).

Decoding and crosschecking work best in tandem. There is good research evidence (see Chapter 3) that crosschecking is an integral part of the process of decoding (Ehri, 1998). If a word has an irregular letter, as in *listen*, a decoding attempt may generate "lis-ten." By crosschecking ("Listen to the music"), the reader can recognize *listen*, which not only allows him to build meaning, but also permits a closer spelling analysis. He can mentally marks the silent *t*, noting it as a letter to include in the spelling but not to pronounce in reading (Ehri & Wilce, 1980).

Decoding is like a jet, context a taxi. If we decide to vacation in Cancun, the jet will take us to the airport, but we still need a taxi to get to the beach. Similarly, decoding will usually give the reader something close to the word, even with irregular spellings, and this approximation can usually be corrected by crosschecking. For this reason, to criticize phonics rules because they don't always generate the exact word is unrealistic (Groff, 1985). Decoding using phonics rules does the important work of generating a pronunciation close enough to correct by crosschecking.

Rereading

Rereading is the third most important strategy for beginning readers. After an unfamiliar word is identified, the young reader should reread the sentence. This accomplishes two things. First, it provides a second opportunity to decode the word, and research suggests only about four decoding trials are necessary to add a word to one's sight vocabulary (Reitsma, 1983). Second, it allows the reader to re-engage with the story and recover the motivation for reading.

Figure 2 shows bookmarks to guide the work of beginning readers and reading teachers. Beginners may benefit from a bookmark that reminds them of their three most useful strategies when they are "stuck on a word," decoding, crosschecking, and rereading. This bookmark may also be a useful physical prop for using coverups. A second bookmark summarizes teachers' five conditional steps for scaffolding young readers' efforts as they read aloud. These conditional scaffolds will be described next page.

Stuck on a word?

Decode it.
Uncover letters slowly to see how you could say the word.

Crosscheck
Finish the sentence to see if your word makes sense. If not, change your word to fit the sentence.

Reread the sentence.
Start the sentence over to get back into the story.

Student stuck on a word?

Wait and write.
Give the student time to decode as you note the miscue for later analysis.

Finish the sentence.
Have the student finish the sentence (or stop the reader at the end of the sentence) to cross-check.

Brief help.
Provide a single brief and unobtrusive scaffold, usually cover-ups.

Provide word.
Don't ask questions, give hints, teach phonics, or ask the student to try again.

Reread.
Have the student reread the sentence to practice the new word and get back into the story.

FIGURE 2: Bookmarks for self-help (Stuck on a word?) and teacher scaffolding (Student stuck on a word?)

Maximizing Motivation

Reading motivation is a crucial element of successful and productive oral reading practice. Two major factors in reading motivation are the reader's expectation of success and his or her engagement with the story. Expert scaffolding encourages successful reading, provided the book is written within the reader's instructional level (Betts, 1946). Engaged reading begins with a book introduction that introduces the problem of the story without showing how the problem is solved (see Practical Chapter 1). Teachers may be interested in a beginner's mastery of short *o*, but the reader is far more interested in finding out how magic may go wrong in *Doc in the Fog* (Cushman, 1990).

To keep the reader focused on meaning, expert teachers keep up a running discussion of the story. A good rule of thumb is *talk before you turn*. Every page or two, make a comment about story events or ask an open-ended question; that is, a question with multiple right answers. For instance, you might ask, "What do you think will happen next?" or "What would you do in that situation?" Illustrations often provide good topics for discussion. Because the words of early readers are kept simple, illustrations provide important clues to flesh out the story. Unfamiliar vocabulary words often invite good questions. For example, in the decodable book *Bo and Rose* (Cushman & Kornblum, 1990), the goat Bo "roams from home." Because the word *roam* is unknown to most beginning readers, establishing the meaning of *roam* is necessary for understanding the story (see Appendix for an example of expert scaffolding with this book).

To keep the reader engaged in the story, all questions from the teacher should focus on story events, not on phonics. Asking, "What does short *o* say?" works against engaged reading. Also crucial for keeping young readers engaged in the story is to have them hold the book themselves. Having the book in the reader's own hands gives ownership to a reading and allows the reader to use self-help strategies like fingerpointing and coverups. Having to lean over to read a book held by a parent or teacher is awkward for the reader, and the teacher can't record observations and miscue notes.

Five-step conditional scaffolds

How do we help a beginner struggling with a word? Observations suggest that teachers simply provide the unrecognized word about half the time (Spiegel & Rogers, 1980), which short-circuits learning. The opposite mistake is to conduct an impromptu phonics lesson that bogs down the reading. Is there a middle ground between simply intervening with every unrecognized word and intervening with decoding instruction that takes the reader away from the story? The solution is to provide a five-step series of conditional scaffolds. By *conditional*, I mean that taking each next step depends on the reader's success with the previous step. For example, if sending the reader on to complete the sentence helps the reader crosscheck to identify a misread word, then there is no need to proceed with the brief help of coverups. However, the final step of rereading is mandatory rather than conditional. Whenever the student has identified an unfamiliar word, we want him to reread the sentence help him learn the word and recover motivation for reading.

1. Wait and Write

Expert scaffolding begins with wait time. Skillful teachers provide enough wait time—5 seconds or so—for a student to "take a shot" by decoding. Wait time after questioning has been shown to result in more and better quality responses (Rowe, 1987), and there is every reason to believe the same is true in confronting an unfamiliar word. Teachers working with a group of children must teach other students to wait, too, rather than calling out unrecognized words. Hearing the word makes it unnecessary to continue studying the spelling and making sense of it. While readers get a word in the short term, they usually don't recognize the same word next time. It takes time to study the spelling of a word and generate a pronunciation, which is the most effective word-learning strategy. Making sense of the spelling as a pronunciation map is the essential way to make a sight word, and this requires decoding, crosschecking, mental marking, and rereading to secure the encoded word in memory.

Wait time is a good opportunity to note the miscue. Reading mistakes are usually called *miscues* (Clay, 2002) to emphasize that the reader is either responding to the wrong cues (e.g., context or pictures) or incompletely responding to the right cues (i.e., using only part of the spelling). A simple way to note a miscue is to write the attempt over the text word, with a dividing line between them. Suppose, for instance, the student read, "I spun the tip" for the sentence "I spun the top." The miscue would be written like a fraction:

tip ← (attempt)
top ← (text word)

When leisure permits, we can analyze miscues for missing correspondences and for strategies. A *correspondence* is a match between a *grapheme* (either a single letter or a digraph) and a *phoneme*, a vocal element in a spoken word, so that the grapheme signals the phoneme during decoding. The first correspondence in the text word not used in the attempt—usually the vowel—is missing from the reader's decoding "toolkit." For example, in reading "tip" for *top*, the student correctly decoded the consonants *t* and *p*, but didn't use the *o* to signal the vowel /o[1]/. An easy shorthand for recording missing correspondences is write down the grapheme and the phoneme, separated by an equal sign (=); in this case, o = /o/, read "o says /o/." If a reader read, "She taps her can" for "She taps her cane," the miscue note would be can/cane, suggesting the reader is missing the correspondence a_e = /A/. Self-corrected miscues suggest missing correspondences, too; self-corrections are made by crosschecking, not by decoding. Of course, irregular words do not suggest missing correspondences because their constituent correspondences are exceptions to the rules.

Sometimes readers will make a miscue that uses the correct vowel but a wrong consonant, such as rib/rid. A likely problem here is that the reader is confusing consonants that look alike (*b* and *d*). Such letter recognition problems are worth noting. They are not missing correspondences to be addressed in

---

1   To avoid diacritical marks in this book, I use lower-case letters in slashes to symbolize short vowels and capital letters between slashes to symbolize long vowels.

phonics instruction, but residual difficulties in recognizing letters, to be addressed with guided printing practice (see Practical Chapter 4). Another likely possibility is that the reader is working so hard at getting the vowel that he doesn't complete the blending work needed for accurate decoding and simply makes a guess. This interpretation is consistent with the typical developmental sequence of learning to decode consonants as phonetic cues during the partial-alphabetic phase before learning to fully decode with vowels during the full alphabetic phase (see Chapter 3). For this reason, I would tentatively catalog any regular vowel in a reading miscue as missing even when the error seems to be with consonants. For example, the miscue rib/rid suggests i = /i/ may be missing in the sense that it has not be thoroughly installed in the reader's decoding toolkit for easy use. If no other miscues with short i present themselves, I might include words with i = /i/ as review words in a letterbox lesson to provide further practice and an opportunity for additional assessment.

Miscue analysis is also important for detecting readers' strategies. When an attempt makes use of graphemes in the text word, the student is decoding; the more letters used in the attempt, the more complete the decoding. When a miscue is self-corrected, or when an attempt makes sense in context, the reader is crosschecking. With developing reading skill, readers make better decoding attempts and crosscheck to correct most of their miscues (Biemiller, 1970), provided they are reading instructional level text with teacher help; at frustration levels, most readers give up on crosschecking. Taking note of students' success with decoding and crosschecking helps us track their progress in learning to read. We make maximum progress when most miscues are self-corrected and when errors that cannot be self-corrected are in the 2-5% range.

2. Finish the Sentence

If the student doesn't recognize the word in a few seconds, expert teachers send the reader on to read the rest of the sentence for a contextual boost. Completing the sentence scaffolds crosschecking, the second-most powerful word-learning strategy. Crosschecking provides contextual help to complete or correct partial decoding. Suppose, for example, a reader began, "I rid . . ." and stopped in confusion. Encouraged to complete the sentence, the reader can make use of helpful context, "I rid . . . my bike—oh, I *ride* my bike." Usually students given a few seconds of wait time will try to decode the word. With something like the word in mind, context will often provide enough information to revise the attempt into the correct word.

Some beginners will stop at an unfamiliar word, but others will not. Frustrated readers may give up on making meaning and keep on going simply to complete the reading task, oblivious to comprehension. In that case, the experts stop the reader at the end of the sentence, saying something like, "I didn't get that. Reading should make sense. Let's take another look at that sentence." In general, the requirements of crosschecking suggest we restrict any intervention to sentence boundaries. If the reader has not reached the sentence boundary, the experts send the reader on; if he continues after a miscue beyond the sentence boundary, they send him back. Gathering in the remainder of the sentence is usually necessary for crosschecking.

Contrary to past advice, reading teachers should not tell the young reader to skip unfamiliar words or say "blank" and continue on. Decoding is the most valuable strategy for adding sight vocabulary (Ehri, 1998). Context is simply not powerful enough to produce the word without a decoding attempt. Following up an earlier analogy, relying solely on context would be like taking a taxi all the way to Cancun. It would cost much more money, use up much of your vacation time, and might break down along the way. Decoding allows the reader to learn the word and store its spelling for sight word recognition.

Saying "sound it out" is equally unhelpful. If you were struggling with a tough math problem, and teacher said, "Figure it out," would that help? Saying "sound it out" is badgering, not helping. Most beginners are trying to decode, but they may be missing vowel or digraph correspondences, or they may not have a good strategy for blending, or they may be daunted by the formidable length of an unfamiliar word. Recall the child struggling to decode the word *house*, only to be told over and over, "Sound it out." I doubt he'd had any instruction on the advanced vowel digraph *ou* to enable him to "sound it out." Rather than exhorting struggling readers to "sound it out," we need to provide an effective decoding scaffold.

3. Brief Help

To avoid a prolonged, motivation-killing distraction from the events of the story, skilled reading coaches keep scaffolding brief by providing a single scaffolding action, as unobtrusive as possible so as not to disrupt reading comprehension. We want to keep our intervention brief so that the student is away from the story only about 5-10 seconds. The least intrusive scaffold is *coverups*, uncovering the word bit by bit to help the student decode. I first observed coverups as a clinical supervisor during a summer reading clinic at the University of Georgia. One clinic room was unusually quiet. The clinician, a doctoral student in school psychology, was tutoring a shy 7-year-old girl. Whenever the girl came to a word she didn't recognize, the clinician would reach over, cover the word with her hand, and slowly uncover it to help the child decode it. This nearly always provided enough help for the girl to identify the word and continue reading, and she made rapid progress that summer.

Coverups work well with most words. The teacher can scaffold the reading of simple words like *soft* by uncovering each letter in sequence with a "coverup critter" (see the section on decoding above). With a word like *shock* with digraphs, the teacher uncovers each grapheme one by one rather than each letter, so that the digraphs *sh* and *ck* are kept intact. With more advanced beginners, teachers can scaffold the reading of multisyllabic words like *interesting*; for such a word, simply uncover the syllable chunks one by one. Exact syllable boundaries are not important as long as vowels are separated within approximate syllables.

Coverups scaffold a procedure young readers can take over as a self-help strategy. After seeing the teacher use scaffolds regularly to break down the task of decoding, many readers begin to use their own coverups to simplify the task of decoding unfamiliar words. If students don't begin using coverups, teachers can provide explicit instruction in the coverup strategy by explaining and modeling how to use coverups and then having the reader practice coverups with unfamiliar words. This fades the instructional scaffold, allowing the reader to take over coverups as a self-help strategy.

Coverups work so well that some teachers use them too soon. Beginning readers need time to study unknown words, generate an approximate pronunciation, and use the sentence context for testing their approximations by crosschecking. If novice teachers jump in too quickly with coverups, they may cut off crosschecking, the reader's second best self-help strategy. For this reason, we only intervene only at sentence boundaries to allow the student to gather contextual information for self-correction. If crosschecking fails, coverups offer a minimal and unobtrusive teacher intervention. In general, allowing wait time and suggesting the reader finish the sentence encourage self-help; coverups provide stronger scaffolding, directing the student to the powerful strategy of decoding.

Sometimes teachers know coverups won't work because the unfamiliar word contains a correspondence the student has yet to learn. For example, if a student were to encounter the word *drew*, coverups would probably not help without knowledge of the digraph *ew*. An alternative scaffold, slightly more obtrusive, is to provide the missing correspondence while pointing to the unknown grapheme *ew* and saying, "This part says /OO/."

In any case, don't fall into the pitfall of asking questions about phonics, which takes the reader far from the story and builds frustration for students already struggling with a word. I often see novice teachers asking questions like, "What's the first letter?" and "What sound does *e* make," as if trying to draw decoding knowledge from the child. Such questions sometimes trigger word identification, but only at a substantial cost in time, frustration, and motivation for reading.

Another common tactic is to give hints about an unrecognized word by pointing to a picture, supplying a rhyme, giving clues about its meaning, or paging back to its last occurrence in the text. Such assistance won't help in the long run because the clues point to extraneous information outside of the spelling and sentence context. Pictures, rhymes, and definitions will not be available the next time the reader runs into the unfamiliar word. To learn a word as a sight word, the reader must study its spelling and understand its alphabetic mapping in a process that begins by decoding the unknown word (Ehri, 1998).

4. Provide the Word

If the first attempt at intervention fails, the expert teacher provides the missing word. Setting a one-failure limit is what keeps help brief so that the intervention is unobtrusive, a minimal departure from the story. If doing one thing doesn't lead to word recognition, tell the student the word. If a coverup or mention of a new correspondence doesn't work, telling the word resolves the crisis. Some novice teachers ask students to "try it again," and then again and again. This can leave the student discouraged by repeated failure, with a consequent loss of motivation for reading.

5. Reread

The final scaffold in helping a beginning reader learn an unfamiliar word is to ask the student who has recovered an unfamiliar word to reread the sentence. This is true whether the word was strategically identified during wait time, corrected by crosschecking, laboriously decoded using coverups, or provided by the teacher. Rereading accomplishes two goals. First, it shifts attention back to the story, recovering the motivation to read and to find out what happens. Second, it gives the reader a second chance to study the troublesome word and add the word to sight vocabulary. Research suggests a new word can be learned as a sight word in as few as four decoding trials (Reitsma, 1983). Rereading provides the second decoding trial, bringing the reader approximately halfway to word learning.

The first four steps—waiting, finishing the sentence, giving brief help, and providing the word—are conditional steps. This means there is no need to take the next step unless the previous step fails. However, the final step of rereading is unconditional. We want the beginning reader to always reread the sentence after struggling with a word. If the student gets the word after a prolonged pause, have the student reread the sentence. If the student gets the word by finishing the sentence and crosschecking, have the student reread the sentence. If the student gets the word with coverups, have the student reread the sentence. If the teacher must provide the word, have the student reread the sentence. Effective teachers are constantly sending students back to reread sentences in which they have struggled with a word. Their students register greater word recognition gains through this repeated sentence reading, and they maintain interest in the stories they are reading.

Sending students back to reread is often a scaffold novice teachers neglect. This is unfortunate because it is wonderfully effective for learning words and recovering the motivation to read. It replaces frustration with success, and it improves reading fluency (Samuels, 1979, 1997). Sending the student on to finish the rest of the sentence is the second most neglected scaffold. Finishing the sentence is necessary for crosschecking. Many novice teachers jump too quickly to coverups. Proficient reading coaches encourage readers to use self-help strategies of decoding and crosschecking before intervening with even a minimally intrusive decoding scaffold.

Special Situations

Sometimes special situations arise in which the five-step series of conditional scaffolds becomes inappropriate. Some minor miscues may not appreciably change either the meaning or the grammar of the sentence. For example, suppose a student reads the sentence, "Maria went with the group to the monkey house" as "Maria went with her group to the monkey's house" (Leslie & Caldwell, 2001). Because the reader can completely construct the meaning of the sentence with this minor misreading, there is little point in disrupting comprehension by taking the reader back to work on *her* or *monkey*. Teachers are better advised to fight such battles another day, when miscues interfere with reading comprehension.

Sometimes a student will encounter a strange word like *tortilla* or *chamois*, or a highly irregular word like *enough* that the reader has little chance of decoding successfully. In this case, it is expedient to simply provide the word with a brief explanation of what it means. As always, have the student reread the sentence with the new word before continuing on in the text.

One other special situation may arise: The student may struggle with many words in a text. Should this happen, the student needs an easier book. We want students successfully reading 95-98% of the words in a text, not counting self-corrections, an accuracy rate characteristic of an instructional level (Betts, 1946). Decades of research in reading have led researchers to the consensus that the best reading progress takes place when a reader struggles with no more than 1 out of 20 running words of text. As a rule of thumb, a reader should not miss more than one word per page. If a student falls below 95% accuracy, we are asking him to read at his frustration level, and that is exactly the result. At the frustration level, students generally stop reading for meaning, abandon crosschecking, and lose motivation for reading. Rather than reading to find out what happens in the story, they begin reading simply to finish a task. Pushing a beginner to read at the frustration level often leads to the development of bad reading habits and negative attitudes. For this reason, a student missing more than 1 word in 20 needs an easier book. If no alternative book is available, skilled teachers simply read the book aloud to the student and bring an easier text for the next lesson. As a less drastic measure with a book only marginally frustrating, the teacher can read every other page, scaffolding oral reading on the student's page, to complete the book.

ORAL READING SCAFFOLDS FOR PARENTS

What about the mother described at the beginning of this article? How could she have made oral reading a successful, engaging, no-tears experience for her son?

Many conscientious parents help their children read aloud every day. While we would not expect them to record miscue notes or analyze missing strategies and correspondences, parents can improve their success by applying the insights of reading teachers. Two areas where parents can improve are maximizing reading engagement and employing a simplified version of the five-step conditional scaffold.

To enhance reading engagement, parents can follow the rule "talk before you turn." All talk should be restricted to story events rather than about phonics. Parents should resist the temptation to turn story talk into a quiz about story details. A simple framework for open-ended questioning was devised by Stauffer (1969), using two stock questions: What do you think will happen, and why do you think so? Unfamiliar vocabulary words and new information supplied by illustrations provide impetus for open-ended questions to discuss before turning each page.

A non-technical version of the conditional five-step scaffold can guide parental help. When skillful parents help a son or daughter read aloud and the child has trouble with a word, they should try a succession of measures one at a time until the reader recognizes the word. First, wait several seconds before offering to help. This allows the reader time to use self-help strategies to figure out the word. Usually the reader will generate a decoding attempt as the parent waits. If the reader doesn't get come up with the word, then send the reader on to read the rest of the sentence to see what word would make sense. If finishing the sentence doesn't resolve the unfamiliar word, the next move is to try coverups. Ask the reader to cover the word with a finger, a small card, or a "coverup critter," and then slowly uncover parts of the word to make it easier to sound out one part at a time. At first, the parent may provide the coverup, but later, the parent should invite the reader to "try a coverup." If the coverup doesn't work, then provide the unrecognized word to lead the reader back into the story as quickly as possible. No matter when the reader identifies the word—after waiting, completing the sentence, coverups, or providing the word—always finish by sending the reader back to reread the sentence to pick up the thread of the story.

SUMMARY

Reading is hard word work for beginners. They need adults to scaffold their reading, which means to support them at a level beyond what they can achieve on their own. Scaffolding can misfire when adults simply provide unrecognized words, or at the opposite extreme, when they launch into a lesson that competes with comprehending the story. Ideally, scaffolding is brief and unobtrusive, and it directs students to use the vital self-help strategies of decoding, crosschecking, and rereading.

Because decoding is the essential first step in making sight words, students should not be encouraged to skip unfamiliar words. They can help themselves decode with coverups, i.e., covering the word and then slowly uncovering letters, digraphs, and later, syllables, to allow a focus on each decoding unit. A coverup "critter" made from a decorated Popsicle stick provides a useful tool for coverups. Once a decoding attempt has been made, the reader should finish the sentence to crosscheck, i.e., to test the attempt to see if it makes good sense in the sentence. If an attempt does not make sense, readers can usually switch over to a sound-alike word that works better in context. Successful crosschecking allows the reader to note silent or irregular letters to mentally mark for storing the annotated spelling in memory. After crosschecking, the reader should reread the sentence to cement word learning and to recover the thread of the story, which is attenuated by word-reading challenges.

Helping young readers use their most productive strategies during oral reading requires keeping motivational factors in mind. Texts should be selected for low error rates of 2-5%, or as a rule, no more than one miscue per page. A good rule for keeping up an engaging discussion of the text is "Talk before you turn." Before turning each page, the teacher or parent should make a comment or ask a question about what is happening in the story. Comments might be cued by unexplained actions by characters, illustrations, or vocabulary that is likely unfamiliar to the reader. Open-ended questions (those with multiple right answers) are more effective than literal questions. In general, all questions should probe story events and no questions should detour from the story into a phonics lesson. Readers need to hold the books they are reading to encourage the use of self-help strategies.

Research supports the use of a five-step sequence of conditional scaffolds to support children's oral reading. Except for the final step of rereading, each successive step is only taken if the previous step fails. The initial step is to provide about 5 seconds of wait time for decoding. Waiting for a decoding attempt allows the teacher time to jot a miscue note, recording the attempt (if any) over the text word. This notation allows miscue analysis to determine which correspondences (usually vowels) are missing from the reader's decoding toolkit. In general, the vowel correspondence in the text word not used in the decoding attempt is missing. Even where the correct vowel is used in the attempt, a reasonable supposition is that this vowel has not been learned well enough to survive the gymnastics of blending. Besides indicating missing correspondences, miscue analysis indicates strategy use. Attempts that make use of graphemes in the text work indicate decoding, and miscues that are self-corrected indicate crosschecking.

If the reader pauses after the attempt, we want to encourage him to complete the sentence to crosscheck, which allows self-correction when the attempt doesn't work by coming up with a sound-alike word that fits. If the reader makes an attempt and keeps going into the next sentence, we want the reader to stop before continuing on. If the attempt is correct, we want the beginner to reread the sentence (unconditional step #5), and if it is incorrect, we want to intervene with brief help (conditional step #3). Two common pieces of advice that do not help are advising the reader to say "blank" and read on, which doesn't provide a useful approximation for crosschecking, and saying "sound it out," which badgers the reader.

If crosschecking doesn't produce the correct word, the briefest and least intrusive scaffold is coverups. Either the teacher can uncover the word grapheme by grapheme, or she can encourage the students to try coverups. Because coverups involve teacher intervention rather than self-help, they should be delayed until after the student has completed reading the sentence, which permits crosschecking for self-help. Coverups may not work if students lack knowledge about a more advanced correspondence (e.g., in *growl*); in this case, it may be better to mention the correspondence (*ow* says /ow/) instead of using coverups. If coverups are successful, have the student reread the sentence and continue with the story. Avoid the common pitfalls of teaching phonics or giving extraneous hints using pictures, rhymes, and definitions.

If your brief help goes nowhere, it is time to provide the word. To minimize discouragement, we maintain a one-failure limit after scaffolding, supplying the misread word before the reading goes any further south. To help the reader learn the new word and recover interest in the story, we ask him to reread the sentence. The rereading step is unconditional and ensues whenever an unfamiliar word is identified—after waiting, after crosschecking, after coverups, or after providing the word. Two special situations don't fit well with five-step scaffolding: If a miscue changes neither grammar nor meaning, it is preferable not to intervene, and if a word is too unusual or irregular to warrant decoding, it may be better to provide it and ask for a rereading. In addition, if a text turns out to be too difficult to read with 95-98% accuracy (usually a maximum of one error per page), the teacher should find an easier text for oral reading so that the reader can improve accuracy and save face. The text that proved too difficult can be read aloud by the teacher.

Most parents can improve their success in helping their own children read by restricting their talk to story events and avoiding efforts to teach phonics. They will maximize their children's success and enjoyment with oral reading by using a simple version of the conditional five-step scaffolds that omits taking miscue notes or analyzing them. While parents are reading with a child and he gets stuck on a word, they follow five steps to encourage successful reading: 1) Wait a few seconds to give him time to use self-help strategies. 2) Send him on to read the rest of the sentence to see what would make sense. 3) If he has not self-corrected, cover the word up and then slowly uncover parts, helping him take the word a chunk at a time. 4) If he still doesn't have it, tell him the word. 5) Whenever he has the correct word, always have him reread the sentence.

Appendix: Transcript of oral reading of Bo and Rose

To illustrate the conditional scaffolds for helping with oral reading, I provide a transcript of part of a lesson with Leslie Downer, a gifted teacher then working on a graduate degree in Reading Education. Mrs. Downer was tutoring a rising second grader I'll call "Jamie" during the Summer Reading Program at Auburn University. Jamie is a bright and verbal youngster, but she was only reading at a primer level at the end of first grade. Through Mrs. Downer's skillful teaching, she attained a first-grade level during our summer program (approximately 9 hours of instruction over 12 sessions). In the transcript that follows, Jamie is reading the decodable book *Bo and Rose* (Cushman & Kornblum, 1990).

Instructional conversation scaffolding reading	Text of book/Comments
Mrs. Downer: We're going to read our new book, called *Bo and Rose*.	
Jamie: Okay.	
Mrs. Downer: Have you ever seen a goat?	
Jamie: Many a time.	
Mrs. Downer: Many a time? Do you know some of the funny things that goats do?	
Jamie: Eat stuff, lots of stuff?	
Mrs. Downer: They do. They love to chew on things. My parents have some goats, and he always eats up her rosebushes. Well, in this story about Rose and Bo, Rose has to take care of her goat named Bo. And when Rose tells Bo no, he thinks she says go. So he ends up running away. He chews through his rope, and he runs away, he roams away, and he gets into all kinds of trouble. Do you think he'll ever come back?	This is the sort of engaging booktalk that motivates engaged reading even with simple decodable text.
Jamie: Umm, he might.	
Mrs. Downer: Maybe? All right, let's read and find out if he does, okay?	
Jamie: Rose has a goat. The goat is Bo. Bo . . . Bo has a . . . has a gray count.	*Rose has a goat. The goat is Bo. Bo has a gray coat.*
Mrs. Downer: All right, let's look at this word.	
Jamie: Count?	
Mrs. Downer: I'm going to give you your bookmark, Jamie, and see if you can kind of cover up and see.	This fades the coverup scaffold by inviting Jamie to take over.

Jamie: Cot.	
Mrs. Downer: Nice try.	
Jamie: Cat?	
Mrs. Downer: Let me tell you something. If I cover up these two, that [oa] says /O/. We're going to work on that, too.	The o_e pattern had been taught, but this book also featured the oa digraph.
Jamie: Coat?	
Mrs. Downer: There you go. Now, coat. Can you read that sentence again for me?	Rereading is always the last step—the only scaffold that is not conditional.
Jamie: Bo has a gray coat.	
Mrs. Downer: Okay, when they say Bo has a gray coat, what are they talking about?	Scaffolding oral reading is often an opportunity to teach or review vocabulary.
Jamie: It has gray fur?	
Mrs. Downer: That's right. Whenever you're talking about an animal's coat, you're talking about its fur, its hair. Are there any kind of other animals that could have a coat?	
Jamie: Umm, a horse. Dogs.	
Mrs. Downer: Um hm. What about an alligator. Would they have coats?	
Jamie: Umm . . .	
Mrs. Downer: Do they have fur or hair?	
Jamie: An alligator? No.	
Mrs. Downer: No, they wouldn't have a coat.	
Jamie: Bo has a rope. Rose . . . Rose ties the rope on . . . at home. Bo bites the rope and goes.	*Bo has a rope. Rose ties the rope at home. Bo bites the rope and goes.*
Mrs. Downer: All right, I told you he was going to chew up the rope. He's goin'. I wonder where he's gonna go.	
Jamie: Umm . . .	
Mrs. Downer: Let's read this page over here.	
Jamie: "No, Bo. You cannot go." "No" means "go" to Bo.	*"No, Bo. You cannot go." "No" means "go" to Bo.*
Mrs. Downer: I liked your expression. Look at the picture for me, Jamie. Where do you think they're at?	Mrs. Downer continually follows the guideline "talk before you turn" to keep Jamie engaged.
Jamie: The farm?	
Mrs. Downer: How can you tell?	
Jamie: Uh . . . because it's big?	

Mrs. Downer: It is big, and I see that there are no other houses very close by. There's lots of green things. That kind of gives me a hint they might be on a farm. And most people that have goats live on a farm, don't they?	
Jamie: Um hm.	
Mrs. Downer: Turn the page for me.	
Jamie: He bounces . . . bents . . . bites the rope. He . . . He runs . . . runs for home. Runs from home.	*He bites the rope. He roams from home. Bo the goat needs to go.*
Mrs. Downer: Did that make sense?	
Jamie: Umm. Yes?	
Mrs. Downer: Yeah, it did. Let's look at this word again. It has that /O/ in there again.	
Jamie: Rose?	
Mrs. Downer: Roams.	Note Mrs. Downer provides the word after brief help fails.
Jamie: Roams. Roams.	
Mrs. Downer: Okay.	
Jamie: He roams from home. Bo is gr . . . goat . . . needs . . . Wait. Bo the goat needs to go.	
Mrs. Downer: Okay, what do you think. Let's see. He bites the rope. He roams from home. Remember you changed it to *runs*. You thought it might be *runs*. So *roams* means kind of when you just leave somewhere. Like, Jamie, if I said I'm going to roam around Haley Center, that means I might just go walk around. Or Bo is roaming around the farm. He's just running around the farm. He doesn't really know where he's going. He's just wandering off. Okay. Can you use that word in a sentence?	
Jamie: What word?	
Mrs. Downer: *Roams.*	
Jamie: You mean this word here?	
Mrs. Downer: Could you make up a sentence? Like I said, I'm gonna roam around Haley Center.	
Jamie: I'm gonna roam in my neighborhood?	
Mrs. Downer: Um hm. Very good. Keep going.	
Jamie: Bo digs holes. He rolls in the mud. Bo roams home to Rose.	*Bo digs holes. He rolls in the mud. Bo roams home to Rose.*
Mrs. Downer: Very nice. Oh, wait a minute. He roams home to Rose. So did he decide to go back?	
Jamie: Yes.	

Mrs. Downer: What do you think that she's gonna do when she sees him? All muddy like that?	
Jamie: Uh. Say something bad to him?	
Mrs. Downer: Let's find out.	
Jamie: Wash him? [Reading.] Look at . . . at you, Bo. /k/ . . . cat . . . coat.	Look at Bo's coat. Mud is on his coat. Bo's coat needs soap.
Mrs. Downer: Okay, let's read it again.	
Jamie: Look at . . . Bo's coat. Mud his . . . Mud is on his coat. Bo can't . . . needs . . . Bo's coat needs soap.	
Mrs. Downer: I like the way you went back and fixed that word. It made more sense, didn't it?	Note Mrs. Downer's use of specific praise to support Jamie's crosschecking.
Jamie: Rose gets hose . . . the hose. She puts the ro . . . hose on Bo's . . . Bo. She rubs on coat with soap.	Rose gets the hose. She puts the hose on Bo. She rubs Bo's coat with soap.
Mrs. Downer: Did that make sense?	
Jamie: Sha . . . soap?	
Mrs. Downer: Look at this word.	
Jamie: Bo's?	
Mrs. Downer: Will you read it from here for me?	
Jamie: She rubs Bo's coat with soap.	
Mrs. Downer: Before you turn the page, take a look at her face.	
Jamie: Mad?	
Mrs. Downer: She looks kind of mad right now, doesn't she. Why do you think she's mad?	
Jamie: Because he got muddy?	
Mrs. Downer: He did. He got muddy, and now she has to wash him.	
Jamie: Bo bites the hose. He . . . The hose gone on Rose. Bo and Rose bram . . . farm and farm.	Bo bites the hose. The hose goes on Rose. Bo and Rose foam and foam.
Mrs. Downer: Let's look at this sentence one more time for me.	
Jamie: The rose . . . hose goes on Rose. The . . . Bo and Rose fromm . . . farm . . . foam and foam.	
Mrs. Downer: Good, now you've got it. Can you read it one more time for me?	
Jamie: Bo and Rose foam and foam.	
Mrs. Downer: Foam and foam. Can you point to the foam in the picture for me?	
Jamie: This?	

Mrs. Downer: Uh huh. All those bubbles and suds, that's all the foam from the washing. Now look at Rose's face.	
Jamie: Laughing?	
Mrs. Downer: Yeah. So she's kind of happy now. I think she's gotten over being mad. What do you think?	
Jamie: Yes.	
Mrs. Downer: Did you like that story?	
Jamie: A little. Not very much.	
Mrs. Downer: Not very much. All right. Well, that was our practice book, to help you work on those words.	The number of miscues Jamie made limited her enjoyment of the story. She needs an easier book to improve her comprehension and enjoyment of reading.

PRACTICAL CHAPTER

How to Teach a Letterbox Lesson

When we tutor beginners in reading, we want to see progress. Nothing is quite so disappointing in education when we teach our hearts out and then fail to detect learning in our students. The letterbox lesson enables novice readers to move forward in reading. They make real progress because they learn new correspondence tools for decoding words. New correspondences unlock unfamiliar words, helping beginners recognize them as words already familiar in oral language.

Learning to decode is an important milestone in phonics instruction. We want young readers to understand spellings so well that they can remember them as sight words for automatic word recognition. A memorized string of letters is very hard to remember. Readers find it far easier to remember words when their spellings make sense as alphabetic maps of their pronunciations. To make sense of a spelling, the reader has to study it, connect letters with phonemes, and mentally mark silent or irregular letters (Ehri, 1985, 1990, 1998; Ehri & Wilce, 1987).

Rationale

The *letterbox lesson* (LBL) is designed to help beginners understand alphabetic mappings by working through spellings. In reading, beginners often use a guessing strategy, sounding out some of the consonants to come up with a word that fits the context. If they guess from consonants, they only remember consonants, which means they cannot store complete spellings for sight word recognition. This forces them to fall back on contextual guessing. However, in spelling, students must analyze phonemes completely, including the vowels, to construct a spelling map. Carefully working through the spelling allows the student to store the spelling in memory. Thus, in the letterbox lesson, the student spells the word *before* trying to read it.

The key to learning how to decode and spell is phoneme awareness. The reader has to scout out the vocal terrain to understand how a spelling can map that terrain. This scouting involves stretching the pronunciation, identifying phonemes in the word, and matching phonemes with letters. Recognizing the spelling as an alphabetic mapping allows the reader to transfer spelling knowledge of the word to sight word recognition in reading. Thus, every letterbox lesson follows up guided spelling by reading the lesson words.

Which readers can benefit from the LBL? Readers must be at least partial alphabetic (see Chapter 3). Novice readers who can decode consonants are ready for letterbox lessons, and more generally, ready for phonics instruction to learn the vowels and digraph correspondences for full alphabetic decoding. Because the LBL is designed for students who know most consonants, the typical lesson teaches a vowel correspondence, enabling students to spell and read words that exemplify this correspondence. Readers who can spell regular, one-syllable words and who are ready to work with multisyllable words with irregular spellings are too advanced for the LBL; they will do better with wordmapping (see Practical Chapter 8).

Materials

The LBL requires letter tiles and letterboxes. Letterboxes are rows of connected squares used to indicate the number of phonemes in words. They are also called Elkonin boxes for Russian psychologist Daniel Elkonin, a pioneer in phoneme awareness research (Zaporozheëtìs & Elkonin, 1971). Cardstock cut into 2.5 to 3-inch squares works well for letterboxes. Using a variety of colors makes the boxes more attractive, and outlining each square with a magic marker visually defines it. A set of six squares and a set of two squares should be plenty; the two-square set is necessary because in folding six squares into two, it is nearly impossible to get the boxes to lie flat. The most important consideration with letterboxes is to get them to lie completely flat. If the boxes "pooch up" during a letterbox lesson, the letters slide off, and you can't hold the boxes down while conducting an effective lesson. Use a single piece of scotch tape to join each box to its neighbor so that the boxes will lie flat. See Figure 1.

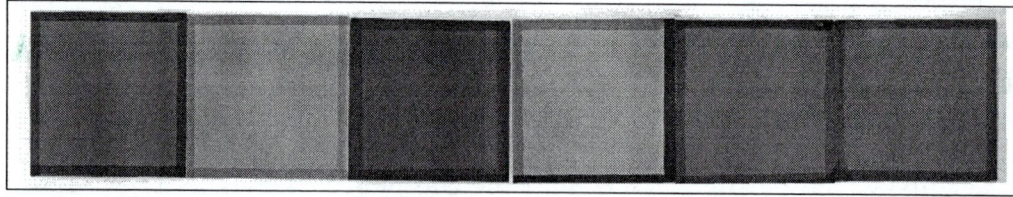

FIGURE 1: A set of letterboxes for the LBL

Letter manipulatives can be made from many materials, but we find plastic letter tiles easier to pick up than paper ones. Because some letters change identities when inverted (*b* and *q*, *p* and *d*, *n* and *u*), a good strategy is to write the capital letter in indelible marker on the back. An inexpensive alternative to plastic letter tiles is to create tables as in Appendix 2, print the first page, turn it upside down in your print tray, and then print the second page on the back. Laminate the double-sided page, and then use a paper cutter to separate the letters.

DECIDING WHAT TO TEACH

A letterbox lesson teaches one new *correspondence*, or match between a grapheme and a phoneme. A *grapheme* is either a single letter or a *digraph* (a 2 or 3-letter spelling for a phoneme, such as *sh*). A *phoneme* is an elemental vocal gesture in the language; for example, /s/, /t/, or /a/. The LBL normally teaches a vowel correspondence—a match between a vowel grapheme and a vowel phoneme. Graphemes are italicized and phonemes are written in slashes without italics. When writing vowel phonemes in this book, we avoid diacritical marks by using lowercase for short vowels and capitals for long vowels. For example, the grapheme *a* represents the phoneme /a/, or briefly, *a* = /a/. The grapheme *ow* represents the phoneme /O/, or briefly, *ow* = /O/. I would read the equal sign as "says," hence "*a* says /a/," and "*ow* says /O/." With silent *e* patterns, the grapheme is a divided digraph, with the place for a consonant marked with an underscore; for example, *i_e* = /I/, read "*i*-blank-*e* says /I/."

The first question to answer in planning the LBL is: What do I teach? We get the answer from miscue analysis. Reading errors are called *miscues* to emphasize that the reader is cuing on the wrong thing (e.g., pictures or context) or not using all the letters in the spelling (usually the reader is missing the vowel). To analyze miscues, we compare the reader's attempt with the text word. To facilitate this comparison, the attempt is written over the text word in the form of a fraction, for example:

$$\frac{\text{died}}{\text{did}}$$

Miscue analysis can provide information about missing correspondences. Here the reader used both consonants in decoding, but misinterpreted the vowel *i*. This suggests that the reader is missing the correspondence *i* = /i/. In general, a missing correspondence is the first correspondence in the text word not correctly decoded in the attempt, and the missing correspondences will usually be the vowel. Consider this miscue:

$$\frac{\text{vorge}}{\text{voyage}}$$

A reasonable guess is that the student does not have the correspondence *oy* = /oi/ in her decoding toolkit. Sometimes consonants seem to be missing in miscues such as this one for the pseudoword *fim*:

$$\frac{\text{fit}}{\text{fim}}$$

Nevertheless, the best interpretation is that the reader has not established the vowel *i* = /i/. My reasoning is that the student is working so hard at getting the vowel that he has run out of resources to complete the decoding.

In Chapter 7, I explain a common sequence for introducing correspondences beginning with short vowels in alphabetical order, interspersing consonant digraphs, and then teaching long vowels in alphabetical order (first with silent-*e* patterns and then covering related digraphs), and concluding with the other vowels. Maintaining this directional path through the correspondences aligns with the introduction of correspondences in decodable books and thus maintains the decodability of the practice texts. In tutoring a single student, we have the luxury of "cutting to the chase," skipping beyond known correspondences, to tackle the next *missing* correspondence. For example, if a student is only missing the short vowel *i* = /i/, we don't need to teach *a* = /a/ or *e* = /e/. Once *i* = /i/ has been mastered, we jump to the long vowels. In this way, we maximize our coverage of phonics in a minimal time. Thus, tutors should not follow lockstep through the phonics sequence, but rather skip through the sequence to secure only the correspondences that are missing.

Making a lesson plan

When the next specific missing correspondence has been identified, you are ready to construct a lesson plan. Create a list of between 3 and 12 simple one-syllable words that illustrate the correspondence. Plan for a lesson time of roughly 10 minutes. Students catching on quickly to new correspondences may study as many as 12 words, but no more than 12 because there are other important lesson activities. If a student is struggling, 3-5 words may be plenty.

Words to Include

Letterbox words must be regular one-syllable words with varied endings, and a lesson must ordinarily include review words, digraphs, and consonant clusters. For example, suppose I am teaching *o* = /o/. I might begin with words like *odd*, *hot*, *rock*, *spot*, *flock*, and *stomp*. Simple digraphs like *ck* and *ss* are easily managed, and they demonstrate from the beginning that phonemes may be spelled with more than one letter. To complete the list, add review words with vowel correspondences already learned, such as *and*, *neck*, and *spin*. For short vowel lessons, review words should feature earlier short vowels in the alphabet; for long vowel lessons (such as *i_e* = /I/), they should feature its short vowel partner (*i* = /i/) as well as previous long vowels. We don't want the new vowel to be a permanent fixture in the lesson words; we want the student to discriminate *when* to use it, as well as to review previous vowels.

Words to Leave Out

The word list must exclude irregular words, words with more than one syllable, and words with consecutive rhymes. For example, for o = /o/, *roll* is out because it is irregular: /O/ is regularly spelled with *o_e*, *oa*, or *ow*. Any multisyllable word like *common* must be ruled out; letterbox words have only one syllable. In multisyllable words, we get spelling complications, like the doubled *m*, and the unaccented syllable changes to a schwa vowel /u/, which is irregular. We also rule out consecutive rhymes, like *hop*, *mop*, *pop*, and *top*. We want students to decide about vowels and consonant endings rather than simply substitute first letters. Finally, avoid plurals and *s*-inflected verbs in letterbox lessons. These present a practical problem when the *s* follows silent *e*. For example, *hopes* has 4 phonemes, but there is no good place in the letterboxes to place the silent *e*.

When you've collected a good set of example words, get a careful phoneme count for each word, and then arrange the words in phoneme-count order, beginning with 2- or 3-phoneme words, and building to 4-, 5-, or even 6-phoneme words, if available. Any one-syllable words with 4 or more phonemes have consonant clusters; for example, *flock* has the cluster *fl* (the *ck* ending is a digraph). Students should work with clusters early to extend their blending skill with consonants and to expand their pool of decodable words. Some phonics programs devote dozens of lessons to teaching each consonant cluster as a separate unit. This needlessly drags out the program by teaching unnecessary units that could be constructed from previous knowledge of consonants. One other reason to include longer one-syllable words with consonant clusters is that students like the challenge of spelling and reading them, and they gain confidence as they conquer these words.

In choosing words for letterbox lessons, it is easier to *find* example words than to work from scratch. *The Reading Teacher's Book of Lists* (Fry & Kress, 2006) contains sample words arranged by phonogram pattern; e.g., all one-syllable words ending in *ell*. When using lists of rhyming words, it is important to select words from a variety of lists to avoid consecutive rhymes, e.g., drawing e = /e/ words from lists using the phonograms –ed, –ell, –en, –end, –ent, –est, and –et. For lists of challenging 4-, 5-, and 6- phoneme words, see Appendix 1 of this chapter.

Your last preparatory step is to write out everything you have planned. List the sequence of words from the fewest phonemes to the most, the phoneme count for each word (it is easiest to bracket a group with the same number of phonemes), and all letters needed to spell the words. Use a checklist as in Figure 2 to make sure your words are well chosen. Collect these letters in an envelope or ziploc bag to save lesson time.

__ At least 3, but not more than 12 words __ All words have regular spellings __ All words have only one syllable __ No consecutive rhymes __ Review words with earlier short vowels __ Words with digraphs __ Words with consonant clusters __ At least one 4-phoneme word	LBL goal: u_e = /U/ 2 [use] 3 [tune, tuck, fuse] 4 [brute, club, crude] 5 [struck] Letters: u, s, e, t, n, c, k, f, b, r, l, d

FIGURE 2: Checklist for letterbox lesson word lists and a sample list

TEACHING THE LESSON

Teaching a letterbox lesson takes four steps: (1) Reviewing the phoneme, (2) modeling how to spell and read words with the new correspondence, (3) guiding the student to spell words, and (4) guiding the student to read words. Each step is vital in accomplishing the goal of helping students understand a new vowel correspondence so thoroughly that it can be added to their decoding toolkits and used to make sight words.

Reviewing the Phoneme

Recognizing the phoneme in the correspondence in spoken words is often the trickiest part of learning that correspondence. Short vowels present a special challenge because the differences between their sounds is slight, and they are formed with subtle differences in mouth shape. As explained in detail in Chapter 6, phonemes are taught by making several memory links from familiar concepts to the unfamiliar phoneme. For a simple phoneme lesson, display a phoneme picture, give the phoneme a meaningful name, and show a hand gesture related to this name. Stretch the phoneme in each word of an alliterative tongue tickler, and have the student test words for the phoneme. For example, to learn the phoneme /e/ (short e), you can introduce it with a phoneme-letter picture as in Figure 3, where the letter name is embedded as a detail in the picture. Phoneme illustrations may be found on the Reading Genie website at http://www.auburn.edu/rdggenie.

To review /e/, explain to the student that when e is by itself, it makes a sound like a creaky door, /e-e-e-e-e/. Have the student pretend to grab the doorknob and slowly pull open the creaky door. Then have the student repeat an alliterative tongue tickler, such as "Eddie the elephant enjoys eggs." Have the student stretch the phoneme /e/ in each word, pretending to open a creaky door. Finally, have the student test some words for /e/: Is /e/ in *green* or *red*? In *start* or *end*? Testing words serves both as practice and as assessment. If the student can't spot /e/ in words, reteach the phoneme, provide more tongue tickler practice, and test additional words.

FIGURE 3: Creaky doorknob *e*

Modeling

Modeling means dramatizing how to solve a problem, playing the role of a savvy beginner. It is more than a demonstration because modeling reveals *how* a problem is solved. Modeling is unlike expert problem solving in that it imagines all the difficulties that might be encountered by a novice reader. Tutors model two types of problems in the letterbox lesson: How to spell an example word, and how to read an example word. For effective modeling, choose words that are relatively challenging examples of the correspondence, words with consonant clusters and digraphs, with at least four phonemes.

To model spelling a word, stretch the pronunciation, simulate finding phonemes, and select appropriate graphemes for each phoneme in the spelling, explaining your choices as you go. Here's how a teacher might model spelling *speck*: "Okay, I want to spell *speck*, like a speck of dust. That's a four-box word, which means it has four different mouth moves. I'm going to stretch out *speck* and try to find four phonemes. Ssspe-e-e-ck; /s/, starts with an *s*. Sssp, sssp, I can feel my lips popping; that's popcorn *p*. I've got two boxes done, *s*, *p*. Spe-e-e. Hey, that's creaky doorknob *e*. I'll put creaky doorknob *e* in the third box, /e-e-e/ [pretending to open the creaky door]. What's left? Ssspe-e-eck. It ends with /k/. Hmm, that could be either *c* or *k*, but I remember that at the end of short-vowel words, it is *ck*. I'll put *c* and *k* together in the last box. Here's my spelling:

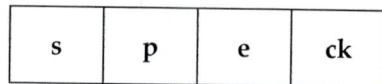

To model reading a word, put aside the boxes and move the letters for vowel-first, body-coda blending. This means to begin with the vowel and then assemble the letters before the vowel; conclude by adding in the letters after the vowel. Here is a modeling example:

Let's say I want to read this word:

fled

A good place to start is with the vowel.

e

That's the creaky doorknob, and it says /e-e-e/ [pretending to open the creaky door]. Okay, I'm going to put the beginning letters with it, *f*, that's /f/, *l*, that's /l/; /f/ /l/ /e/. Fleh?

fle

I've got a chunk, /fle/. Always good to put your chunks together before you go on, /fle/. One more letter to add to the end *d*, says /d/; /fle/, /d/, /fled/, *fled*.

fled

Fled? Oh, I get it, *fled*; it means they ran away. The bad boys fled after they broke a window.

GUIDING SPELLING

Next we want the student to spell all the words from the least challenging to the most challenging, progressively opening up more boxes. Note that the student does not read the words until later in the lesson. We want the student to take a fresh look at each word when it is time to read it. Pass out all the letters needed to spell all of the words. Don't put out all your letters (the student will waste too much time looking for letters), nor at the other extreme, only the letters for the next word (which asks for unscrambling rather than spelling). Ask your student to turn all the letters to the lowercase side and line them up for easy access. Students like to help, and lining up the letters makes them easier to find, especially the reversible letters *b*, *d*, *p*, *q*, *n*, and *u*.

How to Teach a Letterbox Lesson

The letterbox lesson uses letterboxes to scaffold spelling by showing the number of phonemes in the word. Representing phonemes with letters helps the student understand the spelling as a phoneme map, which makes the spelling easy to remember. For this to happen, it is vital to unfold the correct number of letterboxes; in other words, the scaffold requires a correct phoneme count. Digraphs go into a single box. Thus, *thing*, with digraphs *th* and *ng*, would be spelled in three boxes:

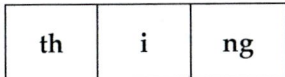

Consonant clusters are broken out into separate boxes; thus the cluster *spr* would be broken out into three boxes, with the vowel digraph *ay* placed in the fourth box:

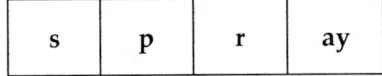

Since the silent *e* functions as a signal letter rather than a grapheme, it is placed outside the last box; thus, *came* would be spelled in three boxes, with the *e* placed outside the third box:

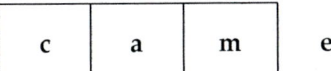

Why does a correct phoneme count matter? Unfolding the correct number of letterboxes provides a visual scaffold for mapping all the phonemes in the word. A wrong phoneme count (e.g., showing the number of letters in *came*) obscures the letter-phoneme mapping and invites a spelling memorization strategy rather than phoneme mapping. Spelling memorization is much more difficult than phoneme matching. It requires an average of 35 trials (Gates, 1931) versus only 4 trials by connecting phonemes with graphemes (Reitsma, 1983).

As you give each word, pronounce it normally, without stretching the pronunciation or segmenting the phonemes. We want the student to stretch and segment phonemes for self-help. Use each word in a sentence so that the meaning is clear. Providing a sentence context can prevent needless frustration when the student is working at a different word than the teacher intended. Some good example words are relatively rare in oral language. Teaching vocabulary is always part of effective reading instruction. For example, in giving the word *lob* to spell, you might say, "Spell *lob*, as in 'Just lob me the ball; don't throw it hard.' *Lob* means toss it slowly, like you'd throw to a little kid."

Scaffolding Misspellings

When a student misspells a letterbox word, the best scaffold is to pronounce exactly what the student has written. For example, suppose we ask a student to spell *spin*, and she spells *sin*, thus:

| s | i | n | |

A good scaffold would be to say, "You spelled *sin*, but we want *spin*. See if you can fix it." Usually students self-correct when the teacher pronounces the misspelling. For an alternative scaffold with a missing grapheme, the tutor can make a show of moving the letters to identify exactly where the phoneme is missing. For the incomplete spelling of *spin*, the letters could be shifted to leave the second box blank, thus:

As in all our tutoring procedures, we have a one-failure limit. If a student cannot correct an error after a single scaffold, don't ask questions to try to draw the knowledge out of your student, or ask him to try again, try again. Asking questions or asking the student to try again usually just adds to his frustration. Instead, model how to spell the word.

Again, modeling means dramatizing how to solve the problem, explaining the reasoning behind each problem-solving step. Modeling reenacts the role of a brilliant beginner. To model spelling *spin*, I would remove all the letters and simulate stretching the word, finding phonemes, and representing them with letters. I might say, "*Spin*. I'll stretch out the word in super slow motion and feel what my mouth is doing: *sssspi-i-innn*. *Sssspin* starts with /s/, like a slithering snake; that's letter *s*. I'll put *s* in the first box. *Sp* . . . /p/, that's popcorn popping *p*, and it goes in the second box. *Spi-i-i*, hey, that's /i/. I'm going to use drippy gooey *i* in the third box. It even looks like drops of gooey stuff, and when it makes your fingers sticky, /i/ [shaking stiff fingers]. *Spinnn* ends with /n/; sounds like a jet ski, /n/. That's letter *n*. *Spin*." After modeling, put a check by that word in your lesson plan. After all the other words have been successfully spelled, come back to any words you had to model, and have your student give them another try. Having observed your model, the student will usually succeed in spelling the word, replacing the previous failure with success.

Some misspellings make good phonemic sense. For example, the misspelling SHOK is a good mapping for *shock*. Compliment such good spellings, show the correct spelling with a brief explanation, and move on to the next word. You might say, "Nice work. You spelled all the sounds in *shock*. However, I'm going to add a *c* before the *k*, because that's how we spell the /k/ ending after a short vowel like /o/. This is what the correct spelling looks like: *shock*." It is important to keep up a brisk lesson pace to maintain student engagement and save time for other lesson activities.

Have the student spell all the words without stopping to read them. If you ask the student to read a word just spelled, no decoding is necessary. The student knows what word she's been working on. To get the reader to take a fresh look at the word, it is necessary to save all word reading until after all words have been spelled.

Guiding Word Reading

The goal of the letterbox lesson is to transfer grapheme-phoneme mappings introduced in spelling to learn to read the words. The student worked through the spellings to learn how the new correspondence works in encoding the words for use in decoding them. Thus, it is crucial that the lesson not end with spelling, but that the student be guided in reading the words. I like to introduce this part of the LBL by saying: "Okay, you've finished the hard work of spelling the words. Now it's my turn to do the hard work, and all you have to do is read what I spell." Giving a list of all the words for the student to read or giving word cards saves time. Teachers presenting a letterbox lesson to a group of students will probably want to display the word list on a chart or overhead for easy visibility.

For reading the words, put away the letterboxes. They are spelling scaffolds, and when it is time to read the words, they are in the way. Letterboxes pregroup digraphs in a way that takes over some of the normal work of decoding; they are too heavy a scaffold at this point. Word reading is a good place to assess understanding of the new correspondence. To assess transfer, include a couple of new words to check to see if the reader can transfer the new correspondence to read untaught words. The added words can be either untaught real words or pseudowords. To make a legal pseudoword, simply replace any consonants before the vowel with other consonants. For example, you could change *rock* to *zock*. This method will keep you from using illegal spellings like *zok* (legal spellings use *ck* after short vowels).

Scaffolding Vowel-First, Body-Coda Blending

Moving letter tiles for vowel-first, body-coda blending is a highly effective scaffold for reading words. The body of a syllable is everything in the spoken syllable through the vowel, and the coda is the remainder of the syllable, any consonants following the vowel. Thus, in *snack*, the body is *sna* and the coda *ck*. In two experiments (Murray, Brabham, Paleologos, Norvell-Hall, & Gaston-Thornton, 2005; Murray, Brabham, Villaume, & Veal, 2002), we found that kindergartners are more successful with body-coda blending (e.g., *sta-mp*) than with other groupings. Arranging body and coda segments makes words significantly easier to blend for young children.

Vowel-first, body-coda blending is scaffolded by moving the letter tiles in a planned order to minimize the difficulty of the blends. For example, to scaffold reading *hot*, first separate out the letters and isolate the vowel *o*. Have the student "say this much." Then move the first consonant and vowel together to form the body, /ho/. It is not sufficient to pronounce the phonemes, /h/, /o/: Have the student blend the two phonemes into a chunk /ho/ to minimize demands on working memory. Finally, move *ho* with the final consonant *t* (the body-coda blend) to identify the word. Figure 4 shows how blending words with digraphs, consonant clusters, and silent-*e* patterns can work with vowel-first, body-coda blending.

Word	Vowel first	Blend body	Add coda	Identify word
thick	i	th-i, thi	thi-ck, thick	Thick slice of bread.
plant	a	p-l-a, pla	pla-nt, plant	Plant a garden.
home	o_e	h-o_e, ho_e	ho_e-m, home	Go home after school.

FIGURE 4: Procedures for vowel-first, body-coda blending

When helping your student read LBL words, don't ask questions. Instead, scaffold reading by moving letters. Use the one-failure-limit rule: Give one chance to read the word with vowel-first, body-coda scaffolding, and if that doesn't work, model how to read the word. If you have to model, put a check by that word in the plan and have the student read it after reading the other words to replace failure with success. To follow up the lesson, have your student read a decodable book featuring the new correspondence. For example, after a lesson teaching *e* = /e/, the student could read *Red Gets Fed* (Cushman, 1990). After learning *o_e* = /O/, the student could read *Is Jo Home* (Cushman & Kornblum, 1990).

The LBL from hell

Imagine getting a letterbox plan to teach *g* and *q* with the words *queen, quick, green, growth, quest, grain,* and *growl*. Do you see any problems with that lesson? To begin with, the LBL teaches a vowel correspondence instead of teaching letter recognition. We teach letter recognition with guided printing practice rather than by guided spelling and reading. Furthermore, the words chosen for this lesson are fraught with difficulty, featuring many untaught correspondences. For example, we have *ow* saying both /O/ and /ow/. Students faced with this level of difficulty will probably not say, "This lesson is too hard for me." They will more likely say, "This is boring." When a student says he is bored, he usually means he is frustrated because the lesson is too hard.

Several errors in design can make a lesson too hard. The lesson may include words like *growl* with untaught correspondences. It may include irregular words, such as *ball* in a lesson teaching *a* = /a/. It may include two-syllable words like *happen*, where consonants double and vowels change their sounds in unaccented syllables. The teacher may provide the wrong number of letterboxes, e.g., asking the student to spell *shape* in five boxes. Memorizing arbitrary spellings is about 9 times harder than understanding alphabetic mappings.

When students are successful, they enjoy the letterbox lesson and think of it as a game they can win. Many say that it is their favorite tutoring activity. With a well-designed, well-modeled, well-scaffolded LBL, the lights come on for beginning readers.

KEY POINTS TO REMEMBER IN TEACHING A SUCCESSFUL LBL

1. Identify the correspondence to teach by analyzing reading miscues. Look for vowels your student is not using in his attempts. Don't teach the next correspondence in the sequence unless you have evidence that your student is missing that vowel.

2. Plan a succession of 3-12 regular, one-syllable words with varied endings, gradually increasing the number of phonemes. Include words with review vowels, digraphs, and consonant clusters.

3. Review the phoneme in the correspondence, especially with short vowels. Display a phoneme picture, give it a meaningful name, and show a hand gesture. Try it out in an alliterative tongue tickler, and have the student test words for the phoneme.

4. Model how to spell a tough word and how to read a different tough word. Choose words as challenging as any words you will ask your student to spell and read. Dramatize, without asking questions, how you would solve the spelling and reading problems.

5. Have your student help you line up the letters needed to spell all the words. Make sure your letterboxes lie flat. If they pooch up, cut them apart and retape them with a single strip of scotch tape.

6. For each word, unfold the letterboxes to show the correct number of phonemes, which is usually different from the number of letters. Digraphs go in one box, consonant clusters are broken up across boxes, and silent *e* goes outside the last box.

7. Pronounce each word to spell without stretching or segmenting it, and use it in a sentence to clarify its meaning. Give the student time to work.

8. If the student misspells a word, pronounce it as it is spelled and ask if he can fix it. For example, if *broke* is spelled BROK, say "That says 'brock.' Can you make it say *broke*?" If the student can't make the repair in one try, model it and come back to the word later.

9. After all the words are spelled correctly, put away the letterboxes and have the student read the words from cards or a list. Include a couple of new example words or pseudowords using the new correspondence to check for transfer.

10. If a student misreads a word, spell out the word with letter tiles and move the tiles to scaffold vowel-first, body-coda blending. In other words, have the student pronounce the vowel, blend the letters before the vowel with the vowel to make a chunk (the body), and then blend the body with any letters after the vowel (the coda).

Appendix 1: Letterbox Example Words With 4, 5, or 6 Phonemes

	a = /a/
4	crab, drab, grab, scab, slab, stab, black, crack, smack, snack, stack, track, glad, brag, drag, flag, snag, clam, cram, gram, slam, camp, damp, lamp, ramp, champ, bran, clan, plan, scan, span, band, hand, land, sand, clang, slang, bank, rank, sank, tank, yank, thank, clap, flap, slap, snap, trap, brash, clash, crash, flash, slash, smash, thrash, trash, brat, flat, scat, fact, tact, raft, shaft, pant, cask, mask, task, cast, fast, last, past, vast, brass, class, glass, grass
5	clamp, cramp, scamp, stamp, tramp, bland, brand, grand, stand, sprang, blank, clank, crank, drank, flank, frank, plank, prank, spank, scrap, strap, tract, craft, draft, grant, plant, slant, flask, blast, scratch, clasp, scalp, splat, scram
6	strand

	e = /e/
4	bled, bred, fled, Fred, shred, sled, sped, smell, spell, swell, bend, lend, mend, send, tend, bent, cent, dent, rent, lent, sent, tent, went, best, nest, pest, rest, test, vest, west, chest, fret, bless, dress, press, left, help, next, weld
5	blend, spend, trend, spent, blest, stress, slept, crept
6	strength

	i = /i/
4	brick, click, flick, slick, stick, trick, grid, skid, slid, swig, twig, drill, grill, frill, skill, spill, still, thrill, trill, brim, grim, slim, swim, trim, grin, skin, spin, twin, bring, cling, fling, sling, sting, swing, kink, link, mink, pink, rink, sink, wink, chink, think, hint, lint, mint, tint, blip, clip, drip, flip, grip, skip, slip, snip, trip, grit, skit, slit, spit, crib, cliff, sniff, stiff, gift, lift, shift, tilt, wilt, swish, disk, risk, Swiss, list, mist, switch
5	sprig, spring, string, blink, brink, clink, drink, shrink, stink, flint, print, strip, split, drift, swift, thrift, brisk, frisk, twist, blimp, crisp
6	sprint, splint, script, scrimp

	o = /o/
4	blob, slob, snob, block, clock, crock, flock, frock, smock, stock, clod, plod, prod, clog, frog, smog, prong, crop, drop, flop, plop, slop, stop, blot, clot, plot, slot, spot, trot, cross, blotch
5	strong, blond, stomp, frost
6	prompt

u = /u/	
4	club, grub, shrub, stub, cluck, pluck, stuck, truck, bluff, fluff, gruff, scuff, stuff, drug, plug, shrug, slug, snug, drum, plum, scum, slum, swum, bump, dump, hump, jump, lump, pump, spun, stun, clung, flung, stung, swung, bunk, dunk, hunk, junk, punk, sunk, chunk, blush, brush, crush, flush, plush, slush, thrush, spud, grudge, bunch, hunch, lunch, munch, punch, bunt, hunt, punt, runt, plus, bust, dust, just, must, rust
5	scrub, struck, strum, clump, grump, plump, slump, stump, trump, sprung, strung, drunk, flunk, plunk, shrunk, skunk, slunk, spunk, stunk, trunk, strut, crunch, blunt, grunt, stunt, thrust, trust, crust

a_e = /A/	
4	brace, grace, place, space, trace, blade, grade, spade, trade, brake, drake, flake, snake, stake, blame, flame, frame, crane, plane, flare, glare, scare, snare, spare, stare, crate, plate, skate, state, brave, grave, slave, stage, grape, blaze, craze
5	scrape, strafe

ai/ay = /A/	
4	frail, snail, trail, brain, drain, grain, plain, Spain, stain, train, spray, stray, braid, stair, claim, faint
5	sprain, strain

ee/ea = /E/	
4	creak, sneak, speak, steal, cream, dream, steam, clear, smear, spear, treat, bleed, breed, freed, greed, speed, steed, treed, creep, sleep, steep, sweep, fleet, greet, sleet, sweet, clean, creek, Greek, sleek, steel, green, sneer, steer, spree, least, feast
5	streak, stream, scream, street, screen

i_e = /I/	
4	price, slice, spice, twice, bride, glide, pride, slide, crime, grime, prime, slime, brine, shrine, spine, swine, drive, thrive, bribe, tribe, spike, smile, gripe, spite
5	splice, stride, strive, scribe, strife, strike, stripe, sprite

igh/y = /I/	
4	bright, flight, fright, slight, spry

o_e = /O/	
4	broke, smoke, spoke, clone, crone, drone, stone, grope, slope, scope, score, store, snore, swore, globe, probe, stole, close, drove, stove
5	stroke, strode

oa/ow = /O/	
4	cloak, croak, groan, boast, coast, roast, toast, bloat, float, throat, blown, flown, grown

u_e = /U/	
4	crude, prude, prune, flute
5	spruce

ew/oo = /U/	
4	screw, drool, spool, stool, bloom, broom, gloom, groom, spoon, droop, scoop, snoop, swoop, troop, smooth

Appendix 2: Sample forms for double-sided letters

A	A	A	B	B	C	C
C	D	D	D	E	E	E
E	F	F	G	G	H	H	H
I	I	I	I	J	K	K
L	L	L	M	M	N	N
O	O	O	O	P	P	Q	Q
R	R	R	R	S	S	S
T	T	T	T	U	U	V	V
W	W	X	X	Y	Y	Z	Z

c	c	b	b	a	a	a	a
e	e	e	e	d	d	d	c
h	h	h	g	g	f	f	e
k	k	j	j	i	i	i	i
n	n	n	m	m	l	l	l
q	q	p	p	o	o	o	o
s	s	s	s	r	r	r	r
v	v	u	u	t	t	t	t
z	z	y	y	x	x	w	w

PRACTICAL CHAPTER

How to Teach Blending, Concepts About Print, and Letter Recognition

Phonemes and letters are the basic building blocks of literacy in an alphabetic language. Fused together into correspondences, they provide systematic access to the lexicon—a reliable way to get to words and their meanings from spelling information. There is a symbiotic relationship between letter recognition and phoneme awareness: Letters and phonemes become more memorable and powerful when they work together. Letter recognition helps phoneme awareness by giving phonemes visible symbols so that they are easier to remember. Phoneme awareness, in turn, makes letter recognition easier because without PA, letters have no meaning. A letter like *h* remains a strange symbol with a weird name—until it comes to mean the "panting dog" phoneme in "Henry held Hannah's hot hand." With letter recognition and phoneme awareness, novice readers have the critical tools for decoding.

In this practical chapter, you will learn how to teach three valuable components in decoding: blending, concepts about print, and letter recognition. With the strategy of blending, novice readers can assemble correspondences to decode words. With concepts about print, they learn to understand teachers' talk about reading. Through instruction in letter formation, they learn to recognize letters automatically, overcoming confusions between letters that can be nagging impediments in reading.

HOW TO TEACH BLENDING

Blending is a critical component strategy in learning to decode. At the beginning of the full alphabetic phase, decoding is a two-step process. First, children have to "sound out" the phonemes signaled by graphemes, i.e., recognize which phonemes are signaled and then pronounce them in isolation. Then, they must blend the phoneme sequence together into a recognizable approximation of the spoken word. To understand the most effective procedures for blending, it is necessary to introduce two ways of dividing the syllable: onset-rime and body-coda.

Onset and Rime

There are four intermediate units in a spoken word larger than a phoneme but smaller than a syllable. Figure 1 shows two ways to divide the word *trust*. The **onset** is the phonological segment of a syllable that precedes the vowel. An onset could be a consonant, a consonant cluster, or nothing, because the onset is an optional part of the syllable, not found when the syllable begins with a vowel. The **rime** is the spoken part of the syllable beginning with the vowel and including any consonants after the vowel. The rime is the part of the syllable that "rhymes," e.g., the common element in *trust*, *dust*, and *must*. Because the vowel is mandatory, the rime is mandatory. Although the *trust* example is presented as a spelling, onsets and rimes are parts of spoken syllables. For example, the rime /At/ is found in *wait*, *gate*, and *freight*. The spelling of a rime is called a phonogram; thus, *ait*, *ate*, and *eight* are phonograms representing the rime /At/.

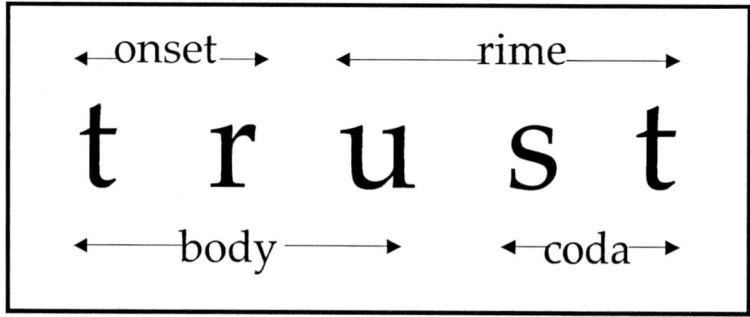

FIGURE 1: How the word *trust* can be divided into onset-time and body-coda segments

Children generally find it easier to segment spoken words into onset and rime chunks than into any other parts of the syllable (Treiman, 1985). In other words, the onset-rime break point, which is immediately before the vowel, is the most fragile place in the syllable. You probably have no difficulty breaking words like *sweet*, *suit*, *brake*, *pie*, and *oak* into onset and rime (*sw-eet*, *s-uit*, *br-ake*, *p-ie*, and *oak*; with *oak*, recall that the onset is optional). If you ask a kindergartner to tell you the first sound in *sweet*, he might well say /sw/, the onset, rather than /s/. Most kindergartners can detect the phoneme /m/ more easily in *match*, where it is the onset, than in *warm*, where it is part of the rime. Most can detect /t/ more easily in *time*, where it is the entire onset, than in *train*, where it is only part of the onset. Adults, too, find it natural to split a syllable into onset and rime. If I asked you to combine the beginning of *blind* with the end of *date*, would you say *blight* or *blate*? Most people say *blate*, even though *blight* may better preserve the meaning of "blind date."

Body and Coda

Though syllables segment naturally into onset and rime, onset-rime blending can be difficult (Murray, Brabham, Villaume, & Veal, 2008). If the onset-rime break point is the most fragile place in the syllable, it is not the easiest place to blend. To make blending easier, we need to work with the phonological segments called the body and the coda (see Figure 1). The **body** is the spoken part of a syllable that includes the onset, if any, and the vowel. Because the body includes the vowel, it is mandatory. The **coda** is composed of any consonants following the vowel, and it is optional. A word like *true* that ends in a vowel has no coda. Because the body-coda intersection is not the natural break point in the syllable, it is slightly harder to break words like *sweet, suit, brake, pie,* and *oak* into body and coda (*swee-t, sui-t, bra-ke, pie,* and *oa-k*; with *pie*, recall that the coda is optional).

The payoff for learning about body and coda segments is that they are easier to blend than onset and rime segments (Murray, et al., 2008). The point before the vowel—the body-coda break point—is the "stickiest" place in a syllable. The "sticky" body-coda breakpoint resists segmentation, but it is the easiest place to blend. For example, /d/ /Is/ is an unnatural and difficult blend, but /dI/ /s/ can be blended easily to identify the word *dice*.

We can introduce blending as an oral language activity. A natural sequence for teaching children to blend is to begin with body-coda chunks and use illustrated words (e.g., pictures of a *mo-p, sui-t, mi-ce, hi-ll,* and *flu-te*). Children can try to guess what is in a hidden picture from body-coda clues pronounced by the teacher. Alternatively, they can answer phoneme riddles, e.g., "I'm thinking of the animal Little Bo Peep lost. It was her *shee-p*." Once children master body-coda blending, they can begin blending with onset and rime chunks (*m-op, s-uit, m-ice, h-ill,* and *fl-ute*), which are slightly harder to blend but allow children to work with only two chunks at a time. After children can blend onset-rime, they can take on the ultimate challenge of blending single phonemes (*m-o-p, s-ui-t, m-i-ce, h-i-ll,* and *f-l-u-te*).

To help children deal with so many segments, teachers should shift to letter tiles to represent the phonemes. The letterbox lesson scaffolds blending by moving letter tiles to identify the vowel first and then blending the body and coda (see Practical Chapter 3). Vowel-first, body-coda blending is the most effective procedure for blending because it works with only a few segments at a time in an optimal order. The vowel is the critical new element to bring to the table first. For example, to blend *stick*, we begin by isolating the letter *i* to sound out the vowel /i/. Next we assemble the body by blending *s-t-i* to make a chunk, *sti-*. Consolidating several isolated phonemes into a single chunk saves mental resources. Finally, we blend in the coda, *sti-ck*, to recognize the word *stick* ("Oh, like a stick fell off the tree").

As children develop blending skill, we can switch over to the more natural left-to-right sequence for blending for reading printed words. A "coverup critter" made from a decorated Popsicle stick is a useful tool to scaffold left-to-right blending. The teacher can cover the word, and then uncover graphemes to reveal the body. With *stick*, this would mean uncovering *s*, *t*, and *i* one at a time to lead the reader to sound out the phonemes /s/ /t/ /i/, and then blending the body, *sti-*. With the body chunk consolidated, the novice reader is ready to blend the body and coda, *sti-ck*, to recognize *stick*. Following the teacher's model, the beginner can take over use of the coverup critter for self-help in decoding.

In sounding out and blending phonemes, teachers have often worried about pronouncing consonants with added schwa, so that they sound like *suh, tuh, i, kuh*. In an experiment, we found that adding the schwa to consonants actually helps children blend, probably by making the segments easier to hear (Murray, et al., 2008). The schwa vowel /u/ acts as a plain brown wrapper. It attaches uniformly to all the consonants, and it is easy to unwrap during blending.

CONCEPTS ABOUT PRINT

Children need a vocabulary for talking about reading, a set of concepts about print. A concept is a general idea of something, abstracted out of many particular instances. For young children, the concept of *dog* may at first include any animal with four legs, including horses and cats. Gradually this concept is refined to eliminate animals with the wrong kind of feet, which have a different looking nose, and which do not bark. Similarly, children gradually discern that the print they see in books, on computer screens, and on billboards has something in common: It is talk written down. When Mommy looks at print on her shopping list, she sees her talk about what to buy written down. The child comes to understand that print is a visual representation of the familiar spoken language.

Concepts about print are best understood as the jargon of reading instruction—the special vocabulary needed to understand talk about written language. It includes key terms like *letter, word*, and *sentence; capital* and *lowercase; period, question mark*, and *quotation marks*. The letter names are print concepts; when the teacher talks about "double-*u*," children need a connection with *w*. Concepts about print also include the tough directional words *left* and *right*. Because print concepts are the essential vocabulary of early reading instruction, they are taught like any other vocabulary (for more information, see Chapter 11). To teach students the meaning of a word or concept, we help them to locate its meaning boundaries with simple explanations, examples, and nonexamples. We show them how to use the word with other words to understand correct usage. We help them extricate the word from its original context to see how it is used in other contexts. Finally, we guide them to generate their own sentences using the new word.

One basic print concept is the concept of word. What is a word? For sophisticated adults, we could talk about free morphemes or phonological structures, but for children, the concept of word is much simpler: A word is a group of letters with space on both sides. This simple concept is sufficient to understand *word* in the vocabulary of reading instruction. Surprisingly, the concept of a spoken word is much more elusive than the concept of a written word. Unlike written words, spoken words have no temporal spacing. A sentence of words sounds like a string of syllables. To learn the boundaries of words, we must study them in print. This is obvious when studying a second language. I listened to a series of Spanish language CDs in my car and learned to say "enseguida" (meaning "right away"), but only recently did I learn that *enseguida* is only one word. Adult English speakers may not be certain about the number of words in *all right, a lot, workbook,* or *time line*.

Dr. George Petrie is a one of the legends at Auburn University—the first football coach, a history professor, and the author of the Auburn Creed. A former student recalled his first encounter with Dr. Petrie:

> The first day of class he walked out, studied the class for a few seconds, and then asked, "Any Yankees in this class?" A New Yorker, I raised my hand, as did a fellow from Connecticut. Then he said with a grin, "I was 21 years old before I knew that damn Yankee was two words. Welcome to the South."

Shared Reading

The two most effective activities for teaching concepts about print are shared reading and the language experience approach. Shared reading with big books is a staple kindergarten activity. A "big book" is a predictable book, enlarged for working with a group. It is not simply any supersized children's book because ordinary stories will not work for shared reading. Predictable big books usually feature patterned language, so that only one or two words change per page. Alternatively, they can be rhyming poetry or cumulative texts that add one new word per page. For prealphabetic children to "share" (i.e., participate in) the reading, they must be able to catch on to the language pattern; they do not need to decode the words. New Zealand author Joy Cowley is well known for creating engaging predictable books for shared readings. Teachers fortunate enough to have the technology to display documents on a screen can save the expense and awkwardness of handling big books.

A shared reading begins with an engaging booktalk (see Practical Chapter 1), and then proceeds with an interactive read aloud. An interactive read aloud provides for frequent interruptions to allow for comments and questions by participants. The teacher then rereads the book, fingerpointing the words (i.e., touching each word as she reads), and invites children to join in wherever they pick up the pattern. Rereadings may continue over several days, and children increase their participation as the text becomes increasingly familiar. Conversations involve not only story events, but also the form of the text. For example, the teacher might point out where to begin reading the page and which direction to read ("I'm starting at the top left, and I'm going toward the right"), demonstrating directionality by fingerpointing the words. The teacher might ask students to count the number of words or point out long words, short words, or repeated words to practice the concept of word.

The best effect of shared reading is to introduce the language of books to children. Book language has a special vocabulary and syntax quite different from the fragmentary exchanges of oral language. To think about this, imagine someone speaking from behind a screen. Could you tell whether the person was talking or reading? The carefully controlled exposition and literary vocabulary of a written text is usually fairly obvious. Book language is different from oral language—it has a different register, i.e., a special form of a language associated with a situation or subject matter. Learning the vocabulary and syntax of book language will eventually improve children's reading comprehension—after they learn how to read words. The patterned language of predictable books is immediately helpful to English language learners, who can internalize the sentence structures of predictable books as well as acquire vocabulary.

However, prealphabetic readers do not learn to read words by engaging in shared readings with predictable big books. They need not even look at the words to use the language patterns and illustrations to remember the text. Sharing the reading of a predictable book is cued recitation, not reading. To learn to read words, students must learn to understand their spellings, which map out pronunciations using letters as phoneme symbols. Learning to read requires learning to understand printed words as meaningful pronunciation maps. There is no progress toward learning to read words in any sort of recitation that does not require decoding.

When prealphabetic readers read predictable books, the illustrations provide the only interpretable cues to the text on the page. Colorfully illustrated books not only have aesthetic value, but also provide reading motivation and enhance comprehension. When partial and full alphabetic readers read decodable books, the illustrations fill in the informational gaps left by the restricted vocabulary. In either case, illustrations are essential to the motivation and delight of learning to read.

The Language Experience Approach

The language experience approach (LEA) was popularized by Roach Van Allen (1976) in hopes of creating a natural bridge between spoken and written language. While no such natural bridge is possible, LEA is probably the single most effective way to teach concepts about print. The language experience approach begins with a vivid experience that children want to talk about. It might be an engaging read aloud, a field trip, or a visit from a DARE officer with a police dog. As children collectively tell a story about the experience, the teacher transcribes their words as a reading text, preserving their exact wording as closely as possible. For example, students might talk about their classroom visitor by saying:

> The dog, he bark real loud. The policeman, he had a big gun. We was scared of the big gun.

It is integral to LEA that the teacher *not* correct children's grammar. The rationale of LEA is that children will understand the text created by the teacher as their own talk written down.

The transcription of children's language in LEA offers an unparalleled opportunity to provide informal instruction in print concepts. As the teacher writes, she models how talk is written down. It is completely natural to point out where to begin writing, which direction to proceed, the importance of leaving a space between each word, and what to do on reaching the end of a line. The teacher can remark about long words ("*Policeman* is certainly a long word") and short words ("Look, the word *a* has only one letter"), and why we make a period to mark the end of a sentence. Talk about print concepts is functional rather than forced; unlike with shared reading, it is a natural narrative for transcribing talk as text. After the story is transcribed, it becomes a text for children to read and reread—or rather to recite by remembering their words, now written down in the LEA.

Is LEA a good way to teach students how to read—to bridge the gap between spoken and written language? We have evidence to the contrary from the First Grade Studies, the large scale experiment in the 1960s comparing the popular beginning reading methods of the day (Bond & Dykstra, 1967). As a method for teaching children how to read, LEA was dismal, no better than the whole-word basals with which it competed. Comparing LEA with what we know is effective in teaching reading shows why. LEA demonstrates reading and writing words, but it provides no instruction in *how* to read words; it is a whole-word method. The texts produced in LEA are not restricted for decodability, which would defeat the rationale for doing LEA. Students do not have the tools for understanding a spelling like *policeman*. They can remember it as "the long word," but they will see many other long words, making it impossible to discriminate which long word it is. The First Grade Studies showed that daily writing is a valuable component in first-grade instruction, but in LEA, the teacher does all the writing. When young children write themselves with invented spelling, they stretch pronunciations to detect and transcribe phonemes, developing their phoneme awareness. LEA is especially weak in developing reading comprehension, which depends on learning new vocabulary, concepts, sentence structures, and text structures. When children's own talk is written down and recycled, they do not encounter the language and vocabulary of books.

Shared reading and LEA are central activities in the emergent literacy view of early literacy, which rests on the assumption that reading develops naturally in the same way children learn oral language. The emergent literacy view proposes that children decontextualize the print they encounter in the natural environment; e.g., by learning to read *STOP* in the context of the familiar octagonal street sign, and by a natural recognition process, learning to read the word *stop* in plain print. However, experimental evidence (Masonheimer, Drum, & Ehri, 1984) shows that such hopes are in vain. When environmental print "experts" were asked to read words from familiar logos in plain print, their "reading" ability disappeared. The ability to interpret logos is simply picture recognition, not reading.

Even skilled readers rarely notice the details of print when they are unnecessary for identification. Try an informal quiz; the answers are at the end of the chapter. Is there a hyphen between Coca and Cola? Is there an apostrophe in the name of the fast-food restaurant with the golden arches? What is printed to the left of Lincoln's collar on a penny? If you answered all three questions correctly, your attention to the superfluous details of print is remarkable, but don't fault your reading ability if you missed any or all of these items. We don't need the details of environmental print to recognize its meaning. We don't learn to recognize words by decontextualizing them, but by decoding them. The effort to immerse children in a print-rich environment is better devoted to teaching them phoneme awareness and letter recognition, the building blocks of decoding.

TEACHING LETTER RECOGNITION

Why is it often hard for children to remember the names of letters? Unlike Chinese characters, letters are simple, spare forms with little detail. This simplicity contributes to the ease of forming letters, but it can make them easy to confuse, particularly the lowercase letters *b*, *d*, *p*, and *q*, which are all the same shape and differ only in orientation. Some teachers have added to the confusion by describing them as made of balls and sticks. Generally, children are taught the capital letters (where *B*, *D*, *P*, and *Q* are not similar shapes) well before the lowercase letters. Acquiring letter names is useful in learning to read. The names are concepts about print, vital vocabulary for understanding reading instruction. In addition, most letter names provide reasonably good hints for phoneme awareness (e.g., *eff* is not a bad approximation of the phoneme /f/). Children's first experience with the alphabet may be to learn to sing the alphabet song, which introduces letter names with a tune originally introduced by Mozart. Figure 2 shows the developmental sequence for learning letters.

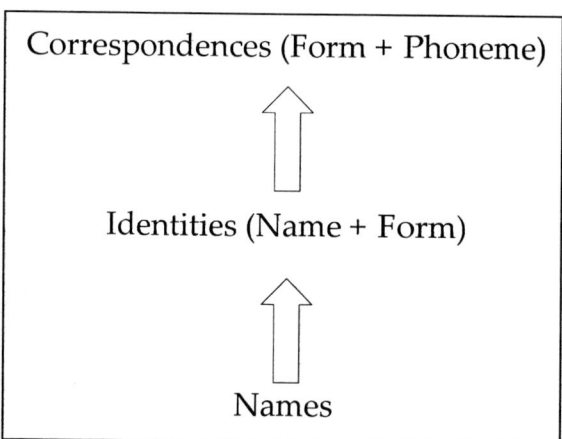

FIGURE 2: Developmental sequence for learning letters

Letter names, essentially nonsense words when first learned in the alphabet song, are linked with letters in learning letter identities. The critical achievement for learning to read is to learn the correspondence between each letter form and its phoneme. Consonants are learned this way in phoneme awareness instruction. At this point, the letter name is replaced by the phoneme so that the letter form signals the phoneme, rather than the letter name. Because the letter name drops out in using correspondences for decoding, teachers should move away from asking, e.g., "What does *h-o-g* say?" In this case, the letter names give misleading signals for the phonemes. It is better to use coverups to reveal the letter forms one by one, to scaffold decoding.

Letter recognition was once thought to be the best predictor of children's success in learning to read (Bond & Dykstra, 1967). Though it has been edged out by phoneme awareness, the combination of letter recognition and PA explains most of the variation in success in learning to read words (Share, Jorm, Maclean, & Matthews, 1984). Letter names are useful for several reasons. First, letter names are concepts about print. Children need the vocabulary of letter names (e.g., *double-u, ex, wye,* and *zee*) to understand the teacher's talk about phoneme awareness and phonics. Second, letter recognition helps phoneme awareness. Having a constant visual symbol for a phoneme makes the phoneme easier to learn. Third, letter names help children learn letter identities by giving the abstract form a name. With a reliable link to the letter identity, correspondences are easier to learn.

The common sense view that we learn letters by memorizing their shapes is wrong. The problem is evident with the letters *b, d, p,* and *q*, which are all the same shape. Recognizing letters is a matter of learning the placement, direction, size, and sequence of letter features (Adams, 1990). It is a mistake to try to teach children letters as holistic shapes, or as assemblages of balls and sticks. Letters are not recognized by shapes, but by their features. For example, the letter *m* is composed of a line segment, a hump, and a second hump, executed from left to right. Learning this sequence is best taught with guided printing practice on lined primary paper, emphasizing the optimal downward and left-to-right sequence of strokes that puts the hand into the right position for the next letter. Sue Dickson, creator of the Sing, Spell, Read, and Write phonics program, devised child-friendly ways to help children learn the placement, direction, size, and sequence of letter features. A summary of her ideas is in the Appendix of this chapter, including a diagram with directional arrows to show the sequence for printing the features and verbal instructions for walking children through forming each letter.

A vital material for helping children learn the placement, direction, size, and sequence of letter features is primary paper, the kind with a dotted line between two solid lines and a generous amount of space for forming the letters. So that children can understand the use of these lines, it helps to give them concrete names, such as the fence (the intermediate dotted line), the rooftop (the line above the fence), and the sidewalk (the line below the fence). The area below the sidewalk, also important in letter formation, might be called the ditch. Figure 3 illustrates these lines with images that will be helpful to prealphabetic readers who can't read the printed labels. The lines act as landmarks to show students the placement, direction, size, and sequence of features in forming the letters. Using plain paper is not more creative: It withholds a crucial scaffold for learning the optimal sequence for forming each letter, the sequence that will make it easiest for the hand and end in the position to form the next letter in spelling words. In general, the easiest sequence is to form letters from top to bottom and from left to right. *Left* and *right* are crucial concepts about print for instruction in forming letters. The directional arrows on the diagram in the appendix show these sequences.

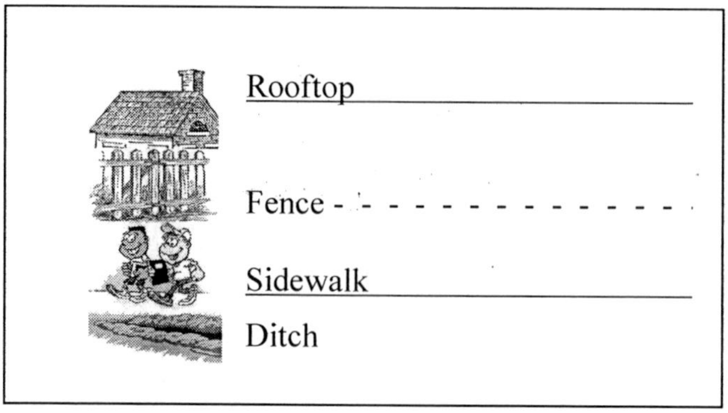

FIGURE 3: Naming the lines on primary paper

The best way to learn letter features is by guided printing practice. Guided printing practice shows the sequence of strokes while explaining and modeling letter formation with simple language. For example, "Letter *c* begins just below the fence, curves up to touch the fence, continues around to the sidewalk, and ends just above the sidewalk. In other words, go up and touch the fence, then around to the sidewalk and up. For letter *a*, make a letter *c*, but keep going back to the place you began and then go straight down to the sidewalk. Go up and touch the fence, then around and touch the sidewalk, around and straight down." Simple directions, coupled with modeling, will help children form the letters in the right sequence and learn the features of letters for automatic recognition. In explaining and modeling letter formation, children need vivid, concrete language, e.g., "To make lowercase b, start at the rooftop and drop straight down to the sidewalk. Then b-b-bounce back up to the fence and around." As children form the letters during their early practice, they should recite a brief version of these instructions as they form the letter, e.g., "Drop down, bounce up, and around."

Should beginners trace dotted letters? The answer is no, because tracing will not guide them through the optimal sequence for forming the letters. If I wanted to show you the way to an unfamiliar place, I could have you follow my car, or I could name the roads, identify landmarks along the way, and give directions a bout which way to turn at each landmark. Having you follow my car would be analogous to tracing dots; you would get there, but you probably wouldn't be able to find your way next time. Noting the key roads, landmarks, and directions would help you learn the route. Similarly, students need printed guidelines and a standard sequence to learn where to begin a letter, which direction to go, and how large to make each part. The idea of drawing the letters is based on the mistaken idea that letters are learned as holistic shapes rather than as sequences of features. Chinese children have much more complicated characters to learn, using guidelines shaped like windows. We can benefit from their insights in using primary paper to help children learn to form letters.

Answers to the Environmental Print Quiz

Yes, Coca-Cola is hyphenated; Yes, McDonald's has an apostrophe; and on a penny, to the left of Lincoln's collar, the printed word is LIBERTY.

APPENDIX

How to Print Letters

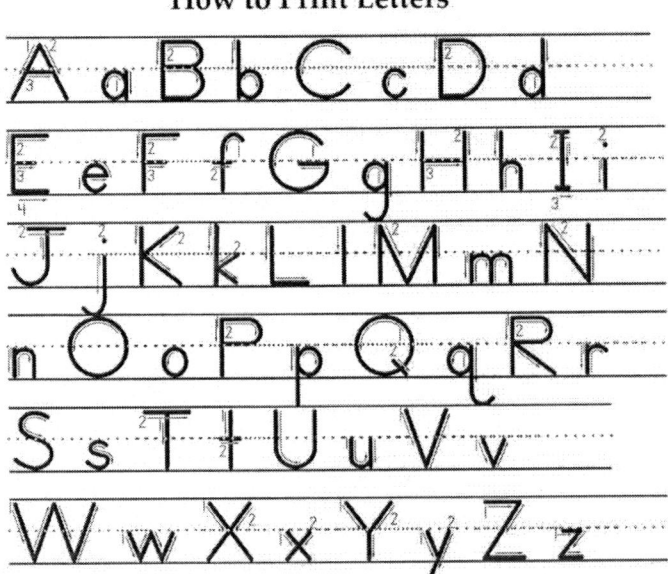

FIGURE 4: Placement, direction, size, and sequence for forming letters, from Zaner-Bloser

Directions for Forming Letters from Sue Dickson, creator of the Sing, Spell, Read, and Write program (http://www.youtube.com/watch?v=TvJ_Chw0Ugg)

Capital *A*: Start at the rooftop, go down the slide to the sidewalk, then down the slide the other way, and cross at the fence. Lowercase *a*: Don't start at the fence. Start under the fence. Go up and touch the fence, then around and touch the sidewalk, around and straight down.

Capital *B*: Go straight down to the sidewalk; around for his big chest, and around for his big tummy. Lowercase *b*: Start at the roof, go down, b-b-bounce up and around.

Capital *C*: Start just below the rooftop, go up to touch, around, and up. Lowercase *c*: Start like little *a*. Go up and touch the fence, then around and up.

Capital *D*: Start at the roof, go straight down, pick up, and go around. Lowercase *d*: First little *c*, then little *d*.

Capital *E*: Go down for a strong backbone, over for his hat, over for his belt, over for his shoes. Lowercase *e*: Get in the center of the space below the fence, go toward the door [right], up to touch the fence, around and up.

Capital *F*: Go down, over for his hat, over for his belt (but no shoes). Lowercase *f*: Start to make a little *c* up in the air, then straighten it out, go down, and cross at the fence.

Capital *G*: Form a big C, then come back to the line to give him a tray to hold straight. Lowercase *g*: First make *a*, then, gee, that's a good idea. If the ball falls, it falls into the basket.

Capital *H*: Down for a wall, down for a wall, and then cross at the fence. Lowercase *h*: Start at the rooftop, come down, and hump over.

Capital *I*: Start with a straight back, then give him his headdress and his moccasins. Lowercase *i*: Go down from the fence, and give him a feather.

Capital *J*: Go down, and turn to make a basket, and put his hat on. Lowercase *j*: Start at the fence, go down through the sidewalk, and turn the same way, then give him a dot.

Capital *K* Go down, come out here, into the center, and down to the sidewalk. Lowercase *k* is just as tall as his daddy. Start at the rooftop, go down, pick up at the fence, into the center and down.

Capital *L:* Go down and turn the corner. Lowercase *l:* Just a straight line down from the rooftop to the sidewalk.

Capital *M*: Go down straight, down the slide, up the slide, and down straight. Lowercase *m*: Go down, hump around, hump around.

Capital *N*: Go down straight, down the slide, down straight. Lowercase *n*: Go down, up, and hump over.

Capital *O*: Always form a C first, and then close it up. Lowercase *o*: Same way. First a little *c* and close it up.

Capital *P*: Go down, pick up, and around to the fence. Lowercase *p*: Start at the fence, go straight down into the ditch, come up and put his chin on the sidewalk.

Capital *Q*: First make a big O, and give the queen her walking stick. Lowercase *q*: Start with an *a*, come down, and give the queen some curly hair.

Capital *R*: Down, pick up, go around to the fence, and then slant down. Lowercase *r*: Down, up, and hook over.

Capital *S*: First form a *c* up in the air between the rooftop and the fence, and then swing back. Lowercase *s*: Form a tiny *c* up in the air, and then swing back.

Capital *T*: Go down and cross at the top. Lowercase *t* is just a teenager, not as tall as his daddy, but not short; cross at the fence.

Capital *U*: Down, curve, and up (no stem). Lowercase *u*: Down, curve up, and straight down for a stem.

Capital *V*: Slant down and up. Lowercase *v*: Slant down and up.

Capital *W*: Slant down, up, down, up. Lowercase *w*: Down, up, down, up.

Capital *X*: Down on a slant, pick up, back in the other direction. Lowercase *x*: Down and back.

Capital *Y*: Start with a *v* up in the air, and put a stem on it. Lowercase *y*: Go down on a slant, pick up your pencil, slant down, touch, and on into the ditch.

Capital *Z*: Make a 7, and then go back. Lowercase *z*: Make a little 7, and then go back.

PRACTICAL CHAPTER 5

How to Assess to Find Out Where Reading is Breaking Down

Before you begin teach reading, you will need to assess your students' reading ability with a series of tests. Notice I just used the terms *tests* and *assessments* in the same sentence. There is an important difference. A test is a one-shot standardized observation of behavior. An assessment, in contrast, is a problem-solving search involving multiple tests and observations. Test is to assessment as battle is to war. Though any one test can mislead, consistent, converging information from multiple tests must be taken seriously.

Why assess? There is only one good answer: to improve teaching. We want to focus teaching where the most good can be accomplished. This means we need to, first, identify students who are struggling in reading. Once we have identified struggling readers, we need to pinpoint areas of weakness to work on in teaching. Just as a physical therapist identifies the particular muscle, joint, or tendon causing pain, the teacher needs to find out where reading is breaking down to correct the problem. We don't want to teach kids what they already know. The world's best teaching addressing a strategy a student already uses is a waste of time. On the other hand, we don't want to frustrate kids with lessons they're not ready for. Frustrated children do not learn much—except poor attitudes. A good assessment allows us to identify the strategies a student hasn't learned but has the ability to learn.

Assessment is quality control for teaching. I can teach what seems to me to be a wonderful lesson, but if students don't learn, I haven't taught well. Teaching is a profession that aims at results. If we give a quiz and our students bomb, that tells us to go back to the drawing board and rethink our instruction.

What if we didn't assess? Without assessment, we can only assume students are learning. This means we will miss the chance to steer our teaching back on track when students aren't catching on. In the long run, we miss the chance to correct reading problems before they pervade a student's entire educational career—and attitude. In general, assessment is a vital part of teaching, showing us which students need special help, which concepts or strategies they need to learn, and which ideas we need to reteach more effectively.

Some say we assess to sort and pigeonhole students, to pin negative labels on them. By analogy, do doctors check blood pressure to sort and pigeonhole patients, and to pin upon them the negative label "hypertensive"? Assessment and consequent labeling—i.e., the summary results of assessment—are important in getting help. Just as patients with hypertension need medicine to restore their physical health, struggling readers need an instructional intervention to gain reading health. Reading assessment tells us who needs special help to catch up, and what kind of help they need.

Many arguments have been fought over whether standardized tests should be included in assessment. In general, we can divide tests into formal and informal measures. Formal assessment is standardized testing. Standardized simply means that there are rules to observe during administration. The rules may range from strict time limits and scripted instructions to simple, paraphrased instructions to work without help. Standardized tests are usually commercially published because producing and validating a test typically involves teams of experts and norming with large numbers of students in national stratified samples. For example, 450,000 students were tested to norm a recent version of the Iowa Tests of Basic Skills (Cross, 1998). To allow for machine-scoring of formal tests, items are typically multiple choice. Most formal tests are norm-referenced, which means they compare a student's performance with the achievement of peers in the norming population. Norms are simply averages, and so a norm-referenced test looks at a student's work in comparison with the average work of students in the same grade.

Informal tests are often called "alternative assessments." While some alternative assessments like portfolios are genuinely unstandardized, most informal assessments are loosely standardized, with some administrative and scoring standards. For example, nearly every test has a rule against helping students during the test because under an administration with help, it is not clear whose results are being reported. Informal tests are usually teacher-made, and because they are usually not experimentally validated, they rarely involve costs other than photocopying. Responses on informal measures usually require more extensive oral or written response; for example, by reading aloud, retelling what was read, or writing as a response to reading. Most informal tests are criterion-referenced, which means a student's performance is compared with a learning standard. For example, a first grader might be expected to successfully name all 52 capital and lower-case letters. Anyone still confusing b, d, p, and q has not met a reasonable first-grade criterion of accurate letter-naming. Figure 1 summarizes these differences.

Should we use formal, standardized reading test or informal, alternative assessments? The best answer is: both. Assessment is a problem-solving search in which we gather and consider all relevant information, presuming that any test considered is a sound measure of reading (Baumann & Murray, 1994). But what makes a test a sound measure of reading? There are two essential standards.

First, the test must be reliable, or in contemporary parlance, trustworthy (Valencia, 1990). Reliability means consistency: You get the same results, no matter who is giving the test, each time the test is taken, barring new learning. If I step on the bathroom scale and it registers 140 pounds, I have no reason to rejoice if in rechecking my weight five minutes later, it registers 180 pounds. An inconsistent measurement cannot be trusted. This explains why scaffolding during a test cannot be allowed: The student will not get the same result with a neutral examiner.

Formal assessment (standardized testing)	Informal assessment (alternative assessment)
Standardized (strict rules for administration, e.g., time limits)	Unstandardized or loosely standardized (leeway in administration)
Commercially published	Usually teacher made
Multiple choice	More extensive oral or written response
Usually norm-referenced (compare performance with achievement of average peer)	Usually criterion-referenced (compare performance with a learning standard)

FIGURE 1: Formal and informal assessment

Reliability is an essential prerequisite for sound measurement. An unreliable test can't be valid. Without trustworthy results, no test can be a believable measure of reading. However, reliability is not a sufficient standard: A test must also be valid, or in contemporary terms, authentic (Valencia, 1990). A valid test measures what it sets out to measure, and a valid reading test gets at processes actually involved in reading. By the validity criterion, we can dismiss measures of perceptual-motor ability, such as walking a balance beam, because perceptual-motor ability is not related to individual differences in reading.

Some reading tests have been attacked on grounds of *ecological* validity; i.e., similarity to real-world reading tasks. An ecologically valid reading test is supposed to resemble typical reading and writing. Typically, we read whole stories or articles, not single words or brief paragraphs, and we talk or write in response to readings rather than answer multiple-choice questions. But real-world reading tasks don't always make valid assessments. With a few long passages, background knowledge looms large. If the reader draws a blank on a topic like mitosis or the Civil War, it will be hard to demonstrate much reading comprehension. Written responses may reflect writing ability rather than reading comprehension. Thus, in ecologically valid assessments, background knowledge or writing ability may conflate reading scores; i.e., they may measure abilities other than reading rather than a pure, unadulterated reading measure. Keith Stanovich (1988, p. 211) poses an analogy from everyday life:

Our family physicians may sometimes make recommendations for healthy living. They may urge us to eat fruits and vegetables and to get adequate exercise. But when we arrive at the physician's office with a health problem, we of course do not expect the doctor to have us run around the block or to have us eat three pears. We find it quite acceptable that doctors do various unnatural things to us: They draw blood, they examine our urine, they tap us with a little hammer. We are not surprised that the methods used to diagnose, to get an underlying cause, to assess a theory of the state of our health, bear no relation to the physician's recommendations for maintaining our day-to-day health.

Reading assessment uses the same logic. Tests designed to get at weaknesses in reading (e.g., naming pseudowords) are nearly always different from the teaching activities designed to strengthen reading. Misplaced concerns about ecological validity may lead teachers to throw out highly valid and pure measures of reading processes.

Useful measures of reading often do not resemble ordinary literacy tasks. We can learn about a reader's phoneme awareness by having the reader break down meaningful words into phonemes, turning sense into nonsense. We can assess a reader's decoding ability by asking her to pronounce decodable pseudowords like *vand*, *zail*, or *screathe*. In assessments, we often ask a student to read a passage aloud without first practicing silently, which violates a venerable rule of reading instruction: Never ask a student to read aloud what he hasn't first read silently. We ask readers to do odd things that would be inappropriate for instruction to isolate hidden strengths and weaknesses in reading ability, in ways that would not be readily discernable from everyday reading. Authentic assessment means getting at processes actually involved in reading, but not necessarily in ordinary literacy work. Often a strange task not valid for instruction isolates a key causal variable of interest.

INFORMAL TESTS OF KEY ABILITIES

Most children struggling to learn to read are experiencing problems in word recognition; they usually have adequate language comprehension to understand the simple books of beginning reading instruction if they can translate the printed words into spoken language. Thus, a useful assessment focuses on the factors that might affect the ability to read words. Figure 2 attempts to capture the abilities that probably underlie fluent word recognition. A similar analysis could probe the component abilities of language comprehension, but in most cases, children's language ability is fully adequate for the simple texts of beginning reading. Thus, we focus on the left side of the diagram to examine the factors that might cause a breakdown in word recognition.

I call this the complex-simple view because it elaborates on Gough and Tunmer's (1986) simple view of reading (discussed in Chapter 11). Word recognition (D in the simple view) depends on fluent, automatic reading. Fluent reading requires a large sight vocabulary and the ability to rapidly size up unfamiliar words by recognizing pronounceable word parts and analogizing. To develop a sight vocabulary requires accurate decoding (see Chapter 3). Decoding accuracy depends on knowing reliable grapheme-phoneme correspondences and blending ability, with the possible addition of understanding concepts about print, the vocabulary of reading instruction. Learning a correspondence depends on recognizing letters and phonemes.

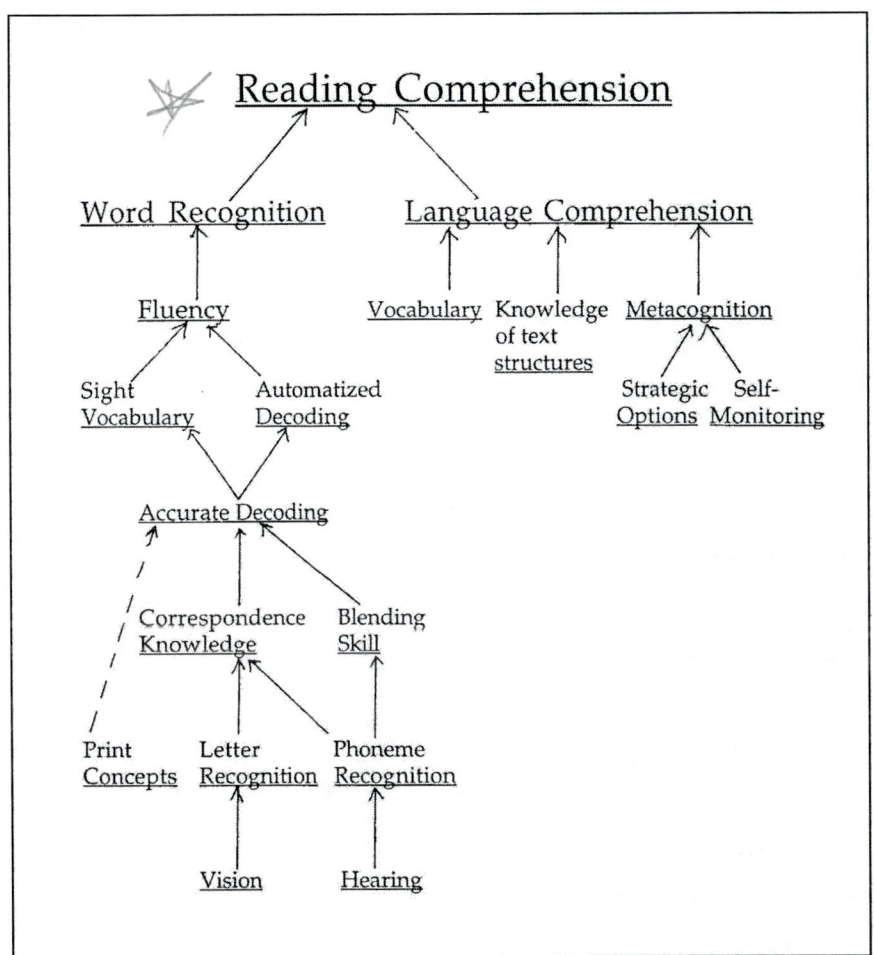

FIGURE 2: The complex simple view

Following this logic, if a student does not recognize words fluently, we can examine each of the component abilities to determine where word reading ability might be breaking down. In particular, we can look at sight vocabulary, decoding accuracy, correspondence knowledge, blending ability, letter recognition, and phoneme awareness. These are the basic abilities to test for when beginners are struggling in learning to read.

Pretest Assessments

We can usually get a reasonably good picture of children's present reading abilities by administering seven informal pretests: the Test of Phoneme Identities (Appendix A), the Letter Recognition Test (Appendix B), the Test of Phonetic Cue Reading (Appendix C), the Pseudoword Reading Test (Appendix D), a set of graded word lists from an informal reading inventory, such as the Basic Reading Inventory (Johns, 2010), Clay's (2002) invented spelling test (Appendix E), and the Roswell-Chall (Chall, Roswell, & Blumenthal, 1963) Test of Auditory Blending (Appendix F). Each test is easy to administer, and directions for administration are included in the appendices, along with posttest versions of several of the tests. For a more in-depth examination of reader's decoding ability, I have included pre- and posttest versions of the Names Test (Appendix G), which probes children's knowledge of the principal vowel correspondences by asking them to read one-syllable names. Figure 3 summarizes the purposes of the seven pretests, the assessment names, and the special materials needed for the assessment. All seven can be given in about half an hour.

Need to know	Test	Special Materials
Letter recognition	Letter recognition test	Stopwatch; student and write-on copies
Phoneme awareness	Test of Phoneme Identities	None
Phonetic cue reading	Test of Phonetic Cue Reading	Cards or list
Decoding	Pseudowords	Cards or list
Sight word knowledge	PP-8th word lists, Basic Reading Inventory	Student and write-on copies
Spelling	Clay Invented Spelling Test	Primary paper, pencil
Blending	Roswell-Chall Test of Auditory Blending	None

FIGURE 3: Materials needed for assessment

As a practical matter, if you are testing in an open area, it is helpful to have a three-sided project display board (or primary-grade lingo, a cubby) to block out noise and distractions. If you will not be working at a table, you will need a clipboard to write on. I strongly recommend a mechanical pencil for recording answers. Pencil marks are erasable (the pencil is the original word processor), and a mechanical pencil requires no sharpener. To engage the student's interest, we find it nearly always helpful to intersperse questions from an interest inventory between tests (Fry & Kress, 2006).

Avoiding Feedback

The goal of assessment is to get an accurate measure of the student's current progress in learning to read. We want to estimate the student's instructional reading level and the Ehri (1998) phase of recognizing words to focus instruction on what the student needs to move ahead, with texts at an appropriate level of challenge. A critical move in getting an accurate assessment is to wear our "psychologists hats." Most of the time, we wear our "teacher hats" and do whatever we can to help our students catch on. However, in wearing the psychologist hat, we commit ourselves to be friendly observers without helping the student succeed. If we help a student achieve what the test is assessing, our results will be unreliable, and an unreliable test is not valid. By helping students achieve what they can't accomplish on their own, we may hide their reading problems and prevent them from getting the instruction they need.

For a reliable assessment, we cannot give any feedback to the student on whether an answer was right or wrong. Feedback is a kind of scaffold, and it invalidates the test results. One solution is to give neutral praise (e.g., "nice work," "good job") provided that praise is given independently of whether an answer is right or wrong. We can always give specific praise for on-task behavior; e.g., "Thanks for your cooperation" or "I like how hard you're working." The response I'm most comfortable with is to repeat each answer with a nod and a smile, meaning "I understand what you are saying, and I appreciate your efforts." In addition, it is important to make a mark for every answer; for example, a checkmark for a correct answer and an X for a wrong answer. If we only make marks when the student makes an error, we are providing negative feedback, which invalidates the test. If the teacher positions herself so that her writing hand is away from the student (e.g., if a right-handed teacher sits on the right side of the student), then the student will rarely be able to see the checks and X's.

Administering Graded Word Lists

The test most useful for quickly assessing sight vocabulary and instructional reading level is a set of graded word lists, such as in the Basic Reading Inventory (Johns, 2010). Most informal reading inventories present 20-word lists at each reading level, typically from preprimer to eighth grade. In a thorough assessment, a reader's success on the word lists directs the teacher to choose reading passages to assess word recognition, fluency, and comprehension by observing the student read passages. The abbreviated half-hour assessment I recommend at pretest uses only the word lists to get a quick and "dirty" view of reading level—dirty because it omits any measure of reading comprehension. This is usually adequate to get instruction underway, but any placement decisions depend on passage reading to determine the level of reading comprehension.

For the quick and dirty method, we can look for the highest list on which the student read 14 or more words correctly as an estimate of instructional reading level. To find this level, we begin at the preprimer list (or well below grade level) and continue giving the next list as long as the student reads 14 or more words correctly. When a student scores less than 14 out of 20, that list estimates the frustration level; this signals the time to terminate the word list test. We are looking for the highest list where the student can read at least 14 words right to estimate the instruction level. This will be the second to last list attempted rather than the final list, which estimates the reader's frustration level.

INTERPRETING THE INFORMAL ASSESSMENTS

In the explanations that follow, I will assume that you have tried giving the seven informal tests to a beginning reader. Interpreting the pretests begins by carefully scoring each test and subtest. To verify the scoring later, it is important to mark each answer right or wrong and to score the number correct for each test or subtest. Assuming that the reader is not yet fluent, we will use this information to look for the point where reading is breaking down. Is the reader struggling with letter recognition? With phoneme awareness? With blending? With correspondence knowledge so that decoding is inaccurate? With reading fluency? Identifying problem areas helps us locate the optimal point to intervene by teaching the strategies that will allow the reader to move ahead.

Phoneme Awareness

PA is the clearest indicator of potential for success in beginning reading. The Test of Phoneme Identities is a forced-choice test in which the reader must choose one of two possible answers, e.g., "Do you hear /z/ in *bug* or *buzz*?" This means we can expect students to get half the items correct (19 out of 38) by chance. The minimal score indicating an awareness of phonemes is 28, which was the average score of the kindergarten norming group. A score of 34-38 indicates well-developed PA; 28-33 indicates growing PA; scores of 0-27 suggest that the student is not aware of phonemes. Students who don't recognize phonemes in spoken words typically make slow progress in learning to read. Thus, with low PA, the teacher should emphasize PA instruction to prepare students to learn to read words (Chapter 6 provides the details).

Letter Recognition

Two scores on letter recognition are of interest: how many of the 54 letters were named accurately, and how fast were the letters named? We hope students can name all letters accurately within one minute as a benchmark of letter naming fluency. Letters not accurately named should be catalogued and taught one by one with guided printing practice (see Practical Chapter 4).

Phonetic Cue Reading

The Tests of Phonetic Cue Reading and Pseudoword Reading are crucial for assessing a reader's phase of recognizing words (see Chapter 3). Recognizing the reader's Ehri phase unleashes a powerful theory to help us understand assessment results and plan effective instruction. Phonetic cue reading is the simplest form of decoding that requires using the initial letter to distinguish between words active in memory. The Test of Phonetic Cue Reading is a watershed test dividing prealphabetic readers from partial alphabetic readers. Like the Test of Phoneme Identities, it is a forced-choice task, which means that a beginner can get 6 out of 12 by guessing. However, a score of 10 could only be obtained by guessing 5 times in 100 tries. Thus, a reader who scores 10-12 correct is probably using phonetic cues, indicating that he is at least partial alphabetic and possibly full or consolidated.

Conversely, a score of 0-9 suggests that the student is prealphabetic. If this finding is consistent with other test scores, the prescription is to teach phoneme awareness to help the reader reach the partial alphabetic phase. We can try teaching very simple letterbox lessons (Practical Chapter 3), with words like *at*, *am*, *an*, *fat*, and *fan*. If the student is unable to spell and read words this simple, the teacher may need to shift to full-scale phoneme awareness lessons with consonants (see Chapter 6). Prealphabetic readers cannot read decodable books, which means teachers should begin with predictable books (see Chapter 8). Predictable books require a different sort of booktalk ("Have you ever . . . ? Well, in this book . . . ."). Because the student can't decode words, the teacher must read part of the book aloud so that the student can pick up the language pattern for cued recitation. It is important for the prealphabetic reader to hold the book and point to the words; fingerpointing the correct words indicates growth into the partial alphabetic phase (Ehri & Sweet, 1991). To detect the vital transition to partial alphabetic decoding, prealphabetic students should be regularly retested in phonetic cue reading. The advent of partial alphabetic decoding signals the student's readiness for instruction in phonics and spelling and a switch to decodable text.

Pseudoword Decoding

The attempt to read a pseudoword—a regularly spelled nonsense word—simulates an encounter with a word never seen before and is thus a pure measure of decoding. The Pseudoword Decoding Test, like the Test of Phonetic Cue Reading, is a watershed test distinguishing partial alphabetic readers from full alphabetic, and full alphabetic readers from consolidated. If a student can read even one pseudoword, we can rule out the prealphabetic and partial alphabetic phases.

Reading a pseudoword indicates at least a toehold in the full alphabetic phase. By reading a pseudoword, the beginner demonstrates the ability to study a word never seen before and to generate a reasonable pronunciation, the defining ability of the full alphabetic phase. This means that the Pseudoword Reading score may provide a correction for a tentative diagnosis of prealphabetic based on Phonetic Cue Reading; a full alphabetic reader may have lost focus during that test. On the other hand, a score of zero pseudowords coupled with a score of 10-12 on Phonetic Cue Reading confirms that the reader is partial alphabetic, i.e., able to use initial letters to distinguish active words but not able to sound out and blend unfamiliar words using their complete spellings.

Scores on each of the three columns on the Pseudoword Reading Test indicate levels of decoding progress. Pseudowords in the first column can be decoded by sequential full alphabetic readers, i.e., by sounding out and blending in a left-to-right sequence. Pseudowords in the second column require hierarchical full alphabetic decoding by recognizing digraphs or silent-*e* signals, which indicates a more sophisticated knowledge of spelling patterns. Pseudowords in the third column are multisyllable pseudowords requiring recognition of pronounceable word parts. Accordingly, readers with 4 or 5 correct in column three are probably consolidated alphabetic readers. If they are not consolidated but read 4 or 5 correct in column two, they are probably hierarchical full alphabetic readers. If they are not hierarchical but read at least one pseudoword, they are sequential full alphabetic readers.

Miscues on pseudowords suggest missing correspondences to work on in letterbox lessons. To analyze a miscue, look for the vowel in the text word not used in the attempt. For example, if a readers said "fun" for *fim*, he seems to be missing the correspondence *i* = /i/. Because the first column of pseudowords feature all five short vowels, it should be possible to see which short vowels, if any, remain to be taught. Other pseudowords and regular real words from the word lists should be analyzed in the same way. By cataloguing all the reader's missing correspondences from the pretest, the teacher should be able to outline a series of letterbox lessons to supply these correspondence tools, giving priority to the short vowels. Vowel correspondences should be taught in alphabetical order to maintain decodability in practice texts, assuming that the decodable series introduces new vowels in alphabetical order.

Word Recognition

Graded word lists from informal reading inventories typically consist of 20 words, with a passing score of 14 or more indicating that the list was read at the instructional or independent level. The highest list read with 14 or more correct estimates the reader's instructional reading level. Because we eventually pushed the reader to a frustration level where his score was less than 14 correct, this final list indicates the reader's frustration level. It is the second-to-last list that estimates the instructional level, i.e., the optimal text level for rapid reading progress when working with a teacher. Figure 4 outlines the expected instructional reading levels in each grade, where the *emergent* level indicates that the student has not yet established an instructional reading level.

Grade	Fall	Midyear	Spring	End of year
Kindergarten	Emergent			Preprimer
First	Preprimer	Primer	First	Second
Second	Second			Third

FIGURE 4: Expected instructional reading levels in the primary grades

As Figure 4 indicates, kindergartners at the end of the year should have reached the preprimer level. First grade is typically a time of rapid progress, with readers reaching the primer level by midyear, first-grade level by mid-spring, and second-grade level by the end of the year. In later grades, we expect readers to begin each year at grade level and to reach the next grade level by year-end. We can use these benchmarks to estimate whether a reader is on grade level or to estimate how far above or below grade level the student is reading. For example, a reader still at the emergent level in mid-first grade is about a half-year below level; a classmate at the second-grade level is about a half-year ahead of the expected grade level.

As important as the instructional reading level is, the reader's phase of recognizing words, or Ehri phase, is even more critical for planning instruction. A reasonable way to state instructional goals for a reader is to anticipate the next Ehri phase (see Chapter 3 for a full discussion of the abilities that emerge during each phase). Figure 5 describes goals for readers based on this next phase.

Pretest phase	Goal phase	Specific goals
Prealphabetic	Partial alphabetic	To recognize phonemes in spoken words; to use consonants to decode words.
Partial alphabetic	Full alphabetic sequential	To use complete spellings in decoding; to recognize words from spellings alone.
Full alphabetic sequential	Full alphabetic hierarchical	To decode words with digraph vowel patterns; to build sight vocabulary.
Full alphabetic hierarchical	Consolidated alphabetic	To build sight vocabulary; to use word chunks to read longer words.
Consolidated alphabetic	Stage of growing independence and fluency	To read fast and effortlessly; to improve reading comprehension.

FIGURE 5: Goals for Ehri phases

Attainment of a new phase of recognizing words indicates that the reader has learned new and productive strategies for reading words, a sort of quantum leap in reading ability that portends more rapid progress toward learning sight words.

Invented Spelling

Clay's (2002) test of invented spelling is an alternative check on phoneme awareness. The test measures the ability to detect each phoneme in words and to record it either with the correct letter or a phonetically related substitute. Only the letters with numbers beneath them are scored, and any letter or digraph that *could* spell each phoneme is acceptable. For example, SKUL is an acceptable spelling for *school* because *k* and *u* capture the phonemes /k/ and /OO/. No points are lost for including extra letters, and if two letters are correct but reversed, only one point is lost.

There are 37 possible points; a score of 32 to 35 indicates above average spelling progress in early first grade, and a score of 36-37 indicates mastery of invented spelling. In terms of the stages of spelling development (see Chapter 8), a score of 9-31 indicates that the student is semi-phonemic, which means he or she is recording at least the initial phonemes of words. A score of 32-37 usually indicates that the student is phonemic, which means that his or her invented spellings typically capture all the phonemes in words. Phonemic spelling is consistent with well-developed phoneme awareness; the student is showing the ability to detect phonemes in spoken words and to record them with phonetically related letters. A mastery score of 36-37 might be consistent with the transitional stage of spelling, in which students begin to mark vowels with digraphs or silent *e* signals. Teachers should analyze invented spellings in messages for confirming evidence.

Blending

For beginning readers, decoding is a two-step process involving sounding out (pronouncing the phonemes signaled by graphemes) and blending (assembling isolated phonemes into a recognizable approximation of the word). The Roswell-Chall (1963) Test of Auditory Blending assesses the ability of beginners to blend phonological segments presented orally by the teacher. A score of 25-30 indicates good progress in learning to blend; scores of 0-24 show that students are struggling with blending. Practical Chapter 4 explained procedures for teaching children to blend. A key procedure is to use letter tiles to lead children through the steps of blending, moving the letters into groups to scaffold assembling the word chunk by chunk. Have students begin with the vowel, which is the vital nerve center of the syllable; backtrack to assemble the body by blending the onset (the optional chunk before the vowel) with the vowel; and finally, blend the body with the coda (the optional chunk after the vowel) to assemble an approximation of the word. Given the irregularities of English, recognizing the word usually requires crosschecking to test the approximation in context (or at least to verify that what has been assembled is a known word).

WHICH BOOK?

An immediate decision in initiating instruction concerns which type and level of book the student is ready to read. The book type and level is suggested by the Ehri phase and by the highest word list on which the reader read at least 14 words. We want the maximum challenge at the instructional level. With books that are either too easy or too difficult, progress grinds to a halt.

Only prealphabetic readers should read predictable books, and they should be weaned from these books as soon as they demonstrate partial alphabetic decoding. Partial alphabetic readers should read decodable books beginning with short vowels. Teachers should monitor students' correspondence knowledge to gear both letterbox lessons and decodable texts to the next vowel the student is ready to learn. Usually, the letterbox lesson teaches the students to read words with this correspondence, and the decodable book lets the reader practice reading these words in a story.

If readers are on a relatively advanced instructional level but their miscues indicate they are missing basic correspondences, I recommend that they work with two books: a lesson book practicing the newly taught correspondence in words, and a "real" book at the reader's instructional level. Thus, a second-grade level reader who has problems reading words with u = /u/ might shore up this correspondence with a letterbox lesson, practice with a decodable book featuring u = /u/, and then move on to an engaging work of children's literature at the second grade level, such as *Sylvester and the Magic Pebble* (Steig, 1969).

Because readers gain fluency by adding unfamiliar words to sight vocabulary, we want to challenge the reader with texts with 2-5% unfamiliar words; i.e., texts at the instructional reading level. Readers who are overwhelmed with more than 5% unfamiliar words give up crosschecking and stop making sight words. Readers who encounter 0-1% unfamiliar words are not building sight vocabulary at an optimal rate. Reading teachers should have both easier and more difficult books on hand in case a text turns out to be either too hard or too easy. A backup book at an easier level will rescue a reader from frustration, and a backup book at a more challenging level will lift a reader from the ennui of reading dull books that are too juvenile and that practice only words already known.

Appendix A: The Test of Phoneme Identities (Murray, Smith, & Murray, 2000)

Materials: None. The test is administered conversationally. Read with expression. Do not emphasize phonemes. Accept any repetition of the sentence that includes the target words, but repeat the sentence if either is incorrect. Require a correct approximation of the isolated phoneme. Repeat the sound-to-word matching question if the response is unclear. Circle the response.

Directions: We're going to play a repeating game. First, I'll say a sentence, then you say it back. Then I'll say a sound, and you say it back. Then I want you to listen for the sound in a word. Let's begin.

Pretest Version

1. Say: We'll see the moon soon. [Wait.] Now say /s/. Do you hear /s/ in *moon* or *soon*?

2. Say: She caught a fish by the fin. [Wait.] Now say /sh/. Do you hear /sh/ in *fish* or *fin*?

3. Say: That bug makes a buzz. [Wait.] Now say /z/. Do you hear /z/ in *bug* or *buzz*?

4. Say: We hid from him. [Wait.] Now say /m/. Do you hear /m/ in *hid* or *him*?

5. Say: Those girls have the same name. [Wait.] Now say /n/. Do you hear /n/ in *same* or *name*?

6. Say: I race to wash my face. [Wait.] Now say /f/. Do you hear /f/ in *race* or *face*?

7. Say: Can you move a moose? [Wait.] Now say /v/. Do you hear /v/ in *move* or *moose*?

8. Say: He gets a badge for taking a bath. [Wait.] Now say /th/. Do you hear /th/ in *badge* or *bath*?

9. Say: This card game is hard. [Wait.] Now say /h/. Do you hear /h/ in *card* or *hard*?

10. Say: His chin is too thin. [Wait.] Now say /ch/. Do you hear /ch/ in *chin* or *thin*?

11. Say: We found him in the gym. [Wait.] Now say /j/. Do you hear /j/ in *him* or *gym*?

12. Say: I brought a scoop to school. [Wait.] Now say /l/. Do you hear /l/ in *scoop* or *school*?

13. Say: There's a rat under that hat. [Wait.] Now say /r/. Do you hear /r/ in *rat* or *hat*?

14. Say: We have tar on our car. [Wait.] Now say /k/. Do you hear /k/ in *tar* or *car*?

15. Say: Would you share a pair of socks? [Wait.] Now say /p/. Do you hear /p/ in *share* or *pair*?

16. Say: The playground is part of the park. [Wait.] Now say /t/. Do you hear /t/ in *part* or *park*?

17. Say: The cub will come when you call. [Wait.] Now say /b/. Do you hear /b/ in *cub* or *come*?

18. Say: She likes to leap into deep water. [Wait.] Now say /d/. Do you hear /d/ in *leap* or *deep*?

19. Say: In this game, you have a new name. [Wait.] Now say /g/. Do you hear /g/ in *game* or *name*?

[Take a stretch break for half a minute.]

20. Say: We hate to wait for the bus. [Wait.] Now say /w/. Do you hear /w/ in *hate* or *wait*?

21. Say: The yarn is in the barn. [Wait.] Now say /y/. Do you hear /y/ in *yarn* or *barn*?

22. Say: He popped the bag with a bang. [Wait.] Now say /ng/. Do you hear /ng/ in *bag* or *bang*?

23. Say: Find a space by the spice. [Wait.] Now say /A/. Do you hear /A/ in *space* or *spice*?

24. Say: This street is straight. [Wait.] Now say /E/. Do you hear /E/ in *street* or *straight*?

25. Say: We go from nine till noon. [Wait.] Now say /I/. Do you hear /I/ in *nine* or *noon*?

26. Say: I have a nose for news. [Wait.] Now say /O/. Do you hear /O/ in *nose* or *news*?

27. Say: Your shoelace is loose. [Wait.] Now say /OO/. Do you hear /OO/ in *lace* or *loose*?

28. Say: He's the last on the list. [Wait.] Now say /a/. Do you hear /a/ in *last* or *list*?

29. Say: I have a red fishing rod. [Wait.] Now say /e/. Do you hear /e/ in *red* or *rod*?

30. Say: On Halloween bring a big bag. Now say /i/. Do you hear /i/ in *big* or *bag*?

31. Say: Move the rock with the rake. [Wait.] Now say /o/. Do you hear /o/ in *rock* or *rake*?

32. Say: Don't cut our kite. [Wait.] Now say /u/. Do you hear /u/ in *cut* or *kite*?

33. Say: I heard a sound in the sand. [Wait.] Now say /ow/. Do you hear /ow/ in *sound* or *sand*?

34. Say: We saw the old barn burn. [Wait.] Now say /er/. Do you hear /er/ in *barn* or *burn*?

35. Say: The fair is far from school. [Wait.] Now say /ar/. Do you hear /ar/ in *fair* or *far*?

36. Say: We'll draw on our pictures after they dry. [Wait.] Now say /aw/. Do you hear /aw/ in *draw* or *dry*?

37. Say: That spill might spoil. [Wait.] Now say /oy/. Do you hear /oy/ in *spill* or *spoil*?

38. Say: Look at the beautiful lake. [Wait.] Now say /oo/. Do you hear /oo/ in *look* or *lake*?

Posttest Version

1. Say: This is a nice night. [Wait.] Now say /s/. Do you hear /s/ in *nice* or *night*?

2. Say: You have dirt on your shirt. [Wait.] Now say /sh/. Do you hear /sh/ in *dirt* or *shirt*?

3. Say: A fly will zoom around a room. [Wait.] Now say /z/. Do you hear /z/ in *zoom* or *room*?

4. Say: The tree made shade. [Wait.] Now say /m/. Do you hear /m/ in *made* or *shade*?

5. Say: The man looked at the map. [Wait.] Now say /n/. Do you hear /n/ in *man* or *map*?

6. Say: The chief had paint on his cheek. [Wait.] Now say /f/. Do you hear /f/ in *chief* or *cheek*?

7. Say: The man was driving a van. [Wait.] Now say /v/. Do you hear /v/ in *man* or *van*?

8. Say: That's the third bird I've seen. [Wait.] Now say /th/. Do you hear /th/ in *third* or *bird*?

9. Say: Jack and Jill went up the hill. [Wait.] Now say /h/. Do you hear /h/ in *Jill* or *hill*?

10. Say: He lost his cap, but he made the catch. [Wait.] Now say /ch/. Do you hear /ch/ in *cap* or *catch*?

11. Say: The bridge is made of brick. [Wait.] Now say /j/. Do you hear /j/ in *bridge* or *brick*?

12. Say: I like to ride my bike. [Wait.] Now say /l/. Do you hear /l/ in *like* or *bike*?

13. Say: There's a sock on that rock. [Wait.] Now say /r/. Do you hear /r/ in *sock* or *rock*?

14. Say: I like your new light. [Wait.] Now say /k/. Do you hear /k/ in *like* or *light*?

15. Say: Don't step on the stem. [Wait.] Now say /p/. Do you hear /p/ in *step* or *stem*?

16. Say: Who took my book? [Wait.] Now say /t/. Do you hear /t/ in *took* or *book*?

17. Say: That toy belongs to the new boy. [Wait.] Now say /b/. Do you hear /b/ in *toy* or *boy*?

18. Say: I had to have some food. [Wait.] Now say /d/. Do you hear /d/ in *had* or *have*?

19. Say: The cookies are in the back of the bag. [Wait.] Now say /g/. Do you hear /g/ in *back* or *bag*?

[Take a stretch break for half a minute.]

20. Say: I know the way to Green Bay. [Wait.] Now say /w/. Do you hear /w/ in *way* or *bay*?

21. Say: Does that shoe fit you? [Wait.] Now say /y/. Do you hear /y/ in *shoe* or *you*?

22. Say: Put a long log on the fire. [Wait.] Now say /ng/. Do you hear /ng/ in *long* or *log*?

23. Say: They like to run in the rain. [Wait.] Now say /A/. Do you hear /A/ in *run* or *rain*?

24. Say: Read the story about the ride. [Wait.] Now say /E/. Do you hear /E/ in *read* or *ride*?

25. Say: We rode a mule for a mile. [Wait.] Now say /I/. Do you hear /I/ in *mule* or *mile*?

26. Say: I took the ham home. [Wait.] Now say /O/. Do you hear /O/ in *ham* or *home*?

27. Say: We burn coal when it's cool. [Wait.] Now say /OO/. Do you hear /OO/ in *coal* or *cool*?

28. Say: You have to be fast to be first. [Wait.] Now say /a/. Do you hear /a/ in *fast* or *first*?

29. Say: In winter we slide on a sled. [Wait.] Now say /e/. Do you hear /e/ in *slide* or *sled*?

30. Say: Look on the table or in the drawer. [Wait.] Now say /i/. Do you hear /i/ in *on* or *in*?

31. Say: Tap the top of the drum. [Wait.] Now say /o/. Do you hear /o/ in *tap* or *top*?

32. Say: The sun will come out soon. [Wait.] Now say /u/. Do you hear /u/ in *sun* or *soon*?

33. Say: That baby can't count. [Wait.] Now say /ow/. Do you hear /ow/ in *can't* or *count*?

34. Say: She threw the dart in the dirt. [Wait.] Now say /er/. Do you hear /er/ in *dart* or *dirt*?

35. Say: We heard the ground is hard. [Wait.] Now say /ar/. Do you hear /ar/ in *heard* or *hard*?

36. Say: On the hike, we saw a hawk. [Wait.] Now say /aw/. Do you hear /aw/ in *hike* or *hawk*?

37. Say: That bowl may boil. [Wait.] Now say /oy/. Do you hear /oy/ in *bowl* or *boil*?

38. Say: I found a weed in the wood. [Wait.] Now say /oo/. Do you hear /oo/ in *weed* or *wood*?

APPENDIX B: LETTER RECOGNITION TEST

Materials: Sheet with capital and lowercase alphabetic (laminated if possible), a mark-on copy, and a stopwatch.

Administration: For each letter named correctly, make a check above the letter on the mark-on copy. If it is incorrect, write what the student said. For example, if the student touches *b* and says "dee," write *d* about the letter *b*. Use the stopwatch to time how how fast the page of letters is named.

Directions to student: Here are all the letters in the alphabet. I want you to touch each letter and say its name as quickly as you can. Ready? Go.

HOW TO ASSESS TO FIND OUT WHERE READING IS BREAKING DOWN

A	F	K	P	W	Z
C	Y	L	Q	M	
D	N	S	X	I	
B	H	O	J	U	
E	G	R	V	T	
a	f	k	p	w	z
c	y	l	q	m	
d	n	s	x	i	
b	h	o	j	u	a
e	g	r	v	t	g

Appendix C: Test of Phonetic Cue Reading

Materials: Make individual cards with the words in the *"card"* column printed in capital letters.

Instructions: I'm going to show you some words, and I'm going to tell you two words it might be. See if you can use the beginning letter to figure out which word it is.

Pretest Version

Card	Question	Circle response	
1. MAD	Is this *sad* or *mad*?	sad	mad
2. FAN	Is this *man* or *fan*?	man	fan
3. SAT	Is this *sat* or *fat*?	sat	fat
4. TEAR	Is this *tear* [TEER] or *near*?	tear	near
5. SELL	Is this *sell* or *tell*?	sell	tell
6. NEST	Is this *test* or *nest*?	test	nest
7. MICE	Is this *mice* or *nice*?	mice	nice
8. LIGHT	Is this *light* or *fight*?	light	fight
9. LOCK	Is this *sock* or *lock*?	sock	lock
10. FOG	Is this *log* or *fog*?	log	fog
11. TOP	Is this *mop* or *top*?	mop	top
12. NOT	Is this *lot* or *not*?	lot	not

Posttest Version

Card	Question	Circle response	
1. PAGE	Is this *cage* or *page*?	cage	page
2. CARD	Is this *card* or *hard*?	card	hard
3. MATCH	Is this *hatch* or *match*?	hatch	match
4. BEAN	Is this *bean* or *lean*?	bean	lean
5. FIB	Is this *fib* or *rib*?	fib	rib
6. WILT	Is this *tilt* or *wilt*?	tilt	wilt
7. LIFT	Is this *gift* or *lift*?	gift	lift
8. HIRE	Is this *fire* or *hire*?	fire	hire
9. SOUTH	Is this *mouth* or *south*?	mouth	south
10. ROAR	Is this *roar* or *soar*?	roar	soar
11. COOL	Is this *cool* or *pool*?	cool	pool
12. LUNCH	Is this *lunch* or *punch*?	lunch	punch

Appendix D: Pseudoword Reading Test

Pretest Version

Materials: Print the pseudowords below on plain cards or on a sheet of paper. Write the response on the line; you may have to invent a spelling.

Directions: I'm going to show you some made-up words. They aren't really words, but some people can read them anyway. I want you to give them a try.

fim _____	yain _____	snitting _____
sep _____	chire _____	bathtail _____
lat _____	nool _____	inteakness _____
dob _____	pot _____	overtodded _____
huzz _____	sheem _____	rebenderable _____

Posttest Version

pid _____	kail _____	plinning _____
lem _____	shipe _____	raincrab _____
san _____	foom _____	undeanful _____
vot _____	chobe _____	pregatted _____
mub _____	reet _____	renackeration _____

Appendix E: Clay Invented Spelling Test (Clay, 2002)

Materials: Paper and pencil.

Directions: I am going to read you a story. When I have read it through once, I will read it again very slowly so that you can write down the words in the story. [Read once at normal speed.] Some of the words are hard. Say them slowly and think how you can write them. After I say each word, you write it down. [Dictate slowly. If the student asks for help, say, "Say it slowly. Write down the sounds you hear." If the student can't complete a word, say, "We'll leave that word. The next one is . . ."]

Pretest Form

I have a big dog at home. Today I am going to take him to school.

```
I  have  a  big   dog   at    home.    Today  I
1   2 3 4  5    6 7 8  9 10 11  12 13  14 15 16   17 18 19 20

a m    g o i n g    to   t a k e    h i m    to   s ch oo l.
21 22  23 24 25 26 27    28 29 30   31 32 33       34 35  36 37
```

Posttest Form

The bus is coming. It will stop here to let me get on.

```
Th e   b u s   i s   c o m i n g.    I t   w i l l
1  2   3 4 5   6 7   8 9 10 11 12 13  14 15  16 17 18

s t o p   h e r e   t o   l e t    m e   g e t   o n.
19 20 21 22  23 24 25  26 27  28 29 30  31 32  33 34 35  36 37
```

Scoring:

Score 1 point for each phoneme the child has recorded that is numbered below.

- If a letter does not have a number under it, it receives no score.

- Additions do not affect scoring.

- Substituted letters are correct if they could spell the phoneme in another word, e.g., SKOOL for *school* and TAC for *take*.

- If the student changes the order of letters, take off 1 point for that word. For example, GONIG for *going* counts as 4 rather than 5.

Appendix F: Auditory Blending (Roswell & Chall, 1963)

Materials: None. This test is strictly oral. Wherever spellings are divided with hyphens, say the sounds rather than spelling out the letters. Say the sounds at approximately one-half second intervals. You'll need to practice this. You can mark the child's responses below by making a check if the answer is correct and writing the response (you may have to invent a spelling) if it is incorrect.

Directions: I'm going to say some words in a funny way. I'll say the sounds one at a time. I want you to put the sounds together and guess what I'm saying. For instance, if I say m-e, what am I saying? [If correct] Right, I said *me*. [If incorrect] No, m-e is a funny way of saying *me*.

Sample words for further practice (give feedback):   s-ing   t-op   s-i-t

Test items (no feedback)

1. a-t	7. b-e	13. pl-ay	19. t-ime	25. g-o-t
2. n-o	8. t-oo	14. b-oat	20. c-all	26. m-a-p
3. i-f	9. c-ow	15. ch-ain	21. c-a-t	27. r-u-g
4. u-p	10. h-e	16. b-ed	22. b-i-g	28. d-e-sk
5. s-ay	11. st-ep	17. c-ake	23. c-u-ff	29. t-oa-st
6. m-y	12. f-at	18. r-an	24. s-a-d	30. p-e-t

APPENDIX G: FIRST NAMES TEST

Adapted by the author from previous versions of the Names Test (Cunningham, 1990; Duffelmeyer, Kruse, Merkley, & Fyfe, 1994). This version restricts names to one-syllable words and covers most regular vowel correspondences in English.

Directions: Pretend you are a teacher who must read a list of names of students in your class. Read the names as if you were taking attendance. I can't help you in any way. Make a guess if you are not sure.

Pretest Version

Jay Clark	Tim Blake	Chuck Hoke	Gus Slade
Glen Wright	Fred Yale	Flo Tweed	Dee Shaw
Grace Swain	Ned Vance	Ron Troy	Joan Brooks
Shane Floyd	Jake Dean	Gene Dale	Neal Wade
Dan Rice	June Hanks	Drew Burns	Ted Ricks

Posttest version

Ann Burk	Shay Crew	Faith Crow	Mark Broils
Trent Nix	Gail Jobe	Jane Sloan	Maud Blunt
Kris Kent	Jack Keen	Rube Chell	Russ Wise
Thor Cox	Tom Snead	Lance Cloud	Dave Groom
Hawk Tubbs	Sky Woods	Fran Blight	Mitch Loyd

PRACTICAL CHAPTER

How to Take a Running Record

Running records are informal assessments of oral reading developed by Marie Clay (1985), a New Zealand researcher who developed the Reading Recovery program (Pinnell, Fried, & Estice, 1990). In Reading Recovery, specially trained teachers tutor struggling first graders with a daily half-hour lesson, hoping to bring them up to grade level before their reading problems worsen and affect everything else. The daily lesson involves reading one or more familiar books, some explicit help breaking the alphabetic code, an introduction and reading of a new book, and writing with invented spelling—all productive and engaging activities for making sight words.

Running records are used to assess the reading of the familiar book, usually at the beginning of the lesson. They should not be used with a new book because helping a student read a new book takes expert scaffolding (see Practical Chapter 2). The intensive, hands-on scaffolding needed to help a struggling reader succeed with instructional level text is not compatible with the restrained, objective evaluation required in assessment. In assessing the reading of the familiar book, we tell students, "This time I'm just going to listen and take some notes to help me remember how you read. I want you to read without any help from me. If you have trouble with a word, just do your best and keep reading."

The biggest advantage of running records is spontaneity. There is no test to buy, no passage to copy, and no advance preparation required. All you need is plain paper and a pencil, which means you can use running records on the spur of the moment with any familiar book. Some teachers learning to take running records copy out the text to mark, which throws away the advantage of spontaneity. There is also no advantage in recopying or typing up a running record later. All we need for assessment is the sloppy copy made in the spur of the moment, annotated with findings in the margin of the page. For best results, try taking running records without "training wheels."

BENEFITS OF RUNNING RECORDS

Running records record miscues for miscue analysis. *Miscues* are simply mistakes during reading, but by thinking of them as miscues, we recognize the reader is either cuing on the wrong thing (e.g., a picture), or cuing incompletely on the right thing (e.g., guessing from consonants). We study miscues in *miscue analysis* to determine which correspondences students are missing. Our goals is to arm beginners with a full toolkit of the 40-some vowel correspondences skilled readers use to unlock the pronunciations of unfamiliar words. We also analyze miscues to see what strategies readers are using so that if necessary, we can help them use the strategies of skilled readers for learning to read words. Skilled readers generate a ballpark pronunciation by decoding, crosscheck to correct a near miss, and then mentally mark any irregular elements so that they can store the complete spelling of the word in memory. When we have a well-spelled word in memory and see that word in print, we can make an instant, automatic match to access meaning information effortlessly and fluently.

Running records go further than miscue notes to adding checkmarks for correct words. This allows us to figure the percent of accuracy in a reading so that we can do the "Goldilocks test": Is the book too hard, too easy, or just right? If it is too easy, there is not enough challenge to make any significant number of new sight words. If it is too hard, reading becomes frustrating and demoralizing. At the frustration level, the reader is rarely learning any new words because he or she gives up on crosschecking and mental marking, the key strategies for making sight words.

The basic procedure of taking a running record is to watch and listen as a student reads, making a checkmark for each word read correctly, and writing a note for each miscue. Practical Chapter 2 introduced the skill of taking miscue notes: We write down the student's attempt (if any) over the text word, like a fraction. For example, if a student tried to read the word *boat* and came up with "bat," we write bat/*boat*. With a pencil, it will look like this:

$$\frac{bat}{boat}$$

When we see such a note, we infer that the reader encountered the text word *boat* and said "bat." We can use information like this from the running record to answer three questions: (1) How hard is the book? (2) What strategies is the reading using with unfamiliar words? (3) What correspondences are missing from the reader's decoding toolkit?

How hard?

To determine the reader's percentage of accuracy, we have to count the number of miscues and the total number of words in the passage and then plug these numbers into a formula (see Figure 1). In the formula, the term "correct words" is the total number of words in the passage minus the number of scorable miscues.

$$\text{Percentage of accuracy} = \frac{\text{Correct words}}{\text{Total words}} \times 100$$

FIGURE 1: Formula for computing the percentage of accuracy

For example, if the passage were 68 words long and the reader made 3 miscues, the number of correct words would be 65, giving us the numbers 65/68, which comes to about .96. We can multiply by 100 to get 96%. But what is the interpretation? Figure 2 gives the benchmarks for accuracy in running records (Betts, 1946). A reading at 96% accuracy is in the instructional range. In the "Goldilocks test," we are looking for reading that is 95-98% accurate, when not counting self-corrections as errors. If we can remember the numbers 95-98% for the instructional level, we can easily figure the percentages at other levels. The percentages for the independent level are 99-100% accuracy, which means the reading is too easy for productive instruction. The percentages for the frustration level are 0-94%, which means the reading is too difficult for the reader to get the message of the text and to add unfamiliar words to sight vocabulary. At the frustration level, the reader cannot succeed even with a teacher's expert help. The reader may struggle through the words of the text, but typically he will have little or no reading comprehension, will not make new sight vocabulary, and will not enjoy even the most delightful text. The reason is that at the frustration level, the readers stops crosschecking and downshifts into survival mode. Unfortunately, this is a common experience for struggling readers, who are all too frequently placed in frustration-level text.

Reading Level	% Miscues	% Accuracy	Description
Independent	0-1%	99-100%	Too easy for productive instruction. Just right for independent reading.
Instructional	2-5%	95-98%	Best level for making sight words and getting the message of the text with teacher scaffolding.
Frustration	> 5%	0-94%	Too hard for instruction. Student stops crosschecking and may go off task.

FIGURE 2: Percent of accuracy at independent, instructional and frustration levels

WHAT STRATEGIES?

As explained in Practical Chapter 2, there are three highly productive self-help strategies for learning to read words. The top strategy for word learning is decoding. When we decode a word, we connect the sequence of letters in the spelling to the sequence of phonemes in the pronunciation, so that the spelling comes to make sense as a map of the pronunciation. When a spelling makes sense, it is easy to store that spelling in memory for sight word recognition. A miscue that shares letters between the attempt and the text word shows decoding. For example, if a reader said "whoa" for *who*, we can infer that he used all the letters in *who* to generate a plausible pronunciation, only to be tripped up by one of the stranger alphabetic mappings in English.

The second most productive strategy is crosschecking. Crosschecking means testing the decoding attempt in context by finishing the sentence and asking if the attempt made grammatical and syntactic sense. If not, the reader thinks of a sound-alike word that fits the context. If our reader finished reading the sentence, saying "Whoa is at the door?" he will probably get enough of a contextual boost to say, "Oh, *who* is at the door?" Crosschecking not only recovers the message of the sentence, but also it allows the reader to mentally mark irregular letters so that the entire spelling can be annotated and stored for sight recognition:

$$\text{wh}\overset{\text{oo}}{\text{o}}$$

Self-corrected miscues shows crosschecking at work. When we mark a miscue SC for self-correction, we infer that the reader could not fully decode the word, but was able to crosscheck to identify the word by testing his attempt in context. Over the course of teaching, we hope most or all miscues come to be self-corrected, a sign that the reader is getting the message of texts and making sight words. To reach this goal, we have to assiduously monitor the reader's success to keep him in instructional-level texts (95-98% accuracy) rather than in frustration-level texts (0-94% accuracy). At the frustration level, readers stop crosschecking, stop making sight words, lose reading comprehension, and over time, develop negative attitudes about reading.

MISSING CORRESPONDENCES?

The third question we can answer with running records is: What correspondences are missing from the reader's decoding toolkit? To find missing correspondences, we compare the reader's attempt to the text word, with particular attention to the vowel in the text word. Generally, the vowel in the text word is missing from the reader's correspondence toolkit. For example, if the miscue was bat/*boat*, the likely culprit is *oa* = /O/. The consonants *b* and *t* were interpreted correctly, but the *oa* vowel did not appear in the attempt.

There are three special cases where miscue analysis can be tricky. First, we cannot infer any missing correspondences when the text word is irregular. For example, if the reader said "wat" for *what*, he made good use of the spelling of *what* but was tripped up by its irregularity. For this reason, we do not use miscues on irregular words to determine missing correspondences. Second, we often encounter miscues where the problem seems to be with a consonant, e.g., trap/*tramp*. However, a possible reason readers would make a miscue with a correct vowel is that they are working so hard at getting the vowel that they run out of resources and are unable to blend. This suggests that the vowel has only been partially learned, so that the reader needs additional work to decode automatically. Thus with such a miscue, we might conditionally list a = /a/ as missing, subject to seeing other corroborating miscues. Of course, in some cases a consonant may be the problem. For example, if a reader said bot/*dot*, the reader is probably mixing up the confusable letters b and d. Third, we may see miscues self-corrected, e.g., saf/SC for *safe*. In this case, the self-correction required crosschecking, but if the reader had learned the correspondence a_e = /A/, decoding would have produced the correct pronunciation. This indicates the correspondence a_e = /A/ is still missing from the reader's decoding toolkit.

MARKING MISCUES

Figure 3 demonstrates how to mark miscues when taking a running record. If there are no miscues, simply make a checkmark for each correct word. When the reader comes to the end of the line of type, start a new row of checks, and at the end of the page, draw a horizontal line to indicate the page break. The most common type of miscue is a substitution, which means the reader says a different word than what is printed in the text. When taking the running record, the teacher writes down the attempt instead of making a checkmark. For the present, we can't stop to write the text word because we need to keep up with the reader. The lines of checks and horizontal lines for page breaks will guide us back to the misread word later. If the reader makes additional attempts, write each successive attempt, separated by slash marks. If the reader self-corrects the miscue, add /SC after the attempt. Two other types of miscues are scored. In an omission, a word is left out, in which case the teacher draws a blank for that word. In an insertion, an extra word is added, in which case the teacher carets that word into the line of checks. When leisure permits, the teacher completes the running record by writing in each text word to allow miscue analysis.

Readings	Meaning	Example	Marking
Correct reading	No mistake.	I saw a pirate.	✓ ✓ ✓ ✓
Substitution	Say a different word than what is written.	I was a pirate.	✓ was ✓ ✓ saw
	Make a second miscue on the same word.	I was, er, say a pirate.	✓ was/say ✓ ✓ saw
Omission	Skip a word that is there.	I saw pirate.	✓ ✓ __ ✓ a
Insertion	Say a word that's not there.	I saw a mean pirate.	mean ✓ ✓ ✓ ^ ✓
Self-correction	Fix the miscue.	I was, I mean, saw a pirate.	✓ was/SC ✓ ✓ saw

FIGURE 3: How to mark running records

Scoring

In scoring a running record, each substitution, omission, or insertion that is not self-corrected counts as one error. When counting omissions, whether the reader leaves out a single word, a line of text, or a whole page, only one error is scored because only a single miscue was made. Of course, the reader receives no checkmarks for correct words either, so the percentage of accuracy is not affected. The accuracy benchmarks in Figure 2 are based on scoring only miscues that are not self-corrected. If other deviations from text are counted, then other benchmarks must be used. For example, some reading specialists count self-corrected miscues as errors and use a range of 90-95% accuracy for the instructional level. This can mislead those who do not count self-corrections as scorable miscues into allowing children to stray far into the frustration level in reading, with all the negative consequences for frustration, a shutdown in word learning, the loss of comprehension, and demoralization about reading. Thus, this is a serious error to avoid.

The reader can deviate from the text in other ways that do not count in the scoring. For example, the reader may repeat words during the reading, e.g., "I saw a . . . I saw a . . . a pirate." Repetition is a good strategy when a reader is struggling with a word because it keeps the previous words in memory until the reader works out the unfamiliar word. For this reason, no error is scored for a repetition. Similarly, there is no error for a parenthetical insertion when the reader makes a self-correction, e.g., "I was . . . I mean, I saw a pirate." In addition, dialect pronunciations are not scored as errors. I once supervised a reading lesson where the student teacher asked children for a word that rhymes with *can*. When a girl suggested *san*, the teacher frowned and said that *san* is not a word. "Sure it's a word," said the girl, "like when you play in the san' in the park." Similarly, "ax" may be a dialect pronunciation for *ask*, and some children "scrap" the baby into the car seat before the car enters the "screet." Such dialect renderings are not reading miscues.

Analyzing a running record

After the checks are made, the miscues noted, and the text words written in under the attempts, we are ready to answer our three questions in the margin of the page. Figure 4 shows a running record for the book *James and the Good Day* (Cushman & Kornblum, 1990), read by "Sara" (pseudonym) as follows:

> James <u>walks</u>—wakes up. / He makes a plan. / It will be a good day. //
>
> James will sail his <u>gut</u>—tug. / He will sail his tug in the tub. //
>
> James makes a lake in the tub. / He <u>wants</u>—waits for a big lake. //
>
> But James can not wait. / He <u>sake—sakes</u>—takes out his games. / <u>His</u>—He plays on the rug. //

HOW TO TAKE A RUNNING RECORD

The lake James made <u>in tug</u>. / The tug sails and sails. / It makes its way out of the tub. //

James plays and plays. / The tug sails /b/ /o/. / It sails on the rug. //

Mom wakes up. / <u>Here fake</u> is /r/ and <u>made</u>. / She has lots to say. //

James has to mop the <u>water</u> mess. / He <u>got</u>—gets a pail. / It is not a good day!

```
✓     wocks/SC ✓            ✓ ✓ ✓ ✓     in  tug
      wakes                             is  big
✓ ✓ ✓ ✓                    ✓ ✓ ✓ ✓ ✓
✓ ✓ ✓ ✓ ✓ ✓                ✓ ✓ ✓ ✓ ✓ ✓ ✓ ✓
_____                     _____

                            ✓ ✓ ✓
✓ ✓ ✓ ✓  gut/SC
         tug                ✓ ✓ ✓   /b/ /o/
                                    down
✓ ✓ ✓ ✓ ✓ ✓ ✓              ✓ ✓ ✓ ✓
_____                     _____

✓ ✓ ✓ ✓ ✓ ✓ ✓              ✓ ✓ ✓
✓ wants/SC ✓ ✓ ✓ ✓         Here fake ✓  /r/ ✓ made
  waits                    Her  face    red   mad
_____                    ✓ ✓ ✓ ✓ ✓
✓ ✓ ✓ ✓ ✓                  _____

✓ sake/sakes/SC ✓ ✓ ✓       ✓ ✓ ✓ ✓ ✓ water ✓
  takes                                    wet
His/SC ✓ ✓ ✓ ✓              ✓ got/SC ✓ ✓
He                            gets
_____                     ✓ ✓ ✓ ✓ ✓ ✓
```

FIGURE 4: Running record for Sara reading *James and the Good Day*.

Interpretation is simply a matter of answering our three questions: (1) How hard is the book? (2) What strategies is the reader using with unfamiliar words? (3) What correspondences are missing from the reader's decoding toolkit?

To find out how hard the reading was for Sara, we use the formula in Figure 1 to determine the difficulty of the reading. Because there were 117 words and 8 miscues, we divide the number of correct words (109) by the total number of words and multiply times 100 to get a percentage, 93%, which indicates reading at the frustration level.

To determine Sara's strategies, we note that most of her miscues used consonants in the text word in the attempts, a partial-alphabetic strategy. Sara self-corrected in the first half of the reading, but she gave up on self-correction later in the reading as frustration set in. This is the usual reaction when we ask students to read text at the frustration level.

To determine Sara's missing correspondences, we look for the vowels in the text words. Sara seems to be missing *a_e* = /A/ in *wakes, takes,* and *face, u* = /u/ in *tug, ai* = /A/ in *waits, i* = /i/ in *is* and *big, ow* = /ow/ in *down, er* = /er/ in *her, c(e)* = /s/ in *face, e* = /e/ in *red, wet,* and *gets,* and *a* = /a/ in *mad*. The next missing correspondences she needs to work on are the short vowels she is missing. Sara needs *e* = e, with a review of *a* = /a/, followed by *i* = /i/. With several missing short vowels, it is no wonder she is frustrated in a long-vowel decodable book that presumes knowledge of all the short vowels.

Using running records

Effective teachers use the information from running records to guide their teaching. They adjust book difficulty to aim at an appropriate level of challenge that is neither too easy nor frustratingly difficult. They track students' missing correspondences to give priority to the earliest missing correspondences in the sequence. This maintains the decodability of practice texts, the best of which accumulate the short vowels in alphabetical order, followed by the long vowels, followed by other regular vowel patterns. We review vowel correspondences until students have mastered them and can apply them automatically in encountering unfamiliar words. Effective teachers also teach students the crucial word-learning strategies of decoding, crosschecking, and rereading the sentence whenever they struggle with a word.

In the long run, the outcome of greatest interest with running records is the evolution of these crucial strategies over time. As we trace running records across the course of teaching, we hope to see that students are using more of the printed word during decoding, eventually using all the letters in spellings to generating pronunciations, and then recognizing pronounceable word parts and analogies in multisyllable words. We hope to see them self-correct more and more of their miscues, indicating a consistent use of crosschecking and an expectation that reading will reveal the messages of texts. Finally, we hope that students will develop the habit of rereading whenever they identify an unfamiliar word to rapidly add that word as sight vocabulary. It only takes about four decodings to make a sight word, and rereading gets the reader halfway there. It is by gaining a wide swath of the words in regular use in English that students become fluent readers.

PRACTICAL CHAPTER

How to Develop Fluency Through Repeated Readings

Fluency means reading with automatic word recognition, so that sight words are recognized effortlessly and involuntarily (see Chapter 9). In practical terms, a fluent reading is one in which most or all the words are in the reader's sight vocabulary. This implies that a reader can be fluent in a specific text, such as this morning's newspaper, but not fluent in another text, such as a chemistry textbook with words like *anhydride*, *deliquescence*, and *ianthanides* that have not yet become sight words. However, with sustained, enthusiastic, engaged reading practice, we can add enough words to sight vocabulary to have general fluency with the bulk of our reading. Automatic word recognition allows us to read quickly and smoothly, to interpret a text expressively when reading aloud, and to read silently twice as fast as we can read orally. Most importantly, automatic word recognition frees up resources for thinking about the messages of texts, thereby improving reading comprehension.

The strongest research evidence for building fluency supports the method of repeated reading (NRP, 2000). The basic idea of repeated reading is simple: Have students reread the same passage under the teacher's guidance until the reading is fluent. The reader continues with the same material until the material is mastered, which is usually defined by a reading rate, e.g., 85 words per minute. Students read and reread a text in a quest to gain specific fluency for that text, i.e., a reading in which most or all of the words in the text have been entered into the reader's sight vocabulary. The goal of this practical chapter will be to familiarize you with the basic procedures for organizing repeated reading. I will thoroughly review the rationale for repeated readings so that you can understand why they work and can adapt them under varied circumstances. It is not enough to have recipe knowledge of teaching activities: To evaluate alternative methods, a teacher must be clear on the governing principles for becoming a fluent reader.

The fluency formula

To build sight vocabulary, fluency work most involve extensive reading, crosschecking, and rereading in instructional-level text. The basic rationale is expressed in what I call the fluency formula, where fluency gains depend on including each element. To be fluent, a reader must:

Read and Reread Decodable Words in Connected Text.

To gain fluency, the student must *read* the words, which includes decoding any unfamiliar words rather than guessing from context. He must finish the sentence to crosscheck any decoding attempts, mentally marking any odd or silent letters in memory, and then *reread* the sentence to begin to secure the annotated word in memory. Fluency also depends on rereading passages, chapters, and stories until they can be read fluently. Fluency progress requires reading *decodable words* so that the reader can experience success with a decoding strategy. To maintain decodability, texts must be chosen to match the reader's decoding ability. For early full alphabetic readers, this means using specially engineered decodable texts where the reader has learned all vowel correspondences for reading the content words. For more advanced full alphabetic readers who have developed the crosschecking and mental marking ability to tackle irregular words, it means using an instructional level text not restricted for vowel patterns, but readable with 95-98% accuracy. Finally, the reader must work with *connected text* rather than with isolated words to use the vital strategies of crosschecking and mental marking for building sight vocabulary. Connected texts are read with greater motivation and a natural time pressure necessary for moving from decoding into sight word recognition.

An analogy to music

To understand the value and motivation of repeated reading in gaining fluency, it is helpful to think about learning to read music. Those who set out seriously to learn to play a musical instrument must learn a musical code analogous to the alphabetic code. A musical text is written with notes on a staff, a field of horizontal lines. The task in reading music is to decode a printed score into a musical performance. The musician begins by learning to read the notes accurately, using the position of each note on the staff to determine its pitch (this can be a special problem with notes written on ledger lines above or below the staff, which may not be recognized automatically), while using other information to determine its duration. Once the notes can be played accurately, the next step is to play them in rhythm. To make this possible, musicians usually begin with a slow tempo and then gradually build toward the tempo recommended by the composer, which requires reading notes with increasing automaticity. As the tempo increases, the musician works to add expression through phrasing, emphasis, and other interpretive techniques.

To make music, it is vital to give less and less attention to decoding the notes and more and more attention to musical interpretation. But skilled musicians have a secret for achieving this goal: They practice small portions of music—a measure, a phrase, or a passage—over and over to mastery. Each measure, phrase, or passage becomes automatic so that it can be incorporated seamlessly into the performance of the musical work. Through repeated playing, the musician learns to recognize the written score effortlessly and automatically, freeing his full attention for musical expression.

INEFFECTIVE MUSIC INSTRUCTION

Imagine a music lesson with an untrained teacher in which students only sight-read music. Perhaps the teacher is anxious to maintain progress through a musical program of studies. The novice student would work through each piece, laboriously working out pitch and time values, plodding through each musical score with many wrong notes, hesitations, and self-corrections. When he finally reached the end of the piece, the teacher would produce a new piece of music to read through. Imagine the frustrations of such lessons, with students stumbling through piece after piece, never getting the notes into rhythm, never bringing the tempo up to the composer's recommendations, and never adding musical expression. This beginner would miss the pleasure of creating music and very likely give up playing the instrument at the first opportunity.

Many reading lessons follow these failed procedures. Perhaps the teacher is anxious to maintain progress through the basal program. Readers may stumble through stories reading word by word, with frequent awkward pauses, miscues, and revisions, never mastering a single page. Determined readers may plod on, identifying words one by one, but at great cost: They become oblivious to the message of the text and miss the pleasure of reading. Like frustrated music students, they will likely give up voluntary reading and read only under coercion. Yet, following the model of music, teachers need not reduce reading instruction to tedium and frustration. Just as the musician develops his performance by practicing a measure, a phrase, or a passage over and over to mastery, the reader can be guided to master each phrase, sentence, or passage of text and incorporate it into a complete, expressive, and comprehensible reading. As unlikely as the name suggests, the most effective way to help beginners enjoy reading is the method of repeated reading.

WHICH STUDENTS?

Repeated reading for fluency is not for everyone. Automaticity must begin with accuracy. In reading, only students who can accurately decode words can develop fluency through repeated readings. Ehri's model of how beginners develop the ability to read words (Chapter 3) shows which readers are good candidates for fluency instruction. Prealphabetic readers are not decoding at all. They need phoneme awareness instruction to begin using consonants as phonetic cues. Partial alphabetic readers decoding consonants are not yet accurate; they need vowel knowledge to use the entire spelling for accurate decoding. Full alphabetic readers can decode accurately, but they are painfully slow; they are the best candidates for repeated reading. Their accurate decoding equips them to learn sight words across repeated readings. Consolidated alphabetic readers who are not yet fluent may also benefit from repeated readings. However, advanced readers developing an extensive sight vocabulary reach a point of diminishing returns with repeated reading. If they are reading 120 words per minute, there is little point in working toward 130 words per minute. Reading silently will allow them to read more text and use more effective strategies. Learning meaning vocabulary holds more promise for fluent readers in improving reading comprehension.

Which books?

Given that fluency comes from gains in sight vocabulary and that sight vocabulary comes by decoding, crosschecking, mental marking, and rereading, what kind of books should be used in repeated readings for fluency? We have to rule out predictable books such as *Brown Bear, Brown Bear, What Do You See?* (Martin & Carle, 1967) because when children recite patterned language using pictures, they are not decoding, crosschecking, mental marking, and rereading. As the fluency formula indicates, students must read words to gain fluency. Decodable text works well for children's first forays into repeated reading because readers have the vowels to read the content words accurately. When children move from predictable books into decodables, they usually slow down dramatically because they have to solve each word by decoding it. They lose the false fluency of recitation and with it, much of the fun of reading. Repeated reading in decodables can help recover the music of language as most or all of the words are added to sight vocabulary.

With a growing correspondence toolkit and the ability to crosscheck to identify words and mentally mark irregular elements, children can enjoy repeated readings of stories at the reader's instructional level, estimated by 95-98% word reading accuracy. However, stories at the frustration level, below 95% accuracy, should be shelved for the present. Reading at the frustration level will not bring fluency because readers give up crosschecking and stop making sight words. Nevertheless, there is a small window of opportunity with moderately challenging text. If a motivated student is reading only slightly below the instructional level (say, 92-94% accuracy), he may be able to gain the instructional level across repeated readings. Teachers should be sensitive to signs of frustration and discouragement with readers operating at these marginal levels.

Whole texts

Readers need engaging stories, chapters, or informational texts for repeated readings. A typical passage may range from 50 to 200 words, which may be a chapter or the entire text of an early decodable reader. Usually a repeated reading takes only a few minutes. One of the worst ideas in recent memory was to try to build fluency by having children read passages to practice for the DIBELS test of oral reading fluency (Good & Kaminski, 2002). With DIBELS, children read for exactly one minute for a quick and dirty measure of reading fluency. It is easy to get a words-per-minute score by having students do one-minute reads, but reading only part of a text thwarts the reader's natural motivation to find out what happens in a story. It is impossible to get the message of a text without finishing it. Moreover, one-minute reads do not require reading comprehension. The reader can skip words and ignore the message of text to get a high word-per-minute count, which defeats the purpose of reading.

WORD OVERLAP

Jay Samuels (1979) popularized repeated reading for teachers by showing that rereading the same text to a fluency criterion not only develops speed and accuracy in the specific text, but also transfers fluency gains to other texts. After reaching criterion on a particular passage (say, 85 words per minute), the reader typically begins the next passage faster than he began the previous passage and takes fewer trials to reach the fluency criterion. However, Rashotte and Torgesen (1985), experimenting with readers with LD, found that fluency gains across successive readings depend on word overlap in the texts. In other words, any speed gains owe to the repetition of the same words across successive texts so that the repeated words can be made into sight words. Unless content words are repeated in the successive texts, there is no fluency gain. In an experiment with normal readers, we found that students reading a chapter with word overlap from previous chapters read 20 WPM faster than a comparable group reading without word overlap (Murray, 2009). I wrote to Jay Samuels to ask him if word overlap might have played a role in the fluency gains he measured back in 1979. He replied (personal communication, May 3, 2010):

> I had [the students] read short passages from a longer story. They practiced in their seats until they could read the passage at a rate of 85 words a minute (my memory for the details may be off but I think I am close to what we used). When they reached the criterion speed, they moved to the next segment of text. Of course, there was word overlap since each passage came from the same text by the same author. If you ask me what text and author, I cannot answer because at the time the word overlap factor had not occurred to me, but it surely must have played a part. Several factors may have worked in addition to word overlap to account for improvements. Students had been learning strategies for study and practice that would lead to improvement, not to mention the increase in self-confidence the student were experiencing. One student came to me and said for the first time he sounded like a good reader.

Thus, for dramatic fluency gains, students must read successive passages or chapters from the same book, where character names and content words overlap across chapters. This word repetition enables fluency gains with the next chapter, where words that have become sight words from reading the previous passage ease the burden of reading the new material. If students read passages without word overlap, they will still make general fluency gains by adding sight vocabulary, but the fluency progress across readings will be much slower and may escape readers' notice.

Explaining and modeling

When first introducing repeated readings, it is important to explain to students why they are reading the same passage over and over rather than moving on to new material. Children may think they did something wrong in the first reading so that repeated reading is a punishment, like having to redo your math homework. A persuasive explanation might include the following talking points:

> Any good reader who is going to read aloud has to practice. When you reread the same story, your reading gets easier because you learn the words so well they jump out at you. Because reading the words is easier, you can pick up speed and read faster. It's also easier for you to understand the story. If you read the story aloud to others, your reading sounds more like storytelling, which makes it easier for your listeners to understand.

Follow up your explanation with modeling, dramatizing how to improve fluency by rereading. Begin by pretending to read word by word, while explaining that even good readers have to practice to make their reading smooth and expressive. On each successive reading, add smoothness and expression while explaining that the reading is getting easier because you're learning the words. Students will not understand how you are getting better without making the decoding step explicit. Simply demonstrating nonfluent and fluent reading and asking students which they like better does not show how to gain fluency. Modeling fluency might sound something like this, using text from Smith's (1997) *The Sunset Pond*:

> The first time I read something, I may make some mistakes, and it takes time to fix them.
>
> Matt and Bud j-jump from thee frahnt steps—front steps—onto thee soft grass. They ran, no run past thee beds of daffy . . . [coverups] daf-fah-dils, *daffodils* . . . and down thee hill to thee sun-set, sunset pond.
>
> Now that I know the words, I can read faster:
>
> Matt and Bud jump from thee front steps onto thee soft grass. They run past thee beds of daffodils and down thee hill to thee sunset pond.
>
> I'm going to try again to make it smoother and add expression:
>
> Matt and Bud *jump* from the front steps onto the soft grass. They *run* past the beds of daffodils and *down* the hill to the sunset pond.

The key message to impart when modeling how to gain fluency is that we get more fluent because we're remembering the words that slowed us down.

TRACKING GAINS

To track reading rates across readings, the formula for words per minute (WPM) is:

$$\frac{\text{words} \times 60}{\text{seconds}}$$

Here *words* indicates the number of words in the passage, and *seconds* indicates the time in seconds to read the passage. The calculation is simple with a calculator, and if the words have been counted in advance to arrive at the numerator, only the reading time is needed to compute words per minute. Recall that having students read for one minute can simplify the math, but it works against the comprehension focus needed for crosschecking, motivation, and reading comprehension.

To motivate repeated readings, fluency scores must be presented on a child-friendly graph. Figure 1 shows one of the most successful graphs we have created. The monkey is a separate laminated figure with a velcro backing. He is trying to move up a tree to retrieve some tasty bananas, which in this case would require a reading at 85 words per minute. The numbers are written with a water-based marker on a laminated background so that the scale can be changed to match the changing fluency goals of readers. Because some readers may be aiming at 40 WPM and others at 100 WPM, the scale must be adaptable. Of course, the image can be changed to fit the interests of individual readers. Sports-minded readers may be motivated to help a basketball player rise high enough to make a slam-dunk. A bird-lover may be willing to work to see a bird fly up to its nest. What is important is that the reader sees himself making progress toward his individual fluency goal.

SCAFFOLDING WITH REPEATED READINGS

Ordinarily in scaffolding oral reading, we would intervene at sentence boundaries to help with unrecognized words (see Practical Chapter 2). However, if we interrupt a reader during repeated readings, we frustrate his drive to increase reading fluency as measured in words per minute. For this reason, we must limit our interventions to the intervals between readings. During reading, teachers can gather valuable information by collecting miscue notes to analyze for missing correspondences. After each reading, the teacher can help a student locate and correct misread words by using coverups; that is, uncovering the word little by little to make decoding manageable. After the teacher helps with coverups a few times, the student can take over. When the reader correctly identifies each misread word, we want him to reread the sentence to learn the word as sight vocabulary;

this rereading is the second of four encounters needed to learn a sight word by decoding (Reitsma, 1983). In addition, it is important to ask an open-ended question after each reading to help readers maintain a focus on the message of text. The question can be about the meaning of a word, a detail supplied by an illustration, an evaluation of a character's actions or motives, or a prediction about what will happen next. The effort to make connections helps the reader focus on comprehending the text, which is the purpose of reading.

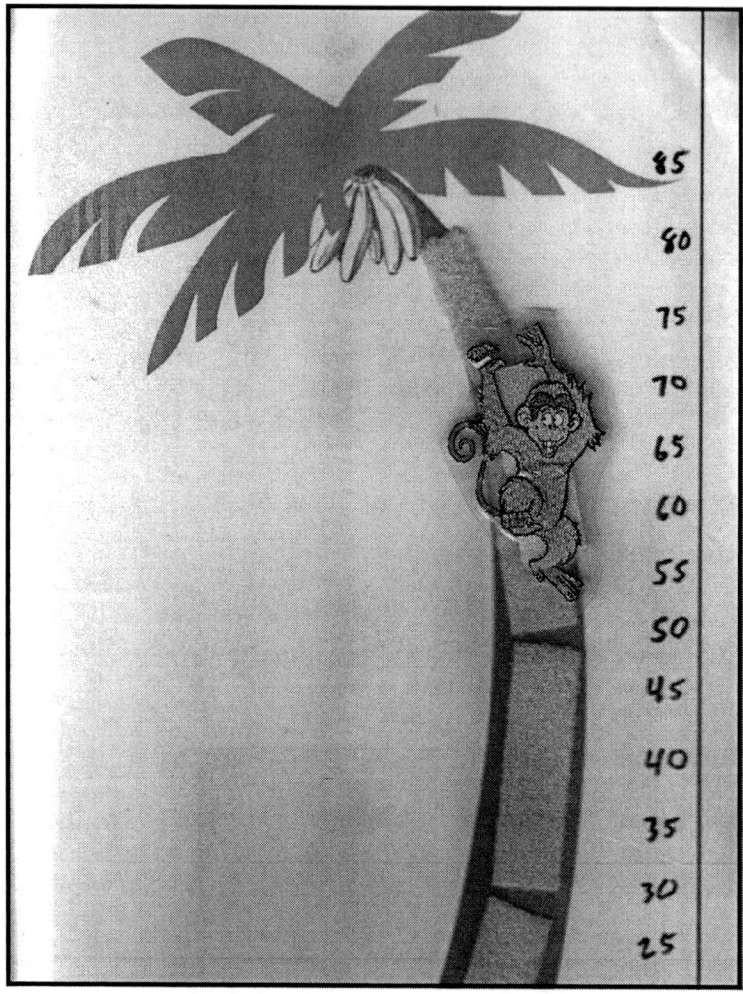

FIGURE 1: Monkey graph for repeated readings.

GROUP REPEATED READINGS

Repeated readings work well in a reading group, and teachers rarely have the luxury of tutoring. To organize group repeated readings, the first reading can be guided. The teacher can give a booktalk and introduce any unfamiliar vocabulary or background information, after which students can read silently, with discussion to review and evaluate story events. Then students return to their places for rereading. Each student comes up to the teacher's desk in turn and reads the selected passage aloud. The teacher times the reading and takes miscue notes. When the reader finishes, the teacher graphs the results, scaffolds a second look at any misread words, and has the student reread those sentences. Then the teacher asks an open-ended question for a brief discussion of the reading. Afterwards, the student returns to his desk to rehearse until his next reading turn, and another student comes up to read. Each student continues taking turns until he reaches his individual fluency goal.

PAIRED REPEATED READING

Paired repeated reading (Koskinen & Blum, 1986) can be an effective and motivating way to organize repeated readings. "Paired" repeated reading was originally designed for peers to work together to help themselves develop reading fluency. It requires a simple pictorial record sheet, such as in Figure 2.

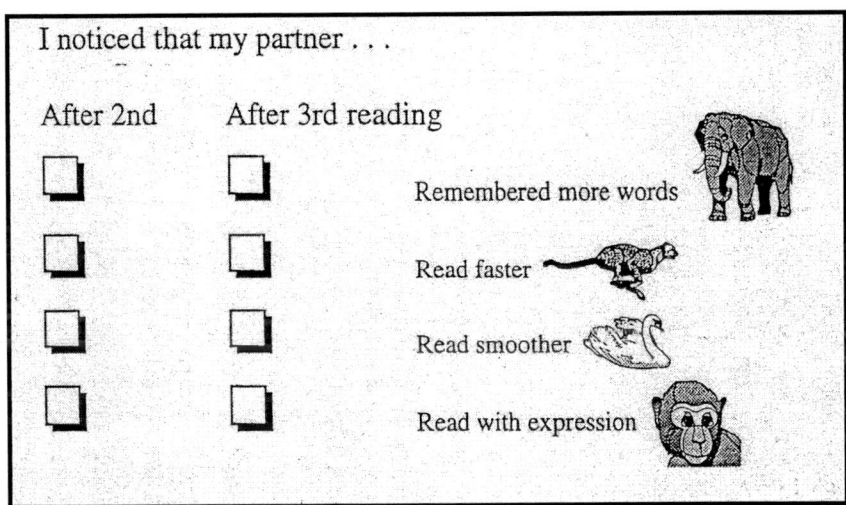

FIGURE 2: Checksheet for paired readings

In paired repeated reading, one student reads a passage three times, while a partner (in tutoring, this is typically the teacher rather than a peer) listens to each reading and gives feedback on fluency progress. The lesson begins by explaining what the partner will listen for: Will the reader remember more words, like the elephant who never forgets? Will the reader read faster, like the cheetah, the fastest of all animals? Will the reader read smoother, like the swan who glides across the water with scarcely a ripple? And will the reader read with more expression, like the monkey who uses his face and voice to dramatize his message?

The first reading serves as a baseline for the next two readings. The teacher or partner recognizes progress by checking the appropriate boxes after the second and third readings. As usual, the teacher follows along with pencil in hand, noting miscues. Between readings, after praising the fluency progress, the teacher points out words that gave difficulty, scaffolds word learning with coverups, and asks the student to reread the sentence. In addition, the teacher makes a comment or asks an open-ended question about a story event, an illustration, or what a word means.

In paired repeated readings, the report is strictly complimentary; there is no option for criticizing the reading or giving advice. If peers are used as partners, they must be given instruction and modeling on how to listen for improvement and to restrict all comments to praise about remembering more words, reading faster, reading smoother, or reading with more expression. In my experience, some children are not used to giving and receiving compliments from their peers. Without firm ground rules, a student may tell a peer that his reading "stunk up the place," which not only fails to encourage repeated reading, but may lead to anything from discouragement to combat.

In general, peer tutoring should be used sparingly and with careful supervision. Most peers do not have the skills to motivate or scaffold repeated reading. Not only have they not learned to provide specific praise for motivation, they don't know how to intervene between repeated readings, to provide word-learning scaffolding and comprehension support. This is not to say that seven- and eight-year old children are unable to develop some routines for helping peers read aloud, but only that motivating and scaffolding reading fluency is difficult even for novice teachers, with all the discipline of adulthood. To expect children to carry out such tasks is unrealistic.

REAL-WORLD REPEATED READING

Historically, schools encouraged repeated reading by requiring students to memorize famous poems, speeches, and historical documents. Students gave oral interpretations of these texts before the public in "recitations." Memorization was also a common task with passages from the Bible. Learning influential works by memory gave students mastery of wonderful language that could become part of their own repetoire of ideas. To learn their recitation texts, students read them over and over again, dozens of times, until they could be remembered—the method of repeated reading. Any motivating activity that gets students reading the same texts over and over builds fluency. Rehearsing parts for a play, practicing choral readings, or learning parts of a reader's theatre script are everyday opportunities for repeated reading, particularly when they motivate readers to prepare to perform for an audience.

SUMMARY

To recap the major ideas of this chapter, research strongly supports the method of repeated readings for improving fluency with novice readers. By reading and rereading an engaging, instructional-level text to a fluency criterion, readers build new sight vocabulary, enabling them to read the text with less effort and greater comprehension. Readers make the best progress with repeated readings under the following conditions:

1. Readers should work with instructional level text in which they will encounter 2-5% unfamiliar words. Working with independent level text will not bring an appreciable growth in sight word knowledge because not enough words will be unfamiliar. Working with frustration level text, where a large percentage of words are unfamiliar, discourages readers to the point where they give up crosschecking, which is essential for learning sight words and gaining fluency. However, in marginal cases where 6-7% of the words are unknown, readers may acquire enough new sight words to bring that text into the instructional level by the second reading.

2. For best results, students should reread the same passage until they reach a fluency criterion defined by reading speed, such as 85 words per minute. A focus on speed rather than accuracy, provided students are reading with comprehension, generally leads to gains in both speed and accuracy. Conversely, a focus on accuracy may actually lead readers to slow down and read less fluently (Samuels, 1979). A fluency checksheet or a teacher's expert judgment can be used to set fluency standards, but a speed target provides an objective, measurable goal for readers.

3. Motivation for repeated reading is enhanced when the reader can see visible progress on a child-friendly graph. A good graph has a movable figure, a well-defined goal, and a scale to measure progress toward the goal. Readers will work hard to move the figure to new heights on the graph, thereby moving their reading to new heights of fluency.

4. Because making sight words requires crosschecking and mental marking to understand spellings so they can be stored in memory, readers must maintain a meaning focus as they work on fluency. Without comprehension, readers will stop crosschecking and stop the mental marking that is crucial for making sight words. Accordingly, they should read intact passages that capture a text message rather than reading for one minute, which usually breaks off reading in the middle of nowhere.

5. To keep students focused on the message of a text, it is vital to ask a different open-ended question after each reading. Because devising thoughtful questions on the spot can be difficult, the teacher should prepare questions in advance. These might be affixed on sticky notes to the teacher's copy of the text.

6. To give students a chance to study newly identified words and add them to sight vocabulary, teachers must scaffold word-learning between readings. Teachers should keep a record of miscues during reading to review when the reader finishes. When the time pressure is relaxed after a completed

reading, teachers should point out misread words in the text (including self-corrections) and scaffold their transformation into sight words. Teachers should help the reader use coverups, complete the sentence for crosschecking, mentally note any spelling oddities, and reread the sentence. Gaining fluency depends on making sight words, and scaffolding word learning between readings builds fluency on the next reading.

PRACTICAL CHAPTER

How to Teach Spelling as Wordmapping

A frustrated mother wrote about her son, whom we will call Terence (J. Berry, personal communication, April 4, 2006):

> Spelling has always been a tremendous problem for Terence. He flunked his first spelling test this year, in spite of copying each word at least ten times the night before the test. Directly after copying the words, he came to me in tears, telling me how stupid he was because he had just copied all those words over and over and still couldn't remember them.

Terence is like many students with limited spelling power, who try to memorize spellings. The sheer number of words to learn and the burden of trying to remember strings of letters without understanding them make a rote approach futile. Students like Terence need strategies for understanding spellings as pronunciation maps, enabling them to generate most of the letters and minimize memorization.

INSIGHTS AT BENCHMARK

Benchmark School near Philadelphia specializes in working with students with learning disabilities in reading. The students at Benchmark are bright, verbal children with a specific weakness in decoding that hinders making sight words—the defining profile for LD. Benchmark teachers developed an analogy approach for reading and spelling words using "key words" posted on a word wall (Gaskins, Ehri, Cress, O'Hara, & Donnelly, 1996-1997). However, many struggling readers at Benchmark were unable to remember the spellings of key words accurately enough to use them in analogies.

> One of our younger students, Adam... gamely attempted to use the analogy approach but rarely could think of a key word with the same spelling

pattern as the unknown word. As a result, he had to resort to searching the word wall for the key word. On one occasion, when he was reading with his teacher and had scanned the word wall in search of a key word, Adam said, "Tell you what, if you tell me the key word, I'll tell you the new word" (p. 314).

Adam's struggles illustrate a natural impediment to analogizing: Without a well-spelled sight word in memory, novice spellers can't generate the spelling pattern for an analogous unknown word. Students like Adam have to internalize the word wall. In other words, they have to store analogy words as well-spelled sight words in memory to decode new words, especially outside of the classroom.

The Benchmark researchers noticed why their students were having trouble remembering the key words: As bright, verbal learners, the children would try to memorize the spellings as soon as they were given new words to learn. Arbitrary letter strings are terribly hard to remember. Imagine trying to memorize a list of 20 phone numbers; it would take hours to learn the list permanently. To head off memorization, Gaskins et al. (1996-1997) developed strategies for learning spellings that entailed withholding the spellings until students had analyzed the phonological structures of the words.

TEACHING SPELLING AS WORDMAPPING

Building on the insights at Benchmark (Gaskins, et al., 1996-1997), I developed a 9-step procedure called wordmapping. Wordmapping directs students to analyze the phonological structure of a word before seeing its spelling, with the goal of recognizing the spelling as a meaningful, hence memorable, map of the pronunciation. In wordmapping, the teacher directs students to pronounce a word by syllables, to stretch each syllable to detect and count phonemes, and to draw blanks for each phoneme—in other words, to construct a blank wordmap. Next, the teacher directs students in filling in the standard spelling grapheme-by-grapheme on the blanks, careting in (^) any silent letters. After students record the spelling to complete the wordmap, they rewrite the intact word and study its spelling, giving extra attention to any odd or irregular elements. Memorization is limited to taking note of any tricky parts in the spelling (e.g., silent, ambiguous, or anomalous letters) rather than the entire letter sequence.

The wordmapping procedure uses five steps to analyze the phonological structure and four steps to recognize how the actual spelling maps this structure. Figure 1 shows how these steps could be used to learn the spelling demon *business*.

HOW TO TEACH SPELLING AS WORDMAPPING

First, examine the mouth moves.

1. Say the word and introduce its meaning. Say the syllables if there are more than one.	Business. *Business* means making and selling things for profit. *Busi-ness.*
2. Stretch the word. Work by syllables for steps 2-5.	/b-i-i-i-zzz/; /b/ /i/ /z/; 3 phonemes. /nnn-u-u-u-sss/; /n/ /u/ /s/; 3 phonemes.
3. Split up the phonemes.	
4. Count the phonemes.	
5. Draw blanks to stand for phonemes. Put slashes between syllables.	___ __ / ___ ___ ___

Then complete the wordmap and study the spelling.

6. Record spelling phoneme by phoneme. Directive: On the __ blank, write [letters]. Caret in any silent letters.	i bus^ /ne ss
7. Write the word.	business
8. Study the spelling. Ask about the tricky parts, or ask how we can remember the spelling.	The *u* says /i/; *s* says /z/; the *i* is silent. You might think of "busy-ness" because business keeps people very busy.
9. Check knowledge of meaning.	What's an example of a business? Chick-fil-A or McDonald's.

FIGURE 1: Wordmapping procedures for the word *business*

To understand the phonological structure, the student is directed to (1) pronounce the word and say the syllables, following the dictionary syllabication; (2) stretch each syllable and (3) segment the phonemes in the syllable; (4) count the phonemes in each syllable; and (5) draw blanks to represent each phoneme, with slashes between the syllables. To recognize how the actual spelling maps the phonological structure, the student is helped to (6) record the graphemes of the standard spelling on the blanks, careting in any silent letters; (7) transcribe the spelling outside the wordmap; (8) study the irregular features; and (9) check his or her knowledge of the word's meaning.

Though nine steps seem extensive, a word can be mapped rapidly in practice. For example, for the word *weird*, the dialogue for the phonological analysis might proceed as follows:

Teacher	Students
Say *weird*.	*Weird.*
Weird means very strange and hard to explain.	
Stretch out *weird*.	/wEEErrrd/
Split up the phonemes.	/w/ /E/ /r/ /d/
How many?	Four.
Draw four blanks.	__ __ __ __

To complete the wordmap, the teacher gets very directive, dictating the graphemes blank by blank and demonstrating visually on a chalkboard or overhead:

Teacher	Students
On the first blank, write *w*.	
On the second blank, squeeze in *ei*.	
On the third blank, write *r*.	
On the last blank, write *d*.	w ei r d
Now write *weird* outside the map to see how it usually looks.	*weird*
What's "weird" about the spelling *weird*?	It breaks the *i-before-e* rule.
Can anybody use *weird* in a sentence?	We watched a weird movie about aliens.

To map a polysyllabic word, it is important to work by dictionary syllables, something the teacher must check in advance. Working with dictionary syllables is especially helpful in learning the boundary letters in syllables. The teacher's instructions for *parallel* might ensue as follows:

Teacher	Students
Say *parallel*.	*Parallel.*
Parallel describes having lines going the same way but never crossing.	
Say the syllables in *parallel*.	*Par-al-lel.*
Stretch out *par*. How many phonemes?	/p-e-e-r/; three.

Notice that explicit phoneme segmentation may be omitted, but if students don't recognize three phonemes, the teacher can ask students to split up the phonemes for a good count, working for consensus.

Teacher	Students
Draw three blanks and a slash.	__ __ __ /
Stretch out *al*. How many phonemes?	/u-u-u-lll/; two.
Draw two blanks and a slash.	__ __ __ / __ __ /

Stretch out *lel*. How many phonemes?	/lll-e-e-e-lll/; three.
Draw three blanks.	__ __ __ / __ __ / __ __ __
On the first three blanks, write p-a-r.	<u>par</u> / __ __ / __ __ __
After the slash on the next two blanks, write a-l.	p <u>a</u> <u>r</u> /<u>al</u> / __ __ __
On the last three blanks, write l-e-l.	p <u>a</u> <u>r</u> / <u>a</u> <u>l</u> /<u>le</u> <u>l</u>
Now write parallel outside of the wordmap.	parallel
What's tricky about it?	Double *l*'s in the middle, one *l* at the end.
Can you think of anything that is parallel?	The lanes on the interstate.

AN EXPERIMENTAL TEST

To test the effectiveness of wordmapping, we tried it out with ninth graders enrolled in Communications Skills, a remedial language arts course (Murray & Steinen, 2011). We randomly assigned students to wordmapping and vocabulary treatments. Each group studied the same 95 challenging words, including *altruism, bearable, camouflage, daunted, embroider, fermentation,* and *gregarious,* at a rate of 12 words per week. However, the wordmapping group worked on understanding the spellings, and the vocabulary group focused on word meanings.

A typical week for the wordmapping group began by studying the first six words using wordmapping procedures: First, each word (e.g., *camouflage*) was explained ("*Camouflage* means hiding things with colors that blend in with the surroundings"). The teacher had students pronounce it slowly (/kam-u-flozh/) and break it into syllables (*cam-ou-flage*); the teacher relied on the dictionary for syllabication. With teacher guidance, students counted the phonemes in each syllable to construct wordmaps on their papers, using slashes to mark syllable boundaries. For example, the analysis of *camouflage* yielded this wordmap form:

__ __ __ / __ / __ __ __ __

Next, the teacher directed students to place the correct graphemes in the blanks, careting in any silent letters:

<u>c</u> <u>a</u> <u>m</u> / <u>ou</u> / <u>fla</u> g ^

Next, students transcribed the spelling from the wordmap into an intact word on their papers and studied the "tricky parts," in this case, the *ou* spelling of /u/, the *a* spelling for /o/, and the *ge* spelling for /zh/. To conclude, the teacher briefly checked understanding of the meaning of the word ("Why would soldiers or hunters wear camouflage?").

The next day, students reviewed the first six words and worked through six more words using the same procedures. On the third day, students enjoyed cooperative learning activities. Some played concentration in groups of 2 to 5 players. Game cards came in pairs, with one card having the correctly spelled word and the other a partial wordmap with one or two clue letters. On a turn, a player turned over a pair of cards, looking for a match; if successful, the player kept the cards. Another favorite was "hangman" (see Figure 2). Students began with a blank wordmap for one of the words and guessed letters, trying to avoid the penalty of adding a body part to a stick figure on a gallows. Other students worked in study-buddy pairs, taking turns mapping words and quizzing each other on spellings.

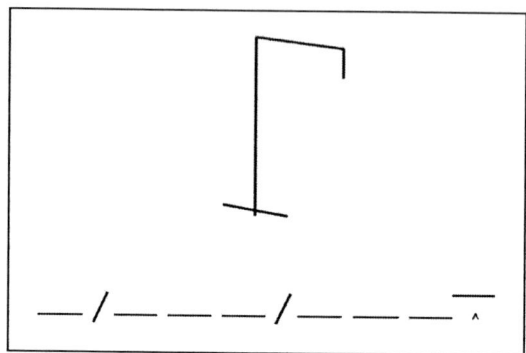

FIGURE 2: Hangman with wordmapping

Another learning activity was a modified spelling bee with spelling teams. While one student worked to construct a wordmap on the board, other team members offered advice and encouragement. The fourth day, the teacher led a review, after which students took a practice test, discussed their spellings, and corrected any errors. To warm up for the spelling test on the fifth day, students chose one of the cooperative learning activities. Afterwards, they took a spelling dictation test for a grade.

Results

We found that using wordmapping improved students' spelling. Not only did experimental students improve their knowledge of the words they studied, but they also improved their spelling ability with words they did not study, as indicated by their statistically significant advantage over the vocabulary group on a standardized spelling test. Why did students' spelling ability improve with wordmapping? As explained in Chapter 10, learning to spell requires learning spelling correspondences, rules, and patterns. Wordmapping may have helped students learn less obvious correspondences (e.g., that *c* followed by *e*, *i*, or *y* represents /s/) or useful rules (e.g., *i* before *e* except after *c*). In learning 95 challenging multisyllable words, they had to learn spelling patterns (e.g., that the final syllable /shun/ is spelled *tion*). Learning to spell such versatile word parts may have contributed most to the spelling gains with wordmapping.

Wordmapping focuses on constructing a spelling map to see how phonemes are represented in syllables. When students learn the regularities in correspondences, rules, and patterns, they can focus attention on spelling irregularities, such as silent letters, and mentally mark these anomalies in the spellings they remember (Ehri, 1980). For example, for students familiar with the *i*-before-*e* rule, the *ei* vowel in *weird* is glaring. The focus on unconventional elements replaces the inefficient attempt to memorize entire spellings, which is costly and unreliable.

APPLYING WORDMAPPING IN THE CLASSROOM

The success of wordmapping in a high school remedial English class suggests ways wordmapping might be adopted as a basic technique for teaching spelling in elementary schools. Since wordmapping aims at teaching spelling correspondences, rules, and patterns, students will make the best progress with word lists selected to reveal correspondences, rules, and patterns. Such patterned word lists are common in spelling basal series, e.g., where a weekly list might include words like *graphic, photography, telegraph, paragraph, autograph, biographer, geography, autobiography,* and *oceanographer*. Studying the common root *graph* is these words provides repeated experiences in varied contexts, which supports pattern learning.

Given the goal of enhancing spelling power, teachers should consider testing spelling power rather than only assessing words taught. This means the spelling test should include a few untaught words that exemplify the correspondence, rule, or pattern students have worked on. For example, students who have studied *presence* should be able to spell *absence*. Teachers may object that it is unfair to test students on spelling words they have not studied, but testing untaught items is typical in other subjects. We don't, for example, test students on the same math or grammar problems they have solved as homework; rather, we give them new problems with the expectation that they can solve similar problems using the strategies they have learned. In the same way, we should expect students to be able to apply their knowledge of correspondences, rules, and patterns to spell other words featuring those same correspondences, rules, and patterns.

Spelling teachers may continue to use the traditional weekly structure for spelling work while modifying it to emphasize wordmapping and cooperative learning. On Mondays, teachers can introduce the spelling pattern to be learned by modeling wordmapping with several exemplary words and guiding practice with others. Tuesdays can be used to review the pattern and guide students in mapping the remaining words.

During the week, students can work in cooperative learning teams with heterogeneous grouping to study the words. Research on cooperative learning suggests that to improve achievement, stronger students must be persuaded to help weaker students. The mechanism for this cooperation is pairing group rewards with individual accountability (Slavin, 1980). To earn a group reward (e.g., extra computer time), students must demonstrate achievement individually (e.g., by achieving a group average of 80% on a spelling test). To help their groups win, stronger spellers are willing to help weaker students learn words for the test.

An effective activity for learning spelling words in cooperative groups, as demonstrated in our quasi-experiment, is for stronger spellers to guide struggling spellers in wordmapping in study-buddy pairs. The engaging activities of concentration, hangman, and cooperative spelling bees, each adapted to use wordmapping rather than oral spelling recitation, provide high interest spelling practice. A pretest would be useful in helping students identify words for extra study before the Friday test. To focus attention on pattern learning, the unit test should include other exemplars of the learned pattern, perhaps explicitly cued by the teacher ("You studied the word *definite*. I want you to spell *infinite*, which has the same spelling pattern").

POSTSCRIPT ON TERENCE

After Terence learned wordmapping strategies, he made a remarkable turnaround in learning spelling words. His mother wrote:

> I sat down with him the next week with his new list, and we studied his words using your method. He was skeptical at first, but I convinced him to give it a shot—it couldn't hurt! We went through the list following your steps.
>
> The next night I sat down with him again, and said I'd give him a practice test over the words he learned the night before. I was hoping he'd be able to spell at least half of them correctly, because typically he wouldn't have remembered the correct spelling for many of them at all. To the amazement of both of us, he spelled every word right the first time. I was stunned, and so was he.
>
> We've continued to use your method, and studying for spelling tests is wonderful now. I told him he wasn't stupid, but the way he was trying to learn his spelling words—just memorizing the letters—would be impossible for anyone. He told me this week how much he liked studying the new way, and said, "It's almost like being a good speller!"

PRACTICAL CHAPTER

How to Write a Literacy Report

A basic task of the reading teacher is to report back to parents, other teachers, or school administrators on the progress a student has made over the course of a teaching program. We can crank out any number of reports that could be filed in some manila folder and safely encased in a filing cabinet, but for a report to have any value in directing future instruction, we must make our reports readable. Several general writing strategies are crucial to persuading our target audience—a busy teacher, a harried administrator, or a concerned parent—to spend time reading the report.

ENHANCING READABILITY

First, a literacy report should be concise, reporting only the necessary information to refocus teaching efforts. As a rule of thumb, two single-spaced pages should be sufficient. A one-page report has usually omitted critical information, and a three-page report is too wordy. If we want our reports to be read, we have to keep them short. Second, a readable report is written in plain language. If you imagine your grandmother as the audience, you will probably be on the right track. Imagine Grandma has a solid high-school education and good reading skills, but her vocabulary does not include the jargon of reading education. A good strategy for writing for Grandma is to season the report with the child's name. Teachers and parents have a powerful personal interest in a child's success, and every mention of that child's name will help maintain their interest. Because Grandma lacks knowledge of jargon, it is important to either translate or omit all jargon from the report. Readers of this book understand what phonetic cue reading means, but not Grandma. A simple translation, in this case, is that "Jeff tried to guess words using only the beginning letter."

Effective writers write strong sentences in the active voice. Passive sentences (e.g., "Stories were not understood") force readers to infer the subject of the sentence. In contrast, sentences written in active voice ("Jeff did not understand the stories") supply the subject for readers. Effective writers give specific examples when making general statements to bring the point home. If no particular examples come to mind, there may be no basis for the generalization. And finally, since the literacy report is a publication, spelling and language mechanics must be perfect. Whether it is fair or not, a single spelling or grammar mistake can destroy the credibility of the writer, especially with parents. Fortunately, modern word-processing software will catch many of our mistakes if we are careful to spell-check. In the spelling and grammar preferences, set the writing style to "formal." In addition, ask another good writer to read over your work, especially a writer who, like Grandma, does not know the jargon of reading education. Your writer-friend will probably catch homonyms missed by the spell-checker and snag the jargon that has become second nature to reading teachers ("A running record—is that like a 50-yard dash?").

Several conventions govern writing about letters and words. We italicize letters rather than underlining them or writing them in quotation marks, e.g., "Jeremy confuses the letters *b* and *d*." Similarly, we italicize partial spellings like digraphs and syllables, e.g., "Erin has begun to use the *sh* digraph and the syllable *ing* in her invented spellings." In addition, we italicize words whenever they indicate words rather than their meanings, e.g., "He spelled *dog* with two *g*'s." In contrast, we write phonemes in Roman, not italics, with slash marks on either side, e.g., "Robin has begun to recognize the phoneme /f/ in spoken words." We can also use slash marks to show pronunciations, e.g., "Janelle read the word hair as /har/." The convention for representing invented spellings is capitalization, and if possible, small caps, e.g., "Jaylen's invented spellings, e.g., 'MY CAT SKRACHT ME,' typically represent all the phonemes in words." Using regular caps suggests shouting.

The literacy report is a standard document rather than a work of creative writing. It conveys very specific information in a very tight structure. To help readers quickly locate vital information, it helps to adopt a standard document form, beginning with a centered headline followed by identifying information set against the left margin, for example:

Auburn University Department of Curriculum and Teaching
Literacy Report and Recommendations

Name of student: Ebony Collins

Grade: 1, Mrs. Longenbach

School: Shelton Mill Road Elementary

Report by: Tamara Brice

Date of report: December 1, 2012

The four sections that follow report on the key data of the teaching program:

I. Behavior observations.

II. Description of instructional program.

III. Assessment of current progress.

IV. Recommendations.

These headers should be indented with the text run into the same line as the header in order to conserve space for the two-page report, as illustrated in the description below.

I. Behavior Observations. One paragraph should be sufficient to explain your behavior observations of the child during teaching. In describing behavior, it is important to focus on what you observed rather than making inferences about the child's feelings, motivation, attitude, or condition, and to cite particular examples of this behavior. Write as a friendly but objective observer, keeping the focus on your student. It is not appropriate to write about yourself, explaining, for example, how much you enjoyed working with the child, or hoping that the child will continue making good progress and become an excellent reader. These are nice sentiments for a friendly letter, but not for a literacy report.

Where behavior observations often go wrong is in diagnosing a condition rather than reporting on behavior. If you tell what you saw, readers can draw their own conclusions about the reasons for the behavior. For example, instead of saying "Marquis was confident," you could say, "Marquis did what I asked without hesitation or looking for approval." Instead of saying "Julie was distractible," you could say, "Julie greeted children passing our cubby, which interrupted our lessons." Rather than saying, "Bob was lazy," you can report an observation, "Bob often lay on the floor and was slow to respond when I asked him to get up." How we can address distractibility or laziness is unclear, but there is a clear course of action in dealing with breaking off the lesson to greet other children or lying on the floor. Nevertheless, there are two important interpretive questions to answer in this section: How motivated was the student to work at the reading lessons, and what can you infer about the student's attitude toward reading and writing outside of tutoring or small-group lessons?

II. Description of Instructional Program. The narration describing the program should be introduced by specifying the teaching goals, which are best thought of in terms of gaining the word-reading strategies of the next phase in recognizing words (see Figure 5 of Practical Chapter 5). For example, if a reader is full alphabetic, the most important strategic goals are those that characterize the consolidated alphabetic phase, e.g., "Amanda needs to build a larger sight vocabulary, including sight words and sight chunks she can use to read multisyllable words."

After stating the tutoring goals, the report should take readers through a brief tour of a typical lesson. Following the adaptations of the Reading Recovery model suggested in this book, this would include assessing the reading of a familiar book; conducting a letterbox lesson; introducing and helping the student read a new book; and helping the student write a message. Keeping Grandma in mind, we avoid the jargon of reading education in preference for describing our activities in plain language. For example, rather than talk about running records, we could say, "I kept track of Carla's mistakes and the word she read accurately." Frequent use of the child's name will personalize the information:

> For each lesson I chose one new correspondence (usually a vowel) that Juan needed work on, and I made a list of example words. I asked Juan to spell these words with paper letters in cardboard squares ("letterboxes") that showed how many sounds were in each word. After Juan spelled all of the words, he read them again without the boxes.

III. Assessment of Current Progress. Section III is the heart of the literacy report. It is the longest section, and it contains the crucial information to direct future teaching. There are seven vital topics to explain in the section, covering the student's reading at the beginning of the teaching program, the progress made during tutoring, and the student's current reading.

Begin this section by explaining the readers' phase of recognizing words at the beginning of the teaching program in plain language (see Chapter 3). Examples of plain-language explanations are as follows:

> **Prealphabetic:** Alex had not yet discovered that word spellings map out the pronunciations of words, and thus he still looked to language patterns and pictures for reading clues.
>
> **Partial alphabetic:** Barbara used the beginning letters in words, along with context and pictures, to identify words, but she did not sound out and blend using the entire spelling.
>
> **Full alphabetic:** Connie could accurately sound out and blend to recognize unfamiliar words, but she read slowly and with considerable effort.
>
> **Consolidated alphabetic:** Darrell could already remember many sight words and word chunks for easy and rapid recognition of new words.

Next, we interpret the seven pretest assessments (see Practical Chapter 5). If possible, summarize each test in a single sentence, avoiding jargon to focus on what the student can do, e.g., "Billy's Phoneme Identity score showed that he can usually recognize phonemes in spoken words, which helps him understand decoding." Numerical results are usually unnecessary, but if they are included, they should be written as numerals to conserve space. In interpreting the results of graded word lists, a key piece of information is the student's instructional reading level at the beginning of the program.

To describe the student's progress during the lessons, consider the student's strategies, skills, and correspondence knowledge. Strategies are problem-solving tactics, especially decoding, crosschecking, and rereading. Fingerpointing words or using coverups may be important in the early phases of learning to read words. Skills are learned automatic responses, such as phoneme awareness, letter recognition, sight vocabulary, fluency, and silent reading. Correspondences should be stated in general terms, such as knowledge of short vowels, or the use of silent *e* in recognizing words with long vowels, or knowledge of vowel digraphs. The shorthand often used in this book (e.g., a_e = /A/) should be avoided because Grandma doesn't understand it.

Generalizations about learning during the teaching program should be documented with examples from running records, written messages, and informal observations. Examples of miscues during a running record could document the growth of strategies. For example, miscues that show better matches with the printed word (smile/*face* in an early lesson, with fake/*face* in a later lesson) demonstrate a growing ability to decode. An increase in self-corrections indicates improvement in crosschecking. Examples of invented spellings that show improvements in mapping the complete phoneme structures of spoken words (e.g., HN/*train* giving way to TRAN/*train*) demonstrate growing phoneme awareness and spelling ability.

Section III ends with an update on the student's current reading ability, based on recent posttests. Begin with the student's phase of recognizing words, again using plain language rather than jargon such as "partial alphabetic." A plain-language translation might be, "Rosie has begun to use the beginning letters in words, along with context and pictures, to identify words." If the student is using similar strategies to those used at the beginning, it is still important to restate these strategies, i.e., "Isaac is still sounding out and blending to identify unfamiliar words, but he is working faster and making better use of vowels in decoding." Interpret each posttest administered, if possible using a single sentence that tells what the score means, e.g., "Andy's pseudoword score at the end of the program shows he has mastered all five short vowels." A vital piece of data concerns the student's instructional reading level at posttest, e.g., "Nyla read enough words on the primer word list to show she is probably reading at the expected primer level at midyear in first grade." Finally, explain what the student still needs to learn. Consider the reader's strategies (e.g., rereading the sentence after identifying an unfamiliar word), skills (e.g., continuing confusions with the similar letters *b* and *d*), and knowledge of correspondences (e.g., knowledge of vowel digraphs).

IV. Recommendations. The recommendations section begins by restating a key finding of the posttest assessment: the reader's instructional reading level. Because we expect some readers to approach the literacy report selectively, we repeat critical information without undue concern about redundancy. In stating the reading level, we need to specify whether the reader is caught up to grade level, and if not, how far the reader is below level. The chart in Figure 1 will be helpful in interpreting the reader's progress toward grade-level reading. In general, the reader should reach the next level by the end of the previous grade. In first grade, we expect a dramatic leap in reading ability over four different reading levels.

Grade	Fall	Midyear	Spring	End of year
Kindergarten	Emergent			Preprimer
First	Preprimer	Primer	First	Second
Second	Second			Third

FIGURE 1: Expected instructional reading levels in the primary grades

The literacy report concludes with recommendations for three key audiences: a future reading teacher, the classroom teacher, and parents. We would like a future reading teacher to have the advantage of the vital practical knowledge we have learned in our teaching program. What worked to help this student forge ahead in learning to read? For example, what type and level of books helped the student make sight words? Were books expressly engineered for decodability helpful in practicing new correspondences in story context, or were they too babyish? Did it work to treat the decodable book as a practice book and then to read a decodable chapter book or early work of children's literature? Did any book or message topic catch the student's imagination? Did particular activities like writing or word-reading review games generate special enthusiasm?

Any tips we can pass on to the classroom teacher may help her build on tutoring gains, but we have to be realistic: With 15-25 other students, teachers do not have the luxury of providing extensive lessons with the individualized activities common to tutoring or small-group instruction. However, the following sample recommendations may be appropriate for helping teachers capitalize on the gains made in the special reading program.

> Because Janelle needs to increase her voluntary reading, she would benefit from daily library visits to find engaging books at her independent level—and to put books back that turn out to be too hard or not interesting. She needs books she can read with 99-100% accuracy. Instructional level books are too difficult for her independent reading because they require a teacher's help to read successfully.

Ben is building a basic sight vocabulary by using decoding to make sight words. He needs decodable books to maintain his decoding strategies. If he is placed prematurely in books not engineered for decodability, he may experience frustration, give up on crosschecking, and fall back on guessing words from context. He will need to learn most major vowel spellings and improve his crosschecking before he is ready for early children's literature.

Yamiyah has responded well to progress charts we used in the special reading program. She may continue to find individualized charts motivating in the regular classroom. Charts that showed how many books she had read and that marked progress in maintaining cooperative behavior motivated her to do her best. Pictures of phonemes we worked on helped her remember correspondences during reading.

Max needs to reread the same book several times to gain reading fluency. His first readings were painfully slow. Charting his fluency progress motivated him to reread books several times, allowing him to pick up speed and add expression. Because building fluency requires a focus on the message of text to motivate crosschecking, fluency readings should involve entire chapters or brief books and should be supported with open-ended questions about story events. One-minute reads will not work because they do not require reading comprehension.

Cali continues to struggle with letter recognition, especially by mixing up the letters *b* and *d*. She would benefit from daily printing practice with lined primary paper to consolidate information on the placement, direction, size, and sequence of letter features.

Kody enjoyed solving words in our letterbox lessons. He especially enjoyed conquering longer words, such as *sprint* and *script*. If he could continue working in small-group letterbox lessons with other children working at about the same level, he could build up his decoding toolkit with other useful vowel correspondences.

The final key audience to address in the literacy report may be the most important for sustaining long-term literacy progress—the parents. While parents cannot be expected to function as expert reading teachers, they can provide vital support for learning the language of books, voluntary reading, and for oral reading practice. Recommendations for regular library visits, nightly read alouds, and constructive support for oral readings would be appropriate suggestions for parents.

> Children need regular opportunities to select appealing and appropriately leveled books from the public library. A weekly scheduled excursion to the library should become part of the family routine. Regular library visits help children discover that there is a world of interesting books about nearly any topic under the sun. Children need very easy books they can read on their own as well as

more interesting books for parents to read aloud to them. Informational books may rival narratives in capturing the interests of many children.

Reading aloud to children should continue as a staple activity of family life. Parents and caretakers should plan a daily time to share engaging books somewhat more challenging than the books the child can read on his own. Read alouds help children learn new word meanings, understand the complex syntax of books, gain a foothold in new topics, and enjoy books at a time when reading can be very hard work. Reading aloud to children is also a crucial part of parent-child bonding. The act of taking time each day to enter the storybook world with a child is probably the single most vital way a parent can share in a child's education.

An effective read-aloud is always a conversation. Story events in a well-chosen book will evoke ideas and questions that invite learning about people and how the world works. To maximize the potential of read alouds, the reading should be slow, which may be counterintuitive in a world that often overvalues reading speed. A slow reading gives the child time to examine the illustrations and to visualize story events. It also gives the reader time to use vocal expression to emphasize important words and bring characters to life.

Children need the help of parents and caretakers to help them read aloud to progress toward reading fluency. To see whether a book is easy enough, parents can use a two-finger test. Have the child read aloud a page of the book while holding up two fingers. If he can't read a word or doesn't know its meaning, have him put one finger down. If both fingers come down, the book is still too hard for independent reading. (The independent level is 99-100% accuracy, and two missed words on a single page would almost certainly indicate a more challenging level than the reader is ready to tackle independently.)

Finally, we need to give parents a simplified version of the five-step conditional scaffold explained in Practical Chapter 2. We might explain how to help as follows, personalized with the reader's name:

> When you help Charlotte read aloud and she has trouble with a word, wait several seconds before offering to help. This allows Charlotte time to use strategies to figure out the word on her own. If she doesn't get it without help, then try these steps as necessary: Send her on to read the rest of the sentence to see what word would make sense. If that doesn't work, cover the word, and then slowly uncover parts of it to make it easier to sound out one part at a time. If that doesn't work, tell her the word. We want her to get back to the story as quickly as possible. No matter when Charlotte identifies the word, always send her back to reread that sentence and pick up the thread of the story.

Although parents cannot be expected to collect and analyze miscue notes, we can advise them to take simple steps toward successful reading: Give the reader some wait time before providing a word. Encourage the reader to finish the sentence for crosschecking before pointing out the misread word. Use coverups to support decoding rather than saying, "Sound it out." Provide the word rather than let the reader become frustrated with repeated failure. Send the child back to reread the sentence to replace the frustration of decoding with the success of word recognition.

Parents can also learn to "talk before you turn." Taking a moment to wonder aloud what will happen next, to assess the motives of a character, to explain an unfamiliar word, or to ask about what is happening in an illustration helps to keep the reader focused on the message of the text. Engaged attention to the events of the story is not only crucial to parent-child bonding in the story-world of texts, but it is also vital to making sight words. Making sense of the language of the text during oral reading motivates young readers to decode unfamiliar words, to crosscheck to nudge a word into clarity, and to mentally annotate any irregularities to store the spelling for sight word recognition. This decoding, crosschecking, and mental marking is the essential work of making sight words.

GLOSSARY

Alphabetic insight: The "aha" experience when children discover that word spellings tell your mouth how to say a word.

Alphabetic principle: The sequence of letters in the written word maps out the sequence of phonemes in the spoken word.

Amalgamation: The process of making sight words by decoding, crosschecking, mental marking, and rereading so that each letter in the spelling is bonded to a phoneme in the pronunciation or annotated as irregular.

Analogizing: The word identification strategy of imagining a well-spelled sight word with a similarly spelled ending to an unfamiliar word and making the unfamiliar word rhyme with this word.

Analytic phonics: Phonics in which children memorize whole words and later analyze them to understand their alphabetic mapping, following the rule that teachers should never pronounce phonemes in isolation.

Assessment: A problem-solving search involving a series of tests.

Auditory discrimination: The ability to perceive differences in spoken words.

Basal reader: A graded reading textbook series, usually consisting of hardbound student texts, spiral-bound teacher's editions, and adjunct materials including workbooks, worksheets, supplemental readers, and tests.

Beginning reading: The developmental stage in which beginners learn to read words.

Blending: Smoothing together isolated phonemes to identify a word.

Body: The spoken part of the syllable through the vowel, e.g., /swE/ in *sweet*.

Booktalk: A brief informal talk that dramatizes the problem of a story without giving away the resolution.

Bottom-up models: Models of skilled reading that assume skilled readers begin at the bottom (the printed words) and work upward toward the message.

Cloze tests: Tests in which readers must supply missing words to complete a passage.

Coarticulation: The overlapping of phonemes in spoken words so that they become physically inseparable.

Coda: Any optional consonants that follow the vowel in a syllable, e.g., /t/ in *sweet*.

Conflate: To get a faulty measure of a trait by mixing valid measures with unrelated information.

Consolidated alphabetic decoding: Using pronounceable word parts or analogizing to identify words.

Consonants: Phonemes made by closing off part of the vocal channel to cause audible friction.

Content words: Nouns, action verbs, adjectives, adverbs, and longer prepositions that carry meaning (see also glue words).

Context processor: The language processor that detects messages in the overlapping meanings of words.

Contextual guessing: Using meaning clues in other words in the sentence to figure out an unknown word.

Control group: Randomly assigned participants in an experiment who do something interesting or useful not expected to improve learning on the variable of interest.

Correlation: An index varying from 0 to 1 (or -1) showing how closely two variables are related.

Correspondence: A learned link between a grapheme (a letter or digraph) and a phoneme so that the grapheme signals the phoneme in decoding.

Coverups: Uncovering difficult words grapheme by grapheme (or pronounceable word part by pronounceable word part) to scaffold decoding.

Criterion-referenced test: A test where performance is compared with a learning benchmark.

Crosschecking: The strategy of examining a pronunciation to make sure it makes sense in context; if not, the reader searches for a sound-alike word that fits.

Decodable text: Text written so that content words are restricted to students' current vowel knowledge while allowing high frequency function words necessary to write any coherent text.

Decode: Translate words encoded in spellings into spoken language, at first by sounding out graphemes into phonemes and then blending phonemes into a recognizable approximation of the word.

Decontextualization of environmental print: Discredited idea that beginners see words on a printed sign in the environment and gradually come to recognize the words out of context when written in plain print.

Deep structure: The hierarchy of main ideas and important details in a text.

Depth-chart model: The view that children gradually become aware of briefer and more subtle linguistic units in spoken language by working their way down from messages to words, to syllables, to onset and rime segments, and finally to phonemes.

Diacritical marks are symbols added to letters to signal how they are pronounced. Common diacritical marks include the macron (ā) for long vowels and the breve (ă) for short vowels.

Digraph: A phoneme spelling such as *sh*, with more than one letter.

Directed reading-thinking activity (DR-TA): A method of arranging silent reading by dividing a narrative text into sections and asking readers to predict what will happen at each stopping point and to justify their predictions.

Dyslexia (see learning disability).

Early intervention: The view that young children need explicit, systematic instruction in phoneme awareness and letter recognition for early success in learning to read.

Elaborated summary: An abbreviated mental model of the writer's message with critical connections to background knowledge.

Emergent literacy: (1) The developmental stage in which beginners acquire phoneme awareness and letter recognition as basic tools of reading words. (2) The view that reading develops naturally in a literate environment.

Experimental group: Randomly assigned participants in an experiment who receive the treatment we think will improve their learning on the variable of interest.

Explicit instruction: Instruction with clear explanations, teacher modeling, and carefully guided practice.

Explicit phonics: Decoding instruction in which the teacher models how to sound out and blend to identify words.

Expository text: Text written to impart information to readers.

Fixation: Gazing fixedly (however briefly) at an object in the visual field.

Fluency: Reading with automatic word recognition.

Frustration level: The level at which a reader can read words with 0-94% accuracy, so that even with teacher scaffolding, the reader cannot comprehend the message of the text.

Full alphabetic decoding: Using the entire spelling of a word to generate a pronunciation for word identification.

Function word (see glue word).

General fluency: The quality of reading achieved when a reader has a sight vocabulary sufficiently large to read the words in a wide range of literature and expository text effortlessly.

Glue words or function words: High frequency words, including linking verbs, articles, pronouns, smaller prepositions, and conjunctions, that show the relations between content words.

Grapheme: A phoneme spelling consisting of either a single letter or a digraph.

Growing independence and fluency: The developmental stage in which beginners build an extensive sight vocabulary for automatic word recognition.

Heuristics: Temporary models designed to establish a strategy, to be discarded when the strategy becomes a skill.

Hierarchical full alphabetic decoding: Decoding words by recognizing syllable patterns such as vowel digraphs or silent *e* signals.

Hierarchy: An organization of ideas in which some ideas are more important and central to understanding the information and other ideas that are less important or trivial.

Homogeneous achievement groups: Children at similar reading levels working together for focused instruction.

Independent level: The level at which a reader can read words with 99-100% accuracy, allowing reading comprehension without teacher scaffolding.

Insertion: In oral reading, saying a word that is not in the text.

Instructional level: The level at which a reader can read words with 95-98% accuracy, allowing reading comprehension with teacher scaffolding.

Intensive phonics: Decoding instruction that teaches about two correspondences per week with the goal of teaching all major correspondences by second grade.

Interactive models: Models of skilled reading that assume skilled readers simultaneously use top-down and bottom-up processes to determine the message of texts.

Invented spelling: A child's phonemic transcription of a word, capturing none, some, or all of its phonemes, e.g., BH for *beach*.

Irregular words: Words with few or no rhyming words that share the same phonogram pattern.

Learning disability (LD), or reading disability, or dyslexia: A condition in which readers have normal or even bright intelligence but specific difficulties with decoding.

Letter: A symbol in alphabetic writing representing a phoneme.

Lexical access: Getting at the verbal information for a word stored in the lexicon.

Lexicon: A reader's interconnected store of words in memory, in which each entry includes a pronunciation, a web of meaning, usage information, and optional spelling data.

Logography: A writing system in which the symbols directly represent meanings.

Long vowels: The five vowels in English pronounced like the letter names *A, E, I, O,* and *U.*

Matthew effects: The eventual pervasive consequences of small, early achievements or deficits in phoneme awareness, affecting everything from decoding skill to verbal intelligence.

Meaning processor: The language processor that activates all possible meaning information (whether relevant or irrelevant) in response to printed or spoken words.

Mental marking: Annotating irregular or silent letters in a spelling in memory after crosschecking to make the spelling understandable.

Metacognition: Executive control over learning.

Metalinguistic: Literally, standing beside language to examine its form apart from its meaning.

Minilessons: Brief explanations with demonstrations, omitting the guided practice, text application, assessment, and reteaching needed for mastery.

Miscue analysis: Examining reading mistakes to determine which correspondences readers are missing and what strategies they are using.

Miscues: Reading mistakes that suggest a reader's strategies and missing correspondences.

Morphemes: Meaningful words or word parts, such as *un, de, cipher,* and *able* in *undecipherable.*

Narrative text: Text written to tell a story.

Norm-referenced test: A test where performance is compared with the achievement of average peers.

Omission: In oral reading, skipping a word, a line, or a page of text.

Onset: The optional spoken part of the syllable before the vowel, e.g., /sw/ in *sweet*.

Open-ended question: A question with multiple right answers.

Orthographic processor: The language processor that analyzes the visual field to detect print.

Ownership of vocabulary: The ability to access word meanings effortlessly and to use words precisely in speaking and writing.

Partial alphabetic decoding, or phonetic cue reading: Sounding out the first consonant or boundary consonants for a pronunciation clue for word identification.

Perceptual skill: The ability to interpret sensory data in order to detect patterns and recognize sounds.

Phoneme awareness (PA): The ability to detect phonemes in spoken words.

Phoneme-direct model: The view that explicit teaching of phonemes is the most efficient path to PA: working with one phoneme at a time, making it memorable, providing practice finding the phoneme in spoken words; and applying PA to read words.

Phonemes: The elemental speech gestures of a language, such as /s/, /O/, and /p/, coarticulated in forming spoken words.

Phonemic spelling: Invented spelling that records a letter for each phoneme in a word, e.g., NIT for *night*.

Phonetic cue reading (see partial alphabetic decoding).

Phonetics: A branch of linguistics that deals with speech characteristics across languages.

Phonics: Decoding instruction.

Phonogram: The spelling of a rime, e.g., *-eat* or *-eet*.

Phonological awareness: The ability to identify any speech unit in the spoken word. It usually involves units larger than a phoneme, especially syllables and rimes.

Phonological processer: The language processor that analyzes sounds and detects the phonological structures of speech.

Phonological structures: Sound constructed of coarticulated phonemes; if linked to meanings, spoken words.

Popcorn reading: Round-robin reading in which the order of readers is not planned.

Prealphabetic reading: Selecting a visual cue in a word and linking it directly to the meaning for word identification.

Predictable books: Books that employ rhyme or repetitive sentence structures to facilitate recitation with children who have not learned to decode.

Prephonemic spelling: Attempting to write without representing phonemes, such as by drawing or scribbling.

Pronounceable word parts: The word identification strategy of recognizing syllables or other familiar word parts and quickly assembling them into words.

Proposition: The smallest unit of information that can be judged true or false.

Pseudoword: A nonsense word with a legal and pronounceable spelling.

Reading disability (see learning disability).

Reading readiness: The view that children need to mature in intelligence and develop perceptual skills before they can learn how to read.

Reading to learn: The developmental stage in which fluent readers begin to acquire facts and concepts by reading.

Reading: Getting the message encoded in a text.

Regularity: The consistency in the spelling pattern of a word commensurate with the size of its word family.

Reliability: Consistency, so that a test gives the same results no matter who's giving it and when it's given, barring new learning.

Rime: The spoken part of a syllable beginning with the vowel, e.g., /Et/ in *sweet*.

Round-robin reading: Arranging oral reading so that each child reads aloud a paragraph or page of a text in a planned order, working around the circle of readers.

Running record: An informal assessment of oral reading in a familiar book, with checkmarks for words read correctly, miscue notes for errors, and analysis.

Saccade: A rapid jump from one fixation to another.

SAT vocabulary: The unique, versatile, and expressive words tested in college entrance examinations as indicators of advanced learning ability.

Scaffold: To support work in a challenging activity at a slightly higher level than the student could work independently.

Scaffolds: Ways teachers support the learning of students, e.g., by preteaching vocabulary or preparing reading guides.

Schema (plural schemata): A reader's generic idea of a situation.

Segmentation: Breaking down a word into its phonological parts.

Semantic group: A collection of words with common meaning elements for vocabulary study.

Semantic map: A graphic organizer displaying a hierarchy of ideas.

Semi-phonemic spelling: Invented spelling that uses letters to represent some (but not all) of the phonemes in words, e.g., JV for *drive*.

Sequential full alphabetic decoding: Sounding out and blending in a left-to-right sequence, without having to reckon with silent letters or digraph vowels.

Short vowels: The five common vowels in English found at the beginnings of the words in "Ask Ed if odd's up."

Sight chunks: Pronounceable word parts like *un* and *able* recognized effortlessly and automatically.

Sight word method (see whole word method).

Sight word process: Learning words as sight words by understanding and storing their alphabetic mappings.

Sight word: Any word recognized instantly and effortlessly.

Skill: A learned automatic response, e.g., automatic word recognition during reading.

Sounding out: Pronouncing isolated phonemes signaled by graphemes.

Specific fluency: The quality of a reading when most or all words in a text are in the sight vocabulary of the reader.

Spelling power: The ability to learn and remember spellings efficiently.

Standardized test: A test administered according to strict rules, such as time limits.

Strategies: Problem-solving procedures readers can use independently of a teacher.

Substitution: In oral reading, saying a different word than what is written.

Subvocalization: Pronouncing words quietly or silently to oneself.

Summarization: Reducing a text into a compact and memorable gist.

Superordinate: An umbrella term for a list of particulars.

Surface structure: The actual words in a text.

Syllabary: A writing system in which the symbols represent syllables.

Syllable: A loud chunk of a spoken word centered on a vowel.

Systematic access: Methodical routines for lexical access that always work for word recognition.

Systematic instruction: Instruction in a planned program where crucial information is built up in small increments in a planned order.

Systematic phonics: Decoding instruction that covers all major correspondences in a planned order.

Test: A one-shot standardized observation of behavior.

Top-down models: Models of skilled reading that presume skilled readers anticipate the message using background knowledge and then sample the text to confirm their predictions.

Topic sentence: A sentence, usually constructed in summarization, that states the topic of a paragraph and the main point the writer is making about that topic.

Transitional spelling: Invented spelling that builds on phonemic spellings by adding conventions of standard spelling, e.g, TAWKED for *talked*.

Validity: Authenticity, so that a test measures what it claims to measure. A valid reading test is a reliable test that measures a process actually involved in reading.

Vowels: Phonemes made by vocalizing (making sounds with the vocal cords) with an open, shaped mouth.

Whole word method, or sight word method: Learning words by rote, i.e., by mechanical repetition without real understanding, analogous to the way we learn phone numbers.

Word family: A group of words that rhyme and share a phonogram, e.g., *pail, rail, mail, sail,* and *trail.*

Word identification: Using conscious problem-solving to figure out a word unfamiliar in printed form.

Word recognition: Effortless, automatic access to a printed word.

References

Adams, M.J. (1990). *Beginning to read: Thinking and learning about print.* Cambridge, MA: MIT Press.

Allen, R.V. (1976). *Language experiences in communication.* Boston: Houghton-Mifflin.

Anania, J. (1982). *The effects of quality instruction on the cognitive and affective learning of students.* Unpublished doctoral dissertation, University of Chicago.

Anderson, R.C., Hiebert, E., Scott, J., & Wilkinson, I.A.G. (1985). *Becoming a nation of readers: The report of the Commission on Reading.* Champaign, IL: Center for the Study of Reading.

Armstrong, D.P., Patberg, J.P., & Dewitz, P. (1988). Reading guides: Helping students understand. *Journal of Reading, 31,* 532-541.

Balmuth, M. (1982). *The roots of phonics: A historical introduction.* New York: McGraw-Hill.

Baron, J., & Strawson, C. (1976). Use of orthographic and word-specific knowledge in reading words aloud. *Journal of Experimental Psychology: Human Perception and Performance, 2,* 386-393.

Baumann, J.F., & Murray, B.A. (1994). Current practices in reading assessment. In K.D. Wood & B. Algozzine (Eds.), *Teaching reading to high-risk learners.* Needham Heights, MA: Allyn and Bacon.

Beck, I.L., McKeown, M.G., & Kucan, L. (2002). *Bringing words to life: Robust vocabulary instruction.* New York: Guilford.

Berdiansky, B., Cronnell, B., & Koehler, J. (1969). *Spelling-sound relations and primary form-class descriptions for speech comprehension vocabularies of 6-9 year olds.* Technical Report No. 15. Los Alamitos, CA: Southwest Regional Laboratory for Educational Research and Development.

Betts, E.A. (1946). *Foundations of reading instruction, with emphasis on differentiated guidance.* New York: American Book Company.

Bond, G.L., & Dykstra, R. (1967). The cooperative research program in first-grade reading in instruction. *Reading Research Quarterly, 2,* 5-142.

Brabham, E.G., Murray, B.A., & Hudson, S. (2006). Reading alphabet books in kindergarten: Effects of instructional emphasis and media practice. *Journal of Research in Childhood Education, 20,* 219-234.

Bransford, J.D., & Johnson, M.K. (1973). Considerations of some problems of comprehension. In W.G. Chase (Ed.), *Visual information processing.* New York: Academic Press.

Brown, D.A. (1982). *Reading diagnosis and remediation.* Englewood Cliffs, NJ: Prentice Hall.

Burke, A.J. (1984). *Students' potential for learning contrasted under tutorial and group approaches to instruction.* Unpublished doctoral dissertation, University of Chicago.

Byrne, B. (1998). *The foundation of literacy: The child's acquisition of the alphabetic principle.* Hove, East Sussex, UK: Psychology Press.

Byrne, B., & Fielding-Barnsley, R. (1989). Phonemic awareness and letter knowledge in the child's acquisition of the alphabetic principle. *Journal of Educational Psychology, 81,* 313-321.

Byrne, B., & Fielding-Barnsley, R. (1990). Acquiring the alphabetic principle: A case for teaching recognition of phoneme identity. *Journal of Educational Psychology, 82,* 805-812.

Carbo, M. (1988). Debunking the great phonics myth. *Phi Delta Kappan, 70,* 226-240.

Carroll, J.B., Davies, P., & Richman, B. (1971). *The American heritage word frequency book.* Boston: Houghton-Mifflin.

Castiglioni-Spalten, M.L., & Ehri, L.C. (2003). Phonemic awareness instruction: Contribution of articulatory segmentation to novice beginners' reading and spelling. *Scientific Studies of Reading, 7,* 25-52.

Chall, J.S. (1967). *Learning to read: The great debate.* New York: McGraw-Hill.

Chall, J.S. (1996). *Stages of reading development* (2nd ed.). Fort Worth: Harcourt Brace College Publishers.

Chall, J.S., Roswell, F.G., & Blumenthal, S. (1963). Auditory blending ability: A factor in success in beginning reading. *The Reading Teacher, 17,* 113-118.

Clarke, L.K. (1988). Invented versus traditional spelling in first graders' writings: Effects on learning to spell and read. *Research in the Teaching of English, 22,* 281-309.

Clay, M.M. (1985). *The early detection of reading difficulties* (3rd ed.). Portsmouth, NH: Heinemann.

Clay, M.M. (1991). Introducing a new storybook to young readers. *The Reading Teacher, 45*, 264-273.

Clay, M.M. (1993). *Reading recovery: A guide book for teachers in training*. Portsmouth, NH: Heinemann.

Clay, M.M. (2002). *An observation survey of early literacy achievement* (2nd ed.). Portsmouth, NH: Heinemann.

Clymer, T. (1963). The utility of phonic generalizations in the primary grades. *The Reading Teacher, 16*, 252-258.

Cross, L.H. (1998). Review of the Iowa Tests of Basic Skills, Forms K, L, and M. In J.C. Impara & B.S. Plake (Eds.), *The thirteenth mental measurements yearbook*. Lincoln, NB: Buros Institute of Mental Measurements.

Cunningham, A.E. (1990). Explicit versus implicit instruction in phonemic awareness. *Journal of Experimental Child Psychology, 50*, 429-444.

Cunningham, A.E., & Stanovich, K.E. (1998). What reading does for the mind. *American Educator, 22*(1), 8-15.

Cunningham, P. (1990). The Names Test: A quick assessment of decoding ability. *The Reading Teacher, 44*, 124-129.

Davey, B., & McBride, S. (1986). Effects of question-generation training on reading comprehension. *Journal of Educational Psychology, 78*, 256-262.

Delpit, L.D. (1988). *The silenced dialogue: Power and pedagogy in educating other people's children*. Harvard Educational Review, 58, 280-298.

Dolch, E., & Bloomster, M. (1937). Phonic readiness. *Elementary School Journal, 38*, 201-205.

Druse, J. (2004). *Booktalks*. Topeka KS: Washburn University.

Duffelmeyer, F.A., Kruse, A.E., Merkley, D.J., & Fyfe, S.A. (1994). Further validation and enhancement of the Names Test. *The Reading Teacher, 48*, 118-128.

Durkin, D. (1984). Is there a match between what elementary teachers do and what basal reader manuals recommend? *The Reading Teacher, 37*, 734-744.

Ehri, L.C. (1980). The development of orthographic images. In U. Frith (Ed.), *Cognitive processes in spelling* (pp. 311-338). London: Academic.

Ehri, L.C. (1985). *Learning to read and spell*. Washington, DC: National Institute of Education.

Ehri, L.C. (1987). Learning to read and spell words. *Journal of Reading Behavior, 19*(1), 5-31.

Ehri, L.C. (1990). Development of the ability to read words. In R. Barr, M.L. Kamil, P. Mosenthal & P.D. Pearson (Eds.), *Handbook of Reading Research* (Vol. 2) (pp. 383-417). New York: Longman.

Ehri, L.C. (1998). Grapheme-phoneme knowledge is essential for learning to read words in English. In J.L. Metsala & L.C. Ehri (Eds.), *Word recognition in beginning literacy* (pp. 3-40). Mahwah, NJ: Erlbaum.

Ehri, L.C., & Sweet, J. (1991). Fingerpoint-reading of memorized text: What enables beginners to process the print? *Reading Research Quarterly, 26*, 442-462.

Ehri, L.C., & Wilce, L.S. (1987). Does learning to spell help beginners learn to read words? *Reading Research Quarterly, 22*, 47-65.

Ehri, L.C., & Soffer, A.G. (1999). Graphophonemic awareness: Development in elementary students. *Scientific Studies of Reading, 3*, 1-30.

Ehri, L.C., Nunes, S.R., Stahl, S.A., & Willows, D.M. (2001). Systematic phonics instruction helps students learn to read: Evidence from the National Reading Panel's meta-analysis. *Review of Educational Research, 71*, 393-447.

Flesch, R.F. (1955). *Why Johnny can't read--and what you can do about it*. New York: Harper.

Flesch, R.F. (1981). *Why Johnny still can't read: A new look at the scandal of our schools*. New York: Harper & Row.

Fry, E.B. (1977). *Elementary reading instruction*. New York: McGraw-Hill.

Fry, E.B., & Kress, J.E. (2006). *The Reading Teacher's Book of Lists* (5th ed.). San Francisco: Jossey-Bass.

Gaskins, I.W., Ehri, L.C., Cress, C., O'Hara, C., & Donnelly, K. (1996-1997). Procedures for word learning: Making discoveries about words. *The Reading Teacher, 50*, 312-327.

Gaskins, I.W. (1988). *A metacognitive approach to phonics: Using what you know to decode what you don't know*. Technical Report No. 424 (pp. 12). Illinois.

Gates, A.I. (1931). *Interest and ability in reading*. New York: Macmillan.

Gentry, J.R., & Gillet, J.W. (1993). *Teaching kids to spell*. Portsmouth, NH: Heinemann.

Good, R.H., & Kaminski, R.A. (2002). *Dynamic Indicators of Basic Early Literacy Skills*, 6th edition. Retrieved March 30, 2012, from http://dibels.uoregon.edu

Goodman, K.S. (1967). Reading: A psycholinguistic guessing game. *Journal of the Reading Specialist, 6*, 126-135.

Goodman, K.S., & Goodman, Y.M. (1979). Learning to read is natural. In L.B. Resnick & P.A. Weaver (Eds.), *Theory and practice of early reading* (Vol. I, pp. 137-154). Hillsdale, NJ: Erlbaum.

Gough, P.B., & Tunmer, W.E. (1986). Decoding, reading, and reading disability. *Remedial and Special Education (RASE), 7*(1), 6-10.

Gough, P.B., & Walsh, S. (1991). Chinese, Phoenicians, and the orthographic cipher. In S. Brady & D. Shankweiler (Eds.), *Phonological processes in literacy: A tribute to Isabelle Y. Liberman* (pp. 199-209). Hillsdale, NJ: Erlbaum.

Gough, P., Juel, C., & Griffith, P. (1992). Reading, spelling and the orthographic cipher. In P. Gough, L.C. Ehri & R. Treiman (Eds.), *Reading acquisition* (pp. 35-48). Hillsdale, NJ: Erlbaum.

Gough, P.B. (1983). Context, form, and interaction. In K. Rayner (Ed.), *Eye movements in reading* (pp. 203-211). New York: Academic Press.

Griffith, P.L., & Klesius, J.P. (1990). *The effect of phonemic awareness ability and reading instructional approach on first grade children's acquisition of spelling and decoding skills.* Paper presented at the National Reading Conference, Miami, Florida.

Groff, P. J. (1985). *Myths of reading instruction* (Rev. ed.). Washington, DC: National Institute of Education.

Guszak, F. (1967). Teacher questioning and reading. *The Reading Teacher, 21,* 227-234.

Hanna, P.R., & Hanna, J.S. (1966). *Phoneme-grapheme correspondences as cues to spelling improvement.* Washington DC: US Government Printing Office.

Harste, J.C., Burke, C.L., & Woodward, V.A. (1982). Children's language and world: Initial encounters with print. In J.A. Langer & M.T. Smith-Burke (Eds.), *Reader meets author: Bridging the gap* (pp. 105-131). Newark, DE: IRA.

Hohn, W.E., & Ehri, L.C. (1983). Do alphabet letters help prereaders acquire phonemic segmentation skill? *Journal of Educational Psychology, 75,* 752-762.

Hoover, W.A., & Gough, P.B. (1990). The simple view of reading. *Reading and Writing: An Interdisciplinary Journal, 2,* 127-160.

Iversen, S., & Tunmer, W. (1993). Phonological processing skills and the Reading Recovery Program. *Journal of Educational Psychology, 85,* 112-126.

Johns, J. (2010). *Basic Reading Inventory.* Dubuque, IA: Kendall Hunt.

Johnston, F.P. (2001). The utility of phonic generalizations: Let's take another look at Clymer's conclusions. *The Reading Teacher, 55,* 132-143.

Jorm, A.F., & Share, D.L. (1983). Phonological recoding and reading acquisition. *Applied Psycholinguistics, 4,* 103-147.

Juel, C., & Roper/Schneider, D. (1985). The influence of basal readers on first grade reading. *Reading Research Quarterly, 20,* 134-152.

Juel, C., Griffith, P., & Gough, P. (1986). Acquisition of literacy: A longitudinal study of children in first and second grade. *Journal of Educational Psychology, 78,* 243-255.

Just, M.A., & Carpenter, P.A. (1987). *The psychology of reading and language comprehension.* Boston: Allyn and Bacon.

Kintsch, W., & Van Dijk, T.A. (1978). Toward a model of text comprehension and production. *Psychological Review, 85,* 363-394.

Koskinen, P.S., & Blum, I.H. (1986). Paired repeated reading: A classroom strategy for developing fluent reading. *The Reading Teacher, 40,* 70-75.

Leslie, L., & Caldwell, J. (2001). *Qualitative reading inventory 3.* New York: Longman.

Lewkowicz, N.K. (1980). Phonemic awareness training: What to teach and how to teach it. *Journal of Educational Psychology, 72,* 686-700.

Liberman, I.Y., & Liberman, A.M. (1992). Whole language versus code emphasis: Underlying assumptions and their implications for reading instruction. In P.B. Gough, L.C. Ehri & R. Treiman (Eds.), *Reading acquisition* (pp. 343-366). Hillsdale, NJ: Erlbaum.

Lytle, S.L. (2000). Teacher research in the contact zone. In M.L. Kamil, P. Mosenthal, P.D. Pearson & R. Barr (Eds.), *Handbook of reading research, Volume III* (pp. 691-718). Mahwah, NJ: Erlbaum.

MacGinitie, W.H. (1976). Difficulty with logical operations. *The Reading Teacher, 29,* 371-375.

Maclean, M., Bradley, P., & Bryant, L. (1987). Rhymes, nursery rhymes, and reading in early childhood. *Merrill-Palmer Quarterly, 33,* 255-281.

Mandler, J., & Johnson, N. (1977). Remembrance of things parsed: Story structure and recall. *Cognitive Psychology, 9,* 111-151.

Manning, G.L., & Manning, M. (1984). What models of recreational reading make a difference? *Reading World, 23,* 375-380.

Masonheimer, P.E., Drum, P.A., & Ehri, L.C. (1984). Does environmental print identification lead children into word reading? *Journal of Reading Behavior, 16,* 257-271.

McGee, L.M., & Ukrainetz, T.A. (2009). Using scaffolding to teach phonemic awareness in preschool and kindergarten. *The Reading Teacher, 62,* 599-603.

McKeown, M.G., Beck, I.L., Omanson, R.C., & Pople, M.T. (1985). Some effects of the nature and frequency of vocabulary instruction on the knowledge and use of words. *Reading Research Quarterly, 20*, 522-535.

McQuillan, J. (1997). The effects of incentives on reading. *Reading Research and Instruction, 36*, 111-125.

Metsala, J.L., & Ehri, L.C. (1998). *Word recognition in beginning literacy.* Mahwah, N.J.: Erlbaum.

Montessori, M. (1966). *The secret of childhood.* New York: Ballantine.

Morgan, R.F., Meeks, J.W., Schollaert, A., & Paul, J. (1986). *Critical reading/thinking skills for the college student.* Dubuque, IA: Kendall-Hunt.

Murray, B.A. (1995). *A meta-analysis of phoneme awareness teaching studies.* Paper presented at the American Educational Research Association, San Francisco, CA.

Murray, B.A. (1998). Gaining alphabetic insight: Is phoneme manipulation skill or identity knowledge causal? *Journal of Educational Psychology, 90*, 461-475.

Murray, B.A. (2009). *So, what is reading fluency, anyway? A defining experiment.* Paper presented at the National Reading Conference, Albuquerque, NM.

Murray, B.A., & Lesniak, T. (1999). The letterbox lesson: A hands-on approach for teaching decoding. *The Reading Teacher, 52*, 644-650.

Murray, B.A., & Steinen, N. (2011). Word/ map/ping: How understanding spellings improves spelling power. *Intervention in School and Clinic, 46*, 299-304.

Murray, B.A., Brabham, E.G., Paleologos, T., Norvell-Hall, B., & Gaston-Thornton, P. (2005). *Does body-coda or onset-rime blending better help kindergartners begin to decode words?* Paper presented at the National Reading Conference, Miami, FL.

Murray, B.A., Brabham, E.G., Villaume, S.K., & Veal, M. (2008). The Cluella study: Optimal segmentation and voicing for oral blending. *Journal of Literacy Research, 40*, 395-421.

Murray, B.A., Brabham, E.G., Villaume, S.K., & Veal, M. (2002). *The effect of three segmentation options on ease of blending for prealphabetic and partial alphabetic readers.* Paper presented at the National Reading Conference, Miami, FL.

Murray, B.A., Smith, K.A., & Murray, G.G. (2000). The Test of Phoneme Identities: Predicting alphabetic insight in prealphabetic readers. *Journal of Literacy Research, 32*, 421-447.

Murray, B.A., Stahl, S.A., & Ivey, M.G. (1996). Developing phonological awareness through alphabet books. *Reading and Writing: An Interdisciplinary Journal, 8*, 307-322.

Nagy, W.E., & Anderson, R.C. (1984). How many words are there in printed school English? *Reading Research Quarterly, 19,* 304-330.

Nagy, W.E., Herman, P.A., & Anderson, R.C. (1985). Learning words from context. *Reading Research Quarterly, 20,* 233-253.

Nolte, R.Y., & Singer, H. (1985). Active comprehension: Teaching a process of reading comprehension and its effects on reading achievement. *The Reading Teacher, 39,* 24-31.

NRP. (2000). *Report of the National Reading Panel: Teaching children to read: An evidence-based assessment of the scientific research literature on reading and its implications for reading instruction.* Washington, DC: National Institute of Child Health and Human Development.

Olson, R.K. (2004). SSSR, environment, and genes. *Scientific Studies of Reading, 8,* 111-124.

Opitz, M.F. (1999). Empowering the reader in every child. *Scholastic Instructor, 108*(5), 35-38.

Perfetti, C.A. (1985). *Reading ability.* New York: Oxford University Press.

Pinnell, G.S., Fried, M.D., & Estice, R.M. (1990). Reading Recovery: Learning how to make a difference. *The Reading Teacher, 43,* 282-295.

Pressley, M., Gaskins, I.W., Solic, K., & Collins, S. (2006). A portrait of Benchmark School: How a school produces high achievement in students who previously failed. *Journal of Educational Psychology, 98,* 282-306.

Pressley, M., Johnson, C.J., Symons, S., McGoldrick, J.A., & Kurity, J.A. (1989). Strategies that improve children's memory and comprehension of text. *The Elementary School Journal, 90,* 3-32.

Rafferty, M. (1968). *Max Rafferty on education.* New York: Devin-Adair.

Raphael, T.E. (1984). Teaching learners about sources of information for answering comprehension questions. *Journal of Reading, 27,* 303-311.

Rashotte, C., & Torgesen, J.K. (1985). Repeated reading and reading fluency in learning disabled children. *Reading Research Quarterly, 20,* 180-188.

Reitsma, P. (1983). Printed word learning in beginning readers. *Journal of Experimental Child Psychology, 36,* 321-339.

Reutzel, D.R., Fawson, P.C., & Smith, J.A. (2008). Reconsidering silent sustained reading: An exploratory study of scaffolded silent reading. *Journal of Educational Research, 62,* 194-207.

Rosenshine, B. (1995). Advances in research on instruction. *Journal of Educational Research, 88,* 262-268.

Rosenshine, B., & Stevens, R. (2002). Classroom instruction in reading. In R. Barr, M.L. Kamil, P. Mosenthal & P.D. Pearson (Eds.), *Handbook of Reading Research* (Vol. 1). Mahwah, NJ: Erlbaum.

Roswell, F.G., & Chall, J. (1963). *Auditory blending test*. New York: Essay Press.

Rowe, M.B. (1987). Wait time: Slowing down may be a way of speeding up. *American Educator, 11*, 38-43, 47.

Samuels, S. (1979). The method of repeated readings. *The Reading Teacher, 32*, 403-408.

Samuels, S.J., & Flor, R.F. (1997). The importance of automaticity for developing expertise in reading. *Reading and Writing Quarterly: Overcoming Learning Difficulties, 13*, 107-121.

Samuels, S.J. (2007). The DIBELS tests: Is speed of barking at print what we mean by reading fluency? *Reading Research Quarterly, 42*, 563-566.

Sanford, A.J., & Garrod, S.C. (1981). *Understanding written language: Explorations in comprehension beyond the sentence*. New York: Wiley.

Saphier, J.D. (1973). The relation of perceptual-motor skills to learning and school success. *Journal of Learning Disabilities, 6*, 583-591.

Schwartz, B. (1982). Reinforcement-induced behavioral stereotypy: How not to teach people to discover rules. *Journal of Experimental Psychology: General, 111*, 23-59.

Share, D.L. (1999). Phonological recoding and orthographic learning: A direct test of the self-teaching hypothesis. *Journal of Experimental Child Psychology, 72*(2), 95-129.

Share, D.L., Jorm, A.F., Maclean, R., & Matthews, R. (1984). Sources of individual differences in reading acquisition. *Journal of Educational Psychology, 76*(6), 1309-1324.

Simon, D.P., & Simon, H.A. (1973). Alternative uses of phonemic information in spelling. *Review of Educational Research, 43*, 115-137.

Slavin, R.E. (1980). Cooperative learning. *Review of Educational Research, 50*, 71-82.

Snow, C.E., Burns, S., & Griffin, P. (1998). *Preventing reading difficulties in young children*. Washington, DC: National Academy Press.

Spiegel, D.L., & Rogers, C. (1980). Teacher responses to miscues during oral reading by second-grade students. *Journal of Educational Research, 74*, 8-12.

Stahl, S.A., & Murray, B.A. (1993). Environmental print, phonemic awareness, letter recognition, and word recognition. *National Reading Conference Yearbook, 42*, 227-233.

Stahl, S.A. (1988). Is there evidence to support matching reading styles and initial reading methods? A reply to Carbo. *Phi Delta Kappan, 70*(4), 317-322.

Stahl, S.A. (1992). Saying the "p" word: Nine guidelines for exemplary phonics instruction. *The Reading Teacher, 45,* 618-625.

Stahl, S.A., Osborn, J., & Lehr, F. (1990). *Beginning to read: Thinking and learning about print - A summary.* Champaign, IL: Center for the Study of Reading.

Stanovich, K.E. (1986). Matthew effects in reading: Some consequences of individual differences in the acquisition of literacy. *Reading Research Quarterly, 21,* 360-406.

Stanovich, K.E. (1988). Science and learning disabilities. *Journal of Learning Disabilities, 21,* 210-214.

Stanovich, K.E. (2000). *Progress in understanding reading: Scientific foundations and new frontiers.* New York: Guilford.

Stanovich, K.E. (2010). *How to think straight about psychology.* Boston: Allyn & Bacon.

Stauffer, R.G. (1969). *Directing reading maturity as a cognitive process.* New York: Harper & Row.

Stebbins, L.B., St. Pierre, R.G., Proper, E.C., Anderson, R.B., & Cerva, T.R. (1977). *Education as experimentation: A planned variation model.* Volume IV-A: An evaluation of Follow Through (No. AAI-76-196A). Cambridge, MA: ABT Associates.

Teale, W.H. (1986). Home background and young children's literacy development. In W.H. Teale & E. Sulzby (Eds.), *Emergent literacy* (pp. 173-206). Norwood, NJ: Ablex.

Treiman, R. (1985). Onsets and rimes as units of spoken syllables: Evidence from children. *Journal of Experimental Child Psychology, 39,* 161-181.

Trelease, J. (2006). *The read-aloud handbook* (6th ed.). New York: Penguin.

Tunmer, W., & Hoover, W. (1993). Phonological recoding skill and beginning reading. *Reading and Writing: An Interdisciplinary Journal, 5,* 161-179.

Valencia, S.W. (1990). A portfolio approach to classroom reading assessment: The whys, whats, and hows. *The Reading Teacher, 43,* 338-340.

Wallach, M.A., & Wallach, L. (1976). *Teaching all children to read.* Chicago: University of Chicago Press.

Wallach, M.A., & Wallach, L. (1979). Helping disadvantaged children learn to read by teaching them phoneme identification skills. In L.B. Resnick & P.A. Weaver (Eds.), *Theory and practice of early reading* (Vol. 3). Hillsdale, NJ: Erlbaum.

Warner, J.M. (1993). Independent strategies. *The Reading Teacher, 46,* 710.

Wilson, P. (1992). Among nonreaders: Voluntary reading, reading achievement, and the development of reading habits. In C. Temple & P. Collins (Eds.), *Stories and readers: New perspectives on literature in the elementary classroom* (pp. 157-169). Norwood, MA: Christopher Gordon.

Wylie, R.E., & Durrell, D.D. (1970). Teaching vowels through phonograms. *Elementary English, 47,* 787-791.

Zaporozheëtis, A.V., & Elkonin, D.B. (1971). *The psychology of preschool children.* Cambridge, MA: MIT Press.

CHILDREN'S BOOKS CITED

Appleton-Smith, L., & Piontek, C. (1998). *Meg and Jim's Sled Trip*. Lyme, NH: Flyleaf.

Arrendo, G. (1997). *The balloon*. San Diego CA: Dominie Press.

Bridwell, N. (1994). *Clifford's first Christmas*. New York: Scholastic.

Cleary, B. (1983). *Dear Mr. Henshaw*. New York: HarperCollins.

Cushman, S. (1990). *A cat nap*. Carson CA: Educational Insights.

Cushman, S. (1990). *Bud the sub*. Carson, CA: Educational Insights.

Cushman, S. (1990). *Doc in the fog*. Carson, CA: Educational Insights.

Cushman, S. (1990). *Red gets fed*. Carson CA: Educational Insights.

Cushman, S. (1990). *Rube and the tube*. Carson CA: Educational Insights.

Cushman, S. (1990). *Tin man fix-it*. Carson, CA: Educational Insights.

Cushman, S., & Kornblum, R. (1990). *Bo and Rose*. Carson CA: Educational Insights.

Cushman, S., & Kornblum, R. (1990). *Is Jo home?* Carson CA: Educational Insights.

Cushman, S., & Kornblum, R. (1990). *James and the good day*. Carson, CA: Educational Insights.

Cushman, S., & Kornblum, R. (1990). *Kite day at Pine Lake*. Carson, CA: Educational Insights.

Dickson, S. (1973). *The Indian book*. Virginia Beach, VA: Sing, Spell, Read & Write.

Flack, M., & Wiese, K. (1970). *The story about Ping*. New York: Viking Press.

Geisel, T.S. (1957). *The cat in the hat*. Boston,: Houghton Mifflin.

Geisel, T.S. (1963). *Dr. Seuss's ABC*. New York: Random House.

Gray, W.S., & Arbuthnot, M.H. (1946). *Fun with Dick and Jane*. Toronto: W. J. Gage.

Gray, W.S., Monroe, M., Artley, A.S., & Arbuthnot, M.H. (1956). *We work and play.* Chicago: Scott, Foresman.

Klein, A. (1996). *I can draw.* San Diego CA: Dominie Press.

Lobel, A. (1970). *Frog and Toad are friends.* New York: Harper and Row.

Lobel, A. (1978). *Mouse tales.* New York: HarperCollins.

Martin, B., & Carle, E. (1967). *Brown Bear, Brown Bear, what do you see?* New York: Holt.

Montgomery, L.M. (1908). *Anne of Green Gables.* Boston: L.C. Page & Co.

Paterson, K. (1978). *The Great Gilly Hopkins.* New York: HarperCollins.

Prince, S., & Curtain, M. (1999). *Playing.* Littleton, MA: Sundance.

Rowling, J.K. (1997). *Harry Potter and the Philosopher's Stone.* New York: Scholastic.

Silverstein, A., & Silverstein, V. (2003). *Nature's champions: The biggest, the fastest, the best.* Mineola, NY: Dover.

Sims, M. (1999). *The tug.* Novato, CA: High Noon Books.

Smith, L.A. (1997) *The sunset pond.* Lyme, NH: Flyleaf.

Steig, W. (1969). *Sylvester and the magic pebble.* New York: Simon and Schuster.

Van Allsburg, C. (1987). *The Z was zapped: A play in twenty-six acts.* Boston: Houghton Mifflin.